THE LIVES OF THE GREAT COMPOSERS
Volume One

Also by Harold C Schonberg

THE GREAT CONDUCTORS
THE GREAT PIANISTS

Harold C Schonberg

The Lives of
The Great Composers

VOLUME ONE

Futura Publications Limited

An Omega Book

First Omega edition published in Great
Britain in 1975 by Futura Publications Limited
Warner Road, London SE5

Publisher's note

The two volumes of THE LIVES OF THE
GREAT COMPOSERS published by Futura
Publications Ltd were originally one volume
entitled THE LIVES OF THE GREAT
COMPOSERS, published by Davis-Poynter Limited

ISBN 0 8600 7722 5
Printed in Great Britain by
Hazell Watson & Viney Ltd
Aylesbury, Bucks

Futura Publications Limited
Warner Road, London SE5

Again, to Rosalyn

Contents

Preface

I have written this book for the intelligent layman, and have tried to organize it so that the consecutive line from Johann Sebastian Bach to Arnold
Schoenberg has been traced. Music is a continually evolving process, and
there has been no genius, however great, who has not taken from his predecessors.

Also, in the process of writing this book, I have tried to humanize the
great composers, to give an idea of what they felt and thought. This approach is somewhat unfashionable today. Many musical scholars insist that
the work rather than the man is the thing; that a piece of music can best be
explained *as music*; that thorough harmonic and structural analysis is the
only valid "explanation." The rest is sentimental program-note writing and
has no real application to the music. I happen to disagree. I firmly believe
that music can be explained by the man; indeed, *must* be explained by the
man and his times. For a man's music is a function of himself, and is a reflection of his mind and his reaction to the world in which he lives. Just as
we see the world through the eyes and mind of a Rembrandt, Cézanne, or
Picasso when we look at their paintings, so we experience the world
through the ears and mind of a Beethoven, Brahms, or Stravinsky when we
hear their music. We are in contact with a mind, and we must attempt an
identification with that mind. The closer the identification, the closer it is
possible to come to understanding the creator's work. That is why the
French pianist Alfred Cortot insisted that his pupils, while studying a piece
of music, also read biographies of the composer, his letters, and the letters of
his contemporaries. Then the pupil had to relate the piece of music to the
composer's entire life and work.

Hence this book is greatly concerned with the biographical aspects of the
great composers. There is little on form and analysis. Technical terminology
is kept to a minimum, though sometimes it is unavoidable, especially in a
discussion of twentieth-century dodecaphonic and serial music. It is easy to
make a mystique out of form and analysis; but are not these topics best left

to the student and the professional? I have always been amused by books supposedly for the layman which are full of complicated musical examples Some of those examples—score reductions and the like—Vladimir Horowitz himself would find difficult to play. A reader who is an able enough musician to play them does not need them, while a reader who has trouble following a single line in C major on a G clef—and that includes the majority —cannot use them.

A glance at the Table of Contents will reveal that most of the greatest composers receive a complete chapter devoted to themselves. Other great composers whose contributions to the history of music are better understood when compared with one or more contemporaries are bracketed with them within a single chapter. And, finally, there is a third kind of chapter devoted to an entire period or a specific time and place, offering general material to supplement the succession of biograhical chapters.

I have started with Bach in volume one, not because there were no great composers before Bach, but because Bach is where the active repertoire really begins. The book ends in volume two with the Second Viennese School. It had to cut off *somewhere,* and the trinity of Schoenberg, Berg, and Webern seemed the logical place. A postlude briefly discusses major trends since 1945. This may be a cowardly evasion, but the development of serial, postserial, electronic, stochastic, aleatoric, and mixed-media music is so complicated and so lengthy a subject that it demands a book in itself.

Orthographical problems always arise in books on music. I have followed normal American professional usage in spelling and terminology. Some British writers have accused my previous books of being too "American" in style. Did they think I was Mongolian? American usage, for example, dictates "twelve-tone music" instead of the British "twelve-note," for reasons explained in the chapter on Schoenberg. American usage dictates, to give two examples, *Harold in Italy* yet, inconsistently, *Symphonie fantastique.* Never have I heard the former work referred to as *Harold en Italie,* just as one rarely if ever hears reference to the Berlioz *Fantastic Symphony.* Generally it is just *Fantastique:* "Bernstein conducted the Berlioz *Fantastique* last night."

Russian and other foreign names pose their familiar problems. The "v" endings are used for Prokofiev, Balakirev, and the others. Yet Rachmaninoff is spelled with the double "f" because that is how he himself signed his name, just as Schoenberg insisted on that spelling and not Schönberg. Similarly, Handel rather than Händel. If there are inconsistencies throughout the book, I apologize.

Some of the material in the following pages originally appeared as Sunday articles in my weekly New York *Times* column, and several appeared as

Times magazine pieces. All have been revised and amplified. I wish to thank the New York Times Company for permission to use that material. A substantial portion of the chapter on Charles Ives originally appeared in the December, 1958, issue of *Esquire,* and is reprinted by permission of Esquire Magazine, Inc. I would like to thank my wife for her constant help and encouragement. Eric Schaal was kind enough to supply several rare photographs of composers from his famous collection, and Rosemary Andersen was extremely helpful in gathering others. And Robert E. Farlow, my editor at W. W. Norton, gave the manuscript a stupendously thorough scrutiny, one unparalleled in my fairly wide experience. In more than one respect it is "our" book.

❧ I ❧

Transfiguration of the Baroque

JOHANN SEBASTIAN BACH

There was a tradition in Leipzig that the body of Johann Sebastian Bach
had been interred near the door of the Church of St. John, approximately
six paces from the south wall. In 1894, St. John's readied itself for
alterations—alterations that would have destroyed the traditional site of
Bach's grave. Whereupon a group of scholars, headed by an anatomist
named William His, started looking for the grave. They had one piece of
information with which to work: in 1750, the year of Bach's death, only
twelve persons had been interred in oak coffins. One of those twelve was
Bach.

Three coffins were dug up near the south wall. Two of them were of
pine. One was of oak and contained a male skeleton in good condition.
Every possible test was made, and a facial mask to cover the skull was contributed by the sculptor Karl Seffner. The mask corresponded closely to the
known portraits of Bach. In his report, published in 1895, Dr. His summarized all evidence and concluded, along with the scientists who had worked
on the project, that the skeleton was indeed Bach's. The remains were then
transferred to a tomb beneath the altar of St. John's.

If the skeleton was indeed Bach's, and there is no good reason to doubt it,
the composer was a man about 5 feet, 7½ inches tall, with a rather massive
head, a strong physique and a solid body, all physical characteristics suggested by the few portraits from life that have come down to us. Bach icon-
ographers have bemoaned the fact that there is so little pictorial evidence,
and a few believe that there is no way of telling what he looked like. But
whatever pictures we do have, all with Bach wearing a wig, according to the
custom of the day (though some scholars have wondered if it covers a bald
head), show many points in common. There are the prominent nose, the
fleshy cheeks, the outthrust chin, the severe lips. It is a tough, strong masculine face, the face of a man who will stand up for his rights. It is an uncom-

13

promising face: not with the look of a fanatic, but certainly with the look of one who is determined to have his own way.

All of this tallies with whatever is known about Bach the man. He was stubborn, he had a temper, he had the reputation of being a hard person to get along with. His pupils, and most likely his children, may have feared this stern figure. He was a religious man, a practicing Lutheran whose library contained an extraordinarily (for the day) large number of ecclesiastical volumes. He seems to have been obsessed with the idea of death, and worried about it far more than his contemporaries even in those days when Heaven and Hell were not abstract concepts but fearful truth. Handel, for instance, was a profoundly religious man, but he *knew* he would be going to Heaven. So, one gathers, did Haydn. Those two men felt that they were friends of God. Not Bach, who stood much more in awe of the Deity. He once said that the aim and final reason of music "should be none else but the glory of God and the recreation of the mind." That he had a strong sexual drive, his family attests; he had twenty children, of whom nine survived him. It was the largest family, by far, produced by any of the great composers: large even for Bach's day, when large families were not unusual. There also is the reproof handed him by the Arnstadt authorities in 1706: "Thereupon ask him further by what right he recently caused the strange maiden to be invited into the organ loft and let her make music there." Victorian biographers of Bach were thrown into sheer consternation by the implication that their saintly hero, the composer of the B minor Mass, could have been interested in strange maidens. It was decided that the strange maiden was his cousin, Maria Barbara, whom he married the following year. But there is no evidence one way or the other.

Bach was a solid burgher, twice married, and as thrifty as a peasant. He never suffered want. Of all the Bachs of his day he was the most affluent and most respected, but he was not above pinching every penny and watching grimly over every expense. Some of his correspondence with his cousin, Johann Elias, is rather amusing in this respect. Indeed, it is virtually the only amusing thing in Bach's humorless life. Did the man ever smile? One wonders. Certainly his music has less humor than the music of any of the other great composers. Even Wagner composed a *Meistersinger*. Bach's musical humor—his *Coffee Cantata,* his *Capriccio on the Departure of a Beloved Brother,* one or two other pieces—bulk infinitesimally small in his output. Anyway, getting back to Johann Elias, Bach writes about a gift of wine that Elias had sent. Some of it was lost in transit, and Bach lamented mightily "that even the least drop of this noble gift of God should have been spilled." Then Bach hastily says he is in no position "to make an appropriate return." Then, finally, there is a postscript: "Although my honored Cousin kindly offers to oblige with more of the *liqueur,* I must decline his offer on account of the excessive expenses here. For since the carriage charges cost 16 groschen, the delivery man 2 groschen, the customs inspector 2 groschen, the inland duty 5 groschen, 3 pfennig, and the general duty 3 groschen, my honored Cousin can judge for himself that each quart costs me almost 5 groschen, which for a present is really too expensive."

Bach was born in Eisenach, Germany, on March 21, 1685, the youngest of the eight children of Johann Ambrosius Bach, who was the son of Christoph Bach, who was the son of Johannes Bach, and so back to Veit Bach, whose birth date is unknown but who died in 1619. Johann Sebastian, who like all the Bachs took great pride in the accomplishments of the family, once started a genealogy named "Origin of the Musical Bach Family." He traced it back to Veit, "a white bread baker in Hungary," who "in the sixteenth century was compelled to escape from Hungary because of his Lutheran faith." In this genealogy, Bach draws a charming picture of old Veit, who "found his greatest pleasure in a little cithern which he took with him even into the mill and played while the grinding was going on. (How pretty it must have sounded altogether! Yet in this way he had a chance to have the rhythm drilled into him.) And this was, as it were, the beginning of a musical inclination in his descendants." Bach always believed he was of Hungarian descent, but most scholars now think that Veit had been born in Germany, had moved to Hungary, and then returned.

In Veit's day there were also Hans Bach and Caspar Bach. Veit fathered Johannes and Lips. From Johannes sprang Johanna, Christoph, and Heinrich. From Lips came the Meiningen line of Bachs. The family was industriously fertile, and for over two centuries bred true, producing one respected musician after another. There were musical Bachs in Arnstadt and Eisenach, in Ohrdruf, Hamburg, and Lüneburg, in Berlin, Schweinfurt, and Halle, in Dresden, Gotha, Weimar, Jena, Mühlhausen, Minden, and Leipzig. They were a close-knit, clannish group who loved to visit one another, making music, exchanging gossip, trying to place members of their own family in important musical posts. Whenever an opening presented itself anywhere in Germany, news raced through the ganglia of the great Bach family, causing twitches and responses. As often as not, the Bachs got their man in.

Johann Sebastian's father, Johann Ambrosius, was a highly regarded church organist in Eisenach. He died when Sebastian was ten (his mother had died the preceding year). Sebastian and his brother Jakob were taken in by their older brother Johann Christoph, who was organist at Ohrdruf. Not much is known about the five years Sebastian spent there. He must have been a gifted child. He was what we would call a senior in the local school at the age of fourteen, and at that time the average age of seniors was nearer eighteen. He also was a good organist and clavier player (the clavier is the generic term for keyboard stringed instruments: harpsichord, clavichord, spinet), a singer, a good violinist, presumably already a composer. But we are not discussing any talented young musician. We are discussing Johann Sebastian Bach, perhaps the most stupendously gifted figure in the history of music, and there is so much more we would like to know about his childhood. When did his extraordinary talent first show itself? Did he have absolute pitch? (He must have had.) The Bach family being what it was, a genetic factor must be taken into consideration. What went on in the boy's head, what kind of musical and physical reflex operated, exactly what kind of training did his father and elder brother give him? We do not know.

We do know the main external events of his life. We know that at the age of fifteen he went to St. Michael's school in Lüneburg; that he visited Hamburg; that already he was a contentious young man; that his life was a series of positions in the service of the court or the church: Arnstadt, Mühlhausen, the ducal court of Anhalt-Cöthen, his final position, which he held for twenty-seven years, as cantor (teacher) of St. Thomas's Church in Leipzig. We know that he was highly respected in his day, though more as an organ player and organ technician than as a composer. Bach, who carried the baroque movement to its peak, lived during a time when radical new concepts were undermining the edifice that to a large extent had been built on polyphony. Indeed, Bach lived to find himself considered an old-fashioned composer, a pedant, whose music was pushed aside in favor of the lighter, homophonic, melodic music of the *style galant*—the elegant, graceful, rather superficial music that made his son, Johann Christian, so popular in London.

The chances are that this did not bother Bach very much. He lived before the romantic notion of art for art's sake, of music composed for eternity. Bach was as practical and as level-headed a composer as ever lived. Like all composers of the day, he regarded himself as a working professional, one who ordinarily wrote to fill a specific need—a cantata for Sunday, an exercise book for the children, an organ piece to demonstrate a particular instrument. He did publish certain pieces of which he was especially proud, but by and large he fully expected the bulk of his music to disappear after his death. When he became cantor in Leipzig, he disposed of all his predecessor's music, and he knew that his successor would just as summarily get rid of whatever Bach manuscripts were around. It was a cantor's job to present music that *he* had composed, not the music of another man.

Of course, he knew his worth. He must have known from the beginning, and if there was anything that drove him out of his mind it was slovenly musicianship, or musicianship of a kind that did not meet his own standards. And those standards were—well, Bachian. His whole life is dotted with episodes that attest to his determination to make music on his own level. As early as 1705, in Arnstadt, he got involved in an argument with a student named Geyersbach. The upshot was that Bach drew his dagger and went for Geyersbach; and, in a trice, the future composer of the *St. Matthew Passion* was rolling on the ground, attempting mayhem on his opponent. On examination it turned out that Bach had once disdainfully called his colleague a *Zippelfaggotist*—a bassoonist who produced sounds like those of a nanny-goat. Bach was reproved, especially as he "already had the reputation of not getting along with the students."

But Bach was incorrigible. It would seem that he knew his potentialities and was determined to have his own way. Nothing could interfere with his vision of music and his drive—no, his compulsion—to saturate himself in his art, to improve himself, to study, to absorb everything that could be absorbed. If somebody interfered, *tant pis!* He is reproved in 1706 for staying away from his duties (he had walked to Lübeck to hear Buxtehude play the organ). He is reproved for his strange harmonies at the organ during services. He is reproved for playing too long and, in defiance, "he had at once fallen into the other extreme and made it too short." He is reproved for being a "loner," for his standoffish, superior attitude. "For if he considers it no disgrace to be connected with the Church and to accept his salary, he must not be ashamed to make music with other students assigned to do so.'

At Weimar he is actually sent to jail, in 1717, for "too stubbornly forcing the issue of his dismissal." Bach wanted to go to Cöthen. In Leipzig he is constantly complaining to the Elector about money matters and his perquisites, and soon becomes very unpopular with the town council, which accuses him of neglecting his duties. Bach's duties were numerous. In his application to Leipzig in 1723 he had written out what he promised to do:

(1) That I shall set the boys a shining example of an honest, retiring manner of life, serve the School industriously, and instruct the boys conscientiously;

(2) Bring the music in both the principal Churches of this town into good estate, to the best of my ability;

(3) Show to the Honorable and Most Wise Council all proper respect and obedience, and protect and further everywhere as best I may its honor and reputation; likewise if a gentleman of the Council desires the boys for a musical occasion, unhesitatingly provide him with the same, but otherwise never permit them to go out of town to funerals or weddings without the previous knowledge and consent of the Burgomaster and Honorable Directors of the School currently in office;

(4) Give due obedience to the Honorable Inspectors and Directors of the School in each and every instruction which the same shall issue in the name of the Honorable and Most Wise Council;

(5) Not take any boys into the School who have not already laid a

foundation in music, or are not the least suited to being instructed therein, nor do the same without the previous knowledge and consent of the Honorable Inspectors and Directors;

(6) So that the Churches may not have to be put to unnecessary expense, faithfully instruct the boys not only in vocal but also in instrumental music;

(7) In order to preserve the good order in the Churches, so arrange the music that it shall not last too long, and shall be of such a nature as not to make an operatic impression, but rather incite the listeners to devotion;

(8) Provide the New Church with good scholars;

(9) Treat the boys in a friendly manner and with caution, but, in case they do not wish to obey, chastise them with moderation or report them to the proper place;

(10) Faithfully attend to the instruction in the school and whatever else it befits me to do;

(11) And if I cannot undertake this myself, arrange that it be done by some other capable person without expense to the Honorable and Most Wise Council or to the School;

(12) Not to go out of town without the permission of the Honorable Burgomaster currently in office;

(13) Always so far as possible walk with the boys at funerals, as is customary;

(14) And shall not accept or wish to accept any office in the University without the consent of the Honorable and Learned Council.

In addition, Bach was responsible for musical programs—the actual music and its performance—in all four of the city's churches. He had to compose a cantata for the weekly service and conduct the performance. He had to provide Passion music for Good Friday. All this was the normal part of any cantor's post. There were extracurricular activities, such as providing motets for weddings and funerals, or festival compositions for the city. From these extracurricular tasks he derived income, and he once pointed out in all seriousness that "when there are rather more funerals than usual, the fees rise in proportion; but when a healthy wind blows, they fall accordingly, as for example last year, when I lost fees that would ordinarily come in from funerals to an amount of more than 100 thaler."

In Leipzig, Bach found neither the co-operation, the income, nor the appreciation he had hoped for, and soon he was as usual at odds with the officials. City Councilor Steger was provoked into saying that not only did the Cantor do nothing, "but he was not even willing to give an explanation of that fact." This probably confirmed the council's secret suspicions about Bach, for he had come to Leipzig because no other candidates who suited the council were available As Councilor Platz had put it, "since the best man could not be obtained, mediocre ones would have to be accepted." Thus did Councilor Platz assure himself of a footnote in history. The "best man" to whom he referred was Georg Philipp Telemann (1681–1767), an incredibly prolific composer who had some 3,000 works to his credit at his death. Telemann, a fine musician and an admirable composer, was very popular in Germany—far more than the less fashionable Bach ever was. Then, in 1736, came Bach's great battle with Johann August Ernesti, the rector of St. Thomas's School. It was an affair that rocked the school, drove the council frantic, and brought out every bit of the considerable stubbornness and fighting instinct of Bach. Ernesti had chosen one Johann Gottlieb Krause to be prefect of the St. Thomas School. But Krause was a poor musician, and Bach was infuriated. He protested to the council. Ernesti answered back. There were charges and countercharges. Bach would not quit. He carried the fight to the consistory and, when he could get no satisfaction, "to His Most Serene Highness, the Mighty Prince and Lord, Frederick Augustus, King in Poland, Grand Duke in Lithuania, Reuss, Prussia, Mazovia, Samogitia, Kyovia, Vollhynia, Podlachia, Lieffland, Smolensk, Severia and Czernienhovia, Duke of Saxony, Jülich, Cleve, Berg, Engern and Westphalia, Archmarshal and Elector of the Holy Roman Empire, Landgrave of Thuringia, Margrave of Meissen, also of Upper and Lower Lausiz, Burgrave of Magdeburg, Prince and Count of Henneberg, Count of the Marck, Ravensberg and Barby, Lord of Ravenstein, My Most Gracious King, Elector and Master." Nobody knows how the affair finally came out. It is assumed that Bach finally won.

The point is that Bach was not a man to be pushed around, and he carried this attitude into his music-making. How he chafed at the mediocrity with which he was surrounded! This complete musician, this incomparable executant, this composer whose vision embraced the then-known musical universe, this titan had to work in Leipzig with wretched students and with personnel far below the strength he needed and wanted. In 1730 he outlined his minimum requirements for church music forces. Every musical choir, he told the town council, should contain at least twelve singers, though it would be better if sixteen were available. For the orchestra there should be eighteen and preferably twenty players. But, complained Bach, what did he have? A grand total of eight—four town pipers, three professional fiddlers, and one apprentice; and "Modesty forbids me to speak at all truthfully of their qualities and musical knowledge." Bach threw up his hands. Such conditions were intolerable, and on top of everything else, most of the students were untalented. This accounted, Bach said, for the decline of performance standards in Leipzig. At the end, he summarizes the quality of the students. Seventeen were "unusable," twenty "not yet usable," and seventeen "unfit." These fifty-four boys constituted the choruses of the four churches in Leipzig. Poor St. Peter's Church got the worst of the lot, "namely those who do not understand music and can only just barely sing in a chorale."

(Note the reference to the "town pipers." Those gentlemen could be well-rounded musicians, and in 1745 Bach examined one of them, a worthy named Carl Friedrich Pfaffe. "It was found," Bach wrote, "that he performed quite well, and to the applause of all those present, on all the instruments that are customarily employed by town pipers, namely: violin, oboe, transverse flute, trumpet, and horn, and the remaining brass instruments, and he was found quite suited to the post of assistant which he seeks.")

That, then, was what Bach had to work with. Every once in a while, for special occasions, he could get more. For the *St. Matthew Passion* he scraped together over forty participants. Bach evidently craved large forces, and it is a mistake today, in the name of "authenticity," to present such large-scale works as the B minor Mass and the two big Passions with a tiny number of participants in line with Bach's memo of 1730. Of course, Bachian textures must be preserved whatever the forces involved, and the music must be presented with perfect clarity. But that does not preclude a big sound.

Bach did his best with the raw material. He could probably play most of the instruments in the orchestra, and he took his forces in charge much as a modern conductor does. Generally he conducted from the violin or the harpsichord. Very little scholarly work has been done in the early history of conducting, and the general assumption is that not until the nineteenth century did a leader actually beat time. Yet there is plenty of evidence from Bach's own day that the person in charge of an ensemble most definitely did beat time. Indeed, when Bach examined the unfortunate Krause, he specifically mentions that the student could not beat time correctly; that "he could not accurately give the beat in the two principal kinds of time, namely even, or four-quarter, and uneven, or three-quarter."

From all eyewitness accounts, Bach at the head of an orchestra was a dominating figure. He was a brilliant score reader. "His hearing was so fine that he was able to detect the slightest error even in the largest ensembles." While conducting, he would sing, play his own part, keep the rhythm steady, and cue everybody in, "the one with a nod, another by tapping with his feet, the third with a warning finger, giving the right note to one from the top of his voice, to another from the bottom, and a third from the middle of it—all alone, in the midst of the greatest din made by all the participants, and, although he is executing the most difficult parts himself, noticing at once whenever and wherever a mistake occurs, holding everybody together, taking precautions everywhere and repairing any unsteadiness, full of rhythm in every part of his body." Thus has Johann Matthias Gesner, the Rector who preceded the troublesome Ernesti, described the great man at work. His son, Carl Philipp Emanuel, remarks that Bach was especially finicky about tuning. To this he paid the greatest attention, both in the orchestra and in his own instruments at home. "Nobody could tune and quill his instruments to please him. He did everything himself. . . . He heard the slightest wrong note even in the largest ensembles." The concept of the conductor, in the modern sense of the word, had not been invented; but, it is interesting to note, Bach was a modern conductor in everything but name —and probably, with his quick temper, a fearsome one.

Exactly how he conducted, we do not know. What were his tempos? Ideas about rhythm? Expressive devices? Today many of the fine points of Bach performance practice have been lost. We can only speculate about things like pitch, instruments, ornaments, embellishments, balances, even the rhythms and tempos. Take the subject of pitch. Scholars have determined that it was often as much as a full tone lower in Bach's day than it is in ours. But there also are organs of Bach's day, still in operation, in which the pitch is *higher*. How Bach himself tuned his instruments we do not know. As for embellishments, books have been written on the subject of written-out embellishments in Bach's music, and often the authorities disagree. Which is not surprising, for authorities in Bach's own day disagreed. In addition there seem to have been many conventions that were not written out, such as holding notes for a longer length of time than they were actually written. At best the conscientious musician can, after much specialized study, make an informed guess.

But where performance practices are transitory, changing from generation to generation, Bach's music remains stronger than it ever was. Stronger, indeed, for we can look at it in historical perspective, comparing it with the music of the other great men of his day—Handel, Vivaldi, Couperin, Alessandro Scarlatti. By any measurement Bach eclipses all. His vision was greater, his technique unparalleled, his harmonic sense frightening in its power, expression, and ingenuity. And while he is not considered one of the great melodists, he could nevertheless spin out tunes of ineffable rapture, such as the aria *Bist du bei mir,* or the slow movement of the Trio Sonata in E minor, which proceeds in calm, immense, noble phrases in a kind of tidal ebb and flow.

Bach was a composer of the Baroque. In music, the Baroque Era runs from about 1600 to 1750. Baroque music, as practiced by its greatest figures, has pronounced mannerist qualities: mysticism, exuberance, complexity, decoration, allegory, distortion, the exploitation of the supernatural or grandiose, all commingled. Where the Renaissance period (and later the Classic) stood for order and clarity, the Baroque (and later the Romantic) stood for movement, disturbance, doubt. The musical baroque started in Italy with such figures as Claudio Monteverdi (1567–1643) and the Florentine group that "invented" opera, and rapidly swept through Europe. The Baroque saw the rise of four-part harmony and the figured bass, in which numerals indicate the harmonies to be used. Another name for figured bass is thorough bass, and to Bach it was equivalent to a system handed down from On High. The thorough bass, he was quoted by a pupil as saying, "is the most perfect foundation of music, being played with both hands in such a manner that the left hand plays the notes written down while the right adds consonances and dissonances, in order to make a well-sounding harmony to the Glory of God and the permissible delectation of the spirit; and the aim and final reason, as of all music, so of the thorough bass should be none else but the Glory of God and the recreation of the mind."

The Baroque also saw the disappearance of the old church modes and the consolidation of the scale and its associated keys that have remained in use to this day. It also saw the development of rhythmic ideas that broke music into accented bar lines. It saw the rise of the forms that were to lead directly into sonata, symphony, concerto, overture, and variation. But the Baroque also had its own free forms—toccata, fantasia, prelude, ricercar.

It was a period that saw the rise of a cultured middle class. Music began to spread from court and church into the city, where many middle-class citizens started demanding musical entertainments. These were the forerunners of today's public concerts. Musicians began to supply those demands, sometimes, as in the case of Handel, on a spectacularly successful financial basis. Musical academies were formed, and even coffeehouses put on musical programs to satisfy their patrons. Bach was involved in such a project, and for many years conducted the weekly concerts at Zimmermann's coffeehouse in Leipzig, on Friday evenings from 8 to 10. The participants (so ran the announcement in 1736) "are chiefly students here, and there are always good musicians among them, so that sometimes they become, as is well known, famous virtuosos."

With Bach the baroque in music came to fulfillment. Bach was all that had gone before, and he anticipated much that was to come. He was not only a learned musician when it came to his own music; he also was a learned musician in all music. He certainly was one of the most cultured musicians of his day, with a tremendous knowledge of what was happening in the European scene. He had a sheer lust to know and to assimilate all of the music then available, ancient and contemporary. It was not that he was a scholar, interested in musical history. There is no evidence that he made any great effort to unearth medieval music, for instance. That probably would not have interested him. What did interest him, overwhelmingly and even compulsively, was technique. How did composers put things together? What was the quality of their ideas? In matters like these, Bach seems to have had insatiable professional curiosity. Was it because, consciously or unconsciously, he wanted to measure himself against other composers? He went to hear new music, wherever it was possible for him to attend, and was constantly reading what he was not able to hear in person. Bach, of course, could read a printed score as easily as an accountant reads a ledger or a commuter the evening newspaper. As a youth he would absent himself from his duties to listen to the great organists—Vincent Lübeck and Buxtehude, among others—and it was one of the great regrets of his life that he never heard the famous Handel. He knew the old music by Palestrina, Frescobaldi, and Legrenzi; new music by Vivaldi, Telemann, and Albinoni. He was familiar with the music of the French school, from Lully to d'Anglebert and Couperin. (There is no evidence that he was acquainted with the music of the English school.) Of the German composers he esteemed the music of Froberger, Kerll, Fux, Schütz, Theile, Pachelbel, Fischer. He knew the sonatas of Domenico Scarlatti and the choral works of Alessandro Scarlatti. As a child he had grown up with an unquenchable musical appetite, and was never able to satisfy it.

To a large extent he probably was self-taught. Musicians on the order of genius possessed by a Bach, a Mozart, or a Schubert do not need much instruction. They have minds like blotters that immediately soak up and assimilate every musical impulse. They merely have to be pointed in the right direction and be given a little push. So it was with Bach. From the very beginning he took from all sources and made them his own. And he did this in every known musical form with the exception of opera. Bach's music has endless variety. At its worst—and Bach could write *dull* music, though never *bad* music—Bach's music bears signs of haste and impatience, and clearly he was dashing off a formula piece to meet the demands of a specific occasion. But his average is very high, and at its best his music is at the summit of the art. Bach could use formulae of the day and make them sound fresh and original, because they were *his* formulae. The forty-eight preludes and fugues of the *Well-Tempered Clavier* are as different from one another as are the Chopin Études. *The Art of Fugue* (*Die Kunst der Fuge*), unanimously hailed as one of the great intellectual *tours de force* of Western man, is a colossal work, an unfinished series of contrapuntal variations, again with unfailing variety and imagination.

Nobody knows how Bach intended the *Art of Fugue* to be played—as an organ work, as an orchestral work, or anything in between. The instrumentation is unspecified, and the German scholar, Friedrich Blume, even suggests that Bach himself was not interested in whether such works as the *Art of Fugue* were ever performed, or were capable of being performed. "In them," Blume writes, "he wanted to continue a tradition of consummate contrapuntal skill, which he had inherited from the Roman school of the

Palestrina period by way of Berardi, Sweelinck, Scacchi, Theile, Werckmeister and G. B. Vitali. It was . . . an 'esoteric' activity, this disinterested transmission of a purely abstract theory." Perhaps, but was there ever a composer who wrote abstract music not to be played? One doubts it. In any case, the *Art of Fugue* carries pure counterpoint to its height. To give an idea of the complexity of the work: it starts with four fugues, two of which present the theme, the others presenting the theme in contrary motion (that is, back to front). Then there are counterfugues, in which the original subject is inverted (turned upside down) and combined with the original. There are double and triple fugues, several canons, three pairs of mirror fugues. In Karl Geiringer's description, "Bach presents all the voices first in their original form and then, like a reflected image, in complete inversion. To make the mirror reflection doubly realistic, the treble of the first fugue becomes the bass of the second fugue, the alto changes into a tenor, the tenor into an alto, and the bass into a treble, with the result that No. 12:2 appears like 12:1 standing on its head."

Musicians for over 200 years have been awed by the incredible technique and ingenuity with which Bach, in the *Art of Fugue,* summarized everything known about counterpoint and then added the full measure of his own mighty genius, creating a score that in its majesty and poetry stands unique. It is Bach's last major composition, and he never finished it. While working on an enormous triple fugue he decided to add as a counterpoint the letters of his own name (B = B flat, and H = B natural in German nomenclature). Just as his name appears, the autograph stops. Some musicians— Tovey, Riemann, and others—have worked out a completion, but those are never played in concert, nor should they be. The emotional shock of hearing the B-A-C-H theme, and then abrupt silence just as the fugue is getting started, is an overwhelming experience.

Polyphony is but one side of Bach. He could write collections of dance movements under the titles of Suite or Partita; or devotional cantatas; or music with the bracing athletic vigor of the *Brandenburg* Concertos; or music as titanic as the B minor Mass and *St. Matthew Passion;* or out-and-out virtuoso pieces for the organ, of grand design, overwhelming sonority, and uninhibited finger and foot display (these organ works should be played on a baroque and *never* on a romantic organ); or involved pieces for solo violin or cello; or a long set of harpsichord variations called the *Goldberg,* which in chromatic intensity (that twenty-fifth variation!) has hardly a peer until Chopin and Wagner.

It is harmonic intensity above all that sets Bach's music apart from that of his contemporaries. Bach had anything but a conventional musical mind. His work is always full of surprises: something unexpected, something that departs from the norm, something that only Bach could have dreamed from the material. A Vivaldi concerto grosso, for example, goes along primarily in tonic, dominant and subdominant harmonies, and any exploration of keys is within safely charted courses. In Bach's music a completely new harmonic language is forged. A superior harmonic sense is the mark of nearly all the great composers, the one thing that sets them off from their more timid and less inventive contemporaries. Where most composers of his day would confine themselves to the rules, Bach *made* the rules. Even as a young man he was industriously investigating the harmonic potential of music. It was for this that he would be reproved. His listeners were not used to such daring. At Arnstadt, the twenty-one-year-old Bach was rebuked "for having hitherto made many curious variations in the chorale, and mingled many strange tones in it, and for the fact that the congregation has been confused by it." As he grew older, his harmonic adventurousness became more and more pronounced.

Taking the forms bequeathed to him, Bach was constantly expanding, refining, improving them. He developed the clavier concerto. His music for solo string instruments has never been surpassed for ingenuity, complexity, and difficulty. One wonders how good a violinist Bach was. Surely none but a master of the instrument could have conceived such figurations. One also wonders how many violinists in the world at the time could have played, with any degree of accuracy, such phenomenally taxing writing. The immense chaconne from the D minor Partita for solo violin is the best-known of these solo string pieces, but the fugue of the C major Sonata is as powerful and magnificent a conception. The fugal movements of the solo suites for cello are also of extreme complexity and difficulty. As one of the outstanding performers of the day, Bach clearly enjoyed an occasional workout. There are bursts of exhilarating virtuosity in his music, as in the clavier cadenza of the D major *Brandenburg* Concerto. And many of his organ works are finger-twisters and foot-tanglers. "There!" one can imagine Bach saying, after the conclusion of the D major Prelude and Fugue for organ. "Beat *that!*"

Bach was the one who, once and for all, established the well-tempered scale used today. Composers had been working in that direction, but it remained for Bach to demonstrate the practicality and, indeed, inevitability of the system. Up to his time, mean-tone temperament was in general use, which meant half tones of different sizes. The problem was how to arrange the tones within the octave so that the scale would have consistent harmonic ratios from tone to tone. In mean-tone temperament, the ratios of the scale in any given key could be worked out, but what was good for, say, C major was not good for F minor. The German theoretician and writer on music, Friedrich Wilhelm Marpurg (who lived in Bach's time), put it this way: "Three scales were made ugly in order to make one beautiful." Or, in the words of the British musicologist, Percy A. Scholes, "It is not possible to tune any keyed instrument *perfectly* for more than one key; if you tune it correctly for key C, the moment you play in another key some of the notes will be out of tune. On the mean-tone temperament just a single key was perfect, but, by a compromise, a certain number of keys were made near enough perfect for the ear to tolerate them, the rest being outside the pale." The compromise mentioned by Scholes involved raising or lowering individual pitches of the scale so that several keys could be accommodated. But, as Scholes points out, certain keys were so outside the mean-tone patterns that they could not be used. In early music such common keys as B major or C sharp minor are very seldom found—except in Bach. Following the lead suggested in Andreas Werckmeister's *Musical Temperament* (1691), Bach divided the octave into twelve approximately even tones. No one key was perfect in this kind of compromise, and there were slight imperfections in all keys, but those were small enough for the ear to tolerate. Bach's system made it practicable to modulate into any other key, and any of the twelve keys could serve as the tonic. He composed the *Well-Tempered Clavier* as an illustration of what could be done with this kind of tuning. The two books of the *Well-Tempered Clavier* contain forty-eight preludes and fugues, two each in all of the major and minor keys.

In recent years a good deal has been written about Bach's use of musical symbolism. Albert Schweitzer was one of the first proponents of the idea. He maintained that not only was Bach essentially a painter in tones, but also that Bach as often as not incorporated into his music specific motives of terror, grief, hope, weariness, and so on. Schweitzer insisted that it is impossible to interpret a Bach work unless the meaning of the motive is known. Most of Schweitzer's ideas along this line are discounted today, though it is still a parlor game among a handful of Bach specialists to read ecclesiastical and even numerical symbolism into Bach's music. The substitution of numbers for the letters of the alphabet seems to have been an occasional practice in Bach's day. Thus, to quote from Karl Geiringer's 1966 biography of Bach, "14, for instance, is the number symbolizing Bach [B = 2, A = 1, C = 3, H = 8]; inverted, it turns into 41, which stands for J. S. Bach, as J is the ninth, S the eighteenth letter, and 9 plus 18 plus 14 makes 41. In Bach's very last chorale arrangement this symbolic method is significantly used."

The temptation is great to say that if this was indeed Bach's method, the less Bach he. Fortunately, his music can be enjoyed without such artificial props, stimulating as such exercises may be to a certain kind of mind. There is no music in the literature that has Bach's kind of *rightness,* of inevitability, of intelligence, of logically organized sequences of notes. And there is scarcely any music by any major composer that is so tied up with religion, specifically, Lutheranism. Bach honestly believed that music was an expression of divinity. He began his scores of sacred music with JJ (*Jesu Juva*, "Jesus, help") and ended with SDG (*Soli Deo Gloria*, "To God alone the Glory"). Unconvincing attempts have been made by one or two scholars to prove that Bach was not really a religious composer. It is hard to follow the reasoning. Bach composed a great deal of church music (including much that has been lost), and in the motets and cantatas, the masses and passions, there is so religious a feeling that the music cannot fully be understood except by one whose religious roots, feeling, and very background run closely parallel to Bach's. In the appreciation of any art, the responder's identification with the mental processes of the composer is critical: the closer the identification, the greater the appreciation. Any of us can get the obvious message of *Christ lag in Todesbanden* or the B minor Mass. But the niceties and refinements of the music in relation to the spiritual message and the actual religious service that it represents are fully open only to those who can identify with the church and the spiritual life of Bach's day. Nor are these remarks necessarily confined to Bach's church music. Certainly a work like the *Art of Fugue* means more to one who has himself struggled with counterpoint, and thus is in a position to recognize the diabolically ingenious way Bach solved the problems, than it means to a listener who cannot even read music. But at least the secular music poses fewer difficulties. It is abstract, and following the lines of Bach's thought, sharing in his mental processes, is one of the intellectual and emotional treats music has to offer.

One of the great problems posed by Bach's music in the twentieth century involves matters of performance practice. Obviously, it is impossible to re-create a performance that would duplicate one in Bach's day. Too many factors have changed. And every age has its own performance style. The romantics, as they did in everything, took a very free attitude toward Bach, and played him in their image. Romantic performance practice has extended into our own day, and it has been only within the last few decades that serious attempts have been made to come to grips with the problem. Musicians, thanks to intense musicological research, now know much more than previous generations did about the salient points of Bach's style in performance. Not enough, however, is known. As a corrective to romantic performance practice, a generation of young artists grew up playing, singing, and conducting Bach with mechanical rigidity, using approved editions and relatively small forces in an attempt to be "authentic." The trouble has been that the music then sounds sterile—a Bach robbed of humanity, of grace, of style, of line. If we know one thing about Bach, it is that he was a passionate man and a passionate performer. He undoubtedly played and conducted his own music with infinitely more dash, freedom, and spontaneity than modern performance practice will admit. Bach himself told a pupil, one Johann Gotthilf Ziegler, that an organist should not merely play the notes. He should express the "affect," the meaning, the emotional significance of the piece. By a strange irony, it might eventually turn out that the derided romantics, even though lacking today's scholarship, were instinctively closer to the essential Bach style than the severe, note-perfect, and literal musicians of today.

After Bach's death, most of his music was shelved, though he himself and a handful of his scores were not forgotten. It seems to be an article of faith among Bach biographers that he was neglected for some seventy-five years. That simply is not true. For one thing, his sons, who had a rather ambivalent attitude toward their father (and toward his second wife, too; they let Anna Magdalena all but starve, and she was buried in a pauper's grave), nevertheless did something to propagandize his music. Johann Christian may have once referred to his father as "the old perruque;" but it was Johann Christian who introduced Bach's music to many of the performers of the day. Carl Philipp Emanuel, who seems to have been a little embarrassed by the old-fashioned quality of Bach's music, and who disposed of the plates of the *Art of Fugue,* nevertheless supplied invaluable material to Johann Nicolaus Forkel, Bach's first biographer (1802).

Indeed, all of Bach's sons spread his name and fame. They all took up music, as was expected. "All born musicians," the proud father said of his boys. But several died young and another was feeble-minded. Four, however, went on to important careers.

Wilhelm Friedemann (1710–1784) went to Halle, then started a wandering life, and finally settled in Berlin. He was eccentric and ill-adjusted and, it is believed, a drunkard. He was very talented, and his father's pride, but he lived an unfulfilled life. Carl Philipp Emanuel (1714–1788) was at the court of Frederick the Great for twenty-eight years, achieving great fame—more than his father ever did—as keyboard player, composer, and teacher. In 1768 he succeeded Telemann in Hamburg. As a composer, Carl Philipp Emanuel represented the new style that was sweeping Europe—the elegant, noncontrapuntal *style galant* that was developed by the Mannheim composers and led into Haydn and Mozart. One curious thing about C. P. E. Bach: he could not play the violin because he was left-handed. Johann Christoph Bach (1732–1795), known as the Bückeburg Bach, served in that city from the age of eighteen until his death, carrying on his father's tradition. Finally, there was Johann Christian (1735–1782), the London Bach, who was one of the few traveling members of the family. He went to Italy, where he called himself Giovanni Bach, and he became a Catholic. His father would not have liked that. Then, in 1762, he went to England, where he was known as John Bach. A big social and artistic success, he composed operas, gave piano recitals and conducted orchestras, taught, was mentor to the young Mozart when the child visited London, went bankrupt and died leaving many debts. He, too, represented the *style galant.*

These four sons of Bach, two of them known all over Europe, helped keep old Bach's memory alive. Several things should be kept in mind when discussing Bach's reputation after his death. The institution of the public concert was in its infancy. When concerts *were* given, at whatever kind of hall could be pressed into service (a nobleman's salon, or a dance hall, or an opera house, or whatever, for there were almost no concert halls as such), it was generally through the efforts of a composer who wanted to introduce his own music. The idea of a concert artist playing other men's music was still in the future. Music until the romantic period was very much a contemporary art, concerned primarily with what was going on, not with what had been. Little interest was paid to music of the past. In any case, it was extremely difficult to hear, or to study, music of the past. Scores were hard to find, performances all but nonexistent.

Yet so great was the power of Bach's music that it remained known to many professional musicians. It even came to pass that Bach's music broke tradition by remaining in the repertory at Leipzig. Johann Friedrich Doles, Bach's pupil and successor as the cantor at St. Thomas, from 1756 to 1789, continued to perform Bach's music at the services. Doles also acquainted Mozart with some Bach scores, and Mozart was entranced. He studied them, arranged some of the music, and was strongly influenced by Bachian counterpoint. Baron Gottfried van Swieten in Vienna was the leader of something that amounted to a Bach cult. He showed Bach scores to Mozart and Haydn, and had musicales at which Bach's music was played. Haydn was well acquainted with the *Well-Tempered Clavier* and the B minor Mass, owning the printed music of both. Beethoven was brought up on the *Well-Tempered Clavier.* The English organist and composer Samuel Wesley (1766–1837), long before Mendelssohn revived the *St. Matthew Passion,* was studying, playing, and preaching Bach—and Wesley had been introduced to Bach by a group of dedicated amateurs and professionals. Johann Baptist Cramer (1771–1858), composer and pianist, was playing Bach in public before 1800, and was followed by such other pianists as Alexander Boëly, Joseph Lipavsky, and John Field. Anybody who takes the trouble to go through European musical periodicals and books of the late eighteenth and early nineteenth centuries can dig out innumerable references to "the famous Bach." Many musical histories state that Bach was forgotten after his death, and not rediscovered until the Mendelssohn *St. Matthew* revival of 1829. But that is a myth. Bach most definitely was not forgotten. Indeed, he bulked large. Not so large, perhaps, as Handel, or Johann Adolf Hasse (1699–1783), the popular composer of now-forgotten operas, but large; and the myth of his "total neglect" should be laid to rest.

With Bach's sons, the great stream exhausted itself. The last male Bach descended directly from Johann Sebastian was Wilhelm Friedrich Ernst (1759–1845), a grandson through the Bückeburg Bach. The strain is still alive. Bachs of the Meiningen and Ohrdruf branches are in existence today, and as late as 1937 there was started a *Bach'ser Familienverband für Thüringen*—the Bach Family Association for Thuringia. But none of the twentieth-century Bachs is a professional musician.

Zenger Collection, Municipal Archive, Augsburg

St. Thomas Church in Leipzig, where Bach worked from 1723 to the end of his life.

❧ 2 ❧

Composer and Impresario

GEORGE FRIDERIC HANDEL

Where Bach was a provincial, a German who never left Germany, his great contemporary George Frideric Handel (so he spelled his name in England, where he spent most of his life) was a cosmopolite, a man of the world, an independent figure, one of the first great composers to be also a business man of music. George Frideric Handel: a big man and a lusty one; a naturalized British subject who spoke English with a heavy accent; a man with an explosive temperament and withal a sweet-tempered and even generous philanthropist; a man who made and lost fortunes in his musical enterprises; the owner of a good art collection, including some Rembrandt paintings; one of the greatest organists and harpsichord players of his day; a man with a simple, uncomplicated faith and an equally simple and uncomplicated view toward life.

Handel first came to London in 1710 and made a shattering impact upon the city. That was no easy thing to do in those days. What an age it was! The London of Handel's day had a collection of wits, litterateurs, eccentrics, dandies, perverts, poets, essayists, politicians, and courtiers that made it one of the great intellectual centers of Europe. It was a closed society and a gossipy one. John Gay would write to Alexander Pope, who would relay the information to Dr. Arbuthnot, who would pass it on to Jonathan Swift. Joseph Addison and Richard Steele were delighting London with their *Tatler* and *Spectator* papers. Sir Isaac Newton, having overturned many mathematical concepts and introduced new ones that would keep scientists busy for generations, was brooding about religion. The wits were running all over London, maliciously telling stories about one another. There were no secrets, especially at court; and when Lord Hervey got into one of his frequent scandals, or when one of the Duchess of Queensbury's ladies-in-waiting flirted with a member of the royal family, or when Lord S. was observed slipping from Lady B.'s boudoir, tongues started to wag simultaneously all over London. But the wits did not claim to be retailing gossip.

Never that, they said, licking their lips. As Swift once wrote to Sir Charles Wogan, "You see, Pope, Gay and I use all our endeavours to make folks merry and wise, and profess to have no enemies except knaves and fools."

Into this society, Handel, the burly stranger from Saxony, simply erupted. Domineering, tactless, he immediately started to make enemies, beginning with Addison and Steele. Addison's position was not exactly disinterested. Shortly before the arrival of Handel, Addison had written a libretto that was set to music by a nonentity named Thomas Clayton. The opera was named *Rosamond,* and seldom has the lyric stage given birth to such a failure. Addison, who had hoped to establish a school of opera-in-English, was still smarting, and when that foreigner Handel made his debut with enormous success, and with an Italian libretto, Addison unleashed his heaviest artillery. The *Spectator* papers dealing with Italian opera are still among the funniest and most venomous contributions to the British polemic style.

Handel set the pace, and for years turned out Italian opera after Italian opera. No composer could stand up against him for very long. Handel made Italian opera the rage; and, as a by-product, he made a great deal of money. The impact was overwhelming. Gay wrote about the fad to Swift, with great disgust: "There is nobody allowed to say *I sing* but an eunuch or an Italian woman. Every body is grown now as great a judge of singing as they were in your time of poetry; and folks, that could not distinguish one tune from another, now daily dispute about the different stiles of Handel, Bononcini and Attilio. . . . In London and Westminster, in all polite conversations, Senesino is daily voted to be the greatest man that ever lived." Senesino, born Francesco Bernardi, was one of the important castrato singers active in London. Of the castratos, more later.

The public, and society, took to Handelian opera, but there were fearsome attacks upon him in the press. Nevertheless, by and large, it was believed by most cultivated Englishmen—and Europeans, too—that Handel was the greatest musician who ever lived. He did not suffer from lack of appreciation in his own time. "Hendel from Hanover, a man of the vastest genius and skill in music that perhaps has lived since Orpheus." That was the entry of Viscount Percival in his diary of August 31, 1731. (Percival, like many in that free and permissive orthographic day, spelled words as they were pronounced. Handel dropped the umlaut from his name after he settled in England, but the pronunciation remained "Hendel," and so it was frequently spelled.) Antoine Prévost, he who wrote *Manon Lescaut,* gave an estimate of Handel in his *Le Pour et Contre* (1733): "Never has perfection in any art been combined in the same man with such fertility of production." These reactions of Percival and Prévost were typical. Few composers in history have been so eulogized in their own time, and few were more written about.

And of none of the famous composers in history, except Franz Schubert, have we such scant personal information. There is an enormous amount of material *about* Handel, as anybody can see glancing through Otto Erich Deutsch's massive *Handel: A Documentary Biography*. But no composer has been so secretive about himself. Gaps exist in the Handel chronology, especially during the years he spent in Italy. We know how much money he made, we know how his music was received throughout his life, but we know almost nothing about what he thought. The few Handel letters that have come down to us are formal, stilted affairs in which he reveals nothing about his personal life. For a man so much in the public eye—as composer, as impresario, as executant, as one of the more colorful figures in a colorful period—this cannot be entirely accidental. It is almost as though the man had some secret to hide. Handel guarded his privacy and went out of his way to keep his public life divorced from his private life.

The main contemporary source of information about him comes from the biography by the Reverend John Mainwaring. This was published in 1760, the year after Handel's death, and was the first biography ever written about a musician. That alone is extraordinary testimony to Handel's fame. (Bach's first biography came in 1802, fifty-two years after his death.) But Mainwaring never even knew Handel. He got much of his information from Handel's secretary, John Christopher Smith (born Johann Christoph Schmidt), and the book is full of inaccuracies. Much Handel material can be found in Charles Burney's *A General History of Music* (1776–1789), which has a sketch of the composer's life and a good deal of miscellaneous information. Burney at least knew Handel, and has given a physical description that can be accepted with confidence. Handel, he says, was large, corpulent (Sir John Hawkins, another British writer on music, says that Handel's thick legs were bowed), unwieldy in his motions, and "his general look was somewhat heavy and sour; but when he *did* smile, it was his sire the sun bursting out of a black cloud. . . . He was impetuous, rough, and peremptory in his manners and conversation, but totally devoid of ill-nature or malevolence." That appears to be a fair judgment. The great composer could go into terrible rages, but there never was any malice in him, and his dealings with all people were invariably honest. Burney says that Handel had "a natural propensity to wit and humor," and was a good raconteur even with his heavily accented English. "Had he been as great a master of the English language as Swift, his *bons mots* would have been as frequent, and somewhat of the same kind." Johann Mattheson, the then-famous composer who as a young man had been very close to Handel in Hamburg, attests to Handel's wry sense of humor. Handel "behaved as if he could not count to five. . . . He had a dry way of making the most serious people laugh, without laughing himself." He retained his sense of proportion and could even joke about the affliction that cursed his late years. During his blindness—he lost his sight in 1752, though that did not stop him from composing and playing the organ—his surgeon, Samuel Sharp, suggested that John Stanley participate in one of the Handel concerts. Stanley was a famous blind organist. Handel is supposed to have burst out in a roar of laughter. "Mr. Sharp, have you never read the Scriptures? Do you not remember, if the blind lead the blind, they both fall into the ditch?"

Much traveled, in contact with many great men of the day, Handel must have been a well-rounded personality. It is known that he was a connoisseur of painting. He studied at the University of Halle, which means that he must have received a good humanistic education. But because of his secretiveness, many guesses have to be made about the breadth of his culture. Also guesses are anything that has to do with his sex life. He never married, and whatever associations he had with women he kept to himself. In his early days there were vague rumors about his liaisons with Italian singers. In a copy of the Mainwaring biography is a scribbled bit of marginalia: "G. F. Handel . . . scorned the advice of any but the Woman he loved, but his Amours were rather of short duration, and always within the pale of his own profession." The handwriting is believed to be that of George III.

Judging from his activities, Handel was a gambler, as all impresarios must be. His temper was legendary, especially with singers who crossed him. The most famous occurrence along that line came when the soprano Francesca Cuzzoni refused to sing an aria—*Falsa immagine* from *Ottone*—as written. Handel lost control, grabbed her and made as if to throw her out of the window, bellowing meanwhile: "Madame, I know you are a true she-devil, but I will show you that I am Beelzebub, the chief devil."

What else? He was religious, but not fanatically so, and he told Hawkins of his delight at setting the Scriptures to music. He was an enormous eater, and the famous caricature by Joseph Goupy shows him with the face of a pig, seated on a wine barrel, surrounded by food. (For this it seems that Handel cut Goupy out of his will.) He moved comfortably in the highest society. He was not one of those art-for-art's-sake musicians (that was, in any case, almost unheard-of in Handel's day). He could easily be persuaded to entertain. There is the charming account of a party, on April 12, 1734, which he attended. Lord and Lady Rich were there, and Lord Shaftesbury, and Lord and Lady Hanmer, and the Percivals. Handel played the harpsichord, accompanied amateur singers, and was at the keyboard from 7 to 11, enjoying himself immensely.

Handel was born in Halle on February 23, 1685, the year Bach was born. Little is known about his boyhood, though by the age of ten he was playing the organ well enough to attract the attention of Duke Johann Adolf of Weissenfels. Handel was sent to study with Friedrich Zachow, organist at

34

the Lutheran church at Halle. If Handel had any teacher other than Zachow, he is not known. By 1702, Handel was organist at the cathedral. But he was not cut out to be a church organist. From the very beginning he was attracted to the theater, and in 1703 he went to Hamburg, one of the busiest and most famous opera centers in Europe. It was there that he made friends with the young German composer Johann Mattheson (1681–1764), and it was there that he started composing in earnest. It was there, too, that his life almost came to an end. Mattheson was as strong-minded and stubborn as Handel, and the two young men got into an argument. *Cleopatra*, an opera by Mattheson, was being produced in Hamburg. In addition, Mattheson sang one of the leading roles. Then, presumably to show his versatility, he descended into the orchestra, where Handel was presiding at the harpsichord, and attempted to relieve him of that task. Handel was not the kind of young man who could be pushed aside. There were words, and the two hotheads marched out and drew their swords. Mattheson lunged at Handel, and the sword broke on a metal button of his opponent's coat. A half-inch in any other direction . . . The two made up, and Mattheson even took the tenor lead in Handel's first opera, *Almira*, composed in 1707.

That same year, 1707, Handel went to Rome. He spent the next three years in Italy, where he was called *Il Sassone*—the Saxon—making a big impression there, as he did everywhere. Very little is known about this Italian sojourn. There are anecdotes. Legend has it that he had a harpsichord and organ duel with Domenico Scarlatti, his exact contemporary (Scarlatti also was born in 1685) and the composer of those remarkable keyboard sonatas or "exercises." Scarlatti composed over 550 of these short, glinting masterpieces. The Handel-Scarlatti encounter took place in the house of Cardinal Ottoboni. As harpsichordists, both were declared equal. As organist, Handel won easily. "Scarlatti," says Mainwaring, "himself declared the superiority of his antagonist, and owned ingenuously, that till he had heard him on this instrument, he had no conception of its powers." Something has gone out of musical life with the disappearance of those duels—the appearance on one program of two major instrumentalists who would try to play each other under the table. Mozart and Clementi fought to a draw before the King of Prussia. Beethoven demolished the Abbé Gelinek and anybody else who came his way. Liszt and Thalberg had it out at the salon of Princess Belgiojoso in Paris.

Another anecdote involves the great violinist-composer Arcangelo Corelli. A work by Handel was being played, and Corelli was having trouble in the high positions. Handel, always impulsive, snatched the violin from the hands of the greatest virtuoso in Europe and demonstrated how the passage should go. Corelli, a sweet-tempered and generous man, took no offense. "My dear Saxon, this is music in the French style, of which I have no knowledge." The point is that Handel achieved the respect of all musicians with whom he came into contact. He met everybody, studied everything, and was influenced by the sunny flow of Italian melody. The music of Alessandro Scarlatti (1660–1725), Domenico's father, made a particular impression on him.

From Italy, Handel went to Hanover in 1710 as court musician to the Elector. Later that year he went on leave of absence to England, where Italian opera was the most fashionable of musical entertainments, and where the castrato singers were astonishing everybody with their vocal power and brilliance. Handel composed an opera for the English. It was named *Rinaldo*, was produced in 1711, and was a tremendous success. He went back to Hanover, and it is easy to guess what went on in his mind: a sleepy little court, with little opportunity, versus the great city of London and the chance to become famous and wealthy. So in 1712, Handel obtained permission to go back to England, with the proviso that he return within a reasonable time. In this case, a reasonable time was forever. On his arrival in England he composed an opera, *Il Pastor Fido*, and, soon after, a grand official piece, the *Utrecht Te Deum*, celebrating the Peace of Utrecht. He also wrote a birthday piece for Queen Anne, who settled upon him a yearly pension of £200. Two years had passed, and Handel definitely was absent without leave from the Hanover court. He may or may not have had thoughts of going back. But matters were taken out of his hands when Queen Anne died in 1714. His employer, the Elector of Hanover, succeeded Anne as George I of England. Handel must have spent some uneasy hours wondering what would happen to him.

Nothing did happen. Before long, he was back in George's favor, with a doubled pension. There is a pleasant story, now considered apocryphal, that Handel was restored to the royal confidence through his *Water Music*. As the story goes, the King so admired the score, which was played in 1717 on the occasion of a royal barge trip on the Thames, that a reconciliation immediately took place. There was such a trip, and it is a matter of record that a suite of Handel's music was played during the festivities. And the *Daily Courant* of July 19, 1717, states that George liked the music so well "that he caus'd it to be plaid over three times in going and returning." Unfortunately for the pleasant legend, however, the reconciliation appears to have taken place before 1717.

In London, mentally at ease now that his relations with the King were established, Handel began his long series of operas, becoming as much tangled up in the economic and producing end as in the creative side. He established permanent liaisons with British nobility, especially with Lord Burlington and the Duke of Chandos. For a time he lived in Burlington's great house in Piccadilly, a fact of which John Gay took careful note. The

36

British wits always were greatly interested in the sponsorship any creative figure enjoyed. Burlington House was an artistic and literary center, and Gay commemorated it in his *Trivia:*

> Yet *Burlington's* fair Palace still remains;
> Beauty within, without Proportion reigns . . .
> There *Hendel* strikes the Strings, the melting Strain
> Transports the Soul, and thrills through ev'ry Vein.

Handel plunged into London's social life, aided not only by the £400 pension from George I but by an additional £200 from the Princess of Wales. He headed opera companies that were underwritten by the nobility, and went to Europe to search for singers. In the meantime, a stream of operas was flowing from his pen: *Il Pastor Fido* (1712), *Teseo* (1712), *Silla* (1718), *Radamisto* (1720), *Floridante* (1721), *Ottone* (1723), *Giulio Cesare* (1724), *Tamerlano* (1724), and *Serse* (1738), among others. He turned these out with amazing speed. The Italian librettist, Giacomo Rossi, was amazed at the way Handel dashed off the music for *Rinaldo* in 1711: "Mr. Hendel, the Orpheus of our century, while composing the music, scarcely gave me time to write, and to my great wonder I saw an entire opera put to music by that surprising genius, with the greatest degree of perfection, in only two weeks." What Rossi did not know was that Handel used for *Rinàldo* some music he had previously written for another opera. But Handel was a very, very fast workman. Before he was through, he was to compose over forty operas. All were in Italian, and all were what today is called baroque opera.

Handelian baroque opera was as strict a form as such later art forms as the sonata and the cowboy film. It was marked by certain conventions. Almost always the libretto was based on a classical or mythological subject. Characters in Handel operas sport names like Bradamante, Oronte, Melissa, Morgana, Alcina. They are as artificial as their names. Little attempt at characterization was made by librettists of baroque opera. Handel's music to these librettos may be gay, or martial, or heartbreaking in its pathos, but it is music that more often defines mood than character. The plots had almost no action, and baroque opera has been described as a concert in costume. Handel's operas were no exception. Dramatically they are close to being entirely static.

Basic to the operas was the *da capo* aria. In the *da capo* aria, the singer goes through all of the musical material and then returns to the first section. On the return the singer was expected to show off his bag of vocal tricks, embellishing, adorning, and ornamenting the melody. Handelian opera is largely a succession of *da capo* arias, with a few duets and occasional larger ensembles thrown in. Choruses and orchestral interludes were few. One other aspect of baroque opera might be noted—the behavior of the audience. Opera-going in Handel's day was not the sedate experience it is today. People went to the opera to be seen, and to follow the vocal gyrations of a favorite singer. At performances they would play cards, chat, move around, eat oranges and nuts, spit freely, hiss and yowl at a singer they did not like. The singers themselves would go out of character, greeting friends in the boxes, or talking to one another while they were not singing. Nobody on stage pretended to act.

For this kind of opera, spectacular singing was needed. Handel had those singers, and vocal art has been in decline ever since the disappearance of the castratos. A great castrato was the vocal wonder of all time: a singing machine, virtually a musical instrument. Even before Handel's time the castratos were idols. They were spoiled, pampered figures of great wealth and vanity, and even greater eccentricity. They were the first performers in musical history to achieve star status.

Castratos are what the name implies—castrated males. They were known to antiquity, and reappeared in the service of the popes in the twelfth century. Women's voices had been banished from the church, and the castratos replaced them. The operation took place before puberty. After years of rigorous training, the singers were sent into the service of the church, having female voices and male lungs. Such was the accomplishment of their singing that they began to appear in public, outside of the church. Baldassare Ferri (1610–1680) was the first of the stars. They could do incredible tricks. Some of them had ranges of *four* octaves, up to the A or even B above high C in full voice. And those were voices that lasted. Caffarelli sounded youthful at seventy. Orsini caused a furor with his beautiful singing in Prague when he was seventy-three, and ten years later was singing before Maria Theresa. Bannieri, who died at the age of 102, was singing at the age of ninety-seven. Often these singers were physical freaks, oversized, fat, with barrel chests and yet with skinny arms and legs. They had a sexless kind of woman's voice, but from all reports the sound they produced was of exceptional sweetness. One of their vocal tricks, and one that astounded audiences every time, was their ability to hold a tone. Some of them could sustain a note for well over a minute, and part of the fun of going to the opera in those days was to cheer an encounter between a castrato and a trumpeter or flutist. All would turn blue in the face, holding on to a single note, but the castrato always won. It is related of the young Farinelli that an oboe player once held on to a note, in unison with the singer, much longer than he had done at rehearsal. Farinelli, still singing, let him run out of breath, after which Farinelli continued on and on, still in the same breath. While the audience sat transfixed, waiting for him to explode, Farinelli added a difficult extempore cadenza; and not until then did he have to pause for air.

The great period of castrato singing was from about 1720 to 1790, a period dominated by such singers as Nicolo Grimaldi (called Nicolini), Francesco Bernardi (Senesino), Gaetano Maiorano (Caffarelli), and the greatest of all, Carlo Broschi (Farinelli). All flourished within the period of about a hundred years—from 1673, when Nicolini was born, to 1783, when Caffarelli died. The last of the operatic castratos was Giovanni Battista Vellutti, for whom Meyerbeer wrote a part in *Il Crociato in Egitto* (1824). The breed became extinct, as far as is known, with the death of Alessandro Moreschi (1858–1922). Moreschi was a member of the Sistine Chapel Chorus and actually made a few phonograph records in the first decade of the twentieth century. The sound on those records makes one shiver. The voice has a timbre like that of an alto who is neither male nor female, and with a strange, sad, pleading quality.

What the castrato stood for, vocally, was control and flexibility. A glance at the score of any Handel opera reveals coloratura passages of running thirty-second notes that seem to continue forever without giving the singer a chance to take a breath. The parts do not run especially high, and in any case, audiences of the day did not care for high notes. The tenor's high C is a romantic invention. As a matter of fact, the starring tenor was largely a romantic invention. In baroque opera, tenors sing secondary roles. It is true that most of the castratos could easily take a high C, and if the flutist-composer Johann Quantz (1697–1773) is to be believed, Farinelli could take an F above high C in full voice. But the castratos did not normally go in for such effects. What they were proud of was their incredible breath control and the ability to negotiate any kind of complicated figuration without a break in register or any evidence of vocal strain.

The women singers of Handel's day also had this ability. Most famous were Francesca Cuzzoni and Faustina Bordoni. Both sang in Handel operas in London, often in the same cast. Cuzzoni was short, fat, ugly, ill-tempered, and no actress at all, just as the castratos tended to be tall, fat, ungainly (the absence of secondary sex characteristics prevented the growth of their beards and often gave them the breasts of a woman), and were no actors at all. Bordoni, on the other hand, was attractive and, for the day, an accomplished actress. Naturally, the two women hated one another, and things came to a climax on June 6, 1727, with a performance of Bononcini's *Astianatte*. Spurred by their supporters in the audience (Bordoni was a favorite of the Burlington faction, and Cuzzoni's admirers were part of Lady Pembroke's circle), the two women made for each other with curved talons, and a great fight ensued, complete with screams and hair-pulling. The newspapers had a great time with it, and a pamphlet was published giving a blow-by-blow report of the "full and true Account of a most horrible and bloody Battle between Madame Faustina and Madame Cuzzoni." The pamphlet proposed that the two ladies fight it out in public. Handel happened to be the impresario that immortal evening. He roared that Cuzzoni was a she-devil, that Faustina was "Beelzebub's spoiled child," and that both were hussies.

Audiences in Handel's day were willing to accept the castrato and the conventions of baroque opera. Later audiences did not. Today, no singer could begin to handle the vocal writing as did the singers of Handel's day, nor can the impossibly stilted librettos compensate for the wonderful music. Highly stylized productions are necessary. Some scholars suggest that the castrato roles be transferred to baritones or basses. In any case, the vocal line has to be simplified today, and much of the *raison d'être* of Handelian opera is thus lost. It can still give pleasure, as revivals of *Julius Caesar* and *Alcina*, among others, have shown, but these modern productions can only be called adaptations of the original.

A surprisingly large part of some Handel operas is not original music. Audiences of Handel's day were prepared to accept his appropriations of other men's music. This always has been a touchy subject in Handel biography, and writers have turned themselves inside out trying to explain it, or apologize for it. To put it bluntly, Handel was a plagiarist, and was known as such in his own day. Early in his career he was drawing upon the music of such composers as Keiser, Graun, and Urio and passing it off as his own. From 1737, the year he became ill, Handel more and more drew on the music of other men. His contemporaries took a lenient view of this practice. The Abbé Prévost wrote in 1733: "Some critics, however, accuse him of having borrowed the matter of many beautiful things from Lully, especially from our French cantatas, which he has the skill, so they say, to disguise in the Italian style. But the crime would be venial, were it certain." One charitable explanation would be that the busy Handel, faced with the administration of an opera house, faced with the personality clashes of his singers, faced with the necessity of turning out new operas, faced with the necessity of writing occasional pieces for the court, simply did not have the time to do everything. So he took other material, generally improving it in the process, and passed it off as his own. A list of Handel plagiarisms would be appallingly large. (Bach rewrote other men's music, but these works were in the nature of adaptations or arrangements, and there is no evidence that Bach ever tried to profit from material not his own. Gluck was a self-plagiarist who plundered his own music rather than the music of other men.)

By the late 1720's, the craze in London for Italian opera began to fall off, and was almost killed by the success of *The Beggar's Opera*—a ballad opera sung in English, full of satire addressed against the Walpole administration. *The Beggar's Opera*, with words by John Gay and music arranged by John Christopher Pepusch (1667–1752), has had a more consistent life than any Handel opera, and has never been out of the repertoire since its premiere in

1728. It is an authentic minor masterpiece. It also contributed to the bankruptcy of Handel's Italian opera company. But Handel had made a great deal of money in the enterprise and was able to put £10,000 of his own funds into his next operatic venture at the King's Theater—a venture that lasted until 1737. It might have lasted longer had not a rival opera company been established at Lincoln's Inn Fields. London was not big enough to support two houses, and this time Handel lost a great deal of money.

Italian opera seemed dead, and Handel turned to something else— oratorio in English. He found a ready public for this. He composed *Saul* in 1738, *Israel in Egypt* in 1739, *Messiah* in 1741. In all he composed close to twenty oratorios, ending the great series with *Jephtha* in 1752. Had not total blindness set in by 1751 he doubtless would have composed many more. Recent years have seen an increasing interest in the Handel oratorios, but most of them still remain unknown.

Why did Handel turn to the oratorio? Older biographers liked to believe that after a stroke and some mental disturbance in 1737, Handel became very religious. The truth is probably more mundane. He was a professional composer largely on his own. He was a businessman-composer. If Italian opera was played out, he would turn to something else. Discovering that audiences would flock to his oratorios, he supplied oratorios. Some Handel scholars, notably Paul Henry Lang, insist that the oratorios are not devotional religious works at all; that they are dramatic works on Biblical subjects, completely divorced from the church. In any case, Handel found that composing oratorios was a most profitable enterprise. He was, after all, one of London's most famous figures, and also extremely popular as a performer. So he saw to it that he appeared as organ soloist on every one of his oratorio presentations, playing a concerto or two as added lure. His blindness aroused pity, and that too helped. When *Samson* was presented, and tenor John Beard stood next to the blind composer to sing:

Total eclipse—no sun; no moon.
All dark, amid the blaze of noon

there must have been an audible gulp from the audience.

The neglect today of most of Handel's operas and oratorios—indeed, of most of his music except for *Messiah*—raises some perplexing questions. In his own time Handel was considered one of the greatest musicians who ever lived, and posterity has seen no reason to change the opinion. His reputation in England immediately after his death and during the nineteenth century remained constantly high, though it was primarily as a composer of oratorios that Handel was held in esteem. His powerful influence had a stifling effect on English music; and, indeed, not until the emergence of

41

Edward Elgar did England produce an internationally famous composer. Thanks to Handel, any British composer had to write elaborate choral pieces to prove himself, and, in effect, England went oratorio-crazy. The craze lasted to the end of the nineteenth century, prompting George Bernard Shaw to observe that "The British public takes a creepy kind of pleasure in Requiems." Choral music was considered the property of the people. Only a year after Handel's death a writer named William Mann was saying that village musical groups all over England "since the rage of oratorio has spread from the Capital to every Market Town in the Kingdom, can by no means be satisfied unless they introduce Chaunts, Services, and Anthems into their British Churches. . . ." A great bourgeois pall descended upon British music, and annual Handel festivals became almost a religious event. Whether or not Handel meant his oratorios as a religious exercise, they were taken as such by the public. The *Chester and North Wales Magazine* of April, 1813, had this to say: "The music of Handel is, indeed, admirably adapted to fill the mind with that sort of devotional rapture which, with the commemoration of our blessed Lord and Saviour, as men we ought to admire, and, as Christians, to *feel*." For well over 150 years, music in England was clutched by Handel's enormous fist, with only Mendelssohn making any other kind of impact. No British composer was strong enough to break free.

But after the turn of the twentieth century Handel's reputation declined even in England. Today it is amazing how little of his music actually is heard in public. His operas were forgotten in his own lifetime. Throughout the nineteenth and most of the twentieth century only one of his works achieved great popularity outside of England. That was, of course, *Messiah*. Seldom did an orchestra perform one of his concerti grossi, and seldom do they do so today. His most popular orchestral work, the *Water Music,* is most often heard in an arrangement by Hamilton Harty. Violinists, if they bother to play Handel at all, turn to such souped-up romanticisms as the Nachez arrangement of the A major or D major Sonatas. His organ concertos contain magnificent music, but almost never are they introduced into the concert hall. Most of his operas remain unknown. In Germany before World War II there was an attempt at a revival of the Handel operas, but the works did not take hold. In effect he turned into a one-work man, and it can be said with complete truth that almost everything by Handel except *Messiah* is out of the permanent repertory, with just a handful of works on the periphery. This is in sharp contrast to Bach, whose music is constantly being presented by orchestras, soloists, and choruses the world over.

The reason for Handel's neglect is hard to determine. Naturally, any performance of one of the operas does pose sizable problems. But no problems are involved with his oratorios, his concerti grossi, his harpsichord suites, his anthems, and cantatas. And this is great music. Through all of it breathes an unusual kind of vigor, breadth, confidence, and invention. It also has a peculiarly British quality, some of it derived from Henry Purcell. Handel's music is, in many ways, more accessible than Bach's: easier to understand, more direct in statement, less complex, more strongly melodic and virile. He did not have Bach's harmonic ingenuity or mastery of counterpoint—who had?—but Handel's counterpoint is nevertheless confident and secure. Handel biographers used to worry about Handel's counterpoint and would compare it unfavorably with Bach's. Comparison is meaningless, for the two composers were after different things. Bach *thought* contrapuntally, as naturally and inevitably as he breathed. Handel used a freer, less textbookish kind of counterpoint only as a tool, for certain effects.

Handel's music awaits rediscovery, a fact that would have come as an overwhelming surprise to his contemporaries. For *they* knew his worth, and Handel himself knew, even unto requesting that he be buried in Westminster Abbey. He died at the age of seventy-four on April 14, 1759, and there was real grief all over England. Handel became the subject of innumerable and elaborate obituaries, of which the one in the *Public Advertiser* of April 17 is typical, complete with acrostic on Handel's name:

> *H*e's gone, the Soul of Harmony is fled!
> *A*nd warbling Angels hover round him dead.
> *N*ever, no, never since the Tide of Time,
> *D*id music know a Genius so sublime!
> *E*ach mighty harmonist that's gone before,
> *L*essen'd to Mites when we his Works explore.

Farinello in abito
che viaggia, che vice
meno i Complimenti
p'lo suo personaggio
nell'anco

in abito da Eullio che prima nobre che
meno à Venetia

Reproduced by permission of S. Karger, Basel/New York
from Moses, P.J.: The psychology of the castrato
voice. Folia phoniat. 12:204–216 (1960).

CONTEMPORARY CARICATURES OF THE GREAT CASTRATO FARINELLI

❧ 3 ❧

Reformer of Opera

CHRISTOPH WILLIBALD GLUCK

Christoph Willibald Gluck's greatest claim to historical fame is as the man who initiated the first great reform in opera. Indeed, he is more famous as a reformer than as a composer. He wrote about fifty operas, of which only one —*Orfeo ed Euridice*—is steadily in the repertory, though *Alceste* and the two *Iphigénie* operas are revived once in a while. Working almost exclusively for the stage, he composed no instrumental music to speak of. Very few, if any, of his early operas have survived. Gluck was a late developer, and not until the age of forty-eight did he compose *Orfeo*. Up to then he had uncomplainingly written a long series of works that followed the established conventions. There was no hint that he was dissatisfied, no indication that in *Orfeo* he would come up with something so spectacularly and radically new.

Had he not met a librettist who stimulated him, Gluck in all probability would never have composed music on the level of an *Orfeo*, nor would he have reformed anything. Ranieri da Calzabigi (1714–1795) was to Gluck what Lorenzo da Ponte was to Mozart. And those two poets had a great deal in common. Both were adventurers, travelers, intriguers, politicians, and rather unscrupulous operators. Both were playwrights with a thorough understanding of, and appreciation for, the musical theater. Both turned up in Vienna just at the right moment. Calzabigi arrived there in 1761 and, in effect, handed Gluck his reform in the libretto of *Orfeo ed Euridice*. Gluck was generous enough to pay full tribute to his collaborator:

> If my music has had some success, I think it is my duty to recognize that I am beholden for it to him, since it was he who enabled me to develop the resources of my art. . . . No matter how much talent a composer has, he will never produce any but mediocre music unless the poet awakens in him that enthusiasm without which the productions of all the arts are but feeble and drooping.

Up to 1762, the year of the *Orfeo ed Euridice* premiere, Gluck had achieved some success, but was regarded as a good professional rather than as the (middle-aged) *enfant terrible* he turned out to be. He was born in Erasbach, in the Upper Palatinate, on July 2, 1714. His father was a forester in the service of great nobles, and the family was constantly on the move. Not much is known of Gluck's early years. He appears to have been well educated, and could play the violin, cello, and clavier. There is evidence that he went to the university in Prague. At the age of twenty-two he went to Vienna, and then to Milan, where he studied with the famous Giovanni Battista Sammartini (1701–1775). Italy claimed Gluck for eight years, and it was there, in 1741, that he composed his first opera, *Artaserse*. It was produced in December of that year in Milan, was a success, and was followed by a series of operas that today are completely forgotten. Even the scores of some of them are lost.

Like Handel, Gluck was a cosmopolite. He drifted to Paris for a brief stay, then to London in 1745. In London he composed two works for the Italian Opera, *La Caduta de' Giganti* and *Artamene*. These were commissioned by Lord Middlesex, proving that Gluck already must have enjoyed a certain amount of fame. In London, too, he made friends with Handel, who is reported to have jeered that his cook knew more counterpoint than Gluck. Considering that Handel's cook, Gustavus Waltz (or Walz), was a bass singer and a well-trained musician, there may have been some truth in the statement. But certainly Gluck, with his kind of training, must have been able to handle the intricacies of fugue. The point is that he was never particularly interested in counterpoint, which is different from saying that he could not manage it. Because Gluck thought homophonically (as opposed to contrapuntally), it has become an article of faith in certain circles that his technique was inferior. Thus Sir Donald Tovey, while pointing out Gluck's constant inspiration, insisted that "his routine technique was and remained poor." Which it was, when measured against the infinite resource of a Bach or Handel. But it wasn't in relation to what Gluck was trying to do. Gluck may or may not have heard Handel's gibe. Certain it is that they remained on good terms, and later in life Gluck had a painting of Handel in his bedroom. He would point to it, saying: "There is the portrait of the most inspired master of our art. When I open my eyes in the morning I look upon him with reverence and awe, and acknowledge him as such."

Gluck's peregrinations took him next to Hamburg, where he directed a touring Italian opera company that visited, among other cities, Leipzig and Dresden. In 1749 he was back in Vienna, and the following year he married the daughter of a rich merchant. From that time he never had to worry about money, which put him in a unique position among the composers of his day. The financial security doubtless accounted for his growing independence—some called it arrogance—and stubbornness. It is easy to tell the world to go to hell when you do not have to worry about the consequences. Gluck composed steadily, and also made a name as a conductor. In 1752 he was appointed kapellmeister of the Imperial Court in Vienna, and in 1754 the director of Prince Hildburghausen's orchestra. In 1756 he received a knighthood from Pope Benedict XIV. After that he insisted upon being called Ritter von Gluck or, in France, the Chevalier Gluck. During these years he composed a series of operas completely forgotten today. They sport such names as *Ezio, Issipile, Le Cinesi, La Dansa,* and *Antigono.*

If his acquaintance with Calzabigi sparked his reform, it can also be said that reform was in the air. Opera had become sheer formula, solidified on the one side by the librettos of Metastasio and disintegrated on the other by the antics of the singers. Pietro Metastasio (1698–1782) was a writer who was especially famous in musical circles for his twenty-seven *drammi per musica.* Most of these were written while he was the Imperial Court Poet of Vienna, a position he held from 1730 until his death. These twenty-seven musical dramas were set by eighteenth-century composers over *a thousand* times. Some of them were so highly regarded that they were set by as many as seventy different composers. No wonder audiences would attend a new opera with the feeling that they had seen it all before. The Metastasian librettos were based on mythology and ancient history, had many characters, and were carefully put together. Tovey describes them as well-constructed and logical, "a very rational musical scheme, according to which each situation was arrived at by a natural and smooth progress of dialogue and action, in order to be marked at every emotional crisis or possible point of repose by a tableau during which the emotion could be expressed in an aria and set to a few lines of pregnant poetry so designed that the words would bear repetition with good musical effect in a musical scheme."

That might have been. But Metastasian opera, and indeed all Italian opera of the time, was a succession of solos and duets dominated by singers who incessantly bawled improvised roulades on a few vowels. And the singers those days were lords of creation who loftily told the composer what to do, and who had no hesitation about altering the music to fit their individual egos and vocal styles. All stage action would come to a stop while they approached the footlights and astounded the audience with vocal pyrotechnics. From the composers, poor things, came occasional objections and pleas for reform. As early as 1720 the Italian composer Benedetto Marcello, in a prose sketch entitled *Il Teatro alla Moda,* satirized Italian opera. One paragraph in it sets forth the relationship between composer and singer: "In working with singers, especially castratos, the composer will always place himself on their left and keep one step behind, hat in hand. . . . He will quicken or retard the tempo of the arias set to the genius of the virtuosos, covering up whatever bad judgment they show with the reflection that his own reputation, credit and interests are in their hands, and for that reason, if need be, he will alter arias, recitatives, sharps, flats, naturals, etc."

It was time for reform. There were factors other than the built-in absurdities of baroque opera. The age of the baroque was being superseded by a new classicism, and the trend was toward simplicity rather than ornateness. Musicians by 1760 had broken completely away from the complicated baroque splendor and were writing in the *style galant,* a simple and melodic style devoid of counterpoint. The thinking of the age was influenced by Rousseau, who came out with his ideal of nature and naturalness in his *Nouvelle Héloïse* (1760) and *Émile* (1762). Johann Joachim Winckelmann, in his famous history of Greek art (1764), reintroduced the classic ideal to Europe. His conclusions, that beauty was a subjugation of details to the whole, that true art consisted of harmony and graceful proportion, greatly influenced the aesthetic thinking of the Enlightenment. Gluck, stimulated by the Calzabigi librettos, did for opera what Winckelmann preached for art and Rousseau for man (Gluck, who obviously had read Rousseau, was always talking about returning to nature in his music, nature meaning not merely trees and sky but life as it actually is lived). Discarding baroque opera, with its embellishments, ornateness, and vocal show, he turned to the classical ideals of purity, balance, simplicity, and even austerity. He was not, however, altogether consistent in his thinking. In the twenty-five years following *Orfeo ed Euridice,* he composed thirteen more operas. Of those, six were "reform" operas and the others in the earlier baroque style. Nevertheless it was Gluck who changed the course of opera, and his ideas did lead to Wagner and even beyond.

His first step was to put the singers in their place, and he did this in two ways. One was by insisting that they remain in character throughout the opera. The other was by modifying or abolishing the da capo aria. No longer could singers insanely improvise on the return to the first section. They had to sing what was written; and the hot-tempered and imperious Gluck, the most demanding conductor of his day, invariably conducted his own operas to make sure that was exactly what would happen. In the Gluck reform operas, arias are much shorter than they were in baroque opera, and there is an increased amount of recitative. Recitative is heightened speech, declamatory in nature, as opposed to sung aria. It is used as a device to further the stage action and characterization, bridging the sung portions of the opera. Gluck all but discarded the old *recitativo secco,* in which the accompaniment is reduced to a chord or two played on the harpsichord. Instead, he used the much more expressive *recitativo stromentato,* with its rather elaborate instrumental accompaniment. He established the overture as part of the drama, strove for emotional realism and development of character,

47

and tried to achieve a complete dramatic unity.

All of this was new in operatic thinking. In a letter to the *Mercure de France* in 1773, Gluck neatly outlined what he was trying to do: "The imitation of nature is the acknowledged goal to which all artists must set themselves. It is that which I too try to attain. Always as simple and natural as I can make it, my music strives toward the utmost expressiveness and seeks to reinforce the meaning of the underlying poetry. It is for this reason that I do not use those trills, coloraturas and cadences that Italians employ so abundantly." Gluck repeated the point to the *Journal de Paris* in 1777: "I believed that the voices, the instruments, all the sounds, and even the silences [in my music] ought to have only one aim, namely that of expression, and that the union of music and words ought to be so intimate that the libretto would seem to be no less closely patterned after the music than the music after the libretto."

Orfeo ed Euridice adheres to these ideals more closely than any other Gluck opera does. The plot lines are clear (even below a minimum of action, some writers have complained), the poetry is simple but elevated, the music is stripped of all superfluities, even of harmonic superfluities. Gluck never was a very inventive harmonist, and was timid about modulations and key changes.

The original 1762 version of *Orfeo* was in Italian, with a male alto as Orfeo. That was the only conventional thing about the score. Musicologists have pointed out that never in the history of opera had such a drastic change in style been accomplished. At first, *Orfeo* was too novel for the Viennese public, but it did not take long before it had enthusiastic adherents. Gluck's next reform opera was *Alceste*, in 1767, again in Italian. It is in the preface to *Alceste* that Gluck fully set forth his theories. As one of the most famous documents of music, it deserves to be reprinted here in a substantially complete version:

When I undertook to write the music for *Alceste*, I resolved to divest it entirely of all those abuses, introduced into it either by the mistaken vanity of singers or by the too great complaisance of composers, which have so long disfigured Italian opera and made of the most splendid and most beautiful of spectacles the most ridiculous and wearisome. I have striven to restrict music to its true office of serving poetry by means of expression and by following the situations of the plot, without interrupting the action or stifling it with a useless superfluity of ornaments; and I believed that it should do this in the same way as telling colors affect correct and well-ordered painting, by a well-assorted contrast of light and shade, which serves to animate the figures without altering their contours. Thus I do not wish to arrest a performer in the greatest heat of dialogue in order to wait for a tiresome *ritornello*, nor to hold him up in the middle of a word on a vowel favorable to his voice, nor to make display of the agility of his fine voice in some long-drawn passage, nor to wait while the orchestra gives him time to recover his breath for a cadenza. I did not think it my duty to pass quickly over the second section of an aria of which perhaps the words are the most impassioned and important, in order to repeat regularly four times over those of the first part, and to finish the aria where its sense may perhaps not end for the convenience of the singer who wishes to show that he can capriciously vary a passage in a number of guises; in short, I have sought to abolish all those abuses against which good sense and reason have cried out in vain.

I have felt that the overture ought to apprise the spectators of the nature of the action that is to be represented and to form, so to speak, its argument; that the concerted instruments should be introduced in proportion to the interest and the intensity of the words, and not leave that sharp contrast between the aria and the recitative in the dialogue, so as not to break a period unreasonably nor wantonly disturb the force and heat of the action.

Furthermore, I believed that my greatest labor should be devoted to seeking a beautiful simplicity, and I have avoided making displays of difficulty at the expense of clarity; nor did I judge it desirable to discover novelties if it was not naturally suggested by the situation and the expression; and there is no rule which I have not thought it right to set aside willingly for the sake of an intended effect.

Such are my principles. By good fortune my designs were wonderfully furthered by the libretto, in which the celebrated author, devising a new dramatic scheme, for florid descriptions, unnatural paragons, and sententious, cold morality had substituted heartfelt language, strong passions, interesting situations and endlessly varied spectacle. The success of the work justified my maxims, and the universal approbation of so enlightened a city has made it clearly evident that simplicity, truth and naturalness are the great principles of beauty in all artistic manifestations. . . .

The third Calzabigi-Gluck collaboration was *Paride ed Elena* in 1770. Then Gluck turned his attention to Paris, where there was great curiosity about his operas. *Iphigénie en Aulide,* with a libretto by François du Roullet, was produced at the Opéra in 1774. Gluck in Paris had the not inconsiderable support of Marie Antoinette. She had been one of his singing pupils in Vienna, and he had no hesitation about dropping her name. Once, dissatisfied at an *Iphigénie* rehearsal, he loudly said: "I shall go to the Queen and tell her that it is impossible to produce my opera. Then I shall get into my coach and go straight back to Vienna." Gluck had his way, as he always did. *Iphigénie* was followed a few months later by the French version of *Orfeo,* in which a tenor replaced the castrato. (The original Italian version with a mezzo-soprano or contralto replacing the male alto. is the one customarily heard today.) Gluck also put *Alceste* into French.

His years in Paris were enlivened by his rivalry with Niccolò Piccinni (1728-1800), a skillful Italian composer who came to Paris in 1776. Piccinni had immediately attracted a group of followers who felt much happier with his traditional operas than with the classical austerities of Gluck. There were great polemics, and Paris enjoyed the controversy as much as it had enjoyed the *Guerre des bouffons* in the early 1750's. That earlier controversy also had to do with opera. Some maintained that the old French opera of Jean-Baptiste Lully (1632–1687) was the only logical course for French opera to take; others insisted with equal fervor that salvation lay only through Italian opera. Rousseau favored the latter, saying that the French language was unmusical and that French opera therefore necessarily had to be an absurdity. Parisians entered the Gluck-Piccinni controversy with equal seriousness. It was reported that men, meeting for the first time, would say: "Sir, are you a Gluckist or Piccinnist?" Benjamin Franklin, in Paris at the time as Commissioner of the new United States of America, listened with amazement to the two factions, who, he wrote:

were disputing warmly on the merit of two foreign musicians, one a *cousin,* the other a *moscheto;* in which dispute they spent their time, seemingly as regardless of the shortness of time as if they had been sure of living a month. Happy people! thought I, you live certainly under a wise, just and mild government, since you have no public grievances to complain of, nor any subject of contention but the perfections and imperfections of foreign music.

Through all this, Gluck and Piccinni remained on good terms, though a note of asperity crept into their relations toward the end of the *affaire*. The consensus was that Gluck had carried the field, especially after *Armide* of 1777 and *Iphigénie en Tauride* of 1779. Some diplomatic observers, however, attempted to smooth things over by saying that Gluck was superior in tragedy, Piccinni in comedy. *Echo et Narcisse,* also produced in 1779, was Gluck's last major work. He had a stroke in 1781 and spent the last years of his life in Vienna, holding court but composing no more.

Gluck was a tough, domineering man with an explosive temper and a genius for self-promotion. In the memoirs of Johann Christoph von Mannlich, a court painter in Paris, there is a good description of Gluck. Mannlich was a little disappointed at first. "Anybody meeting Gluck, wearing his round wig and his large overcoat, would never have taken him for a prominent person and a creative genius." Gluck, says Mannlich, was a little above medium height (which in those days would have put him about 5 feet, 6 inches), "stocky, strong and muscular without being stout. His head was round, his face ruddy, broad and pock-marked. The eyes were small and deeply set." (Dr. Charles Burney agreed, saying that Gluck was "coarse in figure and look.") Mannlich comments on Gluck's "excitable" nature and his devastating frankness or even rudeness. "He called things by their name and therefore, twenty times a day, offended the sensitive ears of the Parisians, used to flattery." The French considered him a very impolite man. "He was a hearty eater and drinker," continues Mannlich. "He never denied being grasping and fond of money, and displayed a goodly portion of egotism, particularly at table, where he was wont at sight to claim first right to the best morsels."

Not only did the Parisians consider him uncouth. As a conductor he was the Toscanini of his day, an irascible martinet, and musicians trembled before him. Or they refused to play in his orchestras. He was a perfectionist who would have the players repeat a passage twenty or thirty times before he was satisfied. Such was the antagonism between Gluck and his players in Vienna that more than once the Emperor himself had to intervene. The gossip was that when Gluck was preparing one of his operas, he had to bribe musicians by offering them double rates. Gluck must have had an extraordinary ear, and the sloppy playing prevalent in his day drove him crazy. He said that if he received twenty livres for composing an opera, he should be paid 20,000 for rehearsing it. Mannlich, who attended the *Aulide* rehearsals, gives an idea of what went on:

> He tore around like a madman. Now the violins were at fault, then the wind instruments had failed to give proper expression to his ideas. While conducting, he would suddenly break off, singing the part with the desired expression. Then, after conducting for a while, he would stop them, screaming at the top of his lungs: "This isn't worth a hoot in hell!" I mentally saw the violins and other instruments flying at his head. . . .

But although Gluck hated to do so, he invariably insisted on preparing his own operas. He knew what would happen if he entrusted them to other hands. As he pointed out to the Duc de Bragance in the dedication of *Paride ed Elena*, "The more one strives for truth and perfection, the more necessary are precision and exactitude." Only the composer, Gluck justly observed, can attain this. "It requires little for my aria, *Che farò senza Euridice,* to turn into a saltarello by Burattini—no more, in fact, than a slight change of expression. . . . Thus the composer's presence at the performance of such music is as necessary as the presence of the sun in the works of nature. He is its very life and soul, and without him everything is confusion and darkness."

To his singers, Gluck was equally abrupt, constantly charging them with

51

screaming, with lack of taste and musicianship. Indeed, to everybody the strong-minded, independent, tactless Gluck was a trial. He always seemed to be saying the wrong things. In retrospect, they have proved to be the right things. Gluck was far ahead of his time as a sociological phenomenon. But that did not make it any easier for his friends to live with him. There was the time he was invited to visit the King at Versailles. On his return to Paris, he dined at the home of a duke. "Were you not pleased at the King's reception?" the grandee wanted to know. Gluck growled that he supposed he should be flattered, but "if I write another opera in Paris, I should prefer to dedicate it to the general collector of taxes, because he may give me ducats instead of compliments." There was consternation among the guests, and the duke quickly changed the subject. Gluck had something remarkably Beethovenian in his nature, and was prepared to dictate to life on his own terms. Thus, in his dealings with the Opéra, he did not ask for but demanded certain conditions. "I must be given at least two months after I arrive in Paris to train my cast; I must have complete authority to call as many rehearsals as I think necessary; there will be no understudies, and another opera shall be held ready in case one of the singers is indisposed. These are my conditions, without which I shall keep *Armide* for my own pleasure." No other composer in Europe could have gotten away with such a *Diktat*.

It was generally realized in Gluck's day that he had revolutionized opera. Dr. Burney, who visited Gluck in 1772, noted that "The Chevalier Gluck is simplifying music . . . he tries all he can to keep his music chaste and sober." Elsewhere: "His invention is, I believe, unequalled by any composer who now lives or has existed, particularly in dramatic painting and theatrical effects." Burney was overwhelmed, as much by the man as by his music, and he relates a charming episode on the occasion of his, Burney's, *adieux*. He visited the Chevalier to say good-bye, "and it was near eleven o'clock when I arrived, yet, like a true great genius, he was still in bed."

Other composers envied Gluck his success, and also were somewhat afraid of him. He was a dangerous infighter. Leopold Mozart told his son to keep away from Gluck. Their paths crossed during Mozart's visit to Paris in 1778. Later, Wolfgang and Gluck met once again in Vienna, and Mozart called him a "great man." It was an indication of the relative position of the two in official eyes that Gluck received 2,000 florins as Royal and Imperial Court Composer of Vienna. When Mozart succeeded Gluck, it was at a pittance of 800 gulden. Leopold Mozart, always a suspicious man who saw conspiracies under the corner of every tablecloth, was convinced that Gluck was jealous of Wolfgang, and was at the head of a cabal to keep his son down.

Gluck's influence turned up only peripherally in Mozart. It is noticeable primarily in Mozart's *opera seria*, *Idomeneo*. Once in a while a melody, such as the one in the slow movement of the D major Flute Quartet, suggests Gluck. The Gluckian spirit was much more pronounced in the works of Spontini, Cherubini, and, to a point, the classicism of Berlioz' *Les Troyens*. Debussy noted that influence in the Berlioz opera and wrote that it was "reminiscent of Gluck, whom he passionately loved." Berlioz did indeed worship Gluck, and as a student he spent hours copying and memorizing the Gluck operas. "The Jove of our Olympus was Gluck." At the Opéra, Berlioz was the watchdog who barked and howled when the conductors touched up a Gluck opera, or otherwise departed from the score. After Berlioz, the direct influence of Gluck is scarcely discernible in European music. Romantic color and Gluck's white classicism did not go together. Modern scholars tend to take Gluck as the end rather than the beginning of a period. Donald Grout's summation (in his *A Short History of Opera*) is representative: "Gluck was, like Handel, the end of an epoch rather than the beginning. He sums up the classicism of serious opera as Handel does of baroque opera." But there is more to Gluck and his influence than that. He did point the way to opera as music drama, as an all-in-one synthesis where song, text, action, dance, and décor were to be united on more or less equal terms. As such, he is the spiritual ancestor of Richard Wagner.

❧ 4 ❧

Classicism par excellence

FRANZ JOSEPH HAYDN

The age in which Franz Joseph Haydn was the most celebrated musical figure was an age that prided itself on its civilization, on its logic, on its emotional restraint, on its *politesse*. It was the golden age of the aristocracy; and also an age in which philosophers honestly believed that reason could direct the working of man and his society. Blood and revolution were to come, near the end of the century, followed by new concepts of society and the role of the artist. But in the eighteenth century, young intellectuals and artists did not walk around wrapped in a mental toga, glorying in their unique gift, making a great to-do about their visions, their sufferings, their ideals and aspirations. That remained for the young romantics of the nineteenth century. The second half of the eighteenth century was an age that looked for proportion in all things. In music, it did not care for fugue or for the immense, complicated forms of the Baroque. It demanded melodic music, homophonic music, music that would entertain, music that would not put too great a strain on the intellect.

Joseph Haydn was *the* composer of the period—the most respected, the most honored, the one closest to the tastes of his public. He was the classic composer *par excellence,* and in his long life, from 1732 to 1809, he grew up with the new musical ideas and, more than any one man, shaped them. In his way he was the typical figure of the Enlightenment, religious but not too religious, daring but not too daring, intelligent but not aggressively so, adventurous but not nearly so revolutionary as Mozart (a much more suppressed, dangerous, rebellious man). With Haydn, everything was in intellectual and emotional proportion.

Physically he was not a prepossessing figure. He was short and dark, his face was pitted by smallpox, his legs were too short for his body. His nose had a polyp that threw it out of shape, and he appears to have been sensitive about it. The famous Haydn never commissioned a portrait. But he must have been a very nice man to know. A person of singularly sweet, kind disposition, he made virtually no enemies at any time. He was even-tempered, industrious, generous, had a good sense of humor, handled his love affairs like a gentleman, enjoyed good health except for some eye trouble and rheumatism toward the end. He may not have been well educated, he was not much of a reader, but he was a practical man with good common sense. He had integrity and intellectual honesty—the kind of honesty that could allow him to say, when Mozart's name came up, "My friends often flatter me about my talent, but he was far above me." He liked to dress well. A Bohemian musician, Johann Wenzel Tomaschek, described the old master receiving guests toward the end of his life: "Haydn sat in an armchair, all dolled up. A powdered wig with side locks, a white neckband with a gold buckle, a white, richly embroidered waistcoat of heavy silk, in the midst of which shone a splendid jabot, a dress coat of fine coffee-colored cloth with embroidered cuffs, black silk breeches, white silk hose, shoes with large silver buckles curved over the instep, and on the little table next to him a pair of white kid gloves."

Haydn lived in a period of patronage. When he entered the service of the Esterházy family—and he was to remain with the Esterházys for a good part of his life—he never did question his position as a servant who wore his master's livery and ate with the help. Yet that never inhibited his strong streak of independence. He was not particularly impressed with nobility and, not being a snob, did not seek contacts with the great. It was not that he felt inferior or knew his position. He simply was not interested, and his feet were too firmly on the ground. "I have had converse with emperors, kings and great princes, and have heard many flattering remarks from them, but I do not wish to live on a familiar footing with such persons, and I prefer people of my own class." Primarily he was interested only in musicians or those who loved music; he was completely apolitical and wanted to be left alone to do his own work. There he was fully aware of his superiority and had no hesitation exercising his authority. One of his masters, Prince Nicholas II, once interfered with a Haydn rehearsal. Haydn all but threw His Grace out. "That, your Highness, is *my* affair." It is reported that Nicholas stomped away in a rage, but made no effort to discipline his famous Kapellmeister. Had he done so, Haydn might have left for good. There were plenty of rich princes eager to have the great Haydn in their employ. Haydn was just as independent with his publishers. He got into a dispute with the firm of Artaria in 1782 and, when matters were not satisfactorily resolved, sent a curt note: "So finish the affair and send me either my music or my money." But there was nothing small or petty about Haydn. He was an authentically big man, a secure man, and never worried about competition. He not only had infinite praise for Mozart, but as early as 1793 he

55

knew enough about the young Beethoven, whom he had briefly taught, to send a tremendous endorsement to the Elector of Cologne: "Beethoven will in time fill the position of one of Europe's greatest composers . . ."

In short, Haydn was a well-adjusted man, and it shows in his music. It is hard to think of the music of any composer that is so free of the neurotic (probably the only comparable body of music in this respect would be Dvořák's). Haydn's music is always sane and healthy. It may have lacked the passion of Mozart's, but a good case can be made that Haydn's music is as consistently on as high a plane as Mozart's, perhaps higher, even if he never reached the mighty levels of Mozart at his greatest. From about 1780 to his death there is scarcely a Haydn symphony, quartet, mass, or oratorio that cannot legitimately be called a masterpiece. The fertility of the man was breathtaking.

But had he died at Mozart's age, thirty-six, he would be all but unknown today. Haydn developed slowly, in a straight line. He was very talented as a child, but was not a Wunderkind, and never dashed off music the way that Mozart, Schubert, or Mendelssohn did. "I was never a quick writer, and composed with care and diligence," he indicated. His career is one of slow growth. He moved along, consolidating his gains. When he started his work, the new music—the music of the *style galant*—was in its infancy and Haydn put everything together. It is not for nothing that he is called The Father of the Symphony. With equal justice he could be called The Father of the String Quartet, or The Father of Sonata Form.

Franz Josef Haydn was born on March 31, 1732, in the town of Rohrau, just on the border of Austria and Hungary. It was formerly believed that the family was Croatian. Modern research has established the fact that the Haydns were Austrian. Mathias Haydn, Joseph's father, was a wagon-maker. The boy grew up virtually as a peasant. But from the beginning he showed unusual musical aptitude. There are pleasant stories of the five-year-old Joseph playing make-believe violinist, sawing at his left arm with a stick. His parents hoped he would become a clergyman, and it was with this aim that Joseph, shortly before he was six years old, was sent to nearby Hainburg at the instigation of a cousin. There he learned to read and write, studied the catechism, and, because of his musical ability, received instruction in wind and string instruments. Haydn himself wrote, in an autobiographical sketch, "Our Almighty Father had endowed me with such fertility in music that even in my sixth year I stood up like a man and sang masses in the church choir and I could play a little on the clavier and violin." But it was not all easy going. Haydn had a miserable life as a child. "More floggings than food," he later remembered. For the most part he had to teach himself. "Proper teachers I never had. I always started right away with the practical side first in singing and playing instruments, later in composing. I listened more than I studied, but I heard the finest music in all forms that was to be heard in my time. . . . Thus little by little my knowledge and my ability were developed."

It was in Vienna that Haydn heard the "finest music." At the age of eight he was recruited into the choir of St. Stephen's Cathedral, where he became one of the star pupils. In 1749 his voice broke, and he was dismissed. Legend has it that his dismissal was accelerated by a schoolboy prank. He is supposed to have cut off a fellow student's pigtail. Haydn was seventeen at the time, and his sole possessions were three old shirts and a worn coat. When he left, the new star pupil was his younger brother, Michael (1737–1806), of whom great things were predicted. Michael seems to have been more gifted than Joseph in everything but composition. He did go on to have a fine career, taking Mozart's place at Salzburg as director of the Archbishop's orchestra. He also composed a large quantity of church music. None of his work, however, has remained in the active repertoire.

For several years after leaving St. Stephen's, Haydn all but starved. As a pianist and violinist he was not on a professional level. He himself admitted that he was "a wizard on no instrument, but I knew the strength and working of all; I was not a bad clavier player or singer, and could also play a concerto on the violin." But many musicians could do that. For eight years Haydn had to "eke out a wretched existence." He lived a Bohemian life, playing at social functions, teaching, arranging music; and, "in my zeal for composition, composed well into the night." He studied the music of C. P. E. Bach and had a few lessons with Nicola Porpora (1686–1767), a famous composer of the day. Little by little he made headway. Possibly his piano and violin playing improved. Certainly his reputation grew. In 1758 he was appointed music director and composer for Count Ferdinand Maximilian von Morzin. Two years later he made the greatest single mistake of his life. He married Maria Anna Aloysia Apollonia Keller.

She was the daughter of a hairdresser, and Haydn was really in love with one of her sisters. Here there is a strong parallel with Mozart, who was in love with Aloysia Weber and then married her sister Constanze on the rebound. Haydn, searching for a wife, was probably talked into marriage by the Keller family. Maria Anna was three years older than Haydn, ugly, ill-tempered, jealous, and a shrew. She did not like music, she was a poor housekeeper, she could not manage money, and she was not thrifty. Small wonder that Haydn quickly became disenchanted, referring to her as "that infernal beast," and turned elsewhere for relaxation. He later rationalized his extramarital affairs by telling his first biographer, Georg August Griesinger, "My wife was unable to bear children, and for this reason I was less indifferent toward the attraction of other women."

57

It was in 1761 that Haydn made the most significant move of his life, entering the service of the Esterházy family as vice-Kapellmeister. Prince Paul Anton Esterházy was head of the greatest and richest family in Hungary, and was a lover of art and music. His castle at Eisenstadt had 200 rooms for guests, and also contained parks and theaters. Haydn moved in, congratulating himself. The terms of his contract are interesting. They give an idea of what was expected from a musician in the service of a great lord:

1st. For many years there has been in Eisenstadt a Kapellmeister Gregorius Werner, who has rendered faithful service to the princely house, but on account of his great age and the incapacity often resulting therefrom can no longer fulfill his duties. He, Gregorius Werner, in consideration of his services of many years, will remain head Kapellmeister, and the aforementioned Joseph Heyden [so his name is spelled throughout the contract] will be Vice-Kapellmeister, subordinate to and answering to Gregorius Werner in choir music; but in all other matters, where music has to be made, everything pertaining to music will at once become the responsibility *in genere* and *in specie* of the Vice-Kapellmeister.

2nd. Joseph Heyden will be considered an officer of the house. Therefore, His Serene Highness graciously trusts that he will, as befits an honest house officer, behave soberly and, to the musicians directed by him, not brutishly but gently, modestly, calmly and honestly, especially when music is to be made in front of His Highness, and not only shall the Vice-Kapellmeister Joseph Heyden together with his subordinates, appear at all times clean and in livery, but he will also see that all those answering to him follow the instructions given to them and appear in white stockings, white shirt, powdered and pigtails dressed alike. Therefore:

3rd. All musicians are subordinated to the Vice-Kapellmeister, consequently he will behave himself in an exemplary manner, so that his subordinates can follow the example of his good qualities. He will avoid any undue familiarity in eating and drinking or otherwise in his relations with them, lest he should lose the respect due him. . . .

4th. At the command of His Serene Highness is required to compose such music as His Serene Highness may require of him. Such compositions are not to be communicated to any person, nor copied, but remain the property of His Serene Highness, and without the knowledge and permission of His Serene Highness, he is not to compose for any person.

5th. Joseph Heyden shall appear daily . . . in the morning and the afternoon in the antechamber and will be announced and will await the decision of His Serene Highness whether there should be music; and having received the order, will inform the other musicians, and not only appear himself punctually at the appointed time but also ensure that the rest appear, and should a musician either come late for the music or even be absent, he will take his name.

6th. Should, regrettably, quarrels or complaints occur among the musicians, the Vice-Kapellmeister shall attempt in accordance with the circumstances to settle them, so that His Grace will not be importuned with trifling matters; but should a more important incident occur that he, Joseph Heyden, cannot himself settle by mediation, he shall faithfully report it to His Serene Highness.

7th. The Vice-Kapellmeister shall survey and take care of all musical instruments . . .

8th. Joseph Heyden is obliged to instruct the female singers, so that they shall not forget in Eisenstadt what they have learned in Vienna . . . and since the Vice-Kapellmeister has experience of various instruments, he will allow himself to be employed in playing all those instruments with which he is acquainted.

9th. The Vice-Kapellmeister will receive herewith a copy of the convention and norms of behavior of his subordinate musicians, so that he will know how to make them behave in service, in accordance with these regulations.

10th. As it is not considered necessary to commit to paper all the services that he is obliged to perform, His Serene Highness graciously hopes that Joseph Heyden will in all matters spontaneously carry out not only the above-mentioned services but also all other orders of His Grace that he may receive in the future, and also maintain the music in good order . . .

11th. The Vice-Kapellmeister will be accorded by His Lordship four hundred guilder annually, payment to be made quarterly by the Chief Cashier. In addition to this,

12th. Joseph Heyden shall receive his meals at the officers' table or half a guilder for board daily. Finally,

13th. This convention was concluded in the 1st May, 1761, with the Vice-Kapellmeister for at least three years, provided that if Joseph wishes to continue in this honor after having served for three years, he must announce his intention to His Lordship six months in advance . . . Similarly,

14th. His Lordship promises not only to keep Joseph Heyden in his service for the agreed period, but if he gives full satisfaction, he may expect the position of Principal Kapellmeister; should the contrary be the case, however, His Serene Highness is free at any time to dismiss him from his service.

But Haydn served with Prince Paul for only a year. Paul died in 1762 and was succeeded by Prince Nicholas, called the Magnificent. Nicholas promptly built himself a new castle and named it Eszterháza. Completed in 1766 at a cost of millions, it was the greatest palace in Europe except for Versailles. It contained a marionette theater and a 400-seat theater for opera. The royal box of the opera house was supported by red marble Roman columns decorated with golden rods, according to a contemporary report, which further went on to say (after describing the lavishness of the building and its surroundings) that German comedies and Italian opera alternated from day to day. "The Prince is always present, and six o'clock is the usual time. The delight for eyes and ears is indescribable. It comes first from the music, since the entire orchestra resounds as a complete entity: now the most moving tenderness, now the most vehement power penetrates the soul—because the great musician, Herr Haiden, who serves the Prince as Kapellmeister, is the director." The Empress Maria Theresa was impressed. "If I want to enjoy a good opera, I go to Eszterháza," she said.

Werner died in 1766 and Haydn became kapellmeister. It was a busy job. He had to direct the orchestra, compose music, be the librarian, take on all administrative duties pertaining to music, hire and fire personnel, be the copyist, arbitrate disputes. He did all this in an unruffled, level-headed manner, stern but always just, often going directly to the Prince to plead for his men. They adored him and called him "Papa."

Nicholas and Haydn got along very well. The Prince, as ardent a music lover as his predecessor, played the baryton, a now obsolete instrument related to the cello. Haydn was expected to compose a great deal of music for Nicholas himself to play, and he obliged with almost 200 pieces for the Prince's favorite instrument, most of which were scored for baryton, viola, and cello. He knew how lucky he was. "My Prince was always satisfied with my work. Not only did I have the encouragement of constant approval, but as conductor of an orchestra I could make experiments, observe what produced an effect and what weakened it, and was thus in a position to improve, to alter, to make additions or omissions, and be as bold as I pleased. I was cut off from the world; there was no one to confuse or torment me, and I was forced to become original."

At Eszterháza, Haydn presided over an orchestra that numbered between twenty and twenty-three players. That was fair-sized for its day. Only a few orchestras in Europe were larger. The finest in the world was at Mannheim, which boasted some fifty players. There was a school of Mannheim composers, represented notably by Johann Stamitz (1717–1757) and Christian Cannabich (1731–1798), both active in Haydn's day and who may have influenced him. Stamitz and later Cannabich directed the Mannheim Orchestra, a group described as "an army of generals." Such precision, power, and virtuosity had been unknown up to then, and even the supercilious Mozart was carried away. Christian Schubart, the composer and critic, was rapturous in his description: "Here the forte is thunder, the crescendo a cataract, the diminuendo a crystal streamlet bubbling away in the far distance, the piano a breeze of spring." This was the famous "Mannheim crescendo," rising from triple pianissimo to crashing fortissimo.

Haydn's orchestra was not on that level, but he made it one of the best in Europe. He was its conductor, and he called himself that. It must be realized that his function as conductor was somewhat different from what is today meant by that term. The day of the virtuoso time-beater with the baton was yet to come. Haydn would have conducted from the clavier or as head of the violin section. In his day it was customary to have two conductors, one leading from the keyboard, the other from the violins. The clavier player would keep the rhythm and correct errant players or singers. The violinist would attend to the general ensemble and the nuances. In Haydn's case there were many nuances, and he insisted on fine degrees of shading, as evidenced in one of his letters explaining how his music should sound. In any orchestra he directed he would have assumed complete control, divided leadership or not, and in effect he would have led his orchestra much as modern conductors lead theirs, dominating the players, setting the tempos, keeping the ensemble together. Only he would have done this seated within the body of the orchestra.

Haydn supplied music for two weekly concerts, Tuesdays and Saturdays, from 2 to 4 in the afternoon. He also was in charge of the opera performances and composed many for the Eszterháza theater (none of the Haydn operas has held the stage, though a few are occasionally revived as novelties). In 1786 alone there were given at Eszterháza seventeen operas (including eight premieres) for a total of 125 performances. The Haydn authority, H. C. Robbins Landon, has estimated that in the course of the ten-year period from 1780 to 1790 Haydn conducted 1026 performances of Italian operas, not to mention the marionette operas and the incidental music to plays. It was hard work, but there were compensations. Haydn had a good salary, a maid, a coachman, a carriage and horses, lived in one of the showplaces of Europe, and had absolute authority over a group of skillfull musicians he himself had selected. He could also pursue his favorite pastimes, hunting and fishing, and to the end of his days would tell of the great occasion when he brought down three birds with one shot.

A considerable spur to his development was his meeting with the twenty-five-year-old Mozart in 1781. The two geniuses admired each other. Not only did Mozart dedicate his great set of six string quartets (Nos. 14-19) to Haydn, but he also defended him in word and deed. Thus when Leopold Kozeluch, a pianist active in Vienna, sneered at a passage in a Haydn quartet, saying "*I* would not have written it that way," Mozart cut him short with "Neither would I. And you know why? Because neither of us would have had so excellent an idea." Haydn reciprocated, and when *Don Giovanni* was criticized in his presence, he said: "I cannot settle this dispute, but this I know: Mozart is the greatest composer the world possesses now." From Mozart, Haydn got new ideas about organization, about key relationship, and, above all, about the expressive possibilities of music. Certain it is that after exposure to Mozart's music, Haydn's became broader than it had ever been, deeper, more expressive. It worked both ways. Mozart learned a great deal about structural organization from Haydn.

By the time of his meeting with Mozart, Haydn already was one of the most famous composers in Europe. As early as 1776 his music was being received with rapture, and one review referred to "Herr Joseph Haydn, the darling of our nation, whose gentle character is marked in each of his pieces. His compositions have beauty, order, clarity, a fine and noble simplicity. . . ." France, Italy, Russia, Spain—all countries admired his music. It was published, then copied and pirated. Invitations for the great Haydn to appear in person came from all the musical capitals. Haydn held fast at Eszterháza. But in 1790 Nicholas the Magnificent died and his successor, Anton, who was not very interested in music, dismissed the orchestra except for a few musicians. Haydn, of course, was kept on. There was little for him to do; and as he was free to go wherever he wished, he moved to Vienna. Late in 1790 he accepted an offer to appear in England. Johann Peter Salomon, a violinist and impresario who had settled in London, made a trip to Vienna to court Europe's most famous composer. All Haydn had to do was go to England, compose music for the public there, make personal appearances, and return to Vienna a rich man. So Salomon assured Haydn, and he was correct. Haydn arrived in England on January 1, 1791, and remained for eighteen months.

No capital in Europe had as much music as London, and the arrival of Haydn created much excitement. Dr. Charles Burney, Handel's old friend, wrote for the new hero a long poem in stately couplets. *Verses on the Arrival of Haydn in England,* it was titled, and it contained such flattering stanzas as:

> HAYDN! Great Sovereign of the tuneful art!
> Thy works alone supply an ample chart
> Of all the mountains, seas, and fertile plains,
> Within the compass of its wide domains.—
> Is there an Artist of the present day
> Untaught by thee to think, as well as play?
> Whose head thy science has not well supplied?
> Whose hand thy labors have not fortified?

Newspapers made much of the event. The *Public Advertiser* of January 6, 1791, discussed Haydn and also gave a list of the musical events to be found in the city, under the heading: *Musical Arrangements for every Day in the Week Through the Winter Season.* The list is impressive:

. . . Our Readers may be pleased to see what will be the arrangements of musical pleasures for the week; even if the coalition of the two Operas should not take place . . .

SUNDAY: The Noblemen's Subscription is held every Sunday at a different house.

MONDAY: The Professional Concert—at the Hanover-square Rooms—with Mrs. Billington.

TUESDAY—The Opera.

WEDNESDAY: The Ancient Music at the Rooms in Tottenham Street, under the patronage of Their Majesties.

THURSDAY—The Pantheon.—A Pasticcio of Music and Dancing, in case that the Opera coalition shall take place; if not, a concert with Madama Mara and Sig. Pacchierotti. Academy of Ancient Music, every other Thursday at Free-Mason's Hall.

FRIDAY—A Concert under the auspices of Haydn at the Rooms, Hanover Square, with Signor David.

SATURDAY—The Opera.

Haydn was taken to the bosom of London society. "My arrival," he wrote to a friend in Vienna, "caused a great sensation throughout the whole city, and I went the round of all the newspapers for 3 successive days. Everybody wants to know me. I had to dine out 6 times up to now, and if I wanted, I could dine out every day; but first I must consider my work, and 2nd my health." The work consisted of a group of six symphonies that turned out to be the first half of his last twelve (Nos. 93-104), all known as the *London* symphonies. (To complicate matters, No. 104 in D is known as the *London Symphony*.) Haydn's first concert took place on March 11, 1791. He conducted an orchestra of forty from the piano. It was the largest group he had ever directed, and he was thrilled by it. His success was tremendous, and the reaction of the *Morning Chronicle* was typical. "Never, perhaps, was there a richer musical treat," the critic wrote, and went on to compare Haydn with Shakespeare. The critic also put out a feeler that was to be re-echoed: "We were happy to see the concert so well attended the first night, for we cannot suppress our very anxious hope that the first musical genius of the age may be induced, by our liberal welcome, to take up his residence in England."

Haydn had a very good time in England. Two of the high spots were his award of an honorary doctorate from Oxford, and his romance with Mrs. Rebecca Schröter, the widow of a well-known pianist. His impressions about musical and social life in England can be found in his diary, the so-called *London Notebooks*, which he religiously kept up.

This diary makes delightful reading, and a good deal about the workings of Haydn's mind can be learned from it. A very attractive personality comes through. Haydn was insatiably curious, and he loved statistics. "The national debt of England is estimated to be over two hundred millions. Recently it was calculated that if they had to make up a convoy to pay this sum in silver, the wagons, end on end, would reach from London to York, that is, 200 miles, presuming that each wagon could not carry more than £600." Or, "The City of London consumes 8 times one hundred thousand cartloads of coal each year; each cart has 13 sacks, each sack holds 2 dry measures: most of the coal comes from Newcastle. Often 200 loaded ships arrive at once. A cartload costs £2½." There are also critical notes: "On 21st Giardini's concert took place in Renelag [Ranelagh Gardens]. He played like a pig." Haydn goes to the races at Ascot on June 14, 1792, and writes down a full description. The observant, curious Haydn was a fine reporter. It is fascinating to read his account of the afternoon he spent, which is, incidentally, one of the earliest descriptive accounts of racing:

. . . When they are ready, the bell is rung a second time, and at the first stroke they ride off at once. Whoever is the first to traverse the circle of 2 miles and return to the platform from which they started receives the prize. In the first heat there were 3 riders and they had to go around the circle twice without stopping. They did this double course in 5 minutes. [Impossible. Haydn's timing is much too fast.] No stranger would believe this unless they had seen it themselves. The second time there were seven riders. When they were in the middle of the circle, all 7 were in the same line, but as soon as they came nearer some fell behind, but never more than about 10 paces; and just when you think that one of them is rather near the goal, and people make large bets on him at this moment, another rushes past him at very close corners and with unbelievable force reaches the winning place. The riders are very lightly clad in silk and each one has a different color, so that you recognize him more easily; no boots, a little cap on his head, they are all as lean as a greyhound and as lean as their horses. Everyone is weighed in, and a certain weight is allowed him, in relation to the strength of the horse, and if the rider is too light he must put on heavier clothes, or they hang some lead on him. . . . Among other things a single large stall is erected, wherein the Englishmen place their bets. The King has his own stall at one side. I saw 5 heats the first day, and despite a heavy rain there were 2000 vehicles, all full of people, and 3 times as many common people on foot. Besides this, there are all sorts of other things—puppet plays, hawkers, horror plays—which go on during the races; many tents with refreshments, all kinds of wine and beer. . . .

Haydn does not say if he came out a winner. He could have afforded a flutter or two, for his London trip was, as Salomon had promised, very lucrative. So lucrative was it that there was every inducement for him to make a return trip, and he did, early in 1794, to remain until August 15, 1795.

Returning to Vienna after the second London visit, he found a new Ester-házy. Prince Anton had died, and the new head of the family, Nicholas II, wanted to restore the orchestra, to be used mostly for church services. Haydn agreed to take it over, and composed a series of great masses, but otherwise he had plenty of time for himself.

It was during these years that he composed the Austrian National Anthem. Haydn had been impressed by the dignity and simplicity of *God Save the King,* and decided that Austria should have an equivalent. The matter was discussed at court, and the imperial chancellor commissioned the poet Leopold Haschka to write a patriotic text. *Gotte erhalte Franz den Kaiser* —"God save Emperor Franz"—was the result, and Haydn set it to music. On February 12, 1797, it was sung in all the theaters of Vienna and the provinces. Later that year, Haydn used the theme for a set of variations in his C major Quartet (Op. 76, No. 3), which of course was promptly nick-named the *Emperor* Quartet.

In 1802 Haydn was released from his official duties. He lived quietly in Vienna, one of the most celebrated figures in Austria. His wife had died in 1800. Illness plagued the last years of his life, and Haydn, who had never complained of anything, who had never had a serious ailment, was largely confined to his house. Rheumatism swelled his legs so that it was painful to walk. He liked to sit at home, the grand old man of European music, and receive visitors. On May 31, 1809, he died. His last musical act was to be carried to the piano, where he played the Austrian hymn three times. That was a day or two before his death. His last reported words were "Children, be comforted. I am well." At the funeral the Mozart Requiem was played. That would have pleased Haydn.

Like so many of the pre-Beethoven composers, Haydn went into eclipse during the nineteenth century. Mozart at least interested the romantics, and *Don Giovanni* was never far from them. But very little of Haydn's music was played in the concert halls except for *The Seasons, The Creation,* and an occasional symphony. It remained for the classic revival after World War I and the extraordinary classic and baroque renaissance after World War II to re-establish Haydn. Up to then he had been largely an admired textbook figure, represented on programs by a few—no more than a half-dozen—of his more than 100 symphonies, and on chamber music programs by a handful of string quartets, and in piano recitals by two works, the F minor Variations and the big E flat Sonata. All of a sudden came the realization of just how significant a creator and innovator Haydn was, and how bracing, inventive, and wonderful his music is.

In his steady output there is surprisingly little change after the early 1780's, in that no matter how much an individual work differs from another individual work, all the music is animated by much the same approach: a pure and perfect technique, a feeling of optimism, a clear layout, masculine-sounding melodies, a surprisingly rich harmonic texture, and a sheer joy in composition. Rococo is left far behind; this is classicism of the purest kind, and the music is big. Emotionally it is uncluttered and uncomplicated. It does not lack feeling or even passion, but the impression it always gives is one of buoyancy. This is true of the symphonies, the chamber music, the masses, and the two great oratorios—*The Seasons* and *The Creation,* both of which also abound in some of the most charming nature painting music has to show.

Haydn's greatest technical contribution was his consolidation of sonata form. In his early years he was content to write tuneful music that had little or no development: arias for instruments, as it were. But as he developed, as he became familiar with the work of the Mannheim school and the early Viennese school, as his vision became bigger and his technique more encompassing, he worked out the sonata principle better than anybody in Europe at the time. Sonata form is essentially contrast and development. That is, the first movement of a sonata is divided into three sections—exposition, development, and recapitulation. The exposition presents the material on which the movement is built. There is a strong theme (first subject), and a more lyric, contrasting theme (second subject). Sometimes, especially in the romantic period, these were called the masculine and feminine elements. In the development one or both of those two themes are manipulated. The quality of the development is the test of the composer's resource, imagination, and technique. After the themes are put through their paces, the recapitulation brings back the two original themes, more or less in their original form. Thus an arch is rounded out. In many classic symphonies the first movement starts with a slow introduction and ends with a snappy coda. A slow, lyric second movement follows; then a dancelike third movement (sometimes this is omitted); and then a finale. Often the finale is a rondo, a form in which subsidiary themes revolve around a main one, in a pattern of ABACA.

Haydn invented none of this, but no composer in Europe so refined the principle. From the 1760's and 1770's to the end of his life he turned out work of miraculous inventiveness, charm, and life, though it was not until after 1780 that he shone with full maturity. He was one of the most prolific composers in history. Standard listings give 104 symphonies, 83 string quartets, 52 piano sonatas, many concertos, much miscellaneous chamber music, a large number of choral works, 23 operas, many songs, 4 oratorios, and many masses. There was no form of music to which Haydn did not turn his industrious pen. And all Europe knew him for the master he was. There was a tendency in some professional circles to underplay his music. It was thought too light, too mellifluous. Haydn never challenged the Establishment, as did Mozart and Beethoven, and there was a tendency to take his music for granted. His lusty peasantlike minuet movements, which so influenced the Beethoven scherzos, were often looked down upon as "common" or "vulgar." So graceful and assured was his writing that some of its remarkable aspects went unnoticed—the daring key structure, for example. In the 1770's Haydn went through what is known as the *Sturm und Drang* period —a period in Europe where creators tried to express a more personal kind of feeling. It was a preromantic urge. *Empfindsamkeit,* it was called in Germany and Austria. Those were the years when Haydn composed music in unusual keys—F minor, E minor, F sharp minor, B major—all "romantic" keys. His choice of keys, indeed, is more adventurous than even Mozart's, though Mozart is more adventurous *within* the key. And Haydn's later music often contains even more anticipations of romanticism. But above all there is that direct, clear, good-natured, un-neurotic view toward life and art. "Since God has given me a cheerful heart, He will forgive me for serving him cheerfully," Haydn once wrote. And that sums it up.

❧ 5 ❧

Prodigy from Salzburg

WOLFGANG AMADEUS MOZART

Wolfgang Amadeus Mozart was the greatest composer of his day. As a composer he was supreme in all forms of music—opera, symphony, concerto, chamber, vocal, piano, choral, everything. He was the finest pianist and organist in Europe, and the finest conductor. Had he worked on it he could also have been the best violinist. There was literally nothing in music he could not do better than anybody else. He could write down a complicated piece while thinking out another piece in his head; or he could think out a complete string quartet and then write out the individual parts before making the full score; or he could read perfectly at sight any music placed before him; or he could hear a long piece of music for the first time and immediately write it out, note for note. He lived but thirty-six years, from January 27, 1756, to December 5, 1791, and in that short span gave the world a legacy of music that shines as bright today as it did in the last years of the eighteenth century.

Mozart was one of the most exploited child prodigies in the history of music, and he paid the price. Child prodigies seldom grow up to lead normal lives. They develop as children cultivating a specific talent at the expense of all others, most of their time is spent with adults, their general education is neglected, they are overpraised. A warped childhood results, and as often as not this leads to a warped manhood. The tragedy of Mozart was that he grew up reliant on his father and was unable to meet the demands of society and life. This was generally recognized in his own day. Thus Friedrich Schlichtegroll, Mozart's first biographer, could write in 1793: "For just as this rare being early became a man so far as his art was concerned, he always remained—as the impartial observer must say of him—in almost all other matters a child. He never learned to rule himself. For domestic order, for sensible management of money, for moderation and wise choice in pleasures, he had no feeling. He always needed a guiding hand." Or, five years later, Franz Niemetschek in his biography of 1798 wrote: "This man, so exceptional as an artist, was not equally great in the other affairs of life." The men who wrote these comments were not Philistines lamenting the fact that Mozart led an unconventional life. They knew what many knew, that Mozart was his own worst enemy.

That Mozart was indeed an exceptional musician, nobody in his day would dispute. At the age of three he started picking out tunes on the piano. His ear was so delicate that loud sounds would make him physically ill. And it was not only delicate, but perfect in pitch. At the age of four he was telling his elders that their violins were a quarter tone out of tune. At that age he also could learn a piece of music in about half an hour. At five he played the clavier amazingly well. At six he started composing, and his father, Leopold, took him on tour with his sister Maria Anna (Nannerl). Nannerl, five years older than Wolfgang, was also a child prodigy, though not nearly as gifted as her brother. Leopold was a good musician, a violinist, vice-kapellmeister in the archiepiscopal court at Salzburg, and the author of a famous treatise on violin playing. But the elder Mozart had not made a great success of his life and was determined to see that his genius of a son should find the best possible position and, incidentally, enrich the Mozart coffers. Leopold wanted security for his old age, a goal about which he kept constantly reminding his son later in life.

Thus from the age of six young Wolfgang was steadily on the road in his formative years, being exhibited to the courts of Europe, to the learned musical academies, to the public. As an adult he made further concert tours, with the result that fourteen of his thirty-six years were spent away from home. In one respect, they were not wasted years. Mozart came in contact with every important musician of the day, and with every kind of music, all of which his incredible brain soaked up and retained. His name was constantly in the news, especially when he was amazing Europe with his fantastic feats as a child. A spate of learned articles was written about the fabulous boy by the musical and scientific community. When Mozart played in Paris, shortly before he was seven years old, Baron Friedrich Melchior von Grimm, writing in the *Correspondance Littéraire,* all but went out of his mind. Mozart went through some of the tricks his father had devised for him, such as playing a clavier whose keyboard was covered with a cloth (not really a very hard task, but one calculated *pour épater le bourgeois*), reading at sight, improvising, harmonizing melodies at first hearing, demonstrating his absolute pitch, and so on. "I cannot be sure," wrote Grimm, "that this child will not turn my head if I go on hearing him often; he makes me realize that it is difficult to guard against madness on seeing prodigies. I am no longer surprised that Saint Paul should have lost his head after his strange vision." All Europe resounded with the praise of this marvelous boy.

A musician with such gifts should have had no trouble landing a lucrative position. But Mozart never succeeded in doing this, though he spent
his whole life looking for one, preferably a position at court, with a large
and guaranteed salary. He grew up a complicated man with a complicated
personality and an unprecedented knack for making enemies. He was tactless, spoke out impulsively, said exactly what he thought about other musicians (rarely did he have a good word to say), tended to be arrogant and supercilious, and made very few real friends in the musical community. He
had the reputation of being giddy and lightheaded, temperamental, obsti-
nate. We can look back upon all this and sympathize. He was Mozart; he
was better than any musician of his time; he *did* unerringly spot the mediocrity around him (and also the great figures: he had nothing but respect
for Haydn), and in his musical judgments he was never wrong. But that did
not make things any easier for him while he was alive. In addition he was
not a glamorous figure physically. He was very short; his face, with a yellow-
ish complexion, was pitted from smallpox; his head was too big for his
slight frame. He was nearsighted, and had blue eyes that tended to pro-
trude, a thick head of hair, a large nose, and plump hands. (Most great pianists have had plump hands with wide palms and a big stretch between
thumb and forefinger. The romantic notion of a great pianist's hand being
long, tapered, and beautiful seldom is borne out in actual life.)

For many years Mozart struggled to escape the domination of his father.
The full story of the relationship between the two remains to be told by a
competent psychiatrist who understands Mozart's music and his time. Leopold Mozart was not a complicated man. He was intelligent but unimaginative and unbending: a precise, pedantic, well-organized, cautious, prudent,
and rather avaricious man. Being a good musician, he immediately recognized the genius of his son. But, much to his grief, he discovered that as
Wolfgang grew older he seemed ill-equipped to meet life on equal terms—
at least, according to Leopold's views about life. Wolfgang, who had constantly been leaning on his father during all those early years, seemed to collapse as soon as the prop was removed. Perhaps there was unconscious
resentment. Perhaps Wolfgang wanted to express himself as a human being
and did not know how. Perhaps it was inevitable that he run wild once the
reins were removed. Whatever the reason, Wolfgang turned out to be the
emotional antithesis of his father—easygoing, gregarious, undisciplined, and
a soft touch.

Leopold was constantly bombarding his son with sage advice. Respect
money. Do not trust strangers. Never go out walking at night. Plan ahead.
Cultivate the right people. Act with dignity. But just as there was a great
deal of Polonius in Leopold, so Wolfgang was Hamlet, with a great deal of
Micawber as well. He never could make up his mind, or strike when the oc-

70

casion was right. That did not seem to worry him. Everything was going to turn out all right. Tomorrow. With Wolfgang it was always tomorrow. "Little by little my circumstances will improve." Wolfgang was always writing these words to his father, but the pot of gold remained eternally at the end of the rainbow. What a trial Wolfgang turned out to be for Leopold! He wasted money, frittered away his talents, cultivated the wrong people, and never learned to assess character. Time and again Leopold writes to his son, warning him about his tendency to like everybody. "All men are villains! The older you will become and the more you associate with people, the more you will realize this sad truth." He begs Wolfgang not to be so easily swayed by flattery.

But Wolfgang goes his merry way. He probably is afraid of his father. Certainly his letters are evasive. Everything will be all right soon. Yes, he has lost money. No, he has not made any decent contacts. But he has prospects, great prospects. In vain Leopold tells his son that "flattering words, praises, cries of 'Bravissimo' pay neither postmasters nor landlords. So as soon as you find there is no money to be made, you should get away at once." Often Leopold loses his temper, especially when Wolfgang writes vague letters full of pious moralizing. "Blast your oracular utterances and all the rest!" Leopold does not want to know what his son thinks of life. He wants to know whether or not a good job is coming up, and where those gold ducats disappeared. He also worries that Wolfgang's loose social habits will make him an object of ridicule. Especially, he warns, keep away from musicians. They are low in the social order and it does not pay to be too friendly with them. That includes composers as important as Gluck, Piccinni, and Grétry. To them, be polite and nothing more. "You can always be perfectly natural with people of high rank, but with everybody else behave like an Englishman. You must not be so open with everyone." Poor Wolfgang probably flinched when he received a letter from his father. Nag, nag, nag. Leopold, of course, meant well. "The purpose of my remarks is to make you into an honorable man. Millions have not received that tremendous favor which God has bestowed upon you. What a responsibility! And what a shame if such a great genius were to founder!"

The upshot was that Leopold all but drove his son from him. Leopold could not change or bend his set of values; and Wolfgang, pushed by a musical genius that demanded a certain kind of evolution, could not be the sober, industrious, thrifty bourgeois his father so earnestly desired him to be. Leopold represented the golden mean. How could a Wolfgang Amadeus Mozart, with the dreams of *Don Giovanni* and the C minor Piano Concerto in his head, represent a prudent golden mean? So Leopold knew his son and did not know his son. Leopold could see nothing but the flaws in his character, and could not respond to an order of genius far beyond his comprehension. He failed utterly to realize how high-strung Wolfgang was, how badly he needed encouragement, sympathy, and support instead of homilies and lectures. Of course, Wolfgang did have those character flaws that Leopold was constantly reminding him of. But many of those flaws can be traced to the unnatural childhood imposed upon him by his father. And so the two, father and son, tortured each other for years in a classic love-hate relationship.

Leopold would have been happy had his son settled in Salzburg as a court musician. That was security. Wolfgang, on the other hand, hated the idea of Salzburg and everything connected with it. He knew his powers and knew they would be wasted in a provincial city. Wolfgang was not one to fight against patronage. Almost every composer had an employer—the church, the court, a rich patron. But he wanted a patron with the imagination and resources to let him exploit the ideas racing through his head. Lacking that kind of patron, he tried to achieve his artistic goal on his own, one of the first musicians in history to make the break. It took determination and courage. Artistically he succeeded, though he died penniless. Throughout his letters, beneath all the nonsense that frequently occurs, is the picture of a creative artist with a goal that had to be achieved. No matter what, he adhered to his vision. He could and did write to order, he could write light music, but he could not write cheap music. Mozart never prostituted himself.

His letters are amazing, and they make wonderful reading. In them everything is laid bare. Traveling as much as they did, the Mozarts were constantly in touch with each other by letter. At first, of course, it was Leopold who wrote home. Then, as Wolfgang grew older, he too took the pen. His life and thought can be traced in his letters—those psychologically complex, bright, observant letters, written in so lively a manner; those nervous letters, so full of bravado; those sad last letters, when he is reduced to abject begging for loans. Mozart was a highly intelligent man. In his youthful letters he could be boyish and affectionate: "Kiss Mama's hands for me 100000000 times." There are ebullient, high-spirited letters to his sister: "If you see Herr von Schiedenhofen"—a family friend—"tell him that I am always singing 'Tralaliera, Tralaliera,' and that I need not put sugar in my soup now that I am no longer in Salzburg." Mozart was fourteen when he wrote this, and already an experienced veteran of the musical circuit. His travels never stopped. There are letters to Salzburg from Vienna, Munich, Coblenz, Frankfurt, Brussels, Paris, London, Lyons, Milan, Bologna, Naples, Venice, Innsbruck, Mannheim. Always he was making music, listening to music, talking with musicians. Even at the age of thirteen he was completely mature when it came to writing about music. Already he is the complete professional, as witness the manner he dissected a performance in Mantua in

1770: "The prima donna sings well, but very softly; and when you do not see her acting, but only singing, you would think that she is not singing at all. For she cannot open her mouth, but whines out everything . . . The seconda donna looks like a grenadier and has a powerful voice, too, and, I must say, does not sing badly. . . . The primo uomo, il musico, sings beautifully, though his voice is uneven." From Bologna he sends home a letter in which he writes out, note for note, a cadenza sung by the soprano Lucrezia Agujari (who, he says, went up to a C above high C in full voice).

In 1777, Wolfgang went on a long tour with his mother. The object was to find a good job. It was his first trip without his father, and thus his first touch of independence. He kept coming up with wildly impractical suggestions, driving his father out of his mind. An air of bravado can be found in these letters from Munich, Mannheim, and Paris; and as one project or another failed, the bravado increased. In Mannheim he made friends with the Weber family, and they were not the kind of friends to Leopold's liking. They had little money, they lived a Bohemian life, and they had been tied up with shady business deals and lawsuits. The father, Fridolin, was a bass singer, prompter, and music copyist at the court theater. There were the mother, a son, and four daughters. Aloysia Weber, eighteen years old when Mozart met her, had a beautiful voice and a promising future as an opera singer. He fell in love with her. Even Mozart's mother, a gentle soul, protested. "When Wolfgang makes new acquaintances, he immediately wants to give his life and property to them." Mozart's ardent friendship with the Webers was temporarily broken when he and his mother continued on to Paris. His mother died there in 1778, and Mozart had to break the news to his father, which he did in a roundabout way. The old man was not deceived. As soon as he read his son's letter, in which he stated that Mama was very ill, he had a feeling that she was gone.

There was no longer any reason for Mozart to remain in Paris, and he returned to Salzburg in 1779—after a long stay with the Webers in Munich. Aloysia had become a prima donna at the opera there, and things were looking up for the Weber family. When Mozart finally reached home, he was a dejected young man. Aloysia had jilted him. She had bigger fish to net. No, there was little to make Mozart happy in Salzburg. He had warned his father in a sort of declaration of independence from Paris: "A fellow of mediocre talent will remain a mediocrity whether he travels or not; but one of superior talent (which without impiety I cannot deny I possess) will go to seed if he always remains in the same place. If the Archbishop would trust me, I should soon make his orchestra famous; of this there is no doubt. . . . But there is one thing more I must settle about Salzburg, and that is that I shall not be kept to the violin as I used to be. I will no longer be a fiddler. I want to conduct at the clavier and accompany arias."

73

At Salzburg Mozart settled in as court organist, with a chip on his shoulder. He was sullen, truculent, and insubordinate. "I shall certainly hoodwink the Archbishop, and how I shall enjoy doing it!" This was not the frame of mind to endear him to the archiepiscopal court. Nevertheless, bored and dejected as he was, he composed steadily. From this period came the first great works of his young maturity. Up to then his music had been fluent and masterfully constructed, but not much had been very striking. Now, however, came the *Coronation* Mass and some other fine church music, the lovely E flat Concerto for two pianos, and the equally lovely *Sinfonia Concertante* for violin, viola, and orchestra. Suddenly Mozart was a great master. He even received a major opera commission, and *Idomeneo* had its premiere in Munich in 1781. It is an *opera seria*—a serious opera along Gluckian and Metastasian lines. Much of it is stiff and formal, but it contains some magnificent music, including a vocal quartet that is as deep and imaginative as anything he ever wrote. *Idomeneo* never has been one of Mozart's more popular operas. During the nineteenth century and much of the twentieth it was out of the repertoire. In recent years, however, it has been picked up by many opera houses.

The year of *Idomeneo* was also the year Mozart broke with the Archbishop, whose secretary, Count Karl Arco, sped his departure with a kick on the backside. Mozart breathed revenge—from a safe distance. "I shall feel bound to assure him in writing that he may confidently expect from me a kick on his arse and a few boxes on the ear in addition. For when I am insulted I must have my revenge." Of course, he never wrote the letter. Poor Mozart was not cut out to be a hero.

After his dismissal, Mozart settled in Vienna. He had no money, and begged his father not to add to his worries by writing unpleasant letters. The Webers were in Vienna, and Mozart moved in with them. On December 15, 1781, he wrote his father a long letter. After a tremendous preamble about the necessity of a young man getting married, he broke the news that he was in love: "Now then, who is the object of my love? Certainly not a Weber? Yes, a Weber, but not Josepha, not Sophie, but Constanze, the middle one. . . . She is not ugly, but by no means a beauty. Her whole beauty consists in two small black eyes and a winsome figure. She is not witty but she has enough sound common sense to enable her to fulfill her duties as a wife and mother. . . ." Leopold's worst fears had come true, and he must have exploded with rage and frustration. His son was to marry a penniless girl from a family of dubious character. Married they were, in August, 1782. Constanze turned out to be a giddy and flirtatious girl, a bad manager, and no help at all to Mozart. But he loved her, and the marriage seems to have been happy, even if Leopold was not. Relations between Mozart and his father cooled off considerably after 1781.

For a while, things looked promising. Mozart got pupils and commissions. His opera, *Die Entführung aus dem Serail—The Abduction from the Seraglio*—was a decided success when it was produced at the National Theater in 1782. He followed this with masterpiece after masterpiece in all forms. In 1786 he met Lorenzo da Ponte, poet for the imperial theaters, and three great operas resulted—*Le Nozze di Figaro* (1786), *Don Giovanni* (1787), and *Così fan tutte* (1790). The first two were immediate successes in Prague, and Mozart had the greatest public acclaim he had ever achieved. How he loved it! On December 2, 1787, he was appointed Chamber Composer to Emperor Joseph II, with a salary of 800 gulden (as against the 2,000 that Gluck had received). At a rough guess (monetary conversions from two centuries back are highly speculative), 800 gulden in Mozart's day would be equivalent to about $1,000 in 1970 American currency. Mozart took the title but was disgusted. "Too much for what I do, too little for what I could do." The subject of Mozart and his income has never been fully investigated. As a successful opera composer and acclaimed piano virtuoso, he *should* have made a great deal of money. For all we know, it was a great deal, but nobody really knows. If he did make a great deal of money, he and Constanze frittered it away. He was constantly on the move, changing residences eleven times in nine years. He became a Mason. He began to run short of money in the last years of his life and constantly was asking his friend and fellow Mason, the rich merchant Michael Puchberg, for a loan. Puchberg generally came through, even though he must have known he would never be repaid. In 1788 Mozart asked Puchberg for 2,000 gulden for a year or two "at a suitable rate of interest." But if that was inconvenient, "then I beg you to lend me until tomorrow at least a couple of hundred gulden as my landlord in the Landstrasse has been so importunate that in order to avoid such an unpleasant incident I have had to pay him on the spot, and this has made things very awkward for me." Later on, Mozart's requests for loans became almost hysterical. In the last year of his life he composed *Die Zauberflöte—The Magic Flute*—which was first performed on September 30, 1791 and which became a smash hit and presumably would have brought in some money. But a combination of overwork and kidney disease sent him to an early death. He received the cheapest funeral available and is buried not in a pauper's grave, as legend has it, but in an unmarked common grave in St. Marx cemetery. Today nobody knows where the body lies.

Mozart's music is at once easy and hard to listen to: easy, because of its grace, its never-ending melody, its clear and perfect organization; hard, because of its depth, its subtlety, its passion. It is strange to say of a composer who started writing at six, and lived only thirty-six years, that he developed late, but that is the truth. Few of Mozart's early works, elegant as they are,

75

have the personality, concentration, and richness that entered his music after 1781 (the year of his final break from Salzburg, significantly). Such works as the little G minor Symphony (K. 183), with its *Sturm und Drang* drama, or the A major (K. 201) and C major (K. 338) Symphonies are exceptions. (The "K" found after Mozart's works refers to a listing by Ludwig Köchel, who in 1862 made a complete chronological catalogue of Mozart's music.) But 1781 marks the period of Mozart's maturity, and virtually every work thereafter is a masterpiece.

Mozart was on his own in Vienna, and it is as if a great psychological block was lifted. He began to write music of much greater depth, confidence, brilliance, and power. This music was not universally admired. There were those who found it turgid, too complicated, hard to follow. Even such professionals as Karl Ditters von Dittersdorf (1739–1799), an eminent violinist and composer who on the whole admired Mozart, was worried. His conventional mind was shaken, even shocked, and he wrote: "I have never yet met with any composer who had such an amazing wealth of ideas. I could almost wish he were not so lavish in using them. He leaves his hearer out of breath, for hardly has he grasped one beautiful thought than another of greater fascination dispels the first, and this goes on throughout, so that in the end it is impossible to retain any one of these beautiful melodies." (We in the late twentieth century, with recordings and radio and concerts in which Mozart is a staple of the repertoire, are apt to forget that in the 1780's even a professional musician could not be sure that the first time he was hearing a work might not also be the last. There were not that many concerts. A new piece of music had to be grasped immediately. It probably would not even be printed. Not until Beethoven and the romantics could a composer be reasonably sure that all of his major works would be published.) Dittersdorf was not the only one a bit puzzled. Others considered Mozart's music too "highly spiced," too "discordant," his operas too richly scored. "Too beautiful for our ears, and far too many notes, my dear Mozart," as Joseph II said.

Mozart's musical development was conditioned by his father and by such composers as Johann Schobert, C. P. E. Bach, and J. C. Bach. Those were the years when the young Mozart was turning out an enormous amount of music in the *style galant,* graceful, well contoured, melodious, and not particularly striking. The first composer who really meant something to Mozart was Haydn, and the younger man studied the six quartets of Haydn's Op. 33 very carefully, using them as a model for the superb series of six quartets he composed between 1782 and 1785. Mozart gratefully dedicated the six to the Austrian master. "I have learned from Haydn how to write quartets," he said. When Haydn heard these quartets, at Mozart's home in Vienna, his reaction was typically unselfish. "Before God and as an honest man," he exclaimed to Leopold Mozart, "I tell you that your son is the greatest composer known to me, either in person or by name."

Later came the influence of J. S. Bach and Handel, especially the former. Mozart came to know Bach's music through the enthusiast Baron Gottfried van Swieten. The Baron, as ambassador to Prussia, had been introduced to Bach's music and brought back to Vienna copies of many Bach works. (He also was a Handel enthusiast.) It was in 1781 that Mozart became friendly with van Swieten, and he writes to his father the following year: "I go every Sunday at 12 o'clock to Baron van Swieten, where nothing is played but Handel and Bach." The Baron lent Mozart some of the music. "When Constanze heard the fugues she fell absolutely in love with them. Now she will listen to nothing but fugues. . . . Well, as she had often heard me play fugues out of my head, she asked me if I had ever written any down, and when I said I had not, she scolded me roundly for not recording some of my compositions in this most artistic and beautiful of all musical forms." It was after this exposure to Bach that a polyphonic texture entered Mozart's music. Mozartean polyphony is not Bachian polyphony, but Mozart was inspired by Bach to introduce all kinds of contrapuntal devices, all used with perfect security and confidence. The culmination is the last movement of the *Jupiter* Symphony, where contrasting themes are lined up, harnessed, and sent galloping down the final stretch in one of the most glorious, tingling, and overwhelming passages in music.

Mozart and opera requires a book in itself. All his life Mozart was interested in opera. He started composing operas at the age of thirteen with *La Finta Semplice,* and a constant stream followed: *Bastien und Bastienne, Mitridate,* and a half-dozen or so more up to *Idomeneo* of 1781. None of these, except the large-scale *Idomeneo,* is a repertory work of the twentieth century, though they do enjoy occasional revivals. The Mozart operas that are in the repertoire of opera houses all over the world are *Die Entführung aus dem Serail* (1782), *Le Nozze di Figaro* (1786), *Don Giovanni* (1787), *Così fan tutte* (1790), and *Die Zauberflöte* (1791). All of these are comedies, including *Don Giovanni,* which Mozart called a "*dramma giocoso,*" or humorous drama. A good deal of comic opera had been written before Mozart's time, but very little of significance. Mozart was the first to make comic opera transcend mere entertainment. He was able to do so because he himself liked people, because he himself had a gay, bubbling, irrepressible streak within him, and because he tried to make his music explain mood, situation, and character. He was the first psychologist of opera.

Mozart realized the supremacy of music. In a letter to his father he wrote that "in an opera poetry must be altogether the obedient daughter of the music." But he did not mean that the libretto was unimportant. Mozart spent a great deal of time looking for workable librettos. More than anything else he wanted to compose operas. To his father, in 1778: "Do not forget how much I desire to write operas. I envy anyone who is composing one. I could really weep for vexation when I see or hear an aria." In 1781 he set to work on *Entführung*, and his letters give an illuminating insight into his approach. He is discussing Osmin's aria and explains to his father that as the character's rage increases, "there comes (just when the aria seems to be at an end) the allegro assai, which is in a totally different measure and in a different key; this is bound to be very effective. For just as a man in such a towering rage oversteps the bounds of order, moderation, and propriety and completely forgets himself, so must the music too forget itself. But as passions, whether violent or not, must never be expressed in such a way as to excite disgust, and as music, even in the most terrible situations, must never offend the ear, but must please the hearer, or in other words must never cease to be *music*, I have gone from F (the key in which the aria is written) not into a remote key, but into a related one, not, however, into its nearest relative D minor, but into the more remote A minor."

Then Mozart discusses Belmonte's aria, *O wie ängstlich* ("Oh, how anxiously"). "Would you like to know how I have expressed it—and even indicated his throbbing heart? By the two violins playing octaves. This is the favorite aria of all those who have heard it, and it is mine also. I wrote it expressly to suit [Johann Valentin] Adamberger's voice. You feel the trembling—the faltering—you see how his throbbing breast begins to swell; this I have expressed by a crescendo. You hear the whispering and the sighing—which I have indicated by the first violins with mutes and a flute playing in unison." In another letter, Mozart ruminates on opera in general: "Why do Italian comic operas please everywhere—in spite of their miserable librettos—even in Paris, where I myself witnessed their success? Just because there the music reigns supreme and when one listens to it all else is forgiven. Why, an opera is sure of success when the plot is well worked out, the words written solely for the music and not shoved in here and there to suit some miserable rhyme. . . . The best thing of all is when a good composer, who understands the stage and is talented enough to make sound suggestions, meets an able poet, that true phoenix . . ."

Mozart at that time (1781) did not know it, but he was shortly to meet his true phoenix. Lorenzo da Ponte, born in 1749 as Emanuele Conegliano, was an Italian priest who had fled Italy because of a scandal. An adventurer and intriguer, he settled in Vienna and in 1783 became poet of the Court Theater in Vienna for Italian opera. (His life ended in New York City in 1838, where he was the first professor of Italian at Columbia College. He wrote an autobiography, mentioning Mozart hardly at all.) Da Ponte and Mozart came together for an operatic adaptation of the Beaumarchais play,

The Marriage of Figaro. It was surprising that the opera which has such an explosive subject—the routing of an aristocrat by a pair of quick-witted plebeians—was allowed to be staged at all. The original play did contain the seeds of revolution, as more sensitive observers, such as the Baroness d'Oberkirch, realized. She watched great lords and ladies chortling at the Beaumarchais comedy and observed: "They will be sorry for it one day." Did Mozart secretly see himself as Figaro? It is not impossible.

The Marriage of Figaro opens the door to a new world of opera. It is a scintillating work with real people in it, and the music exposes them for what they are—lovable, vain, capricious, selfish, ambitious, forgiving, philandering. Human beings, in short, all brought alive by the alchemy of a surpassingly inventive and sympathetic musical mind. In *Figaro* there is not one flawed note, not one situation that rings false. *Così fan tutte,* for instance, has a score on the musical level of *Figaro,* but the libretto written by da Ponte is frankly a farce—a farce with a deep underlying meaning, to be sure, but nevertheless a libretto with an artificially arranged construction. It is an adorable work, but without the humanity of its predecessor. Similarly *The Magic Flute,* in which many see the quintessence of Mozart's music, has a fairy-tale libretto by Emanuel Schikaneder which is full of Masonic symbolism but which, read in cold blood, is as naïve and awkward a pageant as ever disgraced the operatic stage. (The general plan was that of the spectacular comedies popular with Viennese audiences of the time.) All kinds of theories have been advanced about the opera. In 1866 one Moritz Alexander Zille insisted that *The Magic Flute* was an allegory striking back at Leopold II, who was persecuting the Masons. In this interpretation, Sarastro represented Ignaz von Born, leader of Austrian Freemasonry. The Queen of the Night was Empress Maria Theresa, the foe of Masonry. Tamino was Joseph II, Leopold's predecessor, who had been hospitable to the Masons. And so on. Other theories have been advanced. But no matter what is read into it, the libretto is silly and inconsistent. Nevertheless, the Viennese public took it to its heart. It was by far the biggest success with which Mozart had been associated.

The Mozart opera that meant the most to the romantic nineteenth century was *Don Giovanni,* and it is the most romantic of Mozart's operas, just as it is the most serious, the most powerful, and the most otherworldly (the romantics especially loved the graveyard scene and the final appearance of the Commandant). Many consider *Don Giovanni* to be the greatest opera ever composed. The overture sets the mood. With a few diminished seventh chords and a D minor scale, Mozart creates a feeling of anxiety, intensity, anguish, oncoming horror. Near the end of the opera the scale reappears, and one's hair stands on end. It is a colossal effect with the simplest of means. Small wonder the romantics rejoiced. The opera had a moral, and

79

the sentimental romantics liked that too, even if many of them missed the point. What makes the dissolute, cynical, decadent, and rather unsavory Don Giovanni an authentic hero, and a modern hero at that, is the fact that he is willing to die for his principles. "Repent!" cries the apparation of the Commandant. "No!" says the Don. "Repent!" "No!" and Hell opens wide. Carmen was later to be the same kind of heroine. She knows Don José will kill her, but that is less important than giving in to a man she despises. Like Don Giovanni, she dies for a principle.

It was not only in opera, of course, that Mozart's genius shone; it was in every form. The piano concerto is a musical form developed by Mozart into symphonic breadth, and there is not one of his concertos after K. 271 in E flat without its special kind of eloquence, finish, and virtuosity: some gay and happy, as the B flat (K. 595) or the A major (K. 488), even with its elegiac slow movement; some dark and romantic, such as the D minor; some classic and noble, such as the C minor.

The works of Mozart's maturity read like an honor roll: the Clarinet Quintet, the E flat Divertimento, the unfinished Mass in C minor and the unfinished Requiem, the two piano quartets, the last ten string quartets, the five great string quintets, the Sinfonia Concertante for Violin and Viola, the Serenade for Thirteen Winds, the last six symphonies, the Clarinet Concerto, the Adagio and Fugue in C minor. These works stand together as a body of music in which form, expression, technique, and taste are raised to unprecedented heights.

Mozart was constantly talking and writing about "taste," and he had nothing but scorn for the musician who indulged in cheap or meretricious effects. That was one reason why he had hard words to say about the pianist Muzio Clementi—"a charlatan"—for Clementi was out to impress with his technique, with his double thirds, octaves, and virtuosity. (Another reason for Mozart's distaste may have been the realization that Clementi possessed an order of execution as good as his and probably superior.) Mozart was an apostle of proportion. This does not imply sterility or inhibition for Mozart was a very practical composer who was as much interested in the effect of a piece as Verdi or Liszt. He composed his piano concertos as vehicles for himself, and some were frankly virtuoso exercises calculated to make the public—and competing pianists—sit up and take notice. Talking about his Concertos in B flat (K. 450) and D (K. 451) he said that he regarded both as works "bound to make the performers perspire." Similarly as an opera composer he had no hesitation in tailoring an aria for a particular voice, or simplifying the music as necessary to accommodate a singer, as he did for Anton Raaff in *Idomeneo*. Raaff was unhappy about some of the settings and Mozart was only too glad to oblige him. But what always sets Mozart's music apart is its proportion and *rightness*—its taste, if you will. That, and an inexhaustible fund of melody joined to an extremely daring harmonic sense. A fully developed harmonic sense, a feeling for modulation, is the infallible mark of the important composer. It is the mediocrity who sits close to home, who does not have the imagination or the daring to go from key to key. The lack of harmonic richness is what makes so much eighteenth-century music so boring today, that incessant tonic-dominant harmony. Bach had harmonic imagination, and so did Mozart. Mozart's constant and unexpected deviations from the textbook help make his music so entrancing and ever fresh. In a work like the E flat Violin Sonata (K. 481), the first movement touches on the keys of A flat, F minor, D flat, C sharp minor, A major, and G sharp minor. Some of his late piano works, such as the B minor Adagio, have a harmonic texture that actually anticipates Chopin, so varied is the key structure.

Relatively little of Mozart's music was published during his lifetime—144 works in all, a good deal of it light music. He left a very large mass of autographs, and suddenly his widow, who had never been much of a help to him when he was alive, developed into a first-class businesswoman, selling off publication rights for excellent prices, but holding on to the autographs themselves. Thanks to the great success of *The Magic Flute*, there was a Mozart boom at his death, and his music received many performances, though not always as he would have liked. *The Magic Flute*, for instance, was staged in Paris in 1801 as *Les Mystères d'Isis*. The text was changed, harmonies were altered, and sections of other Mozart operas and even of Haydn symphonies were introduced into the score. As far as the age was concerned, however, there was nothing unusual about such a procedure. The concept of fidelity to the printed score was to come much later, in the twentieth century. In any case, Mozart was constantly misunderstood by the nineteenth century. He was called the Raphael of music, and was considered an elegant, dainty rococo composer who just happened to have composed *Don Giovanni*. The humanity and power that animate his music went largely unnoticed.

Nor was Mozart played very much during the Romantic period. When he was, it was with all the exaggerations and trappings of romanticism—inflated dynamics, super-legato phrasings, balance obscured under the heavy color of massed strings. It was not until after the First World War that a serious effort was made to return to the performance practices of Mozart's own day. The battle has not yet been won, however, for orchestras still tend to be out of balance, ruining Mozart's delicate instrumental adjustments. It is not a matter of the size of orchestras. Mozart, like any other composer, was thrilled when he heard his music played by large forces, but he expected the conductor to compensate by adding low-voiced instruments to counterbalance the violins. In 1781 he heard one of his symphonies played by a very large group, and he wrote to his father about it with glee: "The symphony went magnifique and had the greatest success. There were forty violins; *the wind instruments were all doubled,* there were ten violas, eight cellos *and six bassoons.*" (Italics added.) The point is that twentieth-century conductors are still apt to lose the sounds, balances, and adjustments Mozart had in his ear, just as no brilliantly voiced concert grand piano, with its roaring bass and unlimited power, can give an idea of Mozart's piano music, which was composed for a light-actioned Walther piano with a modest dynamic range.

Of course, it is impossible to duplicate exactly the conditions under which Mozart heard his music played. For one thing, pitch has gone up a full half tone since Mozart's day. If he, with his perfect ear, were to hear his G minor Symphony in what to him would be G sharp minor, he would become physically ill. (Musicians with highly organized aural equipment have trouble listening to music played in wrong keys. They hear both keys at once, a semitone or whatever apart, and it is a discordantly unnerving experience.) Instruments, too, have changed. Tempos in Mozart's day are still a mystery. What, exactly, did he mean by "allegro" or andante?" Another problem is that of improvisation. The piano parts of Mozart's concerto scores sometimes are little more than a skeleton of what he actually did on stage. The slow movement of the *Coronation* Concerto as it has come down to us is a good example. It is written in a kind of shorthand, with single notes in the treble and bass. Mozart would have filled in the harmony and embellished the bare melody while playing it. Like all performing musicians of the day, Mozart constantly improvised not only cadenzas but also embellished the melodic line as he went along. It is a mistake to approach Mozart's music with the attitude that the printed note is the final word. Often it is, or should be, just the beginning. If recent research into eighteenth-century performance practice has demonstrated one thing, it is that our forefathers used much more freedom in interpreting the music than many twentieth-century musicians are prepared to admit.

In any case, the music of Mozart today stands rehabilitated, largely freed from the misconceptions of previous eras. The little man from Salzburg was a miracle. More protean than Bach, musically more aristocratic than Beethoven, he can be put forward as the most perfect, best equipped, and most natural musician the world has ever known.

❧ 6 ❧

Revolutionary from Bonn

LUDWIG VAN BEETHOVEN

The difference between Beethoven and all other musicians before him—
aside from things like genius and unparalleled force—was that Beethoven
looked upon himself as an artist, and he stood up for his rights as an artist.
Where Mozart moved in the periphery of the aristocratic world, anxiously
knocking but never really admitted, Beethoven, who was only fourteen years
Mozart's junior, kicked open the doors, stormed in and made himself at
home. He was an artist, a creator, and as such superior to kings and nobles.
Beethoven had decidely revolutionary notions about society, and romantic
notions about music. "What is in my heart must come out and so I write it
down," he told his pupil Carl Czerny. Mozart would never have said a thing
like this, nor Haydn, nor Bach. The word "artist" never occurs in Mozart's
letters. He and the composers before him were skilled craftsmen who supplied a commodity, and the notion of art or writing for posterity did not
enter into their thinking. But Beethoven's letters and observations are full
of words like "art," "artist," and "artistry." He was of a special breed and he
knew it. He also knew he was writing for eternity. And he had what poor
Mozart lacked—a powerful personality that awed all who came in contact
with him. "Never have I met an artist of such spiritual concentration and
intensity," Goethe wrote, "such vitality and great-heartedness. I can well understand how hard he must find it to adapt to the world and its ways." Little did Goethe understand Beethoven. With Beethoven, it was not a matter
of adapting himself to the world and its ways. As with Wagner later on, it
was a matter of the world adapting its ways to *him*. With this high-voltage
personality, coupled to an equally high-voltage order of genius, Beethoven
was able to dictate to life on his own terms in almost everything except his
tragic deafness.

He was able to achieve this despite character flaws and deplorable manners. Never a beauty, he was called *Der Spagnol* in his youth because of his

swarthiness. He was short, about 5 feet, 4 inches, thickset and broad, with a massive head, a wildly luxuriant crop of hair, protruding teeth, a small rounded nose, and a habit of spitting wherever the notion took him. He was clumsy, and anything he touched was liable to be upset or broken. Badly co-ordinated, he could never learn to dance, and more often than not managed to cut himself while shaving. He was sullen and suspicious, touchy as a misanthropic cobra, believed that everybody was out to cheat him, had none of the social graces, was forgetful, was prone to insensate rages, engaged in some unethical dealings with his publishers. A bachelor, he lived in indescribably messy surroundings, largely because no servant could put up with his tantrums. In 1809 he was visited by the Baron de Trémont, and this is how that shocked worthy describes Beethoven's quarters:

> Picture to yourself the darkest, most disorderly place imaginable—blotches of moisture covered the ceiling; an oldish grand piano, on which the dust disputed the place with various pieces of engraved and manuscript music; under the piano (I do not exaggerate) an unemptied chamber pot; beside it a small walnut table accustomed to the frequent overturning of the secretary placed on it; a quantity of pens encrusted with ink, compared with which the proverbial tavern pens would shine; then more music. The chairs, mostly cane-seated, were covered with plates bearing the remains of last night's supper, and with wearing apparel, etc.

The Baron de Trémont's description is one of many along those lines. Beethoven was disorganized in everything but the one thing that really mattered—his music.

His genius was recognized almost from the beginning. A provincial from Bonn, where he was born on December 16, 1770, he was brought up by his father, a dissolute court musician. As a child prodigy, Ludwig was subjected to a severe regimen, and as so often happens in the history of prodigies, it affected his life. Richard and Edith Sterba, who have written a psychiatric study of Beethoven, maintain that "An early rebellion against his father's arbitrariness and unjust strictness laid the foundation for the revolt against every kind of authority which appears in Beethoven with an intensity which can only be described as highly unusual." His father hoped that he would be able to duplicate the feats of the young Mozart. It did not work out that way. The boy was certainly talented enough, and when he was twelve one of his teachers, Christian Gottlob Neefe, said that if he continued as he began, "he will surely be a second Mozart." But although Ludwig was a skilled pianist, violinist, and organist, he was something more than that. From the beginning he was a creator, one of those natural talents, full of ideas and originality.

It was this originality that set him apart. He was a force of nature, and nothing could contain him. He had a few lessons with prominent composers of the day, including Haydn and Mozart, but was dissatisfied with both of those great men and nothing much came of those lessons. It made no difference. Beethoven was not the kind of pupil who can be easily taught. He was too confident of his own genius. Once he made up his mind about something, he *knew* he was right. He always looked with suspicion on "rules" of harmony, and one of his friends once pointed out a series of parallel fifths in his music. In classical harmony, this is the unforgivable sin. Beethoven bridled. Who forbids parallel fifths, he wanted to know. A list of authorities was cited: Fux, Albrechtsberger, and so on. Beethoven dismissed them with a wave of his hand. "*I* admit them," he said. And there exists a notebook in which one harmony exercise is worked out seventeen times to show that one of the "rules" was wrong. Disproving the rule to his own satisfaction, Beethoven added *Du Esel*—you ass—as a comment on the authority who had made the "rule."

He first came to fame as a pianist. By 1791 a critic named Carl Ludwig Junker heard Beethoven play and had a few perceptive remarks to make: "'His style of treating the instrument is so different from that usually heard that it gives one the idea that he has attained that height of excellence on which he now stands by a path of his own discovery." When Beethoven settled in Vienna, in 1792, his style of playing made an overwhelming impression. The Viennese were conditioned to the smooth, fluent style of a Mozart or Hummel. Here came young Beethoven, hands high, smashing the piano, breaking strings, aiming for a hitherto unexploited kind of orchestral sonority on the keyboard. In his quest for more power, Beethoven begged the piano manufacturers to give him a better instrument than the light-actioned Viennese piano, which he said sounded like a harp. Beethoven was the greatest pianist of his time, and perhaps the greatest improviser who ever lived. In the Vienna of his time there was a group of able pianists, in residence or constantly passing through—Hummel, the Abbé Gelinek, Joseph Wölffl, Daniel Steibelt, Ignaz Moscheles. All these Beethoven at one time or another played under the table. None could stand up to him, though the admirable Wölffl, with his classic style, had a strong following among the conservatives. In many respects, Beethoven was the first of the modern piano virtuosos. Where pianists before him suavely and elegantly wooed an audience, Beethoven planted bombs under their seats.

Beethoven was all but adopted by the aristocracy. Fortunately for him, it was a liberal, enlightened, and music-loving aristocracy. Many of the noblemen maintained private orchestras and nearly all had musical salons. Great figures like the Princes Lobkowitz, Schwarzenberg, and Auersperg, Count Heinrich von Haugwitz, and Count Batthyany actually traveled with their orchestras. Prince Grassalkowich had a small wind orchestra. Beethoven moved in these circles and was not in the least awed. "It is easy to get on with the nobility if you have something to impress them with." Haydn and Mozart were expected to dine with the servants. Not Beethoven, who was mighty insulted if he was not at the host's side.

He not only moved in this society. He even had love affairs with its ladies, though the subject of Beethoven and women has been largely unexplored. He is credited by one of his contemporaries with having made conquests that an Adonis could not have made, and he seems to have been in and out of love all his life. Yet there is no real evidence that his amours were ever crowned with physical success. The Sterbas flatly say that Beethoven hated women; that even though he often said he wanted to be married, he subconsciously fled the idea. That is why he fell in love with women who under no circumstances would marry him—women who were already married, or far above him in social station. Nevertheless, there are ardent Beethoven letters to this or that lady, including the famous one to the mysterious Immortal Beloved, whoever she may have been. "My angel, my all, my very self . . . can you change the fact that you are not wholly mine, I not wholly thine . . . Ah, wherever I am, there you are also. . . . Much as you love me, I love you more. . . . Is not our love a heavenly structure, and also as firm as the vault of Heaven . . ." There seems to be no more chance of identifying her than there is of identifying the Dark Lady of the Sonnets, though scholars for generations have been working on those shadowy figures in Beethoven's and Shakespeare's life. However, George Marek, in his biography of Beethoven (1969), has found new evidence that points to Dorothea von Ertmann. She was the wife of an Austrian army officer and a gifted pianist. Beethoven, by the way, was very prudish. He even objected to *Don Giovanni* on the basis of its plot, which he said was immoral.

It is an oversimplification to say, as some music histories do, that Beethoven made his way without patronage. He probably could have been able to do so, but the fact remains that as early as 1801 Prince Lichnowsky settled some money on him. Later, when Beethoven was offered a position in the Westphalian court, the Archduke Rudolf, Prince Lobkowitz, and Prince Kinsky got together and put up 4,000 gulden to keep him in Vienna. That was in 1808. Because of the devaluation of the currency in 1811, that annuity was dissipated. Then Kinsky was killed in an accident and Lobkowitz went bankrupt. Nevertheless, the two noblemen and the Kinsky estate made up the difference, and from 1815 until his death Beethoven received 3,400 florins annually. He was not ashamed to take the money. Quite the contrary. He actually went to court to make the Kinsky estate uphold its obligation. Beethoven did not ask for the money, he *demanded* it. He felt it was his due.

During Beethoven's early years in Vienna, all was rosy. The world was at his feet. He was successful, honored, admired. He had swept all before him as a pianist, and his compositions were beginning to make their mark. His list of pupils boasted some of the most famous names in Vienna. Financially he did very well. "My compositions bring me in a good deal," he wrote to Franz Wegeler, his old friend from Bonn, in 1801, "and I may say that I am offered more commissions than it is possible for me to carry out. Moreover, for every composition I can count on six or seven publishers and even more, if I want them. People no longer come to an arrangement with me. I state my price, and they pay."

But something terrible was beginning to happen. Beethoven's hearing was going.

"My ears buzz continually day and night," he wrote Wegeler. "I can say that I am living a wretched life because it is impossible to say to people: 'I am deaf.' . . . In order to give you an idea of this singular deafness of mine, I must tell you that in the theater I must get very close to the orchestra in order to understand the actor. If I am a little too distant I do not hear the high notes of the instruments, singers, and if I am a little further back I do not hear at all. Frequently I can hear a low conversation, but not the words, and as soon as anybody shouts, it is intolerable." Beethoven tried everything to arrest the aural decay. He even was willing to attempt a cure by galvanism, or by quack doctors.

Naturally, he went through a traumatic experience, and the famous Heiligenstadt Testament, written in 1802 and addressed to his brothers to be read after his death, is a *cri de coeur:* "Oh you who think or say that I am malevolent, stubborn or misanthropic, how greatly do you wrong me. You do not know the secret cause which makes me seem that way to you. . . . Ah, how could I possibly admit an infirmity in the *one sense* which ought to be more perfect in me than in others, a sense which I once enjoyed in the highest perfection, a perfection such as few in my profession enjoy or have enjoyed . . ." There is page after page of lamentation.

He refused to bow to his affliction, though every year saw a further deterioration. By 1817 he was all but stone deaf, though he had his good days in which he could hear some music or speech without an ear trumpet. The cause of his affliction has not been established. It could have resulted from an attack of typhus. Or it might, as some otologists believe, have resulted from syphilis, acquired or congenital. Beethoven's battle with deafness was heroic, epic. He continued to play the piano, and he insisted on conducting his own music even though his wild gestures, coupled with an inability to hear well, completely threw the orchestra off course. The players learned not to look at him, paying attention instead to the first violinist. However, Beethoven, being the musician he was, could actually let sight substitute for hearing. Joseph Böhm, leader of a string quartet, has left us a description of Beethoven at work, and it is heartrending. In 1825, Böhm worked on the E flat Quartet (Op. 127) with the composer present. "It was studied industriously and rehearsed frequently under Beethoven's own eyes: I said Beethoven's *eyes* intentionally, for the unhappy man was so deaf he could no longer hear the heavenly sounds of his own compositions. And yet rehearsing in his presence was not easy. With close attention his eyes followed the bows and therefore he was able to judge the smallest imperfections in tempo or rhythm and correct them immediately."

Nonmusicians find it next to impossible to imagine how a deaf composer can function. But with musicians of a high order of ability, deafness involves only external sounds, not internal ones. Beethoven had absolute pitch, the ability to hear any note or combination of notes and instantly name them; or, on the opposite side, the ability to sing correctly any note without the artificial aid of a piano or tuning fork. That ability is not particularly rare. Any good musician, or even a talented nonprofessional, for that matter, can pick up a score and read it, "hearing" everything that goes on. A good composer does not need a piano to work. Indeed, Beethoven once told his English pupil, Cipriani Potter, never to compose in a room in which there was a piano, in order to resist the temptation to consult an instrument. To many nonmusicians, this ability is on the order of black magic, but professionals take it as a matter of course. Thus Beethoven, with his incredible musical mind, would have had no trouble, no more than Bach or Mozart had, writing music guided only by the sounds in his inner ear.

At the height of his depression, Beethoven was working on the *Eroica* Symphony, which had its premiere in 1805. The *Eroica* is one of the turning points in musical history. Up to then Beethoven had been a composer with roots in the eighteenth century. His music, to be sure, was more rugged than that of Haydn and Mozart. The six quartets of Op. 18 had a lustiness that hinted, but only hinted, at a new world. The first two symphonies pushed the classic symphony to new lengths, both in actual duration and size of the orchestra. The early piano sonatas, especially the *Pathétique*, *Moonlight* (not so named by Beethoven), and D minor, went farther than any of Mozart's or Haydn's piano music in their massive sonority, romantic expression, unconventionality of form, and a new kind of virtuosity. But nevertheless, on the whole, the pre-*Eroica* music is the language of Beethoven's great predecessors. Then came the *Eroica*, and music was never again the same. With one convulsive wrench, music entered the nineteenth century.

The background of the *Eroica* is well known. Beethoven set to work on it in 1803, intending the score to be a tribute to Bonaparte. When Bonaparte proclaimed himself Emperor, legend has it that Beethoven, who preached a kind of democracy, tore up the title page containing the dedication. By May, 1804, the score was finished, and the premiere took place on April 7, 1805, at the Theater an der Wien. History does not relate the quality of the performance. Beethoven's gigantic score must have imposed unprecedented difficulties on the musicians, and the chances are that they played raggedly and out of tune. One wonders, too, what went through the mind of the audience on that historic occasion. It was faced with a monster of a symphony, a symphony longer than any previously written and much more heavily scored; a symphony with complex harmonies; a symphony of titanic force; a symphony of fierce dissonances; a symphony with a funeral march that is paralyzing in its intensity.

Sensitive listeners realized they were in the presence of something monumental. The critics were worried. They recognized the power of the *Eroica*, but very few could grasp its stringent logic and organization. "This long composition," wrote the critic of the *Allgemeine Musikalische Zeitung*, "extremely difficult of performance, is in reality a tremendously expanded, daring and wild fantasia. It lacks nothing in the way of startling and beautiful passages, in which the energetic and talented composer must be recognized; but often it loses itself in lawlessness. . . . . This reviewer belongs to Mr. Beethoven's sincerest admirers, but in this composition he must confess that he finds much that is glaring and bizarre, which hinders greatly one's grasp of the whole, and a sense of unity is almost completely lost." Musical Vienna was divided on the merits of the *Eroica*. Some called it Beethoven's masterpiece. Others said that the work merely illustrated a striving for originality that did not come off. In those circles the feeling was that Beethoven should not continue on this track but should go back to writing music like the celebrated Septet and the first two symphonies. The latter faction outnumbered the admirers of the *Eroica*. At the premiere the audience was not as responsive as Beethoven would have liked to have seen, and he was unhappy, but he refused to change a note. "If *I* write a symphony an hour long, it will be found short enough," he was quoted as saying. His only concession was to suggest that the *Eroica* be played near the beginning of a program, before the audience got weary. The *Eroica* runs about fifty minutes, and even longer if all the repeats are taken. Few, if any, Mozart or Haydn symphonies are over a half-hour long.

The next seven or eight years saw a succession of masterpieces: the first version of *Fidelio* in 1805 (it was not a success until its revision in 1814), the three *Razumovsky* Quartets, the Violin Concerto, the Piano Concertos Nos. 4 in G and 5 in E flat, the Symphonies Nos. 4 through 8, several of the most famous piano sonatas (including the *Waldstein* and *Appassionata*). But around 1811 there was a falling-off in Beethoven's productivity. Several things happened. As his deafness became total, he retired more and more into his inner world. It was a period of gestation from which were to come the *Missa Solemnis* and the final string quartets and piano sonatas—those gigantic, mysterious, mystic creations. Beethoven knew he was in the process of conception even though his pen was idle. "It has always been one of my rules: *Nulla dies sine linea,*" he told Wegeler, "and if I let the Muse sleep, it is only in order that she shall wake up the stronger." In addition, his health was not good. He was bothered by liver and intestinal trouble. But the major factor in his life, one that took up much of his time and conceivably might have robbed the world of some masterpieces, was his relationship with his nephew, Karl.

When Beethoven's brother Caspar died in 1815, the will appointed Caspar's wife, Johanna, and his brother Ludwig, guardian of the nine-year-old child. Beethoven's opinion of Johanna was low to begin with, and to get Karl away from her he resorted to the courts, acting like a wild man, accusing her of character defects and immorality. He did get her guardianship annulled, but she fought back and in 1819 was successful. Beethoven went to a higher court and in 1820 finally won his case. Karl seems to have been a bright, receptive boy, but he could not have found a worse guardian than his doting Uncle Ludwig, who meant well but was alternately strict and easygoing. Karl was driven out of his mind. He learned to take the easy way out and flatter his uncle, but nothing worked. The boy found dubious friends, tried to break away, was unsuccessful and finally, in 1826, attempted suicide. One bullet missed, the other gave him a scalp wound. On recovery, he said that he wanted Beethoven to keep away. "If only he would stop nagging me!" He told the police that Beethoven tormented him. Beethoven took it very badly, and friends said he aged twenty years in those weeks. Eventually Karl, a maligned and misunderstood figure, went into the army. He resigned in 1832, married, inherited the estate of Uncle Johann (Beethoven's other brother), and died in 1858.

Thanks to Beethoven's endless litigation over Karl and his psychopathic determination to thwart his sister-in-law, the period from 1815 to 1820 saw very little music, only six major works in six years. These included the last two cello sonatas, the song cycle *An die ferne Geliebte,* and the Piano Sonatas in A (Op. 101), B flat (Op. 106), and E (Op. 109). The B flat is the *Hammerklavier,* the longest, grandest, and most difficult sonata in history, with a last movement consisting of an all but unplayable fugue. Would he have composed so murderous (technically) a movement had he not been deaf? One wonders. From 1818 he was occupied with the *Missa Solemnis* and Ninth Symphony, finishing the former in 1823 and the Ninth in the following year. The Ninth Symphony had its premiere on May 7, 1824—with only two rehearsals! It must have been a catastrophe. The chorus had trouble singing the music and pleaded for the high notes to be taken down, just as the contralto soloist, Caroline Unger, also begged for changes. Beethoven refused. At the concert, those singers who could not reach the high notes simply omitted them. The scherzo made a big impression, however, and Unger turned Beethoven around so he could see the applause he could not hear. As the *Eroica* was a pivotal point in nineteenth-century music, so the Ninth Symphony was the Beethoven work that above all captured the imagination of the later romantics. Beethoven's last great contributions to music were five string quartets and a fugue for string quartet, the *Grosse Fuge*, originally intended as the last movement of the B flat Quartet (Op. 130).

In his Vienna he was as famous a figure as ever, universally conceded to be the greatest composer in the world, greater even than the composer-pianist Johann Nepomuk Hummel. He also was admired by the Viennese as one of the great eccentrics. His fame, of course, was universal, and people came from all over the continent and England to visit him. He saw them all. He was a familiar figure in the taverns and coffeehouses, where he would hold forth pontifically on all subjects. Self-educated, he was not what could be called an intellectual, and outside of music his mental processes were anything but remarkable. This can be seen in his letters, those infuriating letters, most of which consist of dealing with publishers, or short notes inviting friends for dinner—everything but the things we most want to know: what he thought about music, about his contemporaries, about life. Mozart's letters are revelatory, illustrative of a sharp, quick mind and an endearing, if weak, personality. Beethoven's for the most part (there are exceptions) tell us virtually nothing about himself.

He died on March 27, 1827, after a long illness. If contemporary accounts are to be believed, there was a flash of lightning, a clap of thunder, and the dying man raised himself and defiantly shook his fist at it. The story sounds too pat, too much a romantic invention, to be true, but one hopes it is. Beethoven went through life defying everything. Why not at the end of the struggle, defy the elements and God himself? It is reported that some 20,000 people turned out for the funeral.

This was the man who was the most powerful musical thinker of music. He is often considered a bridge between the classical and romantic periods, but that is merely a label, and not a very accurate one. Indeed, there is surprisingly little romanticism in his music, much less than in the work of Weber and Schubert, two composers active in his time (Weber died in 1826, Schubert in 1828), and much less than in the work of some of the minor figures, such as Ludwig Spohr and Jan Ladislav Dussek. Certain exceptions in Beethoven's music can be cited. The slow movement of the E major Piano Sonata (Op. 109), with its almost Chopinesque melody, has some romanticism in it, for example. But Beethoven simply did not speak the language of the romantics. He had started as a composer in the classic tradition and ended up a composer beyond time and space, using a language he himself had forged: a language compressed, cryptic, and explosive, expressed in forms of his own devising.

Beethoven was a very slow worker. Where Mozart took days or weeks over a work, Beethoven took months and years. Mozart composed his three greatest symphonies within six weeks in the summer of 1788. Beethoven took at least three years, polishing and rewriting, before he thought his Op. 1, three piano trios, was ready for publication. He carried ideas in his head for a long time, and then there was the struggle of getting them on paper. His sketchbooks reveal that he would refine and refine, changing a phrase note by note until it had that definitive quality we recognize as Beethovenian. The theme of the slow movement of the Fifth Symphony must have passed through at least a dozen transformations before Beethoven settled on its final shape. Maturity did not bring relaxation. As Beethoven's musical vision grew, so did his struggles with the material.

Beethoven's music falls into three periods. At the beginning he worked mostly within the forms of the day. His first twenty works or so test the old forms, expanding them, hinting at the explosive power that was to come. Even there, the rough humor and the high degree of expressivity that was to mark the mature Beethoven were already in evidence. The galloping minuet of the First Symphony points the way to the powerful scherzos of the later ones. The intense, beautiful slow movement of the D major Piano Sonata (Op. 10, No. 3) is a minature tone poem. Already Beethoven was a poet in tone, and there is a personal quality to this kind of writing, a direct emotional involvement, a kind of near-romantic melody that is something new in music. The difference between the first movement of the *Pathétique* Sonata and the equally great and powerful C minor Fantasy (K. 475) by Mozart is the difference between the eighteenth and nineteenth century, the difference between a society dominated by the idea of aristocracy and a society dominated by the concept of individuality. In Beethoven's music, the concepts put into motion by the French Revolution and the Industrial Revolution are shaping the destiny of man and art. Beethoven's music has much more personal quality than Mozart's. It is more concerned with inner states of being and the desire for self-expression. Mozart holds himself in classic restraint, while Beethoven bares his soul for all to see.

After the turning point of the *Eroica*, the second period sets in. Beethoven was confident, a master of form, with a fertile mind and an individuality that made its own rules. Under his pen, sonata form underwent a metamorphosis. Beethoven took the sonata form of Haydn and Mozart, and the majority of his great works—the symphonies, concertos, quartets, piano and violin sonatas, trios and other chamber music—are expressed in sonata form, *his* sonata form, not textbook sonata form. The lesser composers of his day used sonata form much as a builder uses a standard architectural plan for a prefabricated house, and the result had as much individuality: Theme A, Theme B, a routine and mechanical development (breaking no rules and using no unconventional harmonies), a recapitulation. But Beethoven bent and twisted sonata form to suit himself and his material. His invention and resource never flagged. He could, in the Fifth Symphony, erect an entire structure on four notes—hammerblows, more a motif than a theme. He could, in the *Appassionata* Sonata, devise a work that breaks all classic rules and erupts wildly all over the keyboard. Lacking the superrefined harmonic sense of a Mozart, he could and did bring something different to music—a propulsive kind of rhythm, a broadening of all musical structures, a kind of development that wrings everything out of the material, a kind of accentuation, often off the beat, that throws the music into uneasy and unexpected metrical patterns, a sheer independence. Beethoven's music is not polite. What he presented, as no composer before or since, was a feeling of drama, of conflict and resolution. But this is conflict expressed purely in musical terms. Beethoven thought only in tone, in musical architecture. He derided program music. While composing the *Pastoral* Symphony he thought about the problem and set down some observations: "All painting in instrumental music is lost if pushed too far. . . . Anyone who has an idea of country life can make out for himself the intentions of the composer without many titles. . . . Also, without titles, the whole will be recognized as a matter more of feeling than of painting in sounds."

Thus, whatever the emotional state of being that any Beethoven score suggests, it is held together by purely *musical* logic, by the composer's ideas of development, contrast, thematic linkages, and rhythm. The music may be a yelp of sheer exultation, as in the last movement of the C major Quartet or most of the Seventh Symphony; or it may be gnarled and cryptic, as in the curious Piano Sonata in F sharp, or it may be a combination of electric virtuosity and pure lyricism, as in the *Emperor* Concerto; or it may be ravishing lyricism throughout, as in the G major Piano Concerto. Whatever it is, it is music governed by the inexorable logic of a great technician and musical thinker.

Then comes the fallow period, followed by the so-called last-period works —the last five string quartets and piano sonatas, the *Diabelli* Variations, the *Missa Solemnis*, the Ninth Symphony. Here we are on a rarefied plane of music. Nothing like it has been composed, nothing like it can ever again be. It is the music of a man who has seen all and experienced all, a man drawn into his silent, suffering world, no longer writing to please anybody else but writing to justify his artistic and intellectual existence. Faced with this music, the temptation is to read things into it in some sort of metaphysical exegesis. The music is not pretty or even attractive. It merely is sublime. At this stage of his career, Beethoven seemed to be dealing as much in concepts and symbols as in notes. Themes can be terse and abrupt or, in such works as the cavatina of the B flat major String Quartet, a long effusion without end. Even silences play a part in this music. Suddenly the trill assumes a menacing importance. The music of Beethoven's last period is full of long, vicious trills that must have had some kind of extramusical significance to him. Form is now not what the professors or the age dictate, but only what the music dictates. The C minor Piano Sonata (Op. 111) has only two movements, the last movement a series of variations ending with a sustained, hushed, mysterious chain of trills. The C sharp minor Quartet has seven clearly defined movements played without a break. The Ninth Symphony has a final movement that uses a chorus and vocal soloists. All of this is music turned inward, music of the spirit, music of extreme subjectivity and extraordinary grandeur.

To this day the last quartets pose problems. Those who will not or can not enter Beethoven's world find them bleak, cold, and incomprehensible, and this is especially true of the great trinity, Opp. 130 in B flat, 131 in C sharp minor, and 132 in A minor. In a way, these three string quartets can be looked upon as one superquartet. They have themes in common, share the same language and feeling, are interrelated texturally and harmonically. Each of these quartets is very long (just as, contrariwise, the last three piano sonatas are relatively short), and each defies description. They are a mystic state of mind as much as music. Their organic developments, the convulsions of the *Grosse Fuge*, the ineffable unfolding of the Lydian slow movement of the A minor Quartet, the fugal introduction to the C sharp minor, the Cavatina of the B flat—all this and much more carry music to a height that actually seems to transcend music.

This concept of Beethoven's musical transcendentalism may have been felt during Beethoven's lifetime, and was certainly adopted by the musicians of the romantic period. In 1859 a scholar named Adolf Bernhard Marx wrote a book about Beethoven that introduced the concept of *Idealmusik*, the idea being that the music of Beethoven had as much to do with ethics as with pure tone. Music as revelation; music as an ideal force (in the Platonic sense); music as manifestation of the Divine. The romantics eagerly embraced the concept. The last five quartets did not mean so much to the romantics, and it remained for the twentieth century to make them its own. But to the romantics, the Ninth Symphony was the beacon. It represented everything the romantics thought to be the essence of Beethoven—a defiance of form, a call for brotherhood, a titanic explosion, a spiritual experience. The Ninth Symphony was the Beethoven work that most influenced

Berlioz and Wagner. It was the Ninth Symphony that remained the unapproachable, unachievable ideal of Brahms, Bruckner, and Mahler. To the romantics, and to many today, the Ninth Symphony is something more than music. It is an *ethos*, and Debussy was not entirely wrong when he said that the great score had become a "universal nightmare." It pressed too heavily on the music of the century. Only within the last generation have there been those who dare criticize the last movement, but not even those critics have anything but awe for the other three movements. And, indeed, the coda of the first movement, with its slippery, chromatic bass and the awesome moans above it, remains a paralyzing experience. *That* is the way the world ends. It is absolute music, but it clearly represents struggle, and it is hard to hear so monumentally anguished a cry without reading something into it. The trouble is that, faced with such music, all of us tend to become sentimentalists, reading into it the wrong message.

Perhaps the true, extramusical interpretation of any Beethoven work would be a long way from what most listeners believe. It might represent nothing more than the strong-minded, even arrogant, reflection of a phenomenal musical intellect who was driven by illness and mental suffering to retreat completely into his own world, his own silent world, the result being sheer solipsism far removed from the lofty ideals attributed by later ages. Beethoven had vague ideas about universal brotherhood and a perfect society, but he would have nothing to do with those abstract concepts when it came to himself. "I don't want to know anything about your system of ethics," he wrote to a friend. "Strength is the morality of the man who stands out from the rest, and it is mine." These are frightening words: a dangerous, ominous, prophetic utterance. But the man was redeemed by his music, and it is the most powerful body of music ever brought together by one composer.

❧ 7 ❧

Poet of Music

FRANZ PETER SCHUBERT

Franz Schubert, who died at the age of thirty-one, lived all his life under the shadow of Beethoven. To the Viennese, and indeed to all of Europe, Beethoven was the great man, and only a few composers—Hummel, Spohr, perhaps Weber—deserved to be mentioned in the same breath. Schubert was not one of them. It is not that he was considered a nonentity. In his own country he had a tidy reputation, though it was primarily as a composer of songs. But his reputation was mostly local. He never moved far from Vienna, except for two short trips to neighboring Hungary, where he taught the children of Count Johann Karl Esterházy, and he was rather shy and retiring. The first great composer in history *not* to be a conductor or public instrumentalist, he could not achieve fame as an executant or push his music through his own virtuosity. He never asked much from life, was something of a Bohemian, and seemed content to pour out page after page of music whether or not it ever was performed. His mission was to create music; that was the only thing he was made for. "The state should keep me," he told his friend Josef Hüttenbrenner. "I have come into the world for no purpose but to compose."

Despite all that has been written about Schubert, he remains a rather vague and even mysterious figure. A great deal is known about the external aspects of his life, but there is surprisingly little about what he said, thought, felt. He left very few letters, and the abortive diary he started in 1816 consists mostly of charming adolescent musings of a general nature. "Man resembles a ball, to be played with by chance and passion." Or, "Happy he who finds a true man friend. Happier still he who finds a true friend in his wife." All very engaging, but nothing specific, nothing that tells us much about the writer. Some forty years after his death, when the world woke up to the fact that Schubert was one of the colossal creative figures of music, efforts were made to get reminiscences from all who knew him. A flood of material resulted, all of which has to be screened with great care. Naturally at that date, anybody who had been associated with Schubert wanted to share in the reflected glory. But of Schubert during the actual period of his short life—January 31, 1797, to November 19, 1828—there remains material only for a superficial biographical sketch. That is why most Schubert biographies concentrate on the music rather than the man. His character is very hard, and perhaps impossible, to evoke.

The main outlines of his life are, of course, documented. He was the twelfth of fourteen children, of whom five survived. His father was the head of his own school, conducted in his own house, where Schubert was born. In 1808, young Franz became a soprano in the choir of the court chapel at the Imperial and Royal Seminary, where he also received a general education. As a seminary student he wore the official uniform: an old-fashioned three-cornered hat, white neckerchief, a dark-colored cutaway coat, a small gold epaulette on his left shoulder, shiny buttons, an old-fashioned waistcoat that reached below the stomach, short breeches with buckles, shoes without buckles. A bright boy, Franz did well in all of his studies, and in music immediately established his superiority. He was the "big man on campus"—a good pianist and violinist, and already a prolific composer. This at the age of eleven. The principal music teacher at the seminary, one Wenzel Ruzicka, found that he had nothing to teach the boy. "This one's learned from God!" he is reported to have said. Another teacher, Michael Holzer, later wrote: "If I wanted to instruct him in anything new, he already knew it. Therefore I gave him no actual tuition but merely talked to him and watched him with silent astonishment." Also in 1808 Schubert made a big enough impression to attract the attention of Antonio Salieri, the court musical director, and became a composition student of that important figure. (Salieri was one of the best-known composers of the day and also was Mozart's bête noire. Salieri had all the contacts and guarded them jealously. Mozart could make little headway against him. After Mozart's death there were weird rumors that Salieri had poisoned him. There is no proof to that absurd contention, but it worked on poor Salieri's mind, and on his very deathbed he kept protesting that he was innocent.) At the seminary Schubert made many friends, and one of them, Joseph von Spaun, remained close to Schubert all his life. From the little that is known about Schubert in the Imperial and Royal Seminary, he was a sweet, uncomplicated boy with a spectacular musical talent. At home he would play chamber music with his brothers and his music-loving father, timidly correcting Papa when the elder man made one of his frequent mistakes.

His voice broke in 1813, but he was kept at the seminary on a scholarship. Later in that year, however, he resigned and started training as a schoolmaster. He loathed the studies and the work, though from 1814–1818

97

he was an assistant at his father's school. During his years as a teacher he composed steadily, turning out song after song, writing symphonies, chamber music, and masses, and also trying to break into the Viennese theater. The time was against him for that. He composed German opera, and Vienna was in the throes of a Rossini craze. It was toward the end of 1816 that Rossini's *L'Inganno felice* created a furor in Vienna, and a succession of Rossini operas followed. Schubert, who never let personal considerations interfere with an objective evaluation of anybody else's music, called Rossini an "extraordinary genius," and some Rossinisms crept into his own music. Perhaps had Schubert found a decent librettist, he might have had a chance. His operas are full of lovely ideas. But seldom has a composer had to set the kind of nonsense Schubert was constantly being saddled with.

In the first two decades of the nineteenth century, music had come out of the courts and salons into the market place. All of a sudden it started to become a bourgeois phenomenon. There was a craze for the waltz, and that influenced serious music. Schubert, like Mozart and to a lesser extent, Beethoven, wrote a very large amount of dance music. Up to the second decade of the century, the minuet, Ländler, and contradance were the popular forms. Then came the waltz. The waltz became fashionable during the Congress of Vienna in 1814–15, and from that time Vienna was the Waltz City. In the 1820's, on the Thursday before Carnival Sunday, the city would offer as many as 1,600 balls in a single night. The bourgeoisie as well as the aristocracy danced to the waltz. The bourgeoisie also heavily supported the Italian opera craze and the German drama. Vienna, not a large city, had four theaters to supply the demand—the Burg Theater, for spoken drama; the Kärntnertor Theater, for opera and ballet; the Theater an der Wien, for drama, concerts, and opera; and the Leopoldstadt Theater for drama and opera. In addition, there were smaller halls—the Josefstadt Theater, the Redoutensaal, the court ballrooms of the Hofburg, the Great Hall of the University, and the County Hall. Many members of the aristocracy maintained their own orchestras and musical salons. Above all, a large group, the cultivated middle class, began to participate in music, associating with composers and making music an essential part of its life.

It was the music-loving, art-loving, intellectual middle-class group with which Schubert was associated all his life. He seldom mixed with the aristocracy, as Beethoven did. He felt comfortable only among the bourgeoisie and the artistic Bohemians of Vienna. When he left schoolteaching for good in 1818, he entered that Bohemian circle and it was for its members that he composed his music. It was a circle of musicians, artists, and literary figures, and most of them were his close friends. There were the poets Johann Mayrhofer and Franz Grillparzer, the painter and illustrator Moritz von Schwind, the composer and conductor Franz Lachner, the singer Johann

Vogl, the dilettante Franz von Schober, and many others. "Our circle," Schubert called them.

He lived *la vie de bohème*, seldom having money, moving in with friends, spending much time at cafés. After 1818 he was on his own, though two years previously he had become a professional. An entry in his diary, dated June 17, 1816, reads: "Today I composed for money for the first time. Namely, a cantata for the name day of Professor Wattrot [Watteroth], words by Dräxler. The fee is 100 florins, V.C." That would be around $50. The chances are that he did not keep the money long. Schubert was always short of cash, and never had enough even to rent a piano, much less buy one. It made no difference, for he did not need a piano for composition. He said it made him lose his train of thought. If he needed a piano, he would go to a friend's house. Among Schubert's closest friends were Schwind and Eduard von Bauernfeld, and the three of them formed a tiny communistic enclave in which there was no such thing as private property. Hats, shoes, clothes, money—all was communal. Whoever was in funds for the moment took care of the bills. Money meant nothing to Schubert, and he was an unaggressive businessman when it came to selling his music and dealing with publishers. Nor did time mean much to him. He would drive his friends to desperation by not turning up when he was expected. A letter from Schwind in 1825 chides him for not showing up for a party, and the letter also gives a clue to the complexity of Schubert's character: "Had you thought of how much affection was waiting for you, you would have come. . . . I am almost afraid of getting as much pleasure from you, seeing how ill I have succeeded all these years in overcoming your mistrust and your fear of not being loved and understood." It could be that Schubert, like many shy persons, was apt to imagine slights and was extremely sensitive about peoples' reaction to him.

Yet there was something in him that made his friends fiercely loyal. And women wanted to mother him. He was a Kewpie doll of a man: tiny (about 5 feet, 1½ inches), dumpy enough to be nicknamed *Schwammerl* (Tubby), with curly brown hair, a stubby rounded nose, a round face, and dimpled chin. His eyesight was bad and he always wore glasses. Generally he was good-natured and could easily be cajoled to the piano to play and improvise waltzes at parties. Sometimes, however, he was moody and irascible, especially during his illness. He contracted venereal disease and went through a bad period in which he temporarily lost his hair and all but retired from society. In Beethoven's conversation book of 1823 there is a note in his nephew Karl's handwriting: "They greatly praise Schubert, but it is said that he hides himself." Schubert's friend Leopold von Sonnleithner said that Schubert "never laughed openly and fully, but only managed a chuckle which sounded toneless rather than bright." His way of life was completely irregular. From about 9 in the morning (unless he was suffering from a hang-over) until 2 in the afternoon, he composed. Then he was on the town. Unless invited somewhere to dinner, or to a party, he frequented the cafés. The Anchor, and Bogner's, were among his favorites. There he would stay until midnight, smoking, drinking coffee and wine, reading the papers, holding court with his circle. On the whole he was a taciturn man. He had affairs with women, but kept them to himself, and not even his friends knew the particulars. He never married. Although never an alcoholic, he sometimes drank more than he could handle. Undoubtedly there were aspects of his life unknown to us. Josef Kenner, another friend, has left some dark hints: "Any one who knew Schubert knows he was of two natures foreign to each other, how powerfully the craving for pleasure dragged his soul down to the slough of moral degradation . . ." This may be mere pious Victorian moralizing; and, then again, there very well may be something to it.

The tentative efforts of Schubert to find a publisher did not get very far. In 1817 he sent Breitkopf and Härtel one of his greatest songs, the *Erlkönig*. Breitkopf and Härtel could not have been less interested, and returned it to the only Franz Schubert they knew, a composer of that name who lived in Dresden. The Dresden Schubert was insulted, and sent a stiff note back to the publishers. Who was the upstart making free with his name? Schubert of Dresden said he would keep the song. "I shall retain it in my possession to learn, if possible, who sent you that sort of trash . . ." In the meantime, Spaun sent to Goethe a group of Schubert songs set to that master's poetry. Spaun hoped to arouse his interest, but Goethe did not even answer. It was not all frustration, however. Little by little Schubert's name became known. Such singers as Anna Milder and, especially, Johann Vogl began to present his music in public; and Schubert's circle, small but influential, made propaganda for their hero. Vogl was of great importance in Schubert's life. When the composer first met him, in the spring of 1817, the baritone was nearly thirty years older and nearing the end of a distinguished operatic career. He looked at some Schubert songs, hemmed and hawed, but was attracted to them and became Schubert's first great interpreter. Vogl was a stout, stern majestic figure, and he and the diminutive Schubert were a sight marching along the streets of Vienna. There is an amusing caricature, believed to be by Franz von Schober, of the two. The fact that so important a singer as Vogl specialized in Schubert was very important for the young composer. Reviewers began to take notice of him, and the notices generally were flattering. A long and understanding review in the *Wiener Zeitschrift für Kunst* flatly called him a genius in 1822; and the following year he was referred to in that publication as "this popular master." Schubert never achieved the fame he deserved, but neither did he work in a vacuum.

The "Schubertiaden" in Vienna were well known. These were evenings sponsored by Schubert's friends in which nothing but his music was performed. With Schubert at the piano, there would be songs, chamber music, four-hand and solo piano pieces. It was this Schubert circle that saw the first group of his songs off the press. As no publisher was willing to print the music, Schubert's admirers got together and raised the money for publication. Franz von Hartmann, a member of the circle, wrote about many Schubertiads in his diary. The entry of December 15, 1826, is characteristic:

> I went to Spaun's, where there was a big, big Schubertiad. On entering I was received very rudely by Fritz and very saucily by Haas. There was a huge gathering. The Arneth, Witteczek, Kurzrock and Pompe couples; the mother-in-law of the Court and State Chancellery probationer Witteczek; Dr. Watteroth's widow, Betty Wanderer, and the painter Kupelwieser and his wife, Grillparzer, Schober, Schwind, Mayrhofer and his landlord Huber, tall Huber, Derffel, Bauernfeld, Gahy (who played four-hand music gloriously with Schubert), and Vogl, who sang almost thirty splendid songs. Baron Schlecta and other Court probationers and secretaries were also there. . . . When the music was over, there was grand feeding and dancing. But I was not at all in a courting mood. I danced twice with Betty and once with each of the Witteczek, Kurzrock and Pompe ladies. At 12:30, after a cordial parting with the Spauns and Enderes, we saw Betty home and went to The Anchor, where we still found Schober, Schubert, Schwind, Derffel and Bauernfeld. Merry. Then home. To bed at 1 o'clock.

As Schubert's reputation grew, a few publishers approached him, but very few of his important works were printed during his lifetime. None of the symphonies appeared in print, only one of the nineteen string quartets, three of the twenty-one piano sonatas, one of the seven masses, none of the ten operas, 187 of the more than 600 songs. From this, according to the estimate of the Schubert authority, Otto Erich Deutsch, Schubert netted an estimated $12,500 spread over twelve years. Not much; but, in Deutsch's words, "Schubert never starved." In the very last years of Schubert's life there were indications that matters would improve. In 1828 the firm of Schott sent him a letter—the address was to "Franz Schubert, Esq., Famous Composer in Vienna"—asking for music. The firm of Probst also was interested. Something might have come of those overtures, especially from Schott, who was looking for a composer to take the place of Beethoven.

Had Schott pursued negotiations in the last year of Schubert's life, the company would have made a great deal of money in the long run. What a tremendous year it was! It was the year of the C major Symphony, the C major String Quintet, the last three piano sonatas, and some remarkable songs. It also was the year of the one and only public concert he had during his lifetime. Again it was the result of his friends, who got together and rented a hall. The concert, given on March 26, 1828, never was reviewed. Paganini happened to be in town and gave his first concert on March 29, following it with thirteen more. Those took up all the space in the papers. As if Schubert was not occupied enough, that last hectic year of his life, he arranged with the theorist Simon Sechter for lessons in counterpoint. Schubert had been reading the music of Handel and decided to study strict counterpoint. "Now for the first time I see what I lack." It was a decision that has amazed later Schubert scholars and admirers, though nobody has raised an eyebrow about Mozart's immersion in Bachian counterpoint, and his enthusiasm for it. But Schubert's lessons were not to be. Early in November he took to his bed and died on the nineteenth of that month from typhoid fever (not typhus, as some biographies have it). He left nothing—no books, no money, no furniture, no estate at all. All that remained were manuscripts scattered all over Vienna. Schubert was buried near Beethoven. His friends were desolate. Schwind wrote to Schober: "Schubert is dead, and with him all that we had of the brightest and fairest." Grillparzer wrote the epitaph on the tombstone: "The art of music here entombed a rich possession, but even far fairer hopes."

In his thirty-one years, Schubert wrote an enormous amount of music. He was a very fast writer, incredibly fast, and while recent scholars cast doubt on some of the stories of his speed, there is no reason to disbelieve the contemporary accounts. They all agree. When Schubert worked, he worked at white heat. Said Schober: "If you go to see him during the day, he says 'Hello, how are you?—Good!' and goes on working, whereupon you go away." Awed friends told story after story of his speed, and those stories are true in essence if not always in detail. Sonnleithner reports that "At Fräulein Fröhlich's request, Franz Grillparzer had written for the occasion the beautiful poem *Ständchen,* and this she gave to Schubert, asking him to set it to music as a serenade for her sister Josefine (mezzo-soprano) and women's chorus. Schubert took the poem, went into an alcove by the window, read it through carefully a few times and then said with a smile, 'I've got it already, it's done, and it's going to be quite good.'" Spaun tells of the composition of the *Erlkönig.* He and Mayrhofer visited Schubert and found him reading the poem. "He paced up and down several times with the book, suddenly he sat down, and in no time at all (just as quickly as you can write) there was the glorious ballad finished on the paper. We ran with it to the Seminary, for there was no piano at Schubert's, and there, on the very same evening, the *Erlkönig* was sung and enthusiastically received." For many years it was believed that Schubert never made sketches even for major compositions like symphonies. Modern research has established otherwise. But there is no doubt at all that Schubert, like Mozart, was one of the fastest writers in musical history: a composer who could conceive a whole work in his head and immediately write it down.

His music is highly original. No composer of the day could entirely escape the influence of Beethoven, Mozart, and Haydn; but Schubert, once his style was formed, broke away more than any composer of the time. Schubert admired Beethoven—from a safe distance. If the two met more than once, history has not recorded it. Beethoven, who knew what was going on everywhere, read through some of the Schubert songs and was impressed. According to Schindler, he said that Schubert had the divine spark. That does not make it a true statement. Schindler often was the victim of his own imagination. But we know from Karl's entry in the conversation books that Beethoven was very much aware of Schubert and his music. Apparently Schubert got up enough nerve to visit Beethoven only once, when Beethoven was on his deathbed. Nothing about the visit is known. But there was really, in Schubert's music, as little Beethoven influence as there was actual personal contact. After experimenting with the forms and textures of Mozart and Haydn in his early music, Schubert proceeded to go along a road of his own without ever turning back.

In his specialty, the song literature, he had relatively little precedent. There were a few composers who had previously added to the German song literature. Among them were Johann Friedrich Reichardt, Carl Friedrich Zelter, and Johann Rudolf Zumsteeg. As a young man, Schubert directly imitated a few Zumsteeg songs. Haydn, Mozart, and Beethoven had given some lovely songs to the world. But Schubert, while he may not have been the first composer to specialize in song (there had been the Elizabethan, John Dowland, for example), nevertheless was the first of the great composers to write a large body of art songs that have remained a permanent part of the active repertoire.

From the very beginning something propelled Schubert into the art song, or lied. He was only seventeen years old when he composed *Gretchen am Spinnrade,* one of the most perfect songs ever written. That was in 1814, and the following year he wrote 145 songs. For his poetry he ranged over the entire field of contemporary German literature. Goethe he found especially attractive, and of his more than 600 songs, about seventy are set to poems by Goethe. He set poems by Schiller, Heine, and Klopstock; poems by his friends Mayrhofer and Schober; poems by Ludwig Gottfried Kosegarten and Wilhelm Müller. In all, lyrics by ninety-one poets are represented. Schubert's basic song forms are strophic or *Durchkomponiert* (through composed). In the strophic song the same melody is used for all the verses. (There also are modifications of the strophic song.) A song that is *Durchkomponiert* follows the poem from beginning to end in a single dramatic or lyric continuity. Often *Durchkomponiert* song suggests the ballad form. It so happens that a composer named Karl Loewe (1796–1869), born a year before Schubert, specialized in the narrative ballad and composed some masterpieces in the form, including a setting of the *Erlkönig*. Schubert's own familiar setting is also a ballad, as purely descriptive as it is emotional, and it strikes far deeper than Loewe's, fine as the latter's is. Schubert was never dogmatic about his song forms. Often he would mix strophic and through-composed writing.

"He bade poetry sound and music speak," said Grillparzer. Schubert's songs are of infinite variety—long and short, lyric and dramatic, simple and complex, strophic and through-composed. Some are ballads. Generally speaking, the ballad is purely narrative while the lied is lyric. Some are declamatory, almost recitations, while others are tiny jewels that flicker gaily through existence. The essence of the lied is the same as the essence of lyric poetry—to heighten an emotion in a brief span. Schubert took his poems and by his own magic illustrated the moods of the words through music so that both elements are heightened.

It is a commonplace statement that Schubert is one of the greatest melodists of music. No song writer can work without an inexhaustible fount of melody, and Schubert above all composers tossed off an extraordinary number of unforgettable melodic ideas—*Auf dem Wasser zu singen, Du bist die Ruh', Horch! Horch! die Lerch!, Liebesbotschaft, Ungeduld, Der Musensohn, Ave Maria*—one after the other in a steady outpouring. Schumann, in an 1829 letter to Friedrich Wieck, used an unforgettable phrase to describe Schubert's melody: "compressed, lyrical insanity." Allied to that fount of melody was a brilliant feeling for modulation. Melodies have to be harmonized, and in his harmonic ideas Schubert was supreme. He would move from key to key in the freest manner, hitting just the inevitable-sounding chord to underline a word or phrase, linking the key changes within a song with rich and unexpected moves that hit the listener with visceral impact. Schubert is a master of the unexpected. It is safe to say that no great music is without the element of the unexpected: the departure that is so original, yet so inevitable. A great composer's mind never works in conventional ways.

Among Schubert's songs are two cycles—*Die schöne Müllerin* and *Die Winterreise*. Many believe *Die Winterreise* (*The Winter's Journey*), composed in 1827, the year before his death, to be the greatest single series of songs in the literature: sad, plaintive haunting, mounting in melancholy and even desperation to the shattering last song, *Der Leiermann*. This song is about an organ-grinder playing his machine in the winter. Nobody gives him any money, nobody listens to his music, nobody cares. Snarling dogs chase him, but he continues to smile and show no disappointment. "*Wunderlicher Alter*," ends the song, "*soll ich mit dir geh'n? Willst zu meinen Lieder dei-*

ner Leier dreh'n?"—meaning, "Mysterious old man, shall I go with you? Will you crank your hurdy-gurdy to my songs?" All this is expressed in a mood of total desolation, with bare fifths in the bass and a scrap of melody, more a motto, really, above it. It is a song that sends icicles of despair through the listener, and it is hard to escape the notion that the words by Wilhelm Müller had an autobiographical significance for Schubert.

Schubert composed in every medium except one. He never wrote a concerto, which is not surprising. For in those days and, indeed, in all music up to then, concertos were composed by musicians who themselves would play the work, and Schubert, though an able pianist, was no virtuoso. A good deal of Schubert's music still goes unheard. His operas are unknown quantities today, and experts say that the librettos are so poor that they cannot be staged. This was also felt in Schubert's time. The reviewer in the *Conversationsblatt* pointed out in an 1820 article on *Die Zauberharfe* that the plot was ridiculous. "What a pity that Schubert's wonderfully beautiful music has not found a worthier subject!" The operas aside, several representative examples of Schubert's work in every form are in today's permanent repertory.

There used to be a tendency to look down on Schubert as a technician. The argument seemed to be that since his ideas of sonata form departed from the classic ideal, since his developments undeniably did have a tendency to wander and become diffuse, since his constructions lacked the organization and power of a Beethoven—ergo, he knew nothing about "sonata form."

Schubert, it is true, was pulled two ways when he engaged sonata form. In the Vienna of his day, a period dominated by Beethoven and the memory of Mozart, all composers wrote sonatas, concertos, and symphonies. Schubert's lyric instinct did have some trouble lacing itself into the corset of the sonata. But he felt obliged to comply. The demands of the day pressed on him. Even though he was one of the most original composers in history, he did not have the kind of mind that gloried in breaking conventions of form. Thus many of his early symphonies, sonatas, and quartets dutifully go through the motions of the sonata mystique. Later, as in the *Unfinished* Symphony and the big C major, he was able to unite content with his own kind of form, and the result is a kind of sonata form just as perfect in its way as Beethoven's was for Beethoven.

There is some confusion about the numbering of Schubert's symphonies. The correct sequence is: No. 1 in D major (1813); No. 2 in B flat major (1815); No. 3 in D major (1815); No. 4 in C minor (1816); No. 5 in B flat major (1816); No. 6 in C major (1818); No. 7 in E major (1821; sketched out and never completed); No. 8 in B minor (the *Unfinished*, 1822); and No. 9 in C major (1828). There also is a mysterious work, of which no real evidence exists, called the *Gmunden-Gastein* Symphony, so named because Schubert worked on it during a summer vacation at those two cities. The manuscript never has turned up. One theory was that Schubert's *Grand Duo* for piano four hands is a reduction of the *Gmunden-Gastein* Symphony, but nobody takes that idea very seriously today. Another theory is that the *Gmunden-Gastein* Symphony later developed into the Ninth in C major. But all that is known is that Schubert did work on a symphony that has been lost.

The first three symphonies are prentice works, though No. 2, bouncing and tuneful, already breathes the essential Schubert. No. 4 in C minor (which he himself named the *Tragic* Symphony), is an underrated work. It is supposed to be Schubert's bow toward a symphony in the Beethoven style, and scholars tend to be condescending about it. As a matter of fact, the music has very little Beethoven in it, and it has a slender, elegiac quality, especially in the last movement, that is of extreme beauty: Schubertian beauty, not Beethovenian. It is amazing how consistently Schubert managed to avoid the influence of his titanic contemporary. Haydn was much more of an influence, and the Fifth Symphony, elegant and lightly scored, is a throwback to the Haydn style. No. 6, with moments of great beauty and also a Rossinian *joie de vivre,* is not a complete success and does not hang together too well—but it is still Schubert.

The *Unfinished,* that universal favorite, is a torso, and millions of words have been written trying to explain it. If the truth about the work has not been discovered by now, it never will be. Schubert gave the score to Anselm Hüttenbrenner in 1822. It was dedicated to the Graz Musical Society, which had just elected Schubert an honorary member, and Hüttenbrenner was supposed to deliver it to the members. Whether or not he did, nobody knows. Whether or not Schubert gave him more than the two movements, nobody knows. The score remained in Hüttenbrenner's possession until 1865, when the conductor Johann Herbeck bribed him out of it by promising to play one of his, Hüttenbrenner's, works in Vienna. Why only two movements? One theory is that Schubert intended to send the other two movements later. Another theory maintains that Schubert felt he could never improve the two existing movements, and thus dropped work on the symphony. It is an unlikely theory. Schubert did not work that way; and the extant manuscript does have sketches for a third movement. Still another suggestion is that Hüttenbrenner lost the final two movements, and this makes the most sense of all.

It was Robert Schumann who unearthed the Ninth Symphony, the "Great" C major. Schumann had known of its existence and on New Year's Day of 1838 he visited Schubert's brother Ferdinand, who showed him piles of manuscripts. Ferdinand allowed Schumann to depart with the score of the C major Symphony, and on March 29, 1839, Mendelssohn conducted the world premiere in Leipzig. There is some evidence that the work was tried out in Vienna in 1828, under Schubert's supervision, and was shelved as being too difficult. In a letter to Clara Wieck, Schumann raved about the score: "It is not possible to describe it to you. All the instruments are human voices. It is gifted beyond measure, and this instrumentation, Beethoven notwithstanding—and this length, this heavenly length, like a novel in four volumes, longer than the [Beethoven] Ninth Symphony." (Schumann was a little too exuberant here. The Schubert Ninth was about fifty minutes, the Beethoven Ninth a little over an hour.) Then Schumann reviewed the Leipzig premiere with his typical understanding and big-heartedness: "The symphony produced such an effect among us as none has produced since Beethoven. . . . Years must pass, perhaps, before the work will be thoroughly understood in Germany, but there is no danger that it ever will be overlooked or forgotten. It bears within it the core of everlasting youth." Schumann, as nearly always, was right. The C major Symphony, in its breadth and passion, has a claim to stand near the Beethoven Ninth. Schubert, in his last year, expanded tremendously. His music is packed with ideas, is enormous in scale, is starting to head in a new direction. On his deathbed he is said to have cried that new ideas were running through his head. What would he not have done had he lived!

Wherever one looks in Schubert's music there is something to love. Always the music is intensely, even piercingly, melodic, the melodies often tinged with a kind of melancholy that can only be described as—well, Schubertian. There are the direct, simple, and lovable waltzes for piano. There are the two piano trios, of which the B flat is the more popular. The slow movement of the B flat Trio contains a wonderful example of Schubert's magic in modulation. The music is going along in the key of A flat and by a twist the music is suddenly in a far remote E major. It takes Schubert exactly a fourth of a measure to get there, and the effect is of the heavens opening up. But all of his music has strokes like this. The last three string quartets (A minor, D major, and G major) are full of them, and so is the great F minor Fantasy for piano duet; and so is the *Trout* Quintet, and so is the lovely and spirited Octet for Winds. The C major String Quintet, one of Schubert's last works, occupies a special niche. Its first two movements have the serene melancholy (there is no other way to describe it) of the *Unfinished* Symphony, that tensile, flawless layout enmeshed in supreme poetry.

It is only in recent years that the piano sonatas have become popular concert-hall pieces. Romantic pianists, by and large, avoided them, and if they played Schubert it was the big *Wanderer* Fantasy or the *Moments Musicaux* (Schubert's own bad French). As far as pianists were concerned, the music was ungratefully written, difficult without any obvious virtuosity, hard to organize. And the music demanded as much from the audience as the player. Not until the 1930's did pianists, following the lead of Artur Schnabel, begin to play the Schubert sonatas with regularity. Today the sonatas have become staples. It took an antiromantic age to make them popular. In Schubert's piano writing—it is true of all his instrumental writing—the piano is merely the medium, not the Thing Unto Itself. The pianist is concerned with music, not with technical tricks (though in order to play the music well, a substantial technique is needed, especially for the three gigantic posthumous sonatas).

It took about forty years after Schubert's death for the world to realize his genius. Today his place is permanently fixed. Although he exerted little influence on the early romantic school, he nevertheless anticipated romanticism in the subjective way he approached music. Schubert was not the first of the romantics, for Carl Maria von Weber was a much more romantic composer, and exerted infinitely more influence on the oncoming generation. But if Schubert was not the first of the romantics, he occupies another and even more significant place. He was the first lyric poet of music.

❧ 8 ❧

Freedom and a New Language

WEBER AND THE EARLY ROMANTICS

By the time Beethoven had died in 1827 and Schubert in 1828, the forces that had been set in motion by the French Revolution and the Industrial Revolution had transformed Europe. Everything was in the process of change. Networks of railroads were beginning to carry people and goods with unheard-of speed. A new class of citizen, the industrial bourgeois, started to amass enormous wealth. Science and medicine were advancing in multiple jumps. Poets were breaking away from couplets, alexandrines, and hexameters, and were writing a new, intensely personal and lyrical kind of verse. New attitudes about life, religion, economics, and politics were in the air. In the arts, everybody was talking about romanticism. Modern man came into being.

Music, of course, reflected the new age. Beethoven had expanded the orchestra to unprecedented size, and the new composers expanded it even further. Hector Berlioz in France dreamed of an orchestra of 467 players supplemented by a chorus of 360. Technology improved the unreliable wind instruments of the eighteenth century, adding keys and valves, and for the first time horns and bassoons could consistently play in tune. As the orchestra grew and as music became more complicated, there evolved the necessity for a controlling force—a man who would undertake all the responsibilities of interpreting a Beethoven symphony. A Vivaldi concerto grosso could run along pretty much by itself, helped by the first violinist and the player at the clavier, but not the complex symphony of Beethoven and his successors. Around 1820 the virtuoso conductor arrived—the man who could stare down the individual egos of the orchestral players and weld them into a single unit. Ludwig (Louis) Spohr (1784–1859), Carl Maria von Weber (1786–1826), and Gasparo Spontini (1774–1851) were among the pioneers of the baton, along with François-Antoine Habeneck (1781–1849), who founded the Paris Conservatory Orchestra in 1828 and led it with a violin bow in lieu of a baton.

Just as technology improved the instruments of the orchestra, so it improved the piano. The delicate Viennese instrument of Mozart's time and the more robust instrument of Broadwood that so delighted Beethoven gave way to a massive engine with a steel frame, and hosts of virtuosos rushed to take advantage of it. They wanted to do on the piano the equivalent of what Nicolò Paganini could do on the violin. Paganini, a graceful but unimportant composer, has an unusually high position in musical history as one who inspired all instrumentalists and instrumental writing of the romantic movement. He was the first of the supervirtuosos, and may have been the greatest violinist who ever lived. Something of a genius, something of a charlatan, Paganini (1782–1840) from 1805 was creating untold excitement wherever he went. There was a feeling of Satanism about this tall, dark, emaciated Italian who could do undreamed-of things on his Guarnerius. Musicians swarmed to his concerts trying to figure out how he achieved his effects. The public also flocked, and many of the more superstitious listeners believed him in league with the Devil. Paganini did nothing to dispel the notion. A great showman, he played up the diabolical quality of his concerts and did everything but come on stage wrapped in a blue flame. He gave saturnalia rather than concerts. One of his tricks was to break a string in the middle of a composition and continue to the end on three strings. Or he would produce a scissors, cut three of the strings, and perform miracles on the G string alone. He greatly expanded the technique of the violin, with new bowings, fingerings, harmonics, double stops of incredible virtuosity. There was not a professional instrumentalist who in his way did not try to duplicate Paganini's hold over an audience. Liszt and Schumann wrote variations on Paganini's famous Twenty-fourth Caprice, trying to achieve the equivalent of Paganini's transcendental technique. Later Brahms, Rachmaninoff, and others used the Twenty-fourth Caprice as a basis for extended piano works.

Paganini was the archetype of the Virtuoso-as-Hero, though there had of course been famous virtuosos before him. Any time an instrumentalist or singer does something better than anybody else, he can count on fame and fortune. Italy in the eighteenth century had some extraordinary violinists, and one of them, Giuseppe Tartini (1692–1770), anticipated Paganini, in a way, by writing a satanically difficult work named *The Devil's Trill*. The great castrato singers also were matinee idols. Toward the end of the eighteenth century appeared a group of pianists, headed by Johann Baptist Cramer, Ignaz Moscheles, Jan Ladislav Dussek, and John Field, who linked the classic school with the oncoming romantic. But no instrumentalist in history caused the sheer mania that Paganini did, nor had anybody else ever brought such a element of calculated, brilliant showmanship to his work. To Liszt fell Paganini's tradition, and those two mighty instrumentalists helped make the nineteenth century an era of rampant virtuosity. The public demanded virtuosity—the heroic virtuosity of Liszt as well as the tinkling, top-of-the-keys virtuosity of Henri Herz, that popular pianist who charmed audiences for several decades. Liszt, a trail-breaker in so many ways, was the first pianist in history to give a concert entirely on his own, unassisted by fellow artists who occupied the program while the Great Man was resting.

To take care of the demand, concert halls were being built all over Europe. Musical associations were created, permanent orchestras formed. In the opera houses, Rossini, Bellini, and Donizetti, starting shortly after the turn of the century, were writing music in which the emphasis was on the voice: *bel canto,* beautiful singing. Again there had been precedents for this kind of singing, but the term *bel canto* is applied specifically to the operas of those three composers. In *bel canto* singing, the emphasis is on flexibility, purity of line, ease of technique in coloratura passages, and careful shaping of vowel sounds. As the century progressed, the emphasis shifted to a more dramatic type of singing, much to the distress of Rossini and other lovers of the *bel canto* style. To them, Meyerbeer, Verdi, and Wagner had murdered pure vocalism. Such great singers as Giovanni Rubini, Luigi Lablache, Maria Malibran, Wilhelmine Schröder-Devrient, Pauline Viardot-Garcia, Gilbert-Louis Duprez, and Enrico Tamberlik were as popular as the pianists and violinists. Duprez was the first tenor consistently to sing a high C in full voice. Rossini, with great disgust, described that note as sounding "like the squawk of a capon whose throat is being cut."

In the first half of the nineteenth century, as before, the great instrumentalists were also the great composers. Weber, Mendelssohn, Chopin, and Liszt were the four greatest pianists of their time. Berlioz, Mendelssohn, Weber, and Wagner were the four greatest conductors. Midway in the century came something new in history—executants who were not themselves composers. Such pianists as Hans von Bülow and Karl Tausıg made arrangements of music by other men, but they themselves did next to no serious composing. They were pure virtuosos. Today, virtuosity is something of a dirty word. It carries the implication of vulgarity, of excess, of exploitation of the composer for the performer's nasty little ends. But the nineteenth century did not look on virtuosity in that respect. Nobody has ever written a definitive history of musical virtuosity and its implications, but it seems clear that the great performers of the nineteenth century had considerable influence on the thinking of the composers. Music is no good on the printed page. It has to sound, and it can only sound through the fingers, voices, and brains of performers. In the eighteenth century and before, composer and performer of instrumental music were almost always the same. In the nineteenth century, with the advent of the specialist-virtuoso, a composer's music began to be refracted through the prism of a different mind. That could, and did, create problems. There always have been virtuosos willing to submerge beautiful music in a welter of cheap effects. But the composers of the nineteenth century, by and large, were perfectly willing to ally themselves with the virtuoso, even if they occasionally grumbled. Composers, on the whole, are more permissive about their music than many modern musicians realize—certainly the romantic composers were—and they above all realize that notation is an inexact medium.

The early romantics were especially permissive. With romanticism came the burgeoning of the Ego, a striving for an intensified kind of personal expression, the ideal of art for art's sake. Beethoven may have been the first composer to work on that premise. Jean-Jacques Rousseau had stimulated his own age with his doctrine of the natural man and the concept of a man's individual worth. Man's feelings, said Rousseau, serve us more reliably than reason. Express yourself and your feelings, said Rousseau. The romantics, who took him very seriously, did exactly that. Johann Paul Friedrich Richter, the great German writer known to the world as Jean Paul, had laid down some ground rules of romanticism as early as 1804 in his *Vorschule der Aesthetik*. The decisive element of romanticism, he said, is expanse. "Romanticism is beauty without bounds—the beautiful infinite." Or, "If poetry is prophecy, then romanticism is being aware of a larger future than there is room for here below."

Much has been written about romanticism, and the subject often is befogged, but its main lines are clear enough: content more important than classical form; alliance of literature with the other arts; an expanded horizon; an interest in the supernatural; a constant experimentation with new forms, new colors, new textures. Within one decade, roughly 1830–1840, the entire harmonic vocabulary of music changed. It seemed to come from nowhere, but all of a sudden composers were using seventh, ninth, and even eleventh chords, altered chords and a chromatic as opposed to classical diatonic harmony. Generally speaking—exceptions, of course, can always be pointed out—composers from Bach through Schubert wrote in diatonic harmony, with a sparse use of accidentals. They might range far afield in their key structures, but the basic tonality always was clear, and the actual chord structure seldom exceeded an octave. Nor was there much in the way of augmented or diminished intervals.

But the romantics reveled in unusual tonal combinations, sophisticated chords, and dissonances that were excruciating to the more conventional minds of the day. Chopin had no hesitation about using minor ninths, and musicians of an older generation were appalled. Ignaz Moscheles (1794–1870) was a fine composer, and he was one of the best pianists in Europe; and he also was as noble and dedicated a musician as ever lived.

When he first encountered Chopin's music he did not know what to make of it. "My thoughts, however, and through them my fingers, stumble at certain hard, inartistic and to me inconceivable modulations." Musicians brought up as Moscheles had been, with the emphasis on clarity, purity, proper voice leading, and spare use of the pedal, could not understand romantic music because they did not understand its aesthetic and acoustical premises. Pure *sound,* sound as sound, was very important to the romantics, and they brought new ideas of technique and composition to express those new concepts. It was not until Moscheles actually heard Chopin play that he realized his error, and handsomely admitted it. For Chopin's new kind of technique, his kind of legato playing supported by nuances of the pedal, enabled him to smooth out those dissonances.

Romantic music thus had its own sound—a rich, sensuous, colorful sound —and that is probably the most important single aspect of the period. Of course there were many other aspects that set romanticism off from the previous periods. Romantic music to a surprisingly large extent is nonabstract music. It might be that the composer followed a specific program in his music, as Berlioz and Liszt so often did. Or more often the program was there but unspecified. In the idealistic age of romantic music, with its close alliance to literature, and with the broader general culture of most composers, one of the favorite games was to read implied programs into music. No music was exempt, and the finest musical minds of the day read the most incredible things into any score. Music, it was felt, expressed specific states of mind and feeling. Schumann was always reading things into music, and the greater the piece, the more he read into it. "The more special a work is, the more individual pictures it spreads before the listener, and the more lasting it will be for all time. Such special traits are especially common to Beethoven and Franz Schubert." Wagner also was constantly reading things into music, portentously so. So did most of the performing artists. In one of the more delirious episodes in this kind of exegesis, Hans von Bülow saw in Chopin's E major Prelude the composer striking his head with a hammer. "The sixteenth and thirty-second notes are to be carried out in exact time, indicating a double stroke of the hammer." And Wagner interpreted the *Eroica* as a dialogue between Man and Woman, ending with the overwhelming power of Love. "Once more the heartstrings quiver, and tears of pure humanity well forth; yet from out the very quick of sadness there bursts the jubilant cry of force—that force which lately led itself to Love and—helped by that—the whole, the total Man now chants to us in avowal of his godhead." Reconstructions like this were common throughout the nineteenth century, and not until the objective outlook of a later age was there a change. Arturo Toscanini was to have his comment about the *Eroica,* contemptuously dismissing the romantic outlook: "Some say this is

Napoleon, some Hitler, some Mussolini. Bah! For me it is simply allegro con brio." Almost everybody today would take the Toscanini point of view.

Toscanini's remark was made in the 1920's and represented an attitude that more and more took hold, to a point where, by mid-century, the principles of romanticism had been all but forgotten—as forgotten as the principles of Mozartean performance practice were in the 1840's. The subject deserves mention, for the relationship of romanticism to the late twentieth century is a complicated one. Much of the present-day repertory is romantic or late romantic, and it seems to be an article of faith that musicians understand this kind of music but are less equipped to handle the classic and baroque repertory. As a matter of fact, the reverse is true. Thanks to a generation of concentrated musicological research, from Mozart back to the Renaissance, young musicians today have a better idea about preromantic music than about music from 1830 to 1900, which means the bulk of the repertory.

This is ironic but true. Today, every educated musician knows a good deal about performance practice in Mozart's time, but the Liszt tradition has all but vanished. Next to nothing has been written about the performance practice of the romantics, for most musicological research centers on problems (and mostly archival problems) in early music. And musicians of the middle third of the twentieth century were brought up in an antiromantic era, one in which the traditions of romanticism were suspect. Many young musicians today do not even know how to realize the notes of a romantic piece. A composer like Schumann, for instance, took great pains to indicate inner-voice relationships, carefully marking the phrases, notating the flags of individual notes so that they stand out clearly, putting legato phrase marks over bass or tenor lines. Schumann did not do this idly. There is a harmonic and polyphonic meaning. But hardly any musician notices those markings when he plays the *Carnaval* or *Kinderszenen,* just as he fails to bring out stepwise bass notes, a convention universally practiced by the romantic pianists and expected by the romantic composers. The romantics expected a slowdown between first and second themes; they expected contrasting sections to be carefully set off; they expected a great deal of rubato and dynamic extremes; they expected constant fluctuation of tempo. Above all, they did not object to discreet tampering with the text, which was anything but sacrosanct. The better musicians, from all that can be gathered, never were anarchic about their modifications, but there was not one who would not unhesitatingly change or reinforce a passage for optimum effect or for the grand gesture. He did this because he honestly believed it was in the spirit of the meaning of the music. In short, the romantics approached music with a freedom forbidden a hundred years later.

With the attitude of the romantics toward music as free and as literary as it was, and with the kind of freedom the nineteenth century gladly gave its vocal and instrumental virtuosos, it was no wonder that all preromantic music was misrepresented during the nineteenth century and especially during the earlier period of romanticism. The early romantics had a tendency to see everything in their own image. There was no concern for scholarship, nor was there a discipline of musicology. When Mendelssohn revived the St. Matthew Passion in 1829, it was shortened, revised, reorchestrated, and, in sections, recomposed. Mozart was a heavy sufferer, as was Beethoven. The romantics idolized Beethoven, but again in their own image. They considered him the greatest of all revolutionaries and ascribed an ethical ideal to his music, but that did not deter them from altering his scores to bring them "up to date." Wagner reorchestrated Gluck, and Liszt "improved" Schubert's piano music. They honestly considered it an act of homage. As Wagner put it, in his Beethoven revisions, "I never carried my piety to the extent of taking his directions absolutely literally." A mind as musically sensitive as Wagner's could not commit mayhem on the Beethoven symphonies, certainly not the mayhem that Mahler committed on the Schumann symphonies later in the century, but Wagner and Mahler both did try to "improve" the music. The conducting of both might sound startling to today's ears.

Many things entered music with the romantics. Sentimentalism appeared. Nationalism became firmly fixed, first with Chopin and his mazurkas and polonaises, then with Liszt and his Hungarian rhapsodies, and later with the Bohemian and Russian nationalists. Opera changed, and the formula bel canto operas gave place to the grand spectacles of Meyerbeer, the red-blooded melodrama of Verdi, and the music drama of Wagner. Along with these came a new and dramatic style of singing and acting. All this took place within twenty-five years, beginning with the first group of romantics, born within five years of one another: Mendelssohn in 1809, Chopin and Schumann in 1810, Liszt in 1811, Wagner and Verdi in 1813. But in music, as in life, nothing springs full-grown. Everything has its predecessors, and the romantic period had some interesting and important precursors.

One of the significant figures was E. T. A. (for Ernst Theodor Amadeus) Hoffmann, a legend to the German romantics, especially Schumann. Hoffman (1776–1822) was everything—poet, painter, novelist, theater manager, singer, composer, conductor, critic, public official, and he seems to have been good and even distinguished in everything. He was one of those people who are always interested in the avant-garde, a sort of Cocteau of his time. Long before the musical romantics appeared on the scene he was writing about romanticism, insisting that "music is at home only in the realm of romanticism," calling music "the most romantic of the arts—in fact, one might almost say, the only genuinely one . . ." This was in 1813, in an essay on Beethoven's instrumental music. "Every passion," Hoffmann continued, "love, hatred, anger, despair, and so forth, just as the opera gives them to us, is clothed by music with the purple luster of romanticism." There is much in Hoffmann's writings about "the faraway spirit realm of sound," "the unknown realm," "the spirit world of the infinite," "the monstrous and immeasurable," "the eternal dances of the spheres," "endless longing," "jubilant song," "inner being." The romantics loved it. Hoffmann's writings about music are high-blown, sentimental and, by modern standards, all wrong; but he was a standard-bearer well in the vanguard, and the romantics were enthusiastically guided by his ideas. He preached a break from the past, looking forward to an idealistic, personal kind of music. In 1815 he composed *Undine,* an opera that in its supernatural subject matter links up with Weber's *Der Freischütz.* Weber praised it as "one of the more spirited works that the newer period has given us."

Another precursor was Muzio Clementi (1752–1832), a pianist-composer who set modern piano technique on its way. He specialized in virtuoso work, especially thirds and octaves, then new, and pianists followed his lead rather than the classical style of Mozart, who was an infinitely greater artist but not as exciting an executant. John Field (1782–1837), a pupil of Clementi, was also an important pianist of the day, representing an incipient romanticism. His graceful series of nocturnes were directly imitated by Chopin. Another fascinating transitional figure was Johann Nepomuk Hummel (1778–1837), whose roots were in the eighteenth century (he was a pupil of Mozart), but who composed some music that strongly verges on romanticism. In Vienna, he was considered Beethoven's only real rival, and for the first half of the nineteenth century it was taken for granted that Hummel was one of the immortals. His Septet for Piano and Winds introduced a harmonic vocabulary much more "modern" and sophisticated than Schubert's, and a style of piano writing that led directly into Chopin. Hummel composed several piano concertos, notably one in A minor; and Chopin's E minor Piano Concerto owes a strong debt to the Hummel. Very little of Hummel's music is in the twentieth-century repertoire, but he was an inventive composer and his work deserves revival.

The music of Ludwig (Louis) Spohr (1784–1859) also warrants a hearing. Spohr lives today by a single violin concerto, the *Gesangszene,* but in his time he experimented with chromatic textures and his music was considered extremely daring. There was a curious dichotomy in Spohr's career. He was the greatest classical violinist of his time, he was of the Mozart school, and he was no great friend of the romantic composers (though late in his career, when he was court conductor at Cassel, he espoused the cause of Wagner). Yet much of his own music looks forward rather than back, and in one of his operas, *Kreuzfahrer* (1845), he anticipated Wagner by "through-composing" the work "somewhat as a musical drama, without superfluous textual repetitions and ornaments, and with ever-increasing action." Previously he had composed an opera, *Jessonda* (1823), that was greeted with almost as much enthusiasm as Weber's *Der Freischütz*, and he had also composed a popular opera on the Faust legend. Spohr was one of the most admired and respected composers of his time.

History is apt to judge a period only by its greatest figures, but at any single time most people are uncomfortable in the presence of greatness and flock to a host of lesser figures who will satisfy their unsophisticated needs. In the 1830's, for example, the average music lover would have said that Beethoven, Mozart, and Hummel were the three greatest composers; but, at the same time, the average music lover was much more comfortable with the music of such as George Onslow (1784–1853), Ferdinand Ries (1784–1838), Henri Herz (1803–1888), Franz Hünten (1793–1878), and Friedrich Kalkbrenner (1785–1849). *Those* were the composers most often played— the commercial men of the period. They provided the music that offered no problems for anybody. They cooked up tasteful overtures, potpourris, and paraphrases, and they supplied the young ladies of Europe with appropriate music to place on their pianos. They wrote the battle pieces and the sentimental ditties and the arrangements for flute, harp, and piano that graced the music rooms of the bourgeoisie and enriched the music publishers.

Kalkbrenner can be taken as a representative example. He was an elegant, flawless pianist whose high reputation was exceeded only by his fine opinion of himself. It was to Kalkbrenner that young Chopin turned when he arrived in Paris. *This*, Chopin exulted, was piano playing! Kalkbrenner's music was extremely popular, and he turned out piece after piece. Probst, his publisher, could not waste much time with Schubert because the firm was engaged in bringing out the complete works of Kalkbrenner. The poet Heinrich Heine, who was a brilliant and acerbic reviewer, has left an amusing description of a Kalkbrenner concert: "On his lips there still gleamed that embalmed smile which we recently noticed on the lips of an Egyptian pharaoh when his mummy was unwrapped at the museum here." And Clara Schumann has left an even more penetrating description of Kalkbrenner "smiling sweetly and highly satisfied with himself and his creation. He always looks as if he was saying 'Oh, God, I and all mankind must thank Thee that Thou hast created a mind like mine.' " The point is that Kalkbrenner was rich, famous, and everybody had to take notice of him. Composers like Kalkbrenner are always around, forgotten a generation after their death, but extremely popular until then. It is that kind of composer who makes up the bulk of the active repertoire of his time, not the four or five geniuses who happen to be active at the same time.

To the early romantics the big man—Beethoven always excepted—was

Carl Maria von Weber, and a good case can be made for him as the first of the true romantics. He met most of the specifications. He was a major pianist and a touring virtuoso; his music was in advance of the day; he wrote operas on supernatural subjects; he dabbled in literature; he had the fashionable disease, consumption. Today very little Weber remains in the repertoire except for *Der Freischütz*, the overtures to three operas, and once in a while the *Concertstück* for piano and orchestra or one of the sonatas. There also is the *Invitation to the Dance*, but that is almost never heard in its original form as a piano solo. Thus it is hard to realize the overwhelming impact of Weber on the oncoming romantics—on Mendelssohn, Berlioz, Liszt, Marschner, and, especially, Wagner. Heinrich Marschner (1795–1861) was a once-popular opera composer—two or three of his operas still hold the stage in Germany—who in such works as *Der Vampyr* took his cue from *Der Freischütz* and raised the hair of audiences in the 1830's and '40s with his ghosts and demons.

The full influence of Weber on Wagner remains to be told, though anybody can listen to those strange harmonies in Weber's *Euryanthe* Overture and hear in them anticipations of the *Ring* cycle. At one time, in 1813, Weber was about to write an opera on the Tannhäuser legend. That would have anticipated Wagner by thirty years. Weber anticipated Wagner in other ways. As a conductor, he was one of the first to demand full control over all aspects of an operatic production, one of the first to institute section rehearsals, one of the first to exercise full authority. Wagner adopted many of his ideas. Weber, too, like Wagner, had pronounced pan-Germanic ideas about opera. He sought, as he explained in 1817, "a fully rounded and self-contained work of art in which all the ingredients furnished by the contributing arts disappear in the process of fusion, and in thus perishing help to form an entirely new universe." This is much the Wagnerian concept of the *Gesamtkunstwerk*—total art work—forty years before Wagner expounded *his* theories.

To the romantics, Weber was the one who unleashed the storm. If any single composition can be said to have set off the Romantic age of music, it was *Der Freischütz*. The scene in the Wolf's Glen, with its mystery and enchantment, its evocation of the power of evil, its nature painting and sheer color, its power and imagination—all this hit Europe with tremendous force, and helped launch the new movement.

Weber was born on November 18, 1786, and died on June 5, 1826, at the age of forty. He died a year before Beethoven and two years before Schubert. He had composed *Der Freischütz* in 1820, and it was unlike any other opera that had ever been written. *Oberon* and *Euryanthe*, which followed, suffered from impossible librettos and are not staged very often today, but those two operas also dealt with the supernatural and the exotic, and to the romantics they opened a new world. Around 1840 the English critic Henry Fothergill Chorley wrote an estimate of Weber that can stand as the typical reaction (and it should be emphasized that Chorley was a reactionary who promptly frothed at the mouth when the names of Schumann and Wagner were brought up). Weber's music, wrote Chorley, "is instinct with the spirit of that olden time, when there were omens whispered in the woods, and battles foretold by the blood-red phantoms that brandished their arms and waved their banners in the West. The fancy of it is not untinctured with superstition; the hue upon it is either the pearly tent of Dream-land, or that gorgeous tint which streams through some blazoned window garnished 'WITH MANY A QUAINT DEVICE.' " Chorley fancied himself as a literary stylist. But his response is genuine. Weber was all that to the romantics. His piano music was as popular as his operas. When Wilhelm von Lenz, that pushy young man who collected names and piano teachers and later wrote books about them, introduced Liszt to the *Invitation to the Dance* and the Sonata in A flat, in the 1820's, the great pianist all but shrieked his admiration to the skies. Liszt and the other romantic pianists were constantly playing Weber.

Weber was a slim, sickly, consumptive man who had been born with a diseased hip and walked with a limp throughout his short life. When he died, it was as much from overwork as anything else. But in his forty years he contributed much to music. His talents were manifold. He was one of the great pianists of the day, and the layout of his piano music is far beyond anything that Beethoven and Schubert conceived. Much of it is frankly virtuosic, with a few technical idiosyncrasies. The short Weber had an enormous pair of hands, and some of the stretches he wrote cannot be played by normal human beings. As a touring pianist very much aware of the public, Weber could be guilty of some meretricious effects, and a good deal of his piano music has more glitter than substance. But when everything came together, as it did in the *Concertstück,* the music approaches sublimity. Today his four piano sonatas, his variations, and such virtuoso pieces as the *Polacca brillante* are almost out of the repertoire, but during the entire nineteenth century they enjoyed enormous popularity.

It was not only as a pianist and composer that Weber achieved fame. As the most important conductor of his period he opened the gate to a group of followers, and it was not long before conductors were the dominating musical forces in the world. As early as 1804, when he was eighteen, Weber became chief conductor at the opera house in Breslau, where he encountered tremendous opposition, for both his youth and his novel ideas about leadership. The first violinist, a great dignitary named Joseph Schnabel, even left the orchestra rather than submit to the indignity of being directed by a "child." Weber left Breslau in 1806 and after various minor appointments and some concertizing, became director of the opera house in Prague in 1812. From there he went to Dresden where he was summoned by the king of Saxony late in 1817 specifically to found a German opera house as a counterattraction to the Italian opera craze. Rossini had swept Germany, and in 1820 in Berlin the redoubtable Spontini had established a dictatorship as conductor and as composer of such popular operas as *La Vestale* (so beloved by Berlioz) and *Fernand Cortez*. Weber, a brilliant organizer, turned the Dresden opera house upside down and reconstructed it in his own image, even having Italian and French librettos translated into German. He made himself the dominating force. Wagner not many years later was conducting at Dresden, and picked up many of Weber's ideas. Weber, at Dresden, was a fierce disciplinarian who had to have everything right. He went through all the scores, correcting errors; his demands at sectional rehearsals were legendary; he took charge of all aspects of production from scenery and staging to casting, rehearsing, and conducting. When he conducted the finished performance, it was indeed a finished performance.

Then in 1821 came *Der Freischütz*, which made Weber the founder of romantic German opera. Before him there was very little German opera—at least, very little that was in the repertoire. Three of the four great Mozart operas were in Italian, and the German *Die Zauberflöte* no more started a school of opera than Beethoven's *Fidelio* did. Schubert's operas lay forgotten, gathering dust, and they still do. But *Der Freischütz* led directly into the very popular, though mostly forgotten, operas of Marschner, Spohr, and Lortzing, and thence to Wagner.

Weber had the kind of restless mind typical of the romantics. He dabbled in lithography, was one of the first virtuosos on the guitar, and he was a passably good singer, though he permanently ruined his voice in 1806 by accidentally drinking a glass of nitric acid. For a time his life was in despair. He found time for some lusty love affairs and spirited dissipation. He turned to literary work and, from 1809 to 1818, wrote book reviews, poems, an unfinished novel, and a large amount of journalism, including some music criticism. Weber had the reputation of being a stringent, uncompromising critic, and even had some derogatory words to say about Beethoven. He went into criticism with the same energy and enthusiasm he applied to everything, and was one of the founders of an association named *Harmonischer Verein*. The idea was to introduce and explain the principles of romanticism. All the members of the *Verein* (meaning society or club) were required to be a combination of composer and literary man, and the motto was "The elevation of musical criticism by musicians themselves." Each member adopted a pseudonym. Weber's was Melos. He also wrote under the signatures of "Simon Knaster" and "B.f.z.Z.," meaning *"Beharrlichkeit führt zum Ziel,"* or "Perseverance leads to the goal"—his own motto. Not many years later, Schumann was to operate his musical journal on much the same premise, pseudonyms included. Schumann called his group the *Davidsbündler*. None of Weber's prose has been translated into English. He was a fascinating figure, this aristocratic, intelligent, forceful man: an authentic genius whose greatest tragedy was that he was born about thirty years ahead of his time.

❧ 9 ❧

Romantic Exuberance and Classic Restraint

HECTOR BERLIOZ

Hector Berlioz was the first important composer in the history of music *not* to come up by way of being either a prodigy or an immensely gifted child. That goes far toward explaining his strengths and weaknesses. Child prodigies, instinct in music from babyhood, develop a certain kind of aural and digital response, and before they arrive at their teens they already are masters of technique. They have imbibed the literature from the cradle, have physically grappled with it, have become secure craftsmen, can do anything they want to do as easily as breathing. As they mature, they go as far as their imaginations allow, but always they develop into masters of form. Some remain merely technicians; some become innovators; some constantly grow; some disappear. But always there is the sense of professionalism in their writing.

But Berlioz! Berlioz never even learned to play a useful instrument correctly. All he could do was pluck a few chords on the guitar or tootle a few notes on the flute or flageolet. Not very much is known about Berlioz' childhood at Saint-André in Isère, where he was born on December 11, 1803, but it is clear that his musical education was sketchy. His father, a physician with a liberal bent, saw to it that the boy was well educated; but when it came to music, neither Dr. Berlioz nor anybody in the vicinity could help Hector very much. There was an old flageolet in the house, and Dr. Berlioz showed his eager son how to finger it. Then he got a flute for the boy and arranged for lessons. Hector also learned the fingering of the clarinet. That was about all. A mighty impulse was present, and there are notebooks filled with rudimentary compositions. From the beginning Hector wanted to be a composer, and he taught himself everything he could about composition. His father would not have encouraged these experiments. Hector was to be a doctor.

Thus Berlioz never did have the ease in manipulation of one who has grown up from the beginning with the materials of music. As a result, the forms he used were different and self-evolved. Sometimes his ideas turned out brilliantly successful, and sometimes they did not come off very well. Often there is a feeling of struggle as he tried to shape his materials. Or there may be a lack of point to his writing. But he did have one thing working for him: genius. If he lacked certain ABC's of his craft, his super-heated imagination could turn that very lack to advantage by making him think differently from all other composers.

He was aware of this. He realized how useful a tool the piano is to a composer. "But when I consider the appalling number of miserable platitudes to which the piano has given birth, which would never have seen the light had their authors been limited to pen and paper, I feel grateful to the happy chance that forced me to compose freely and in silence, and this has delivered me from the tyranny of the fingers, so dangerous to thought, and from the fascination which the ordinary sonorities always exercise on a composer, to a greater or lesser degree. Many amateurs have pitied me for this deprivation, but that does not bother me very much." In any case, if he could not play an instrument, he could play on a hundred instruments—the symphony orchestra.

So he developed into the first French romantic and the first true exponent of what Europe later was to call The Music of the Future. It was Berlioz who, by creating the modern orchestra, demonstrated a new kind of tonal power, resource, and color. It was Berlioz who was the first to express himself autobiographically in music, bringing a new dimension to the psychology of the art. It was Berlioz who, in the detailed program of his autobiographical *Symphonie fantastique,* led to the symphonic poems that so afflicted the latter part of the nineteenth century. It was Berlioz who broke away from the classic rules of harmony to explore hitherto forbidden chord progressions and an entirely new kind of melody. It was Berlioz who emerged as one of the seminal forces of the nineteenth century—the composer studied by Liszt and Wagner, by the new Russians, by Mahler and Richard Strauss, by the new generation of French composers. He had no direct followers, for his ideas were too unorthodox for his immediate contemporaries to absorb; but later composers did absorb his message, and his influence extended to every sector of the musical avant-garde.

Liszt realized this. When he sent Berlioz a copy of Wagner's *Tannhäuser* Overture he wrote on it: "You will rediscover your own." And Wagner, whose *Tristan und Isolde* stems in a way from Berlioz' *Roméo et Juliette*—sections of the latter achieve a *Tristan*-like intensity and unbroken melodic stream—sent Berlioz a score of his masterpiece with the inscription: "To the dear and great composer of *Roméo et Juliette,* the grateful composer of

Tristan und Isolde." Gounod, who turned out to be the new leader of the French school after Berlioz, was another composer influenced by *Roméo et Juliette.* He heard it in 1839 and called it "a strange, passionate, convulsive music that opened up such new and colored horizons for me."

Berlioz was not only the first true French romantic but also the first of music's true romantics anywhere, anticipating Chopin and Schumann by a few years. He was an enthusiast, a natural revolutionary, the first of the *conscious* avant-gardists. Weber would not have considered himself of the avant-garde, nor would have Schubert. But Berlioz was the first of the young Turks, the wild men of music. Uninhibited, highly emotional, witty, mercurial, picturesque, he was very conscious of his romanticism. He loved the very *idea* of romanticism: the urge for self-expression and the bizarre as opposed to the classic ideals of order and restraint. It is romanticism that animates his music and runs riot through his wonderful autobiography, that revealing, magnificently written document. Fancy sometimes outran fact in this book, and some of it indeed is downright fiction. But in all his writing —Berlioz wrote an enormous amount of criticism in his day—he was a brilliant stylist, one who added something not only to musical but also to world literature. His prose as well as his life presents a man with a vivid imagination, a lust for life and battle, and a degree of self-revelation unique in musical annals. (Mozart's letters were not written for publication.) Compared to this, Wagner's autobiography is a dull, gray compilation, part fact, part metaphysics, entirely lacking the civilized, ironic style of Berlioz.

He was an unusual man. Everything about him was unusual. Almost singlehandedly he broke up the European musical establishment. After him, music would never be the same. And what he did, he did all by himself, impatiently brushing aside convention and the old way of doing things. Only a genius could have overcome his lack of basic knowledge. But only his lack of basic knowledge could have led him into the paths he took.

It was in Paris that his genius blossomed. His father had sent him there to study medicine. How Berlioz hated it! At his first dissection, he fled. He is very funny about it in his autobiography:

> When I entered that fearful human charnel house, littered with fragments of limbs, and saw the ghastly faces and cloven heads, the bloody cesspool in which we stood, with its reeking atmosphere, the swarms of sparrows fighting for scraps, and the rats in corners, gnawing bleeding vertebrae, such a feeling of horror possessed me that I leaped out of the window and fled home as though Death and all his hideous crew were at my heels. It was twenty-four hours before I recovered from the shock of this first impression, utterly refusing to hear the words anatomy, dissection or medicine, and firmly resolved to die rather than enter the career that had been forced on me.

. . . I consented to return to the hospital and face the dread scene once more. How strange! I now felt merely cold disgust at the sight of the same things that had before filled me with such horror. I had become as callous to the revolting scene as a veteran soldier. It was all over. I even found some pleasure in rummaging in the gaping breast of an unfortunate corpse for the lungs, with which to feed the winged inhabitants of that charming place.

"Well done!" cried Robert, laughing. "You are growing quite humane! Feeding the little birds!"

"And my bounty extends to all nature," I answered, throwing a shoulder blade to a great rat that was staring at me with famished eyes.

It did not take long for medical studies to take second place to music. Berlioz spent much more time at the Opéra and the library of the Conservatoire than in the medical school at the Hospital of Pity. Finally he managed to overcome the resistance of his father and, equally important, his mother. She was a pious woman who sincerely believed that anybody becoming a professional musician was automatically on the road to Hell. Berlioz was admitted to the Conservatoire, overcoming the objection of the director, Luigi Cherubini, and on his fifth attempt won the Prix de Rome in 1830.

Even as a student he was unforgettable. Berlioz shocked people in his day. "He believes in neither God nor Bach," said the composer-pianist-conductor Ferdinand Hiller, properly scandalized. Hiller has left us a fine description of Berlioz: "the high forehead, precipitously overhanging the deep-set eyes; the great, curving hawk nose; the thin, finely-cut lips; the rather short chin; the enormous shock of light brown hair, against the fantastic wealth of which the barber could do nothing—whoever had seen this head would never forget it." Berlioz was a striking figure and, consciously or unconsciously, was always attracting attention to himself. At the Opéra, where he held court in the balcony surrounded by fellow students, he would rise in wrath and let the world know if something foul was going on. Ernest Legouvé, the dramatist, was at a performance of Der Freischütz one evening when there was a commotion in the gallery. As Legouvé described it:

One of my neighbors rises from his seat and bending towards the orchestra shouts in a voice of thunder: "You don't want two flutes there, you brutes! You want two piccolos! Two piccolos, do you hear? Oh, the brutes!" Having said this, he simply sits down again, scowling indignantly. Amidst the general tumult produced by this outburst, I turn around and see a young man trembling with passion, his hands clenched, his eyes flashing, and a head of hair—such a head of hair. It looked like an enormous umbrella of hair, projecting something like a moveable awning over a beak of a bird of prey.

125

There were those who found Berlioz objectionable. Mendelssohn, a reserved and rather prissy man, was repelled on their first encounter, which took place in Rome. He thought Berlioz affected. "This purely external enthusiasm, this desperation in the presence of women, this assumption of genius in capital letters, is insupportable to me." But even Mendelssohn had to admit that Berlioz was interesting. Schumann was more sympathetic. "Berlioz does not try to be pleasing and elegant. What he hates, he grasps fiercely by the hair; what he loves, he almost crushes in his fervor."

Berlioz was far from being a mere braggart. He had the authentic big vision, and in certain areas the twentieth century has not even started to approximate it. Take his vision of the symphony orchestra. In the 1830's the orchestra seldom went over sixty players. Berlioz, the greatest orchestral innovator in history, had in mind an ideal orchestra, the only orchestra that could properly play his music. As early as 1825 he had brought together an orchestra of 150, but that was as nothing to his dream orchestra. It numbered 467 (to which would be added a chorus of 360); and in addition to the 242 strings there were to be such groupings as thirty harps, thirty pianos, twelve cymbals, sixteen French horns, and an exotic variety of percussion. No wonder his friends considered him impractical and his enemies crazy. Berlioz was unperturbed. "Vulgar prejudice," he said, "calls large orchestras noisy, but if they are well balanced, well trained and well led, and if they perform true music, they should rather be called powerful."

From the beginning his big orchestral conceptions startled Europe. Somehow this relatively untrained composer, this ex-medical student who could not play a respectable musical instrument, had the ear to conceive tonal combinations undreamed-of until then. The *Symphonie fantastique*, whatever it may have owed to Beethoven, had concepts of color and sonority that forced all future composers to revise their estimates of orchestral sound and of the capabilities of the symphony orchestra. The *Fantastique* was Berlioz' first major work. He finished it in 1830 before graduating from the Conservatoire.

Certainly none of the early romantics—the prim and classic Mendelssohn; Chopin and Schumann, who thought primarily in terms of the piano; Liszt, also a pianist who did not compose any significant orchestral works until the middle 1850's—certainly none of those men were thinking along such lines. Berlioz, so far ahead of his time, influenced Wagner and Richard Strauss much more than his contemporaries. Even today the last two movements of the *Fantastique*, which depict a march to the scaffold and a hallucinated witches' Sabbath, remain shockers.

The five-movement symphony is music of youth, of abandon, music that received its initial impetus from De Quincey's *Confessions of an Opium Eater*, music in which the classic emotional amenities are discarded. Berlioz had an imagination that ran as much along literary as musical lines, and it could be triggered very easily. From any other composer the descriptive effects that abound in his music would be superficial. They are not in Berlioz because he was so original, so much his natural self. Defiantly he set about expressing *himself* in his music: *his* loves, *his* attitude toward the world, *his* kind of experience. Not even Schumann, that most personal of composers, ever attempted so graphic a picture of the artist as a young man as Berlioz did in the *Fantastique*.

Here the problem of program music enters. The *Symphonie fantastique* is the first great piece of program music (*i.e.*, a piece of music that tells a story), though there had been many precedents. Even Bach had written a piece on the departure of a beloved brother. How does one listen to program music? Must the story be constantly in mind? Can the story be disregarded and the music listened to merely as music? Aestheticians for a century and a half have been arguing about the problem. It so happens that for the *Fantastique*, Berlioz used some music he had composed long previously for other purposes—music that had nothing to do with the program of the *Fantastique*. It also happens that the *Fantastique* divorced from its program is in many respects an orthodox symphony, with an allegro in sonata form, an adagio, scherzo, and finale. So what price program music? There is no easy answer. Everybody listens to music his own way. The less sophisticated listener often needs some kind of prop and he tends to "see" pictures in all kinds of music. The professional listens differently, concentrating on form, line, and shape, and, as often as not, he completely ignores any program in any type of music. (Arnold Schoenberg has confessed that for years he listened to, and loved, the Schubert songs—songs are in essence a kind of program music—without having the slightest idea of their texts.) In any case, no music can specifically describe anything. Anybody hearing the *Symphonie fantastique* for the first time—or Liszt's *Les Préludes,* or Strauss's *Till Eulenspiegel,* or Debussy's *La Mer*—without knowing the superimposed literary content of the work, would find it impossible to guess the program. At best, music can express only mood and emotion. It would take a dull listener indeed who did not realize that the second movement of the *Fantastique* is a waltz; or that the last movement is a wild, snarling, and turbulent evocation of *something*. And that is as far as anybody can go. A program may give an idea of what went on in the composer's mind, but music succeeds or fails on purely *musical* terms, and this is true even in opera, where extramusical associations necessarily play a part. No opera has ever remained in the repertoire because it has a great libretto. It remains because the music is great.

Berlioz needed some extramusical stimulus to set him off. In the *Fantastique* he expressed his own fantasies, and the thing that triggered them was his affair with the Irish actress Harriet Smithson. To say merely that he was in love with her would be like saying that the oceans have some water in them. It was more than love on Berlioz' part; it was a force of nature that all but drove him out of his mind. He wept to his friends. He raved. He disappeared into the fields outside of Paris, and on one of those occasions Liszt, Mendelssohn, and Chopin went out looking for him, convinced that he was going to destroy himself. Berlioz wrote about his "anguish," his "interminable and inextinguishable passion," his body shuddering with pain. "If she could for one moment conceive all the poetry, all the infinity of a like love, she would fly to my arms though she were to die through my embrace."

Miss Smithson did not reciprocate his great love, and for a good reason. She did not know Berlioz. They had not met, and all she knew about him was contained in the violent letters he sent her. They scared her to death. She thought he was mad and would not see him. He went to the theater to watch her. When he saw her in the arms of her stage lover, he screamed in pain and rushed from the house. Out of all this came the *Fantastique*. He heard rumors that she was carrying on with another man. Very well. He would show her. He put her into the last movement of the symphony as a whore at the witches' Sabbath. Later, learning the rumors were false, he removed the reference to her as a courtesan, but she still attends the Sabbath.

There had been program music before, but nothing like this. The *Fantastique* was first performed in 1830, and bemused listeners followed the progress of Hector and Harriet through five movements of tumultuous upheaval. Naturally, few understood what was going on. Liszt of course knew, and promptly made a piano arrangement of the work, movements of which he played at concerts. One of his tricks was to have the orchestra play the *March to the Scaffold*. Then Liszt would grandly dismiss the orchestra and play his solo version of the movement, building to immense sonorities that made an even grander effect.

One technical idea in the *Fantastique* made a big impression. The hero of the symphony, the young musician in love with Her, never thinks of his beloved except as associated with a musical thought, and Her theme runs through the entire symphony, presenting for the first time the *idée fixe* that eventually was to lead into the Wagnerian leitmotif. The *Fantastique* has its flaws. There is some overwriting, some self-conscious posing, some melodic material less than stimulating, some awkward transitions. But these shrink to nothing before the power and originality of the work, its brilliant orchestration, its ardent romanticism.

This mixture of flaw and genius is true of almost any Berlioz work. Moments of inspiration can alternate with banalities or interminably stretched-out passages. Even by Berlioz' own loose standards his forms sometimes are unsatisfactory. Some composers can get away with deficiencies of form. Schubert and Schumann could because of their extraordinary melodic gifts and the intrinsic quality of the material. Berlioz could because of his hyper-sensitive imagination and unparalleled ear for color. He never was the most disciplined of composers, nor was he the most facile of melodists, though occasionally he could come up with an inspired tune, as in the love music of *Roméo et Juliette* or the first song of the *Nuits d'Eté* cycle.

Berlioz eventually married his Harriet, after six years of siege, but not without a few interesting intervening episodes. There was, for instance, the Marie Moke caper. After the fuss created by the *Fantastique* Berlioz went off to Rome, having temporarily forgotten about his Harriet. His new love was a talented pianist named Marie Moke. In Italy he learned that Marie had married the piano manufacturer Pleyel. Berlioz in his autobiography has some fun with this episode. "I was beside myself with passion, and shed tears of rage; but I made up my mind on the spot what to do. My duty was clear. I must at once proceed to Paris and kill two guilty women"— Marie's mother was the other—"and one innocent man. After that, of course, it would be incumbent upon me to commit suicide." He arranges for a coach, first taking time out to orchestrate an unfinished work. Business before pleasure. He procures a dress and accessories so that he can disguise himself as a lady's maid, gets a pair of pistols, a bottle of laudanum and a bottle of strychnine. Loaded with this conspicuous example of overkill, breathing fire, he reaches Nice and suddenly finds himself cured. At Nice he spends the three happiest weeks of his life. Berlioz narrates all this with high good humor. He is playing a part and poking fun at himself, and he wants the reader to join the fun. It is utterly charming.

In 1832 he returned to Paris and the following year married Harriet. She turned out to be a shrew and, soon, an alcoholic. They fought like Balin and Balan. At intervals between bouts, Berlioz plunged into the European musical life and immediately became the leader of the avant-garde. He was interested only in the future. "If you were to produce one of Sebastian Bach's works I probably should take flight at one of his fugues." Many of the romantic composers either disliked classic music or paid mere lip service to it. Berlioz in his dislike of the early composers was more frank than most. He did not care for the music of Haydn and ignored most of Mozart. The big musical inspiration of his life, as to all the romantics, was Beethoven. Before Beethoven, little music existed for Berlioz, except for the operas of Gluck and Spontini. Yet, paradoxically, in literature he had a great love for the past: Homer, Virgil, Dante, Shakespeare. Shakespeare above all. "Next to God, it is Shakespeare who has created most." At parties he would declaim *Hamlet* for hours to his bored friends. "To have reached the age of 45 or 50 and not to know *Hamlet*—it's like having lived all one's years in a coal mine!" Berlioz could be an inconsistent man. With all of his screams against tradition, there nevertheless was a great deal, of tradition in his music, as recent scholars have been pointing out. As he grew older, the classical tradition in his music became ever more pronounced, and sections of his last opera, *Les Troyens,* are as chaste as anything in Gluck. It was not, of course, an eighteenth-century classicism. Rather it was a classicism in which the uncontrollable instincts of youth are tempered by restraint, clarity, and proportion. Berlioz was French, with all the logic and mental organization that implies.

Even with that classically controlled current running beneath his frequently wild music, the important thing about Berlioz was that he was in every way a revolutionary, a man fully prepared to throw established and even sacred notions into a garbage can. The nineteenth century knew it. "He sought the impossible and would have it at any cost," Saint-Saëns said. Théophile Gautier, in his *Histoire du romanticisme* (1854), placed Berlioz with Hugo and Delacroix as the three great French romantics. To Gautier, Berlioz represented "the romantic musical idea." In his comparison of Berlioz with Hugo, Gautier pointed out that "Their first thought . . . has been to free themselves from the old classical rhythm with its unending drone, its obligatory cadences and its predetermined pauses. Just as Victor Hugo replaces caesuras, uses enjambment and varies, by all kinds of devices, the monotony of the poetic phrase, Hector Berlioz changes rhythm, deceives the ear, which was expecting a symmetrical occurrence, and punctuates as he sees fit the musical phrase. . . . With both there is . . . the same disdain for the too bare, the too simple, line of classical art." Berlioz represented an anti-German type of romanticism: less thick, less sentimental, more aristocratic. As he grew older he shunned such extroverted fantasies as the *Fantastique* and said that "one must try to do coolly the things that are most fiery."

His unique series of scores came in steady progression—*Harold in Italy* in 1834 (where Byron had gone, the romantics were not far behind), the Requiem (1837), *Roméo et Juliette* (1839), *La Damnation de Faust* (1846), the *Te Deum* (1849), the oratorio *L'Enfance du Christ* (1854), the operas *Benvenuto Cellini* (1838), *Les Troyens* (1859), and *Béatrice et Bénedict* (1862). These are the major scores; there also were many choral works, songs, and other material. Often the music is in bastard forms of Berlioz' own devising. *La Damnation de Faust*—what is it? Oratorio? Opera? Berlioz called it "a concert opera." *Roméo et Juliette*—what is it? A choral work? Berlioz called it a "dramatic symphony." No matter. Each work must be judged on its own, not on *a priori* concepts of what constitutes "form." In the case of the *Damnation* the listener, only too conscious of some awkward settings and interminable recitative, can nevertheless thrill to the *Rákoczy* March and feel his skin prickle during the ride to the abyss. Those snarling trombones and bassoons under the whistling of the wind: what a stroke! Or, quite different, the intimate *L'Enfance du Christ,* with its quiet sounds and infinitely appealing tenderness. Or the power of the Requiem, with its secondary brass orchestras, its sensuousness of sound (Berlioz was the first composer to use sound for its own sake—to make an aesthetic of pure sound). No normal set of values can be put to much of this music, for normal values do not apply. The constructions are too unconventional, the melodies too asymmetrical, the harmonic language too personal. The music has a peculiar kind of *essence* that is immensely meaningful to some listeners and rather negative to others. The ever-increasing classic strain in Berlioz involves something more internal than external: quality of line rather than sound. As Gerald Abraham, in *A Hundred Years of Music,* puts it, "The history of music records few more striking paradoxes than this: that when the romantic movement had conquered the whole world of music in the nineteenth century, the only important composer who went on composing serenely beautiful music, filled with the classical spirit and fulfilling the classical ideal, was he who a quarter of a century earlier had been considered the most extravagant of the romantics."

Through these years Berlioz was in constant trouble: trouble at home with his wife (it did not take him long to find a mistress, a second-rate singer named Marie Recio, and he eventually married her after Harriet's death in 1854), trouble with his colleagues, trouble with the French public, which was puzzled by his music. He did have a following. Great composers have always had a following. There is no such thing as a completely misunderstood genius. But it was a small and predominantly professional following, nothing like what the mighty Giacomo Meyerbeer, the hero of the Opéra, could command. Berlioz had to fight every inch of the way, enmired in debt, trying to make the world understand his idiom. Paganini once bailed him out with a gift of 20,000 francs (probably close to $20,000 in 1970 American currency). Paganini said that Berlioz was the only man capable of making Beethoven come alive again.

Musicians of an older school resisted Berlioz' innovations or simply ignored them. His relations with Habeneck were typical. François Habeneck was a nice old boy who had founded the Concerts du Conservatoire in 1828. But he was a conservative and Berlioz had little respect for him. In 1836, Berlioz obtained one of the few official commissions of his career. The Minister of the Interior appointed him to compose a Requiem, and it was scheduled for performance on the day of the annual service commemorating the dead of the 1830 Revolution. The premiere took place the following year, Habeneck conducting. Berlioz was disturbed. Habeneck was the last man he wanted. As he explains the situation, Habeneck had not spoken to him for years. "His behavior to me was rude and incomprehensible." But there was little Berlioz could do, for the premiere was under government auspices, and Habeneck was in charge of the music at all important state musical occasions. The day of the premiere came, and in his autobiography Berlioz described what happened:

My forces had been divided into several groups spread over a wide area; necessarily so because of the four brass bands which I use in the *Tuba mirum*, and which have to be placed beyond the main body of performers, one at each corner. At the point where they enter, at the beginning of the *Tuba mirum*—which follows the *Dies Irae* without a pause —the music broadens to a tempo twice as slow. First, all four groups break in simultaneously—at the new tempo—then successively, challenging and answering each other from a distance, the entries piling up, each a third higher than the one before. It is therefore of the utmost importance to indicate the four beats of the slower tempo very clearly the moment it is reached; otherwise the great cataclysm, a musical representation of the Last Judgment, prepared for with such deliberation and employing an exceptional combination of forces in a manner at the time unprecedented and not attempted since—a passage which will, I hope, endure as a landmark in music—is mere noise and pandemonium, a monstrosity.

With my habitual mistrust I had stayed just behind Habeneck. Standing with my back to him, I supervised the group of timpani (which he could not see), as the moment approached for them to join in the general tumult. There are perhaps a thousand bars in my Requiem. In the very bar I have been speaking of, the bar in which the tempo broadens and the brass proclaim their tremendous fanfare—the one bar, in fact, in which the conductor's direction is absolutely indispensable—Habeneck laid down his baton and, calmly producing his snuffbox, proceeded to take a pinch of snuff. I had been keeping my eye on him. In a flash I turned on my heel, sprang forward in front of him and, stretching out my arm, marked out the four great beats of the new tempo. The bands followed me and everything went off in order. I conducted the piece to the end. The effect I had dreamed of was attained. When, at the final words of the chorus, Habeneck saw that the *Tuba mirum* was saved, he said: "God! I was in a cold sweat. Without you we would have been lost."

"I know," I replied, looking him straight in the eye. I did not say another word. Had he done it deliberately? Was it possible that this man, in collusion with X (who hated me) and with Cherubini's friends, had actually planned and attempted to carry out an act of such base treachery? I would rather not think so. Yet I cannot doubt it. God forgive me if I am doing him an injustice.

Ernest Newman, in his edition of the Berlioz memoirs, doubts that any such incident ever took place. Newman is wrong. Charles Hallé, the pianist and conductor, specifically mentions Habeneck's lapse in his reminiscences. Berlioz to the end of his life believed that Habeneck had tried to sabotage him.

To have some sort of steady income, Berlioz turned to criticism. In 1853 he became critic of the *Journal des Débats*, a position he held for ten years. He also contributed to other publications. Berlioz was the greatest music critic of his time, possibly of all time, but he hated the idea of criticism and he hated to write, even though his prose flows so easily and with so fresh a style that it always appears spontaneous. He was voluble on the subject of his mental blocks when it came to writing, and his memoirs are filled with great moanings about the unhappiness of his lot. He said that he could spend eight consecutive hours on his music, but that he had to fight with himself to begin a piece of prose, and he describes the state of mind so many writers get into:

> About the fourth line or so I get up, walk around the room, look out into the streets, take up a book. . . . My brain seemed ready to burst. My veins were burning. Sometimes I remained with my elbows on the table, holding my head in both my hands. Sometimes I strode up and down like a soldier on guard in a frost 25 degrees below zero. . . .
> And when, on turning around, my eyes fell on that accursed title inscribed at the head of that accursed sheet of paper, still blank and obstinately waiting for the words with which it was supposed to be covered, I felt simply overcome by despair. There was a guitar standing against the table. With one kick I smashed it in the center. . . . On my chimney two pistols were looking at me with their round eyes. I stared at them for a long time. I went so far as to bang my head again and again with my fist. At last, like a schoolboy who cannot do his homework, I tore my hair and wept with furious indignation.

There have been music critics (not many) with Berlioz' technical expertise. There also have been critics (even fewer) with a livelier writing style. But the combination of knowledge and vivacity makes his writing unique. He was very conscious of style. The fear of being dull or monotonous, he said, "makes me try to vary a little the turn of my poor sentences." On the passing musical scene he wrote with warmth, fairness, and good humor. Unfortunately, most of his reviews remain untranslated and have to be dug out of the *Journal des Débats* or the *Gazette Musicale*. Some of his pieces have been reproduced in the volume *Soirées de l'Orchestre*, a collection that contains some of his funniest essays. One of them is a feat of imagination that would have done credit to E. T. A. Hoffmann. It is an account of a piano competition at the Conservatoire. Thirty pianists are assembled to play the competition piece, Mendelssohn's G minor Concerto. After thirty performances the piano, a noble Érard, starts playing the concerto by itself. Nobody can stop it. They send for the manufacturer and Érard himself rushes over. The piano has gone berserk and will not listen to orders. Érard sprinkles the piano with holy water. That does not help. They remove the keyboard, which continues to play, throw it in the courtyard, and Érard has it chopped up with an axe. Now each piece of the keyboard dances around. Finally they throw it into a fire. "There was no other way to loose its grip. But, after all, how can a piano hear a concerto thirty times in the same hall on the same day without contracting the habit of it? M. Mendelssohn won't be able to complain that his music isn't being played. But think of the damage!"

In the latter part of his life, Berlioz spent much time conducting. He turned to the podium because nobody seemed capable or desirous of conducting his music. After a conductor—his friend, Narcisse Girard—messed up the premiere of *Harold in Italy* in 1834, Berlioz resolved in the future to conduct himself. As a musician with ideas, as a forceful personality, as a man with a vision of how music in its ideal state should sound, he was able to get more from an orchestra than anybody of his time. Wagner heard Berlioz conduct in 1839 and was more than impressed; and Wagner was not the man to pass compliments around: "I was simply all ears for things of which I had not dreamed until then, and which I felt I must try to realize." Berlioz was a volatile and extravagant figure on the podium, one of the first of the choreographic conductors. But no matter how much he gyrated, his beat remained clear and his interpretations must have been lucid, logical, and proportioned. As a conductor he was at the opposite pole from Wagner. Wagner stood for egocentricity, constant fluctuation of tempo, expression of self as much as expression of the composers' ideas. Berlioz did not admire this approach and once remarked of Wagner's conducting that it was in much too free a style, "like dancing on a tightrope, *sempre tempo rubato.*" Wagner, on the other hand, thought Berlioz superficial in everything except his own music. (German musicians have always had a tendency to regard French musicians as superficial, and that remains true today.) The odds are that Berlioz' style rather than Wagner's would be much more palatable to twentieth-century tastes.

Berlioz and Wagner: two of the biggest men of the avant-garde. Their careers only slightly intersected, for Wagner came to maturity in the 1860's, after Berlioz had stopped writing. Berlioz never heard any of Wagner's great works, the *Tristan* Prelude being the only work of Wagner's maturity he came across. Berlioz was puzzled and did not like it. Reviewing the piece, he called it "a sort of chromatic moan, full of dissonant chords, of which the long appogiaturas that replace the real note only increase the cruelty." Yet both composers were of the vanguard, and Berlioz of all people should have been responsive to the new speech of his great contemporary. He himself had been knocked from pillar to post, and in his lifetime did not achieve even the slightest foothold in Paris.

It was in London, in 1855, that the two men got to know each another. Both were there on conducting assignments. Wagner has left a record of one evening, not realizing how unconsciously funny it was. Wagner was always a compulsive talker, full of ideas about everything, and his pontifical speech was governed by an underlay of Kantian, Schillerian, and Schopenhauerian aesthetics and metaphysics. On this particular evening in London, Wagner was holding forth in grand and unintelligible manner: "Life's impressions hold us captive, as it were, until we rid ourselves of them by the formation of inner soul forms, which are by no means called forth by those impressions, but are only aroused by them from their deep slumbers so that the artistic image is not the result of the impressions but, on the contrary, a liberation from them." Wagner talked, Berlioz gravely listened. Whereupon, Wagner says, Berlioz smiled in a "condescending, sagacious sort of way," and said: "*Nous appelons cela digérer.*" Wagner had no sense of humor at all, and did not see the point of Berlioz' remark, "We call that digestion." But how deftly it pricks Wagner's inflated and self-satisfied theorizing!

No, the two men could not ever come together. Berlioz had too much of a classic feeling, was too realistic, too urbane, too witty—as urbane and witty as Wagner was egocentric, selfish, and philosophically muddle-headed. As the two most publicized leaders of the avant-garde, it probably was inevitable that they be set up against each other. Liszt and his group solved the problem by joining with Wagner and following him, all united under the banner of The Music of the Future. Berlioz could never have joined that party. He had been first in the field, to begin with, and his style was fully formed long before *Tristan*. He also may have felt, and resented, the fact that the wave of the future was with Wagner. Berlioz was a loner. He left no disciples, and it was Wagner to whom most of the younger generation flocked. Yet in 1860 Wagner, writing to Liszt, shows that he was perfectly aware of Berlioz' high and lonely position. To Wagner, there were only three composers worth taking notice of—Liszt, Berlioz, and Wagner. Or, as Wagner put it, "In the present period we alone are on a par—that is, You, He and I." Characteristically, Wagner omitted the name of Verdi. Otherwise, he was completely accurate. In 1860 Schumann, Mendelssohn, and Chopin were dead, and the great postromantic composers had yet to make their mark.

Berlioz found himself living too long. Ill, dejected, he spent the last half-dozen years of his life waiting for death in a small apartment he named Caliban's Cave. Once in a while he made public appearances, as when he went to Vienna to attend performances of his *Damnation de Faust* and *Harold in Italy*. But music was passing him by, and the great romantic became an anachronism. Liszt, Meyerbeer, Auber, Gounod, Thomas—these were the new heroes in Paris. Berlioz attempted to relieve his physical and emotional pain by taking opium. On March 8, 1869, he died. Thomas and Gounod were among the pallbearers. Cherubini, Gluck, Mozart, and a part of the Berlioz Requiem figured in the funeral service. If Berlioz had not been popular during his life, at least his death attracted some notice. According to newspaper reports, the way to the Montmartre Cemetery was lined with considerable crowds. A band of the National Guard played funeral marches during the passage of the procession. Musical pundits all over Europe wrote estimates of Berlioz' life and work. He was condemned by some as being an evil influence on the development of music. But there was one sensitive and appreciative estimate by Oscar Comettant, the critic of *Le Ménestral*. Among Comettant's observations was a paragraph on what Berlioz' music meant when it was first heard:

> *Roméo et Juliette*, when I first heard it many years ago, with an imposing orchestra and a numerous chorus, under the direction of the composer himself, produced in me one of those profound but indeterminate sensations which do not command enthusiasm though they inspire respect. I saw before me a great artist; I felt I did; my reason told me that I was listening to grandiose music, full of poetry; but it was only with difficulty that my ear, then inexperienced, could follow its ingenious and bold development. On the other hand, the accents of the melody, chaste, voluptuous, fantastic, gloomy, brilliant, ardent, impassioned in turn, but always bearing the stamp of genius, that is to say of originality, merely glided lightly over my heart without penetrating it. In the presence of this original work I remained cold but dazzled, as an inhabitant of the plains of Texas, or of the volcanic mountains of Peru, would be if suddenly transported without any preparation from those solitary and distant regions to the midst of a city like Paris, on some grand fête day.

To this day listeners first coming into contact with the music of Berlioz still have the feelings described so accurately by Comettant in 1869.

Although Berlioz was never entirely out of the repertoire after his death, he was represented only by a handful of works, and only one large-scale piece, the *Symphonie fantastique*. He had some champions, such as Felix Weingartner, but on the whole was a marginal figure until his rediscovery after World War II. In England especially there was a strong revival, and even his operas were staged, to vast acclaim. The Berlioz revival has not spread as strongly in the United States, though much more of his music has been heard since 1950 than ever before. Perhaps Berlioz will always remain the object of veneration by a strong and articulate minority. He could not speak to Everyman. But there is not one piece of his that lacks its incandescent moments. And then Berlioz is seen plain, his eagle beak defiantly thrust at the heavens, glorifying in a kind of tonal magnificence and an ideal of self-expression that make the concept of romanticism very clear.

❧ 10 ❧

Florestan and Eusebius

ROBERT SCHUMANN

With Robert Schumann romanticism came to full flower. Every aspect of romanticism was reflected in him. He was introspective, idealistic, closely allied spiritually with the literary aspects of the age, an innovator, a critic, a propagandist for the new—and a great composer. His music at first almost entirely dispensed with old forms (later he was to write more orthodox symphonies and quartets). He was the first of the completely anticlassic composers, and form as it previously existed meant little to him, though he was a superior theorist and as well informed as any musician then alive. While composers of his day were writing sonatas, symphonies, and variations, Schumann was writing music named *Intermezzi, Arabesque, Davidsbündlertänze, Kreisleriana, Carnaval, Kinderszenen*. These are caprices bundled together; they are spiritual diaries as well as music. A critic once rebuked him for not writing orthodox sonatas. Schumann's response was fervid, and it represented the romantic attitude: "As if all mental pictures must be shaped to fit one or two forms! As if each idea did not come into existence with its form ready-made! As if each work of art had not its own meaning and consequently its own form!" This is a very important, and very modern, statement. For the first time in music is found the expressed statement that content and idea dictate form, not the reverse. More than any composer, more even than Chopin, whose forms also to a large extent were anticlassic, Schumann established an entire aesthetic that verged on impressionism. In this concept, a short statement can be as valid as a long speech, and perhaps more so. Schumann, along with Chopin (the two worked independently of each other), demonstrated that forms existed not for the academicians but for the creative mind: that pure idea could impose its own forms, and that a small but perfect form, one that captured and exploited a single idea, could be its own aesthetic justification.

Mood, color, suggestion, allusion—these were important to Schumann, much more important than writing correct fugues, rondos, or sonatas. Invariably his music has a capricious and unexpected turn, a kaleidoscopic texture and emotion, an intensity of personal utterance that can be measured only in astronomical units. Naturally every pedant and academician in Europe promptly set Schumann up as a whipping boy. To them his works were the end of music, a sign of the degeneracy of the times. His music appeared strange, formless, anarchic, from the void. It was a music tied up with poetry, painting, personal allusions, and romantic aesthetics. To Schumann it was all one. "The esthetic experience," he once wrote, "is the same in any art, only the materials differ." Few major composers have been so disliked in their own time, and even fewer have been so little performed. Wagner, for instance, was hated in many quarters, but he received plenty of performances, and his work was discussed all over Europe. Wagner knew how to promote himself. The gentle Schumann never did. A quiet man, medium-sized, with a sensitive face and lips that were always pursed as though he were whistling to himself, he never really fought back, as Wagner and Berlioz did. When he did fight, and he did so as a critic, it was for the new music and not for himself. Big-hearted, generous, dedicated, in love with music, he lent a helping hand to all young talent. In the meantime his pungent harmonies, his unusually strong dissonances and syncopated rhythms, his new concept of free but functional form—all were being described by the conservatives as the work of a madman. To Henry Fothergill Chorley, the critic of the *Athenaeum* in London, Schumann's music represented the art of "covering pages with thoughts little worth noting and of hiding an intrinsic poverty of invention by grim or monotonous eccentricity." Chorley smelled the end of civilization as he knew it. "Decadence!" he thundered. Fortunately, Schumann had friends and disciples, and his admirers saw to it that his music was spread around. He also had a wife who was one of the best pianists in the world. Little by little his music made progress, though it was not until after his death that he was accepted as one of the immortals.

If ever a composer was doomed to music it was Robert Schumann. There was something of a Greek tragedy in the way music reached into his cradle, seized him, nourished him, and finally destroyed him. From the beginning his emotions were overstrung, abnormally so. His mind was a delicate seismograph upon which music registered violent shocks—shocks that would not even be noticed by people with less sensitive receiving apparatus. He himself once described how, as a child, he stole at night to the piano and played a series of chords, weeping bitterly all the while. He was so moved by the writings of Jean Paul that the intensity of the pleasure drove him (in his own words) to the verge of madness. When he heard of Schubert's death he wept the whole night. Anybody with sensibilities refined to such a pitch is apt to lose control, and Schumann eventually did. Sometime around 1851,

139

five years before his death, he began having hallucinations. He would hear harmonies from heaven. One night he imagined that the spirits of Schubert and Mendelssohn had brought him a theme, and he leapt out of bed to write it down. Like William Blake, he had visions. Unlike Blake, he could not live with them, and his mind finally gave way.

But he accomplished much in the forty-six years of his life. His daemon dictated to him a kind of music that no composer up to that time had begun to visualize. The derivative forces in the music of Bach, Haydn, Handel, Mozart, and Beethoven can easily be traced. Berlioz owed a large debt to Beethoven. Even in so amazing a genius as the young Chopin there can be found influences of earlier composers—Field, Weber, Hummel. But Schumann from the beginning struck off entirely on his own, and it is hard to find a precedent for his music.

Basically he was a self-taught composer. Certainly there were no musical antecedents in his family. He was born on June 8, 1810, in the little town of Zwickau in Saxony. His father, August, was a bookseller and, like Robert, a rather shy and retiring person. In addition to selling books, he undertook publication, in German translation, of the complete works of Scott and Byron. But most of all he liked to sit in his study, smoking pipe after pipe, and writing romances. There was a bad strain in the family. August had what was called a nervous disorder, and was anything but normal in his last years. His daughter, Emilia, was a mental and physical defective who committed suicide. Many years later, Robert was also to try to kill himself. Even as a young man, Robert was afraid that he too would become insane, and the thought plagued his whole life. August died when Robert was sixteen.

With all the books in his father's shop, and with his natural, eager intelligence, it was no wonder that Robert was constantly reading. He especially loved reading the romantics—Ludwig Tieck, Jean Paul, Novalis (the *nom de plume* of Georg Friedrich Philipp von Hardenberg), E. T. A. Hoffmann, Klemens Brentano. Robert grew up conditioned by literature, and in no other composer is there such an attempted fusion of sound with literary idea. His favorite writer was Jean Paul, and that great romantic and visionary was constantly making remarks about music—remarks that the young Schumann devoured. "Sound," wrote Jean Paul, "shines like the dawn, and the sun rises in the form of sound; sound seeks to rise in music, and color is light." Or, Jean Paul would write, it is music alone "which can open the ultimate gates to the Infinite." To Schumann, romantic literature in general and Jean Paul in particular were governing processes of life itself. "If everybody read Jean Paul," he wrote to a friend when he was eighteen, "we should be better but more unhappy. Sometimes he almost clouds my mind, but the rainbow of peace and the natural strength of man bring sweet tears, and the heart comes through its ordeal marvellously purified and softened."

Inspired by his literary heroes, Schumann tried his hand at poetry and fiction. He also attempted composition. Indeed, he had been doing so from the age of seven. He had easily learned how to play the piano and had a strong talent for improvisation. But his musical education was almost nil, and he had to pick everything up by himself. There were musicales and literary readings in Zwickau, and Schumann was the star at those affairs. In music and literature, however, he could be called only an amateur.

At the death of his father he was still wavering between a career in music or literature. His mother had different ideas. She could see no future for Robert in either field, and she sent him to Leipzig to study law. Leipzig was the wrong place for so impressionable a young man as Robert. There was too much music in the city. He would go to concerts at the Gewandhaus, or to the musical services at St. Thomas (Bach's old church), or to the performances of the Euterpe choral society. Or he would get up early and, in a spasm of activity, practice the piano eight or nine hours a day, smoking innumerable cigars in the process. At night he would summon his friends and play for them. Or he would read Goethe, Shakespeare, Byron, and of course Jean Paul, committing to memory page after page of their work. He was a romantic *par excellence*, affecting a Byronic pose, falling in and out of love, dabbling in the arts, arguing about music, life, and aesthetics through the night and well into the morning. He did not study much law in Leipzig. Nor did he study much more in Heidelberg, where he went for a year. One of his closest friends was there, and there also was a law professor, one Justus Thibaut, who had written a book on musical aesthetics and was a great music lover.

All this was very fine, but musically speaking it was not very professional. Not until Schumann was eighteen did he take his first serious musical instruction. In 1830, on his return to Leipzig, he came across a piano teacher named Friedrich Wieck. The best testimonial to Wieck's pedagogical theories was his daughter, the nine-year-old Clara. She was a formidable prodigy and she developed into one of history's outstanding artists. Wieck was enthusiastic about Schumann's potential. He wrote to Schumann's mother, promising that Robert would "be one of the greatest pianists within three years. He shall play with more warmth and genius than Moscheles, and on a grander scale than Hummel." Mrs. Schumann was not happy about the turn events had taken, but there was little she could do about it. Schumann moved into Wieck's house, practiced hard, started composing, and also took lessons in composition with Heinrich Dorn, conductor of the Leipzig opera. But his career as a professional pianist ended before it started. Trying to achieve a short cut to finger independence, the impetuous Schumann invented a contraption that permanently ruined one of his fingers. He does not appear to have been greatly distressed by the accident. Already he must have known that his future was in composing. In 1831 his first published composition appeared, the *Abegg* Variations. Characteristically, he constructed the theme on the letters of a girl's name. Soon came his Op. 2, the *Papillons*, a musical rendering of the ballroom scene from Jean Paul's *Flegeljahre*. This appeared in 1832, and Schumann saw the whole world opening up to him:

> On sleepless nights I am conscious of a mission which rises before me like a distant peak. When I wrote *Papillons* I began to feel a certain independence. Now the butterflies [papillons] have flown off into the vast and magnificent universe of spring; the spring itself is on my doorstep looking at me—it is a child with celestial blue eyes.

His head was full of new music, and he started putting it on paper. He also started reviewing concerts and new music for the *Allgemeine Musikalische Zeitung* and the *Komet*. One of his first reviews in the *Zeitung*, in 1831, brought Chopin to the attention of German readers. Schumann came across the *Là ci darem* Variations (Op. 2), and wrote an enthusiastic review that contained the famous line: "Hats off, gentlemen! A genius!" The review, written in Schumann's best Jean-Paulese, is an amazingly sympathetic and prescient summary of Chopin's startling new music and what it stands for. In 1833 he decided to start his own music magazine, and the first issue of the *Neue Zeitschrift für Musik* appeared in 1834. And he fell in love with Clara.

They became engaged in 1837. Old Wieck took it hard. More than that, he did everything in his power to stop the marriage. History has labeled him the prototype of the hard-hearted, selfish, ambitious father. Yet one can see his point of view. He had made Clara the outstanding pianist of her sex. Now, just when he was ready to reap the financial rewards, she was throwing herself away on a penniless composer, a vague idealist, a radical musician whose theories were being called mad, an impractical and disorganized man. Wieck looked around and could find plenty of material to support his arguments. Nobody thought much of Schumann's music. In Paris, Chopin was poking fun at it. Mendelssohn, who was the strongest musical power in Germany, and who liked Schumann personally, could find little to praise about his music. (Later, when Schumann started composing symphonies, Mendelssohn did bring them to the public.) Liszt himself, the great Liszt, had tried to play some Schumann music in public and had failed. If Liszt, the greatest of matinee idols, could not establish Schumann's music, who could?

But, much as one can see Wieck's point of view, his tactics in trying to stop the marriage were distressing. He spread rumors that Schumann was a dipsomaniac, unreliable, incapable of taking care of a wife. He used every trick to tear the lovers apart, maligning him, lying, growing frantic with rage, anxiety, and frustration. He would tell Clara that Schumann was lazy, and she would relay that bit of information to him. Schumann answered her letters. "Your father calls me phlegmatic. *Carnaval* and phlegmatic! F sharp minor Sonata and phlegmatic! Being in love with such a girl and phlegmatic! And you can listen calmly to all this? He says that I have written nothing in the *Zeitschrift* for six weeks. In the first place, that is not true. Secondly, even if it were, how does he know what other work I have been doing? . . . Up to the present time, the *Zeitschrift* has had about eighty sheets of my own ideas, not to mention the rest of the editorial work, besides which I have finished ten major compositions in two years, and they have cost me some heart's blood. To add to everything else, I have given several hours of hard work every day to Bach and Beethoven, and to my own work, and conscientiously managed a large correspondence, which was often delicate and complicated. I am a young man of twenty-eight, with a very active mind, and an artist in addition. . . . And you mean to say all my industry and simplicity, all that I have done, is quite lost upon your father?" Finally the lovers had to go to court for permission to marry without Wieck's consent. They were married in 1840.

It turned out to be an idyllic marriage, the union of two extraordinary minds. She was the stabilizing force in his life; he was the spiritual beacon in hers. Adjustments had to be made. His work came first, even if it meant that she had to go long periods without practicing; and she worried about that. Practicing, to the professional instrumentalist, becomes compulsive, and there can be a psychic wrench if the normal six or seven hours a day are missed. But Clara had to forego her practicing while *Der Meister* was at work. And Schumann was difficult when he was in one of his moods. At such times he could be the Prussian type of husband. Once he accompanied Clara to Russia on a concert tour, and they were taken on a sightseeing tour of St. Petersburg by the great pianist Adolf Henselt. They came to a tower that gave a fine view of the city, but Schumann refused to climb. "No, it will make me dizzy." Schumann was deathly afraid of heights; he always lived on the ground floor of any house. Mme. Henselt then invited Clara to ascend. "No," Schumann growled. "Clara does not go where I do not go." Mme. Henselt, who told the story, said that Clara apologized meekly and quickly sat next to Robert with a scared look. He still may have been smarting about the remark of the nobleman to whom he was introduced at one of Clara's musicales in St. Petersburg. "Are you, too, musical?" the nobleman wanted to know.

In one respect Clara was a bad influence on Robert. Musically she had been brought up "correctly," and was conditioned to believe that the "best" composers wrote symphonies and operas. Much as she loved Robert and his music, she nevertheless felt that he would not fully realize himself until he entered the arena in competition with Beethoven and the other symphonic heroes. Perhaps it was also a subconscious wish for Schumann to be "respectable." So she pushed him into areas for which he was emotionally, intellectually, and technically unfitted. She wrote in her diary before they were married: "It would be best if he composed for orchestra. His imagination cannot find sufficient scope on the piano. . . . His compositions are all orchestral in feeling. . . . My highest wish is that he should compose for orchestra—that is his field. May I bring him to it!" Clara was monumentally wrong. She was also blind to many of his other musical lapses, and became infuriated when it was suggested that her Robert had better refrain from conducting. This was in Düsseldorf, where he went as musical director and promptly ran the orchestra and chorus into the ground. Clara fought for him, though by then she must have realized his problems. She meant well, but her interference in his life was not always for the best.

Even with his mental handicap, which became progressively worse during the last fifteen years of his life, Schumann did an enormous amount of work. Composition was but a part of his activity. He taught at the Leipzig Conservatory, appeared here and there as a conductor of his own music, made his house one of the centers of progressive musical activity in Europe, and carried on his duties as editor of the *Neue Zeitschrift für Musik*. The journal continued to be run on personal, romantic lines; it was a reflection of Schumann himself. When he and his friends decided to put out the magazine, the idea was to provide a forum in which good music could be praised and bad music spanked. The early 1830's were dominated by a good deal of inferior commercial junk, and the popular composers were such footnotes to history as Henri Herz and Franz Hünten, who industriously provided titillating potpourris for the salons of Europe. As Schumann explained the aims of the magazine in 1834, Rossini reigned on stage, "and at the piano nothing was heard but Herz and Hünten; and yet only a few years had passed since Beethoven, Schubert and Weber lived among us. Then one day awoke the thought: 'Let us not look on idly, but also lend our aid to progress. Let us again bring the poetry of art to honor among men!' "

In his own publication, Schumann could indulge his fancy for romantic byplay. He invented a society known as the *Davidsbund*—the band of David—and gave pen names to the members who would discuss music and write reviews. Schumann himself had two names—Florestan, reflecting the exuberant side of his nature, and Eusebius, the reflective side. There were Master Raro, Chiara, Jonathan, and so on. All were real people. Chiara was Clara; Master Raro was Friedrich Wieck; Jonathan was Ludwig Schunke. All of the Davidites were leagued together to combat the Philistines, those unimaginative bourgeois or pedants or musical tricksters who immersed themselves in safe or meretricious music.

As a critic Schumann was knowledgeable, conscientious, and open-minded. He did not have the flash, brilliance, and wit of Berlioz, but a more generous critic never lived. He was ready to praise a composer unreservedly if he detected any sign of talent. Schumann has been censured for his praise of composers who today are considered second-raters. But men like Niels Gade (1817–1890), William Sterndale Bennett (1815–1875), and the others he helped launch are second-raters only in retrospect. In their own day they achieved big reputations, and they *were* talented and honest musicians, the best of the crop. As a matter of fact, Gade was a really fine composer, and his music deserves to be heard. His String Quartet in F minor, for one, is something of a masterpiece.

Schumann was merciless toward sham and pretentiousness in music, and he was not afraid to engage those current heroes, Rossini and Meyerbeer, in combat. The test of a great critic, in any case, is not how many talents he overpraises, but how many geniuses he fails to recognize. On these grounds, Schumann's record is near-perfect. One of his very first reviews introduced Chopin, and his very last introduced Brahms. He had some reservations about Berlioz, but his long and detailed critique of the *Symphonie fantastique* is a model of fairness and understanding. Mendelssohn he adored, and Liszt he respected, though he told Clara that Liszt's world was not his. Some think that he did not understand Wagner, but that is not true. He did point out the weaknesses of *Tannhäuser*, which indeed does have weaknesses. However, he did not hear any of the music of Wagner's maturity, and thus should not be criticized for something out of his control. As for his writings on past composers, Schumann's appreciative and enthusiastic articles helped clarify the music of the late Beethoven and the virtually forgotten Schubert; and his many articles on Bach were a vital part of the Bach renaissance. In short, here was a writer on music with vast knowledge and impeccable taste, doing what a critic should do—conveying his enthusiasms and educating the public. "It is not enough that a newspaper mirrors the present," he wrote. "The critic must be ahead of his times and ready armed to fight for the future." That was Schumann's credo as a critic, and he adhered to it, as he adhered to all of his principles. "I love not the men whose lives are not in unison with their works," he once made Florestan say.

Schumann's last years were sad, and his illness must have left a permanent scar on Clara, who outlived him by forty years, dying in 1896. As his mind became progressively unbalanced, Schumann withdrew into his own world. He kept hearing in his inner ear an incessant A that prevented him from talking or thinking. Always taciturn, he said less and less, and visitors could not get a word out of him. Wagner once came to his house and, as was his custom, inundated him with talk. But even Wagner, who was notably insensitive, and who liked to hear his own opinions and nobody else's, was bothered. "An impossible person," he indignantly said of Schumann. "You can't always talk *alone*." Toward the end, the Schumann family was in trouble. It was a large family (the Schumanns had eight children, of whom five lived), and there was not much money around. Schumann was not able to work, and he started having hallucinations. Early in 1852 he went through an entire week during which he said that angels were dictating music to him while devils in the form of tigers and hyenas were threatening him with Hell. On February 27 he attempted suicide by throwing himself off a bridge into the Rhine. At his own request he was placed in an asylum. Clara had to leave him and go on tour to bring money home. She was called back from a concert at his last moments. There are harrowing accounts of Schumann's last days, written by Clara and friends of the family; and also by Johannes Brahms, who had been living with the Schumanns. At least there was the consolation that at the time of Schumann's death, on July 29, 1856, his music had started to make an international reputation. The A minor Piano Concerto was popular, and other works were beginning to enter the repertoire.

Although Schumann, as a critic, could well understand and explain to the public the views of other composers, few could understand his. His message was too unconventional and too personal. He realized this, but could write only the way his genius dictated. He was, after all, one of the great melodists and he easily could have turned out pretty, salable items. The thought never once occurred to this most uncompromising of idealists. How wistful is one of his letters to Clara: "I confess it would be a great delight to me if I succeeded in writing something which, when played by you, would make the public dance with delight." But as a young man he had taken up the fight against the Philistines, and to his own self he had to be true.

The unconventionalities aside, what made his music hard to understand fully—the same is true today—is the personal nature of the content. It is almost autobiographical. "I am affected by everything that goes on in the world—politics, literature, people—I think it over in my own way, and then I long to express my feelings in music. That is why my compositions are sometimes difficult to understand, because they are connected with distant interests; and sometimes unorthodox, because anything that happens impresses me and compels me to express it in music." These are the words of a true romantic, and in writing them, Schumann was merely expressing a romantic article of faith. Novalis, one of the leaders of the early German romantic movement, had previously expressed the same thought: "The soul of the individual should be one with the soul of the world." Or Henrik Steffens, the German natural philosopher: "The external world is itself an aspect of our internal being." Schumann was only dropping the small change of the intellectual currency of the time. But he not only echoed it. He applied it.

Nearly everybody, for instance, loves Schumann's *Carnaval,* and pianists love to play it. But it also has to be heard on a secondary level, with a knowledge of the vast extramusical symbolism it contains. This has nothing to do with program music. It merely explains what was going on in the composer's mind. *Carnaval* cannot be fully understood without realizing that it is a picture gallery in which are painted the two sides of Schumann's own nature (Florestan and Eusebius), in which appear Clara, Chopin, Wieck, Paganini, Mendelssohn, and others; that the entire work is based on four notes—ASCH (in German, E flat = S and B natural = H)—Asch being a city in which a lady friend of the composer lived, and also a city that contained four letters that occur in the composer's last name; and that the final march is a musical illustration of Schumann's determination to lead his band of righteous musicians into the enemy camp of Meyerbeer, Herz, and Hünten and demolish them. There are other symbols in *Carnaval,* but this is the general idea. Many of Schumann's works were conceived this way, and many of the allusions he makes have long since lost their meaning. We can only guess, building on a knowledge of Schumann's style and symbolism.

He himself often did not know what his music meant. Some of it was written in what amounted to a trance. First he wrote it. *Then* he looked it over, giving the work a title. That was his standard practice, and nearly all of his pieces were named after they were written. The name merely gives a clue to the mood, and is not to be taken as a guide to a story. "In my latest songs," he told Clara, "I often hear many things that I can hardly explain. It is most extraordinary how I write almost everything in canon and then only detect the imitation later, and often find inversions, rhythms in contrary motion, etc." Schumann's rich, complicated harmony did indeed have a strong polyphonic texture, a fact not generally realized, especially by the young pianists who play his music today. Schumann's careful indications of secondary and inner voices pass largely unnoticed by modern pianists. One musician who did realize the density and polyphonic complexity of the seemingly simple Schumann compositions was Alban Berg. In 1920, Berg had been attacked by the conservative composer-critic Hans Pfitzner for his "lack of melody." Why, asked Pfitzner, could not Berg, Schoenberg, and Webern write a pretty, uncomplicated, melodic work like Schumann's *Träumerei?* Berg demolished Pfitzner by publishing, in a Viennese music magazine, a structural and harmonic analysis of the *Träumerei.* Far from being uncomplicated, Berg demonstrated, the Schumann piece is not only amazingly sophisticated harmonically but is also "a strict piece of four-part writing," so rich in its polyphony that it "could easily be given to a string quartet or wind ensemble, or even to the four singing voices."

Like Chopin, Schumann started as a composer of piano music, and his first twenty-three works are for solo piano. In this series are three sonatas and the three-movement Fantasy in C major, which can loosely be called a sonata. The rest are, for the most part, small pieces bundled together under a name. Sometimes, as in the *Études symphoniques* or *Carnaval*, a unifying structural idea runs through the work, but more often there is no pretense at unity. It was a kind of piano music that had little to do with the pianistically more graceful, glittering piano music that Liszt, Thalberg, and Henselt were turning out. Their piano music was virtuoso material, and the concert hall and audiences were always in mind. Schumann's piano music can be equally difficult, but it is normally not showy. There are exceptions, as in the second movement of the Fantasy, but even there the bravura element is dictated by the content. The Fantasy, Schumann's greatest and largest work for solo piano, is, with Chopin's B flat minor Sonata and the Liszt B minor Sonata, one of the trinity of pieces upon which all romantic piano music rests. In Schumann's piano music are no show-off passages, none of the flashy octaves and finger work characteristic of the age. Schumann had nothing but scorn for virtuosity as an end in itself. "As if there were nothing higher than the art of pleasing the public!"

Not that the music is reticent. Quite the opposite. The Schumann piano works are exuberant, poetic, introspective, grand, and intimate in turn. Schumann's particular musical charm is hard to describe, even with its pronounced idiosyncracies—those syncopations, those altered seventh chords, that thick texture. It is a soaring kind of music, imbued with the romantic ideal, out to do for music what Jean Paul did for literature. In his piano music, Schumann is never far from Jean Paul. To Jean Paul, music represented man's efforts to achieve the infinite. "So life fades and withers behind us, and of our sacred and vanished past, only one thing remains immortal —music," Jean Paul wrote. Schumann had the same feeling. Music was the mysterious art, the art that picked up after poetry and, indeed, life itself had ceased. In expressing all this in his music, Schumann approached mysticism, composing in a state of what might be described as ecstasy, a vision always before him. This sounds sentimental, but it was not sentimental to Schumann. It was what made him go.

From piano music Schumann turned to song, and in 1840 composed a remarkable series of cycles and individual songs—the two *Liederkreis* sets, *Myrthen, Frauenliebe und Leben,* and, above all, the *Dichterliebe* to Heine poems. The sixteen songs of *Dichterliebe* rank with Schubert's *Winterreise* in the hierarchy of song cycles. Schumann took up where Schubert left off, broadening the concept of the art song, making the piano an even more subtle partner, adding piano preludes and postludes. Schumann and the lied were made for each other, for his gift was essentially lyric, his melodic ideas were unique in their taste, imagination, and refinement, and he thought naturally in small forms. In all, he composed over 250 songs throughout his career, including a series of ravishing vocal duets.

When Schumann started to explore a new form of writing, he dropped everything else. Thus, after piano and song, came symphony, and the year was 1841. Clara's dearest wish came true. It took Schumann only four days to sketch out his First Symphony, in B flat, which he himself called *Spring*. Three months later, in March, the scoring was complete, and Mendelssohn conducted the world premiere in Leipzig. In April Schumann finished a score that he called an Overture, and the next month he added two more movements, naming the work at first a suite and later referring to it as a "symphonette." Today the work is called Overture, Scherzo, and Finale, and it lacks only a slow movement to be a full-scale symphony. It is a beautiful piece of music that, for some reason, has been passed over by conductors. In May came a one-movement Fantasy for Piano and Orchestra. Clara played it, and then Schumann put it aside for four years. It eventually emerged as his most popular work, the A minor Piano Concerto.

Immediately after completing the Fantasy, Schumann set to work on a symphony in the key of D minor. This was finished in September and also put aside, emerging ten years later as the Symphony No. 4. Then Schumann started another symphony, this one in C minor. It, too, was put aside, and nothing came of it. The work we know as the Second Symphony was published in 1846, and the Third (*Rhenish*) in 1850. Schumann seems to have spent himself on orchestral writing in 1841. The following year he turned to chamber music, and within six months wrote all of his important works in that form—the three String Quartets, the E flat Piano Quartet, and, above all, the radiant Piano Quintet in E flat.

All four Schumann symphonies are very much in the repertoire, and this despite structural and orchestral flaws that commentators have been pointing out ever since they were composed. There is no argument that Schumann was a weak orchestrator; he thought pianistically rather than in terms of the orchestra, and conductors have always found it necessary to touch up the scoring. Today those emendations are done in a discreet manner, which was not true at the turn of the century, when such conductors as Mahler decided to help Schumann by virtually rewriting his music. It also is conceded that Schumann was unhappy working within the strictures of sonata form. His transitions can be labored and his developments very awkward. At that, Schumann was full of original ideas in his symphonies, including ideas about thematic linkages. This was carried to its ultimate in the one-movement Symphony No. 4 in D minor, in which four movements are packaged into one, and in which a kind of theme transformation is used that foreshadows the Liszt B minor Sonata. What keeps the Schumann symphonies alive is their special glow, the high quality of the musical ideas. Each of the symphonies has its special characteristic: the ebullience of the *Spring* Symphony; the flaming romanticism of the Second (with its mournful adagio movement, one of the most beautiful ever written by any composer); the bigness and pride of the *Rhenish* Symphony, in which Schumann, like Berlioz in the *Fantastique*, composed five movements; and the innovations of the Fourth Symphony, which is also the most "feminine" of the four. Pedants may worry about certain inaccuracies in the scoring, and foolish writers may downgrade the Schumann symphonies by putting them on a scale weighted on the other end by the Beethoven symphonies. But if listeners are content to accept the Schumann symphonies for what they are, they are among the most inspired creations of the nineteenth century.

Schumann achieved success in all musical forms except one, opera. He spent much time over *Genoveva*, which achieved no fame in its day and has had very few performances since. He also wrote a large quantity of choral music, including *Paradies und die Peri*, the *Requiem für Mignon*, and *Der Rose Pilgefahrt*, none of which is much encountered any more. Indeed, a surprisingly large amount of Schumann's music is no longer played. He is not a composer to everybody's taste. As the arch-romantic, the most personal and least objective of the great composers, his message ran counter to the aesthetic that dominated the Western world after 1918. To many of the intellectuals in the period from 1920 to 1940, Schumann was a rather embarrassing relic of the early romantic period. He was considered sentimental, self-indulgent, and one step above a salon composer—at best, a sweet singer without emotional discipline. The whole point of his music was missed—that perfect weld of form and content in his shorter works, that overwhelming daring and originality, that basic purity even in moments of extravagance. Purity is not a word normally used in association with Schumann, but everything about him was pure—his life, his love, his dedication, his integrity, his mind, his music.

11

Apotheosis of the Piano

FRÉDÉRIC CHOPIN

Most of the romantic composers had a *parti pris* about romanticism. They were propagandists; they played or conducted one anothers' music; they wrote reviews and articles about the new styles and theories; they helped one another as best they could; and as teachers, some of them passed their aspirations to the oncoming generation. Not Frédéric Chopin. He would have none of it. Indeed, he disliked romanticism. He thought Liszt's music vulgar, did not like Schumann's music at all, had nothing to say about the works of Berlioz or Mendelssohn, though he was the friend of all of those great men. He approached Beethoven with a mixture of admiration and dislike; the thunderer was too big and uncouth, and Chopin felt uncomfortable in his presence. If he heard any music by Schubert, he did not mention it. The only two masters who meant anything to him were Bach and Mozart. For them he had nothing but praise. He also adored the operas of Bellini.

He was not widely read, nor did he respond to romantic art. Delacroix was one of his best friends, but Chopin would look at a Delacroix painting and mumble something noncommital, not wanting to hurt Delacroix' feelings. His teaching—which was how he supported himself in grand style— was private and largely confined to society. Elegant pupils would enter Chopin's studio and put their twenty or thirty francs on the mantelpiece while he looked out of the window. He was a gentleman, and gentlemen did not soil their hands with anything as vulgar as business transactions. He liked to move in aristocratic circles, and was greatly concerned with style, taste, clothes, and *bon ton*. He could be witty, malicious, suspicious, ill-tempered, charming. There was something feline about Chopin.

One of the greatest pianists in history, he gave very few concerts during his life and was primarily a salon pianist. Short, slim, fair-haired, with blue-gray (some say brown) eyes, a prominent nose, and an exquisite bearing, he was physically frail and his playing at best never had much sonority. Toward the end it was a whisper. Early in life he learned that he should never play in large halls, and his last public appearance in Paris took place on April 26, 1835, when he was twenty-six. For the rest of his life—he died in 1849—he gave only three more recitals, and those were semiprivate, at the salon of the piano manufacturer Pleyel, before a carefully selected audience that never numbered more than 300. He did do a great deal of playing at musical parties. What evenings those must have been! Chopin and Liszt playing four-hand music (Chopin playing the bass; Liszt was not going to drown *him* out), perhaps Mendelssohn turning pages while awaiting his turn at the keyboard. Around the piano might be Berlioz, Meyerbeer, Eugène Sue, Delacroix, Heine, and George Sand, with Ary Scheffer making sketches in the background.

Chopin fit beautifully into the mad, bad, sad, glad Paris of the 1830's and 40's. Although he did not have many close friends, he knew everybody, and everybody liked and respected him. They knew he was a genius. And Paris those days was highly experienced in judging genius. It was the intellectual and artistic capital of the world. Hugo, Balzac, Sand, Vigny, Lamartine, Heine, Gautier, and Musset were among the literary figures living there. Delacroix and Ingres were at the height of their careers. Liszt, Meyerbeer, Rossini, Berlioz, and Luigi Cherubini made Paris their home. Mendelssohn was in and out. Paris had three good orchestras and the greatest opera house in Europe. Malibran, Pasta, Lablache, Rubini, and Nourrit could be heard in opera, and they supplied a kind of florid, virtuosic singing that must have been hair-raising. Paris was the headquarters of European pianism, with Kalkbrenner, Thalberg, Herz, Heller, Litolff, and Prudent in residence. Politically Paris was temporarily stabilized. *Les Trois Glorieuses* of July, 1830, had put Louis-Philippe on the throne and, as the uprising had been a popular movement, there were concessions to popular taste. The *bourgeoisie* was raised to power; and while the lower classes did not have much more than they ever had, there was a kind of national revival and prosperity that manifested itself in a sudden flowering of the arts. Paris in the 1830's was experiencing the kind of renascence that London had experienced in the latter days of Elizabeth I.

Chopin had arrived in Paris in 1831. He spent the rest of his life there. When he came to Paris, it was as a provincial from Warsaw. His birthplace was in Zelazowa Wola, near the Polish capital, and there is some confusion about the date. The parish register says February 22, 1810, but Chopin's mother insisted it was March 1, and that was when she celebrated her famous son's birthday. Some scholars have dug up evidence that suggests 1809 as the year of Chopin's birth. The matter has not yet been resolved. Chopin's father was an émigré from France, his mother a Pole. Frédéric was the second of four children and the only son. His musical talent showed up early and he was a good pianist at the age of six. Adalbert Zywny, his teacher, was a cultivated musician who fed his genius of a pupil plenty of Bach. (Bach in Warsaw in 1816! And they say he was forgotten after his death!) At the age of eight, Chopin saw his first composition in print. It was a polonaise. From 1826 to 1828 he studied composition with Joseph Elsner, a man who had the wisdom to realize that Chopin was something special, to be treated with special care. As an academician, Elsner fervently wanted Chopin to compose symphonies, sonatas, and perhaps Polish national opera. But he never forced Chopin's style and did everything he could to let the young man develop naturally. That may have been his biggest contribution, and one for which posterity must be grateful. For in a way Chopin was a musical freak, more so than even most prodigies. He was not only a genius as a pianist, he was creatively a genius, one of the most startingly original ones of the century.

From where did he get his ideas? Warsaw was a little removed from the cosmopolitan centers of Europe, though it was visited by important artists. Chopin did have the opportunity of hearing some—Hummel, Paganini, and the soprano Henrietta Sontag among others. The genesis of some of Chopin's music can be traced in the work of Moscheles, Hummel, and Czerny. But that does not explain the revolutionary qualities of Chopin's thinking—his development of an altogether new kind of piano playing; his daring, yet refined, harmonic sense; his experimentation with a kind of piano sonority that once and for all released the instrument from the past. All that can be said was that in the young Chopin a musical fermentation went on, and he found that he had to change the rules. How much was conscious in his new way of thinking, how much unconscious, is anybody's guess. He was a genius, and was born with certain reflexes in fingers, ears, and mind that less fortunate musicians never attain. Certainly he came to full maturity earlier than most composers, and everything seemed to come easy to him. "You know," his father wrote, "that the mechanics of piano playing occupied little of your time, and that your mind was busier than your fingers. If others have spent whole days working at the keyboard, you rarely spent an hour playing other men's music." Thus as a musician Chopin was one of the lucky ones—a natural technician with an easy style, a composer who decided early to write only for the instrument that he loved. His work turned out to be mostly in the smaller forms, but he helped change the face of music, and most of his contemporaries recognized him for the revolutionary he was. "Cannon buried in flowers," said Schumann of Chopin's music.

In Warsaw it was realized that young Chopin was something exceptional, though nobody could have guessed to how fantastic an extent. The first inkling came when Chopin left Poland for Vienna, to put himself on exhibition as a pianist-composer. This was in 1829, and he gave several concerts, startling the experts with the novelty of his music and his approach to the keyboard. Like all virtuosos of the day, Chopin concentrated on his own music. In his letters home he wrote modestly and even deprecatingly about his reception, though he did say that "the journalists have taken me to their hearts," and that when he improvised on some Polish tunes, "my spies on the floor of the house declare that people were dancing up and down in their seats." Among the reactions of the Viennese was one expressed again and again. How, they kept asking, could Chopin have learned so much in *Warsaw?*

Back in Poland, he had a puppy-love affair, composed steadily, went to the opera, was feted and pampered, and then decided to make his career in Paris. On November 2, 1830, he left Poland for good, with very little money and supreme confidence in his ability. He played in Vienna once again, made contacts, visited musicians, and listened to competing pianists. Sigismund Thalberg, the new pianistic lion, was one, and Chopin had left a devastating pen portrait of him: "Thalberg plays famously but he is not my man. He is younger than I, popular with the ladies, plays potpourris on themes from *Masaniello,* produces *piano* with pedal rather than the hand, takes tenths as easily as I take octaves, wears diamond shirt-studs." Chopin could have made a career in Vienna, but Paris was his goal, and he arrived there late in 1831, awed by the great men around him. Almost immediately he involved himself in one of the more delirious episodes of musical history.

Chopin, twenty-one years old, a genius with a perfectly formed and original pianistic style, heard Friedrich Kalkbrenner play and was overwhelmed. Kalkbrenner was undoubtedly a wonderful pianist, but he was a classicist of the old school. Preromantic pianists like Kalkbrenner, Moscheles, Hummel, and Clementi would run well-drilled notes up and down the keyboard, with little or no pedal. Using high finger strokes, playing from hand and wrist rather than elbow and arm, they had little idea of the coloristic resources of the piano (an instrument that by 1830 was very close in action and sonority to the concert grand of today). As a group, the classic pianists had no sympathy with romantic music. Kalkbrenner was probably the most proficient of the group. He was one of the most popular pianists of his day, and a conceited popinjay to boot. For some reason Chopin became entranced with his way of playing. He hastened to Kalkbrenner for lessons, and the great man gravely listened to his younger colleague. Then he told Chopin that he had talent, and that he would develop into a fine artist if he spent three years at the Kalkbrenner studio. Chopin promptly notified his family of the step he was going to take. His father and Elsner, both horrified, sent frantic letters from Poland. Fortunately, Chopin came to his senses and made his Paris debut on his own, early in 1832. Liszt and Mendelssohn were present, and the recital was the talk of Paris. After that there was no more nonsense about Kalkbrenner.

Chopin began to move in the highest circles. Through his titled Polish friends he became acquainted with the Rothschilds, and that alone was a passport. Almost immediately he had more pupils than he could handle— Princess this, Countess that. From that time the pattern of his life was set until he met George Sand. He traveled a little. In 1834 he visited Aachen and renewed his friendship with Mendelssohn; the following year he made a trip to Dresden and met Schumann, who idolized him. There was another meeting with Schumann in Leipzig in 1836. Chopin owed a good deal to the generous Schumann, whose review of the *Là ci darem* Variations had introduced him to Germany, and who, in the *Neue Zeitschrift für Musik,* was enthusiastically reviewing every Chopin piece that came his way. (Chopin had been, or pretended to be, vastly amused when, in 1831, he read Schumann's famous review of the Variations. "In the fifth bar of the adagio he declares that Don Giovanni kisses Zerlina on the D flat. Plater [Count Ludwik Plater, a friend in Paris] asked me yesterday where her D flat was, etc.!") But for the most part Chopin stayed in Paris, composing, socializing, making important friends. "I have found my way into the very best society," he wrote home with great satisfaction in 1833. "I have my place among ambassadors, princes, ministers. I don't know by what miracle it has come about, for I have not pushed myself forward. But today all that sort of thing is indispensable to me: those circles are supposed to be the fountain-head of taste. . . . I have five lessons to give today. You will imagine I am making a fortune—but my cabriolet and white gloves cost more than that, and without them I should not have *bon ton* . . ." Chopin was in a position to charge as much as thirty francs a lesson, an enormous sum in those days. He lived in luxury. He also had the quota of love affairs that any spirited and unattached male has. Before tuberculosis weakened him, his sexual habits were perfectly normal. He was neither effeminate nor chaste, though he kept his love affairs to himself and could be prudish.

Chopin's life changed when he was introduced to George Sand by Liszt. He was twenty-six and she was thirty-two years old, already a famous novelist, equally notorious for her independence and her disdain for the proprieties. Her real name was Aurore Dudevant, but she adopted the pen name of George Sand for her novels *Indiana* (1831) and *Lélia* (1833). Both books attracted wide attention for their attacks on conventional morality, especially marriage. She was a short, rather dumpy woman of sharp intelligence, and she was constantly in the public eye. For a time she wore men's clothes, smoked cigars, and had a succession of lovers. The woman who had been the mistress of Jules Sandeau, Prosper Mérimée, Alfred de Musset, Michel de Bourges, Pietro Pagello, and, most likely, Franz Liszt, did not lack experience. By her husband, Casimir Dudevant (they were separated in 1836), she had two children, Maurice and Solange. If a letter of one of Chopin's friends is to be believed, he was repelled at first by George Sand. The love affair progressed slowly, but by 1838 they were living together, and they spent the winter of 1838–39 in Majorca.

The trip had been intended as an idyll, and it turned out to be pure hell. The weather was bad, there was constant rain, the house in which they lived was eternally damp, and Chopin's weak lungs acted up. He all but died. As Sand admitted, the trip was a fiasco. She had to nurse him back to health, and brought him to Marseilles more dead than alive. Chopin sent a wry note to a friend: "The three most celebrated doctors on the island have seen me. One sniffed at what I spat, the second tapped where I spat, the third sounded me and listened as I spat. The first said I was dead, the second that I am dying, the third than I'm going to die." Despite his ill health, Chopin did some important work at Majorca. It was there that he finished his set of twenty-four préludes. One of them, the *Raindrop,* is supposed to be a musical interpretation of the rain dropping relentlessly on the villa in which the lovers were staying. But that title is a later invention, and nobody knows which prélude it is—even if the story were true, which it probably isn't. Some plump for No. 15 in D flat, with the reiterated notes in C sharp minor section, while others with equal insistence say that the *Raindrop* is really the B minor Prélude, with its regular, mournful left-hand pattern.

The relationship between Chopin and George Sand lasted until 1847. During the years of their liaison they were never far apart. In Paris they lived in adjoining houses. In the summer they went to Sand's house at Nohant, staying there about four months. It was at Nohant that Chopin composed his greatest music. Sand babied him, mothered him, looked after him. It seems that after a short time the relationship between them was platonic. Sand appeared content, and there is no evidence that she had any lovers during her long affair with Chopin. The breakup was sad. Sand's children, spoiled and undisciplined, were the agents. Maurice and Chopin did not get along very well, and his favorite was Solange. In 1847 she married a sculptor of dubious reputation named August Clésinger, after breaking off an engagement with a young man that both Chopin and Sand liked. Within the family there were fights and recriminations, lies and charges of bad faith. Solange actually accused her mother of having an affair with one of Maurice's friends. Sand did not want to have anything to do with Solange and her husband, while Chopin took Solange's side. When the smoke cleared away, Sand and Chopin were permanently estranged. During all this she carried herself with great dignity, and she cuts a better figure than Chopin, who seemed eager to believe the lies Solange poured into his ears. After the break they met once, by accident. Chopin was leaving a party, Sand entering. They had a few words in front of the door. "She asked me how I was," Chopin wrote to Solange. "I said I was well, and then I called for the concierge to open the door. I raised my hat and walked home to the Square d'Orléans." With these banalities they parted forever.

Chopin had only a year to live. He was already in a terminal stage, and was spitting blood. In 1848 he visited England at the urging of Jane Stirling, a friend and pupil. She was a very rich maiden lady from Scotland who probably was in love with Chopin. He thought he had nothing to lose by accepting her invitation. The Revolution of 1848 had broken out in Paris and Chopin's pupils had fled, leaving him without a steady source of income. So he dragged himself to England and Scotland. He was in dreadful shape, and was so weak that he had to be carried to his bedroom and undressed by his valet. In England he played for the best society, observed the people and their customs, and hated every bit of it. His letters to Paris give the picture of a man exasperated beyond endurance. He describes a party in his honor given by a titled Scots lady: "After I had played, and other Scottish ladies had sung various songs, they brought a sort of accordion and she [his hostess], with the utmost gravity, began to play the most horrible tunes on it. But what can you expect? It seems to me that every one of these creatures is crazy. . . . The ones who know my compositions ask 'Play me your *Second Sigh* [the Nocturne in G] . . . I love your bells.' And every comment ends with the words: 'Leik Water,' meaning that the music flows like water. I have never yet played to an Englishwoman without her saying: 'Leik Water!!' They all look at their hands and play wrong notes most soulfully. What a queer lot! God have pity on them."

Back in Paris, away from the suffocating clutches of Miss Stirling, Chopin did almost no work, waiting for the end. He was mentally depressed. "I have not yet begun to play, and I cannot compose. God knows what sort of fodder I shall have to live on before long." He was helped by Miss Stirling and her sister who, learning of Chopin's desperate condition, sent him an anonymous gift of 25,000 francs. His sister Louise came from Warsaw to nurse him during his final illness. George Sand sent Louise a letter that she would like to see Frédéric before it was too late. Louise did not answer. It was not George Sand but Solange Clésinger who was at Chopin's side when he died on the morning of October 17, 1849. Also at the bedside were Louise and Princess Marcelline Czartoryska, a friend of the family. In later years there were legends about Chopin's last hours, and wonderfully romantic stories about this or that countess singing sad songs while he died.

Chopin had no false modesty about himself and his work. As early as

1831 he was writing about his "perhaps too audacious but noble wish and intention to create for myself a new world." He did precisely that. As a pianist he created a style that dominated the entire second half of the nineteenth century and was not substantially changed until Debussy and Prokofiev came along. It was a style that broke sharply from everything that went before it. For the first time the piano became a *total* instrument: a singing instrument, an instrument of infinite color, poetry, and nuance, a heroic instrument, an intimate instrument. Schumann's piano music, wonderful as it is, original as it is, sounds thick by comparison. Chopin's music flowed naturally out of his own way of playing the piano, and as a pianist he was light-years ahead of Schumann, exploiting the instrument in an idiomatic and completely modern manner. In any case, the piano music of Schumann exerted relatively little influence in its day, whereas the new ideas about pedaling, fingering, rhythm, and coloristic resource that Chopin invented were immediately taken up by every one of the younger pianists.

Many professionals of the day could not follow him. Moscheles was not the only one who was perplexed. Even so fine a musical mind as Mendelssohn's was disturbed at first. Mendelssohn, who had been trained by Moscheles in a classic style—hands close to the keyboard, little pedal, a minimum of rubato or tempo change—had to become seasoned to Chopin by exposure before he was won over. But Mendelssohn surrendered, as did everybody else. "There is," Mendelssohn wrote, "something entirely original in his piano playing and it is at the same time so masterly that he may be called a perfect virtuoso. . . . He produces new effects, like Paganini on the violin, and accomplishes things nobody could formerly have thought practicable."

Even the great Liszt was not too proud to learn from Chopin. Between the two was an uneasy friendship. They saw a great deal of each other, but there may have been an unconscious hostility. Chopin envied Liszt his strength, his extroversion, his virility, his power to hypnotize large audiences. "Liszt is playing my études," he wrote to Stephen Heller, "and transporting me outside of my respectable thoughts. I should like to steal from him the way to play my own études." But there was an element of vulgarity and fakery to Liszt that repelled Chopin. Occasionally Chopin burst into spitefulness, as in a letter to Jules Fontana: "One of these days he'll be a member of parliament or perhaps even the King of Abyssinia or the Congo —but as regards the themes from his compositions, well, they will be buried in the newspapers."

Liszt, on the other hand, sincerely admired Chopin's pianism and adopted many of his ideas. Chopin showed that the piano could be much more than a virtuoso instrument even in virtuoso music; and, more important, Chopin's music showed that even the wildest flights of virtuosity could have a musical meaning. Chopin's filigree and bravura, in his mature works, never are merely show-off. He introduced the concept of functional ornamentation. Up to the time he met Chopin, Liszt was primarily a banger. After exposure to Chopin's playing and music, he tried to modify his bravura into a more poetic style. But could Liszt have felt a little uncomfortable in Chopin's company? The elegant Pole was an aristocrat, while there was something about Liszt that made him a social climber rather than a natural inhabitant of the great salons. He dressed too flashily, spoke a little too loudly, bragged too much, could not hold his liquor as a gentleman should. Definitely he did not have *bon ton*. Occasionally the sparks flew between him and Chopin. Liszt, who was always "improving" somebody else's music, once played a Chopin nocturne, adding all kinds of embellishments. Chopin, according to an anecdote that appears in Josef Nowakowski's study, snapped at Liszt, telling him to play the music as written or not play it at all. But the two greatest pianists of their time nevertheless did continue to see each other, and as late as 1848 Chopin was referring to "my friend Liszt."

Two things about Chopin's piano style—and by extension, as always, his music—are of extreme importance: his ideas about rubato, and his classic bent. Rubato, which had been the subject of much discussion by performers as far back as Mozart and C. P. E. Bach, is a kind of displacement in which the rhythm is delicately altered but never the idea of the basic meter. It gives variety and added interest to a phrase. Every sensitive musician uses it; the device is equivalent to variation of line in a drawing by a master. Chopin, with his Polish dance heritage, used such a pronounced rubato that listeners unaccustomed to it were taken aback. Meyerbeer, himself a fine pianist, was convinced that Chopin played two-four instead of three-four in his mazurkas. Charles Hallé, another fine pianist, noted that a remarkable feature of Chopin's playing "was the entire freedom with which he treated the rhythm, but which appeared so natural that for years it had never struck me." Hallé also insisted that Chopin in some of his mazurkas played in duple rather than triple time.

Yet despite his romantic rubato and his extremely romantic music, Chopin had a strong classic streak in him. He always had a metronome on his piano, insisted that his pupils play in strict time, gave them plenty of Bach and Mozart, and went into a tantrum when rhythmic liberties were taken. His own playing was pure, and he insisted on purity from his pupils. That, and complete flexibility plus a singing line. "Yesterday we heard Henri Herz," wrote Joseph Filtsch to his parents. "His execution is elegant, agreeable and coquettish, but without subtlety. What a difference between him and Chopin, whose fingers sing and bring tears to your eyes, making anybody who is sensitive tremble with emotion. His delicate and slender hands cover wide stretches and skips with a fabulous lightness, and his finger agility is so marvelous that I am ready to believe the amusing story that he has been seen to put his foot around his neck! Moreover, it is thanks to this flexibility that he can play black notes with his thumb, or a whole series of notes with two fingers only, passing the longer finger over the shorter and sliding from one note to another." These were practices condemned by the classic teachers. Black notes were not to be played with the thumb. Filtsch goes on to describe Chopin's rubato. "To his pupils he says: 'Let your left hand be your conductor and keep strict time.' And so his right hand, now hesitant, now impatient, is nevertheless constrained to follow this great rule and never weaken the rhythm of the left hand." (Mozart had said almost the exact same thing over a half-century previously.) Joseph Filtsch, incidentally, was a pianist who had come from Hungary with his younger brother Karl to study with Chopin. Karl was enormously gifted and was by far the best pupil Chopin ever had. Liszt heard him and said that when the youngster started playing in public, then he, Liszt, would shut up shop. Poor Karl died at the age of fifteen.

As a composer, Chopin has survived all changes of fashion and is as popular today as he ever was. Almost everything he composed is in the active repertoire. Can this be said of many other composers? He found his style very early—before he left Poland for Paris, in fact. In later years a greater depth was to enter his music, but very little in the way of technique, harmonic ideas, or melody. After the Études of Op. 10, many of which had been completed before his arrival in Paris, there was no substantial change. He also had worked out the basic style of his mazurkas and nocturnes in Poland. The nocturnes were derived from John Field's compositions. Chopin took the form of the Field nocturnes and refined it into something much more aristocratic, with a more interesting arpeggiated bass and melodies resembling the long-breathed cantilenas that can be found in Italian bel canto opera. If there was one thing Chopin loved, it was beautiful singing, and many of his melodic ideas came from the great vocal stylists of the day.

Another aspect of his musical style was Polish nationalism, as represented by the mazurkas and polonaises. To Europe, these were strange and exotic. Chopin was the first of the great nationalists. The great nationalists do not copy folk melodies. They do not have to. The folk tradition is part of their background, their racial subconscious. It emerges as an evocation of homeland, even if (as in the case of so many nationalists) no actual folk-tune quotations are used. In his mazurkas and polonaises, Chopin echoed the melodies with which he had grown up. In his other music he was much more a cosmopolitan, though here and there, as in the middle section of the B minor Scherzo, a folk tune can make its appearance.

Chopin was an "absolute" composer, and never gave anything but abstract titles to his music. In this he was different from the other romantics. Even the classicist Mendelssohn supplied descriptive titles to some of his *Songs Without Words* and other pieces. Chopin, never. *Black Key* Étude, *Winter Wind* Étude, *Little Jew* Mazurka, *Raindrop* Prélude, *Military* Polonaise—all these are romantic inventions, generally supplied by publishers. In none of Chopin's music are there any programmatic implications, though it is claimed that the four ballades were inspired by poems by Adam Mickiewicz, the Polish patriot. If this is true, Chopin was remarkably quiet about it. The supposed Mickiewicz background to the ballades is probably another romantic invention. The only names Chopin gave to the overwhelming majority of his music (the Polish songs, of course, excepted) were generic: waltz, mazurka, étude, polonaise, nocturne, scherzo, prélude, fantasy, impromptu, ballade, variations, sonata, concerto.

In his youth his music was graceful, exuberant, inventive, full of brilliance, marked by a decided predilection for virtuosity. Like all composers up to then, Chopin composed his music as vehicles for public performance, and naturally he tailored it to his own pianistic specifications. There are the two concertos, the *Là ci darem la mano* Variations for piano and orchestra, the early études, the *Krakoviak* for piano and orchestra (seldom played, but it is a haunting work). All are marked by an extension of piano technique as it was then known. Schumann, working independently in Germany, was writing piano music in which the *music* was the thing. Chopin turned out music in which there was more of a balance between music and the piano as thing-unto-itself. His music is much more idiomatic than Schumann's in terms of the keyboard. It fits the hand, where Schumann often is awkward. It is often breath-taking music, sparkling and coruscating, taking complicated figurations and breaking them up or spreading them over the keyboard so that the notes scatter like pinpoints of flame.

Now, there were composers around who could come near matching Chopin in mere technical display. Moscheles and Kalkbrenner were among them, and so was the young Liszt. What immediately set Chopin's music off and made it different was a combination of melodic and harmonic resource of unprecedented charm and richness. Few composers have had Chopin's ear, his gift for modulation, his taste in combining pure virtuosity with an aristocratic and poetic kind of melody. That could be heard from the beginning, and he never changed his approach. But as he grew older his forms became tighter. There was less padding, and every note had a point. The music could be difficult, but it also was condensed and under perfect control. It had dissonances, including harsh seconds and ninths, that sounded intolerable as the classic pianists played them, and the new generation of pianists had to learn how to handle them, how to make them glint and resolve through a skillful use of the pedal. Those chromatic and daring harmonies were a seminal influence on nineteenth-century musical thinking. Chopin as a harmonist influenced Wagner and even later composers. The *Barcarolle* actually anticipated Debussy, with its free-floating pedal effects and near-impressionist harmonies. The delicate, sickly Polish composer put a mighty hand on the future of music.

Delicate and sickly; but that does not mean his music lacks power. The scherzos and ballades, the F minor Fantasy, the last polonaises (especially the heroic one in F sharp minor, an even more thrilling and masterly work than the popular A flat Polonaise), the last two sonatas (he composed three, but the C minor is a student work no longer in the repertoire), all contain majestic utterances. These are clothed in forms perfectly appropriate to the material, forms that were dictated by the music. Except in the sonatas, he did not try to impose form on idea. Lyric and spontaneous as his music often sounds, it was the product of much work and thought. He did not rush his ideas to paper, as Mozart and Schubert so often did. Chopin was a slow worker who would not let a piece of music be published until he was satisfied that it was as jeweled, as flawless, as logical as he could make it. His initial ideas came fast, but working them into the appropriate form could be excruciating. Many of his compositions resulted from improvisations, and Filtsch has described the way Chopin worked: "The other day [this was in March, 1842] I heard Chopin improvise at George Sand's house. It is marvellous to hear Chopin compose in this way. His inspiration is so immediate and complete that he plays without hesitation as if it had to be thus. But when it comes to writing it down and recapturing the original thought in all its details, he spends days of nervous strain and almost frightening desperation. He alters and retouches the same phrases incessantly, and walks up and down like a madman." Even when a work was published, Chopin was not satisfied. He would make changes whenever he could, and in many of his works there are differences between the French and German editions, some of them significant.

His music is all of a piece. Whether tiny, as in the Prélude in C sharp minor of Op. 28, which lasts no more than twenty seconds (is there a shorter piece in the entire literature?), or extended, as in the B minor Sonata, it is highly idiosyncratic music characterized by graceful, often melancholy, melodies and a richness of harmonic texture almost Franckian in its chromaticism. But it is not a cloying kind of chromaticism. Chopin's mind was too precise to allow color to dominate form. It is for the most part a highly precise, condensed form of music in some of which a single idea is exploited. The single-idea aspect of Chopin comes in the études, preludes, mazurkas, and nocturnes, though in the longer mazurkas and nocturnes subsidiary ideas make their appearance. The works in larger form—the scherzos, ballades, F minor Fantasy—are Chopin's own solution of the problem of sonata form. Classic sonata form did not interest him very much. In the B minor Sonata he dutifully goes through the motions of exposition, development and recapitulation, achieving a copybook form that just passes. What saves the sonata, and has made it so popular, is the wealth of its ideas and the freedom with which it moves once the first movement is past. The earlier B flat minor Sonata, the one with the *Funeral March,* is completely alien to the concept of the classic sonata, and even so dedicated an admirer as Schumann threw up his hands. This is not a sonata, he said. Chopin has merely assembled for his four movements "four of his wildest children." Ironically enough, the first movement happens to be Chopin's most successful experiment with sonata form. It is tidy, well organized, and consistent all the way through. After that movement, Chopin and sonata part company. Most puzzling of all is the finale, a sotto-voce, murmuring mystery in fast unison scale passages that lasts no more than a minute and a half. It could have been one of the préludes, and for all we know was originally intended as one. The Prélude in E flat minor (No. 14) is close enough in mood, layout, and technique to be a sister of the finale of the B flat minor. Both were composed about the same time. The B flat minor Sonata dates from 1839, and the Préludes between 1836 and 1839.

Toward the end of his life Chopin began to introduce polyphonic textures into his music. There always had been a classic strain in this most romantic of composers, classic in the sense that his forms were tightly organized, classic in their elegant workmanship, classic in that the works of his maturity avoided empty passagework. No matter how effective, glittering, and even spectacular the writing may be (as in the last section of the Impromptu in F sharp major or the cascading figurations of the Scherzo in C sharp minor), each note has an expressive or coloristic meaning that far transcends mere display. Never is it vulgar, never is it effect for effect's sake. There are other things in Chopin's music that suggest classicism and, in particular, his beloved Bach. The twenty-four Préludes follow the idea of the *Well-Tempered Clavier,* going through all the major and minor keys in the circle of fifths. (Hummel had done the same, also in a series of tiny préludes composed at least fifteen years before Chopin's.) Could the very first Prélude by Chopin, the C major, be an implied compliment to the C major Prelude that opens Bach's great series? If Chopin's is played at a very slow tempo, there is a startling relationship between the two. And in the Études Chopin also started an interrelated key scheme, but never carried it out. Later, as in the F minor Ballade or the ending of the Mazurka in C sharp minor (Op. 63, No. 3), are passages in canonic imitation. Polyphonic writing occurs in many of Chopin's late works. To Chopin, fugue was the ultimate in musical logic, and he said as much to Delacroix, who dutifully noted Chopin's comments in his diary: "To know fugue deeply is to be acquainted with the ele-

ment of all reason and consistency in music." This is a side of Chopin unknown to many. He composed only one known fugue; it is a student work
and not in the repertoire.

Once Chopin had established himself, there was remarkably little criticism of his music. It was accepted as the work of a master, and even such
doubters as Ludwig Rellstab, the critic from Berlin, and James William
Davison, the pundit from London, eventually came around. As Liszt wrote
in 1841, "This exquisite, lofty and eminently aristocratic celebrity remains
unattacked. A complete silence of criticism already reigns about him, as if
posterity already had come." Liszt was only stating a fact. Certainly the informed men of the day—Liszt, Mendelssohn, Schumann, Berlioz—knew
that Chopin was an immortal; that within his self-imposed limitation he
was perfection itself. To be a great pianist in the nineteenth century, it was
necessary to be a great Chopin pianist. This was even true in the antiromantic days after World War I. It is less true today, now that romantic performance practice is almost a lost art. Yet even today, Chopin's music figures as
strongly on piano recitals as the work of any other composer, and certainly
much more than the music of the other romantics. Other composers have
had their ups and downs. Chopin goes steadily along, and the piano literature would be inconceivable without him. He seems impervious to changing
tastes.

Virtuoso, Charlatan—and Prophet

FRANZ LISZT

If Chopin was the pianist's pianist, Franz Liszt was the public's pianist—the showman, the Hero, the one who made inarticulate apes of his audiences. He had everything in his favor—good looks, magnetism, power, a colossal technique, an unprecedented sonority, and the kind of opportunism (at least in his early years) that could cater to the public in the most cynical manner. He had the Aura. Before Liszt, pianists kept their hands close to the keyboard, playing from wrist and finger rather than arm or shoulder. But not after Liszt. He established once and for all the genre of the bravura pianist, the pianist who would haughtily come out, cow the audience, lift hands high, and assault the instrument. Even musicians who hated everything he represented, the "pure" musicians, could not but be impressed. Mendelssohn, who was the South Pole to Liszt's North, had to admit that Liszt was unparalleled, that he could play with "a degree of virtuosity and complete finger independence and a thoroughly musical feeling that can scarcely be equaled. In a word, I have heard no performer whose musical perceptions so extend to the very tips of his fingers." Contemporary pianists, such as Charles Hallé, heard Liszt and were in despair. They could not possibly begin to compete with that combination of brilliance and sheer aura. Clara Wieck, no mean technician herself, was completely taken aback because "Liszt played at sight what we toil over and at the end get nowhere with."

It was as a pianist that Liszt made his initial impact on Europe. Later he became everything—composer, conductor, critic, littérateur, Don Juan, abbé, teacher, symbol, and, at the end, The Grand Old Man of Music. He was born on October 22, 1811, about the same time as the other early romantics, but he far outlived them all. Mendelssohn died in 1847, Chopin in 1849, Schumann in 1856, Berlioz in 1869. Liszt died on July 31, 1886, the last of the great musicians who had been a close friend of the early heroes, the man who had met Beethoven and had actually (so it was believed) been kissed by the lips of the Immortal. Franz Liszt: a great man, a complicated man, a man all things to all men. He had genius, yet there was a great deal of the charlatan about him. He was pulled to the church, yet even after becoming an abbé continued the sexual escapades that were the talk of Europe. He had a fine musical mind, one of the strongest in history, yet in his recitals he could not keep from tampering with other men's music, cheapening even Beethoven by added effects. He could be kind and generous, yet could turn around and be arrogant and capricious. He was vain and needed constant adulation, yet he could be genuinely humble in the presence of a genius such as Wagner. Yes, he was all things to all men, and as a result not many have been able to see him whole. Perhaps Liszt himself never could. To many he was the Renaissance Man of music. His admirers could see only his good points. To others he was all tinsel and claptrap—" a talented humbug," as the conductor Hermann Levi scornfully said. His enemies could see only his bad points.

It would take volumes to sift fact from fancy, and it would take a battery of psychiatrists to attempt an explanation of Liszt's motivations. But the general outlines are clear enough. Born in Raiding, Hungary, he was playing the piano very well at the age of seven, composing at eight, making concert appearances at nine, studying with Czerny and Salieri in Vienna at ten. On all of these trips he was accompanied by his father. Adam Liszt, a steward in the service of the Esterházy family, was a skilled musical amateur who fully realized the enormous talent of his son. So did a group of Hungarian noblemen, who subsidized the studies of young Franz. Musical Europe fully endorsed their high opinion of the young genius. The boy startled audiences wherever he appeared. Only a few years after his work with Czerny in Vienna he was a veteran of the concert stage, having made his debut in Paris and London, and having toured Europe. At the age of sixteen he was experiencing doubts and nervous exhaustion, and was talking of quitting everything and joining the church. Throughout his life he was always talking about joining the church; that was part of the romantic posture. Of course it was mostly talk. Even when Liszt did join, late in life, he had the best of both worlds, and probably never took his religion very seriously. He only made a great show of taking it seriously.

Not until the age of nineteen did he more or less settle down. He made Paris his headquarters in 1827, after the death of his father, and worked to remedy gaps in his education. Like most Wunderkinder, he had had only a sketchy general education, and he had an immense amount of study and reading to do once he decided to catch up. Liszt eventually was to pass as a cultured man, and that was a triumph of his industry, for he did it all by himself. "My mind and fingers," he wrote in 1832, "have worked like the damned. Homer, the Bible, Plato, Locke, Lamartine, Chateaubriand, Beethoven, Bach, Hummel, Mozart, Weber are all around me. I study them, I devour them with fury." He moved in intellectual circles, welcome because of his genius and good looks. He mowed down the nubile young ladies of Paris. And he heard the three musicians who so decisively influenced his development.

Berlioz was the first. From Berlioz, Liszt discovered the meaning of color, and also the meaning of Thinking Big. The Berlioz approach was congenial to Liszt. It introduced him to the visionary kind of romanticism, its stirrings and yearnings, its subjectivity and love of the monumental. Liszt tried to do on the piano what Berlioz did with the orchestra, and even transcribed for solo piano several major orchestral works of Berlioz. Among them was the *Symphonie fantastique.* He actually played it in concert, and one of his tricks was to follow an orchestral performance of the *Fantastique* with his piano version of the *Marche au supplice,* the fourth movement, with an effect (wrote Hallé) "surpassing even that of the full orchestra and creating an indescribable furor." Liszt was the first to *orchestrate* on the piano, achieving the wildest of dynamic extremes, the maximum of color, and using the entire compass of the keyboard in a pile-up of sonorities. For all this he was in debt to Berlioz.

The second influence was Paganini. Here the impact was purely instrumental rather than aesthetic or philosophical. In 1831 Liszt heard Paganini for the first time, listened carefully, and was thunderstruck. He immediately decided to transfer Paganini's effects to the piano. There were two goals to this quest: transcendental technique and showmanship. One of the first things he did was to transcribe for the piano six of the Paganini *Caprices* for solo violin, heaping difficulty upon difficulty. Probably nobody but Liszt himself could play them at the time, and very few can today. Liszt's *Paganini Études* are an amazing pianistic equivalent of the original violin pieces. In addition the music, played as only Liszt could play it, drove audiences to a wild excitement comparable to that exerted by Paganini himself.

Finally, Liszt heard Chopin, and realized that there was poetry as well as bravura to piano playing, that the instrument was capable of subtle washes of color as well as of heroic storms, that decoration could be functional to the musical ground plan rather than flashy and vulgar excrescences.

Thus when Liszt resumed his European tours, it was as a finished artist, and he swept all before him. His recitals were a series of triumphs. Women were especially attracted to his concerts, as they later were to Paderewski's, and there were scenes of actual frenzy in which impressionable ladies fainted or would fight over the gloves he negligently tossed on the stage. Heinrich Heine, attempting to describe the phenomenon, spoke of "magnetism and electricity; of contagion in a sultry hall filled with innumerable wax lights and some hundred perfumed and perspiring people; of histrionic epilepsy; of the phenomenon of tickling; of musical cantharides; and other unmentionable matters." Liszt well knew the impression he was making. Everything was calculated. That included his programs, which seldom had much meat on them. In his own studio he played everything. He probably had the entire literature, as it was then known, committed to memory. But at his big public concerts he would play sure-fire, attention-getting music, for the most part. Generally the music was his own. He would enter the stage, clanking with decorations suspended on chains. His hair was down to his shoulders. He would survey the audience and slowly remove his gloves, tossing them to the floor. Until 1839 he followed the established format for concerts, which meant that he shared the time with other artists or an orchestra, and he would be heard only for part of the program. A typical Liszt contribution to one of his recitals would be his transcription of Rossini's *William Tell* Overture, his fantasy on Mozart's *Don Giovanni,* his transcriptions of Schubert's *Erlkönig* and Beethoven's *Adelaide,* and his *Galop chromatique.* This was the actual program he once played in St. Petersburg.

Naturally it would have had to be Liszt, that great egomaniac, who in 1839 invented the solo recital as it is known today. Why should he share a program with anybody else? At first he called his purely solo appearances "soliloquies," and he described them to the Princess Belgiojoso: ". . . these tiresome *musical soliloquies* (I do not know what other name to give these inventions of mine) with which I contrive to gratify the Romans, and which I am quite capable of importing to Paris, so unbounded does my impudence become! Imagine that, wearied with warfare, not being able to put together a program that would have common sense, I have ventured to give a series of concerts all by myself, affecting the Louis XIV style and saying cavalierly to the public, *le concert, c'est moi.*" Later the soliloquies began to be called recitals, and the term aroused great merriment in England. "What does he mean? How can one *recite* upon the piano?"

If Liszt came early to maturity as a pianist, most likely the greatest pianist the world has ever known, he was somewhat late in his development as a composer. His early music no longer has any interest. Most of it is empty virtuoso material. He did compose an opera, *Don Sancho,* at the age of fourteen. That too has been forgotten. From 1829 to 1834 he was busy transcribing various material—Berlioz orchestral works, the Beethoven symphonies—or making operatic paraphrases. Not until 1835 did he start the series of works that were to remain in the repertoire. The four years after 1835 are the years of the *Transcendental Études,* the *Paganini Études,* the first two books of the *Années de Pelérinage,* the arrangements of Schubert songs, the series of Bach organ works transcribed for piano. After 1840 came many of the Hungarian Rhapsodies, the large-scale operatic paraphrases, and a remarkable series of songs that are seldom sung today but should be.

In 1847 Liszt stopped being a "professional" pianist—that is, touring and giving concerts for money. Up to that time his life had been a hectic musical and emotional outburst, and it had included a love affair that had all Europe wagging its head in disapproval (a disapproval perhaps tinged with secret envy). Liszt had met the Countess d'Agoult in 1834, and the following year she deserted her husband and ran off with Liszt to Switzerland. Three children resulted from the union. Two died young, but Cosima, born in 1837, later married Liszt's first great pupil, Hans von Bülow, and then deserted *him* for Wagner. She was a chip off the old block and, like her father, she enjoyed a long life, dying in 1930 at the age of ninety-three.

The Countess d'Agoult had literary aspirations, and it was due to her urging—and, most likely, with the assistance of her editing and rewriting—that Liszt started writing criticism and essays. He and the countess settled in Geneva, where he taught, and it was the headquarters from which he set out on tour after tour. In 1842 he was appointed Grand Ducal Director of Music Extraordinary at the Weimar court, but did not take up serious duties there until 1848. In the meantime, his relations with the countess were cooling, and they separated in 1844. She returned to Paris and, under the pen name of Daniel Stern, wrote a novel named *Nélida*. Liszt cuts a pretty poor figure in it.

On his last tour as a virtuoso, Liszt played in Russia. In Kiev he met the Princess Carolyne Sayn-Wittgenstein. He was thirty-six years old. She was twenty-eight, the daughter of a Polish landowner, and had been married at the age of seventeen to Prince Nicolas of Sayn-Wittgenstein. After a few years they separated, and she lived alone on the estate in Kiev. Not very attractive physically, she was something of a religious fanatic, strong-minded and rather masculine. But she *was* a princess, if only by marriage, had immense wealth, and Liszt made of her still another of his conquests. She was not going to let him go. She joined him at Weimar in 1849, scandalizing the court. Try as she could, she could never get a divorce. In any case, there was very little sexual relationship between Liszt and her after a few years. She was one of those women who wants to guide a man's mind, not his body, and she took Liszt in hand. A writer herself, and a pompous, inferior one, she probably wrote a good part of the material that appeared under Liszt's name. Thanks to her, and her ideas about literary style, Liszt's biography of Chopin, which could have been a primary source about the man and his piano playing, degenerated into a series of vague, purple-prose passages in which Chopin plays a minor role. History has good reason to dislike Carolyne Sayn-Wittgenstein. In the latter years of her life she lived in Rome, working on her great project, a series of books named *Causes intérieures de la faiblessse extérieure de l'Eglise* ("Interior Causes of the Exterior Weakness of the Church"). It was published in twenty-four volumes, most of the volumes over 1,000 pages each. In her room were a printing press, fourteen busts of Liszt, and hundreds of strong cigars made especially for her. The tobacco, so ran the report, was dipped in iron filings to make it stronger.

At Weimer, Liszt plunged into work and made the little city the headquarters of the progressive musical movement. He presented the music of Wagner, Berlioz, Schumann, and such composers of the oncoming school as Raff, Cornelius, and Verdi. Pianists from all over Europe flocked to Weimar to study with him. The most outstanding was Karl Tausig, who died in 1871 at the age of thirty. Tausig, from all accounts, was a stupendous pianist who could do anything Liszt could do, though without Liszt's flair. It was at Weimar, too, that Liszt started conducting. The importance of Liszt as a conductor has not been generally realized. He brought to the podium many of the characteristics of his piano playing. It was free conducting that he represented. Rather than confining himself to the bar line and conducting with regular accents, as so many conductors did and still do, Liszt looked for metrical pliancy, drama, and color. His highly unorthodox beat outlined the rise and fall of a phrase rather than coming down heavily on the first beat of the bar. "We are pilots and not mechanics," he would say. Wagner was another conductor more interested in phrase than accent, and Wagner, like Liszt, took great liberty in matters of tempo. There was no *one* tempo when Liszt or Wagner conducted; there was a series of fluctuating tempos linked by an over-all conception. The chronology is hard to establish, and it is impossible to determine how much Liszt influenced Wagner as a conductor, and how much Wagner influenced Liszt. The two were constantly leaning on each other. But Liszt was there first, as a pianist, and his free ideas about interpretation were carried over into his conducting. The chances are that Liszt, as in so many things, influenced Wagner more than Wagner influenced Liszt.

Because of a hostile demonstration at the premiere of *The Barber of Baghdad* by Peter Cornelius, in 1858, Liszt resigned his position at Weimar. At least, that was the reason he gave. Liszt was no longer happy at Weimar. His first employer, the Grand Duke Charles Frederick, had given him complete authority and a generous budget. But Charles Frederick died in 1853 and his successor, the Grand Duke Charles Alexander, showed little interest in music. Nor was the Grand Duke happy with the expense of the orchestra and opera house. Liszt's position was not improved by the presence of his mistress. When the Cornelius opera was booed, Liszt knew that the demonstration was as much directed against himself as against the composer.

But although Liszt relinquished his duties as director of music, he retained close ties with Weimar. For the rest of his life he established a routine that had him alternating between Rome, Budapest, and Weimar, but also turning up anywhere and everywhere in Europe to lend his services to a good cause. Always he was followed by pupils and adoring young ladies. He took four minor church orders in 1865 and henceforth wore a cassock and was addressed as the Abbé Liszt. "Mephistopheles in a cassock," was one description. He composed steadily, he taught up to the last year of his life, he moved among royalty as royalty.

From the beginning of his career he had insisted on being accepted as an equal by the aristocracy. When young, he had played in the great salons and noted that "artists of the first rank, such as Moscheles, Rubini, Lafont, Pasta, Malibran and others are forced to enter by the service stairs." Liszt would have none of that. If he could not mingle on equal terms with the guests, whoever they were, he would not play. In the course of his career he insulted nobles and even kings when their manners were rude while he was playing. He was Liszt, the only one of his kind, and royalty had to bow to his will. As Liszt grew older, he actually acted like royalty and expected the perquisites. But once homage and adulation were given—Liszt unfortunately was a snob—he could be sweet and generous, and there were very few talents who crossed his path and did not go away rejoicing. Young composers from all over Europe and even the United States brought him their music. He would go through it with unfailing politeness, encouraging such composers as Grieg, Smetana, Borodin, Rimsky-Korsakov, Balakirev, Mac-Dowell, and, for a while, even Brahms. That flirtation with Brahms, who visited Weimar in 1853, did not last long. Brahms represented the "pure" classical school that stood for the old forms of symphony and the sonata principle. Liszt and his group stood for free forms, romantic excess, and a kind of music triggered by extramusical associations. In 1860 Brahms, Joachim, and several others signed a proclamation against the Music of the Future represented by the Weimar school. Brahms was to emerge as the leader of the opposition, the Keeper of the Faith, but history was not on his side. He and his followers, such as Max Reger, had very little impact upon twentieth-century music, whereas Liszt and Wagner led directly into Strauss, Mahler, the young Arnold Schoenberg, and, eventually, the twelve-tone school and its derivations.

As a piano teacher, too, Liszt's influence was to extend far. He turned out two generations of epigones, all of whom spread the style and the teachings of the master all over the world. After von Bülow and Tausig there were such pianistic giants as Sophie Menter, Eugene d'Albert, Moritz Rosenthal, Alfred Reisenauer, Alexander Siloti, Arthur Friedheim, Frederic Lamond, Rafael Joseffy, Emil von Sauer, and Bernhard Stavenhagen—all Liszt products, and most of them teachers who passed on the Liszt tradition. There were, literally, hundreds of others, all trained by Liszt, all representing a now-departed school of romantic pianism.

During the first Weimar period, 1848 to 1858, Liszt was at his creative peak. With an orchestra at his disposal, he started a new phase of composition. At first he had his scores orchestrated for him by August Conradi, Joachim Raff, and other talented young composers in his circle. By 1854 he was confident enough to do his own orchestration. From this period come the twelve symphonic poems, a new musical form invented by Liszt. These are examples of program music, in one movement, inspired by an external stimulus—a poem, a play, a painting, anything. The name of the symphonic poem and, often, a literary excerpt published in the score, supply the clue: *Les Préludes, Orpheus, Hamlet, Mazeppa.* The music specifically illustrates the program; though it may be as strictly organized in its way as a sonata is in its. After Liszt set the example, the vogue of writing symphonic poems swept Europe. Another Liszt contribution was a concept that involves thematic transformation. In such works as the massive one-movement B minor Sonata, or the E flat Piano Concerto, a theme is made to do multiple duty. It may be altered to turn up as a second subject, it may later serve in still another form as the subject for a finale, but it remains recognizably the same theme throughout. Liszt was very inventive in this kind of thematic juggling, and it often served as a formal principle with him, giving his music its own kind of unity without falling back on old forms. Liszt and the classic style had nothing to do with each other, ever. Even Chopin, in his three sonatas and the Cello Sonata, made a bow toward the old sonata principle. Liszt never did. He always invented his own forms.

His tremendous operatic paraphrases for solo piano were also something new. Composers like Herz and Hünten made a good living by filling the demand for operatic paraphrases. They would write a flashy introduction—difficult, but not too difficult for the young ladies who were their customers—and then introduce the theme of the work, following it with a series of standard and uninventive variations, ending with a coda full of scales and arpeggios. Compared to these, Liszt's paraphrases and fantasies on operas are as a bolt of lightning against the flicker of a candle. He threw themes together in a contrapuntal mélange, he changed harmonies, he exploited to the utmost every technical resource of his pianistic genius. The result is music for supervirtuosos only: original compositions (whatever the source) on a heroic and even explosive scale. Music like this has fallen into disfavor during the twentieth century, though recently there have been signs that it is beginning to edge back. The music does contain great ingenuity, and it does bring to life as no other music a specific period in musical history, a period in which the virtuoso was king and virtuosity an end in itself.

The Weimar period also brought forth such ambitious works as the *Faust* Symphony, the *Dante* Symphony, the astounding *Totentanz* for piano and orchestra, a large amount of organ and religious music, and many extended works for solo piano, including an intense, fascinating set of variations on a theme from Bach's cantata *Weinen, Klagen, Sorgen, Sagen*. All of this music is as hard to describe as the man himself, for it is a combination of nobility and sentimentality, poetry and vulgar effect. But one thing the music of his maturity uniformly has, and that is a harmonic outlook of the most original, daring, and even extreme order. Underneath all the effects, underneath the emphasis on manner over matter, is a startlingly unusual musical mind. Liszt's chromaticism could be more extreme even than Chopin's, and it was to lead directly into Wagner. There is a Liszt song, *Ich möchte hingehn*, that contains the famous *Tristan* chords note for note, with one slight change (D natural in the very first chord instead of D sharp). It was composed in 1845, long before Wagner had started thinking of *Tristan und Isolde*. One story, possibly apocryphal, has Liszt and Wagner sitting in a box as the *Tristan* Prelude starts. "That's *your* chord, Papa," Wagner says. To which Liszt answers, sourly, "At least, now it will be heard." Wagner admitted his debt to Liszt. "Since my acquaintance with Liszt's compositions," he wrote in 1859, "my treatment of harmony has become very different from what it was." Liszt's bold strokes and frequent dissonances were copied by young composers everywhere, and between Liszt and Chopin, a new language entered music. Chopin was the pioneer, first in the field. Liszt's harmony, which does owe something to Chopin's, was much more extroverted than the more refined, subtler harmony of the Polish composer. But it was just as personal, just as idiosyncratic, just as far-reaching.

Otherwise Liszt's music is music of dash and bravura, of carefully calculated effect, of defiant pose, of the triumphant resolution of massive technical difficulties. It is kinetic music. It is music intended to amaze. Later in his life, there were to be some significant changes. But to describe Liszt's music as pure effect and little substance, as some have done, misses the point. No music of such harmonic daring can be entirely superficial. Nor can many of Liszt's long-breathed melodies be dismissed. He was a superior melodist, even if his tunes pose just a shade too long, are just a little too determined to attract attention. The music has genuine fascination, but one of the difficulties in understanding it is that it is so heavily dependant on performance. This is especially true of the piano music. The romantic tradition of Liszt playing began to disappear after World War I, and today there are very few who have the combination of *diablerie* and imagination to bring it off successfully. If a pianist approaches the notes literally, he is lost. The music then sounds like empty, rattling, scales and arpeggios. If a pianist uses too much leeway, on the other hand, the music can sound vulgar and self-indulgent. Liszt's piano music needs pianists of unbounded technique, of daring (those careful pianists who never take a chance because they fear to hit a wrong note can never be convincing Liszt players), of great sonority, of delicate shadings, of exhibitionism and extroversion tempered with an ability to float an aristocratic line, of steady yet flexible rhythm. It is not only the pianistic layout that is difficult. Much more difficult these days is an identification with Liszt's mind and world.

Late in life Liszt began a group of curious experiments. In such piano pieces as the *Czardas macabre* and *Nuages gris,* virtuosity is all but eliminated. Harmonies are dissonant, bare, and open. Impressionism and even expressionism are suggested. In recent years there has been considerable study of these late pieces of Liszt. In them are the seeds of Debussy, Bartók, and the other moderns. They remain largely unknown, for very few pianists play them in public. Many are sketches rather than fully worked-out compositions. But they are prophetic and even spooky: the old Liszt idly sketching music that hints at a world still unknown, merely to amuse himself, not caring if the music was ever played or, indeed, ever saw the light.

Liszt in his old age was an institution. He was constantly surrounded by young pianists, young composers, journalists, sycophants, and hangers-on. Occasionally he would appear in public, and he still had the ability to make his listeners swoon. Nor did age, white hair, and a notable collection of warts dim the ardent lover in him. Women remained attracted to the great man, and there was a fine scandal when his pupil, the rich Olga Janina ("the Cossack Countess") tried to shoot him and then herself. His life was constantly being discussed. Everything about the man was of interest to a gossip-hungry world. The hands of the greatest of all pianists received special attention. Plaster casts were made of them, and his pupils wrote prose poems about them. The prevailing notion was that he had a tremendous hand, which was not true. He could span comfortably only a tenth. Just as phrenologists were anxious to examine the bumps on Liszt's head, palmists were eager to look at Liszt's hand, and one American lady, Anne Hampton Brewster, actually did. She sent a report to the Philadelphia *Evening Bulletin,* dated March 22, 1878, and part of it is worth reproducing as a curiosity:

What a proof of Desbarolle's theory is to be found in the hand and fingers of this celebrated artist! It is a mixed one; that is, the fingers are varied, some are round, some square and some flat or spatula; this is the true hand of an artist, for it betokens form and idea. The palm is covered with rays, betraying that his life has been an agitated, eventful one, full of passion and emotion—but the philosophic and material *noeuds,* or knots, on the Apollo and Mercury fingers, the logic and will on that wonderful long thumb, which extends beyond the middle joint of the forefinger, shows how this remarkable man has been able to conquer instincts and govern temperament. According to palmistry this self-control is shown in the palm lines, which are a little defaced. Serious, severe work, and study of a high and noble character, have effaced the impressions of a stormy youth and placed him in old age on a lofty plane where he enjoys serenity and peace. The line of life is the strongest I ever saw; and numberless lines start out from the Jupiter mount. The fingers are remarkable. The Jupiter and Saturn fingers are square; the ring, or Apollo, and little, or Mercury fingers are spatula, flat and broad. The second phalange of the Jupiter finger is longer than the first, which denotes ambition. The Saturn finger is full of knots. There is a wart on the Apollo finger of the right hand. The force of the little finger on both hands is tremendous; the knuckle seems as if made of iron. The knuckle of the Apollo finger is very strongly developed. The knuckle of the Saturn finger is like a hinge. A line starts from the root of the Apollo finger and traverses all the joints; it is strongly marked; this means great reknown.

But there also were those who found Liszt's posturings, and his affectations as an abbé, intolerable. *Le Charivari* in 1877 described his profile as that of a Mephistopheles "who, touched by the death of Marguerite, was meditating a slow conversion." Liszt, said *Le Charivari*, feigns an aged and impoverished air, but "Do not believe in it; it is merely the affectation of humility, and his cassock can scarcely contain the bounding of his still youthful soul. . . . You should see him issue from the Pasdeloup concerts with lowered eyes and modestly enter a princely equipage that a great name has placed at his disposal." *Le Charivari* goes on to describe Liszt's way of life, his eating habits, the small and very bad Roman cigars to which he was partial, the *café noir* he was sipping all day, the oysters he ate for breakfast. "One last word," the article concludes. "Liszt's face is adorned with some moles, politely called grains of genius. Formerly he had four, now their number is more than doubled. It is said that it is his faith coming out."

Yes, they could poke fun at Liszt, and his foibles were fair game. But when he died, genuine sorrow swept the world. It was not only that the last great link with the days of early romanticism had gone. Liszt, as teacher and composer, as pianist and matinee idol, had been an inspiration—the archromantic, the man who had made his own rules, the exceptional figure who could have his cake and eat it. He was everything his friends and his enemies had always said he was. Look at him one way, and he was a genius. Look at him another, and he was a *poseur*. But one *had* to look and make up his own mind. From the moment Liszt broke upon the world, he could not be ignored.

To many today, Liszt's music remains vulgar and second-rate. To others it is eternally fascinating. It is so much like Liszt the man—always original, always full of ideas, often flawed in character, often with a pseudonobility. It is eternally varied music, from the delicate intimacy of that delicious piano piece *Au bord d'une source* to the Mephistophelean posturings of the

175

enormous *Faust* Symphony. With Liszt there is always flesh and the devil on one side, the angelic choir on the other. His works of diabolism are consistently more interesting than his religious works (as has constantly been pointed out, sin is more interesting than virtue). Liszt's music can be as empty-headed as the *Grand galop chromatique,* as visionary as the B minor Sonata, as simple as the *Canzonetta del Salvator Rosa,* as complicated as the *Don Juan Fantasy,* as muted as *Il Pensieroso,* as glittering as *Les Jeux d'eaux à la Villa d'Este.* It can be nationalistic, as in the often-derided *Hungarian Rhapsodies* (somebody once pointed out that nobody would have ever objected had Liszt named them *Gypsy Rhapsodies*), or Bachian, as in the various transcriptions of Bach's organ music, or saintly, as in the oratorio *Christus.*

Above all there were the new concepts of form and harmony that Liszt brought to music. Béla Bartók, in an essay on Liszt, pointed out certain obvious deficiencies in his music. But, said Bartók, those were not important. "The essence of these works we must find in the new ideas, to which Liszt was the first to give expression, and in the bold pointing toward the future. These things raise Liszt as a composer to the ranks of the great." Among Liszt's contributions, Bartók cited:

. . . the bold harmonic turns, the innumerable modulatory digressions, such as the juxtaposition, without any transition at all, of the two keys most distant from each other, and to many other points that would require the use of too many technical terms. But all these are mere details. What is more important is the absolutely new imaginative concept that manifests itself in the chief works (the Piano Sonata and the two outer movements of the *Faust* Symphony, for instance) by reason of which these works rank among the outstanding musical creations of the nineteenth century. Formally, too, though he did not break with tradition completely, Liszt created much that was new. Thus one finds in him, in the E flat Piano Concerto for instance, the first perfect realization of cyclic sonata form, with common themes treated on variation principles. . . . It is humanly very understandable that he did not reject his romantic century, with all its exaggerations. From this comes his own exaggeratedly rhetorical pathos, and no doubt it also explains the concessions he makes to the public, even in his finest works. But whoever picks out only these weaknesses—and there are still some music lovers who do—does not see the essence behind them.

- Bartók was one of the first to hail Liszt as the seminal force he was. Brahms and Wagner were to eclipse Liszt as a creative figure during the nineteenth century, and he was all but ignored during the second quarter of the twentieth century. But it may yet turn out that the prophetic Liszt had more to do with music as it actually developed than any single composer of his time. The full story of his majestic place in musical history has yet to be told.

❧ 13 ❧

Bourgeois Genius

FELIX MENDELSSOHN

Of the early romantics, it was the most natural musician of them all who turned into the neoclassicist, the upholder of the traditions, the "pure" musician. Berlioz, Schumann, Chopin, Liszt—all were geniuses, but as a musician Mendelssohn was something unparalleled, and none but Mozart was born with such gifts. Indeed, Mendelssohn developed faster than Mozart, for he composed the fine Octet in E flat at the age of sixteen and the *Midsummer Night's Dream* Overture at seventeen, far eclipsing Mozart—or anybody else in musical history, for that matter—at an equivalent age. Mendelssohn was no musical specialist. Like Mozart, he could do anything. He was one of the finest pianists of the day, the greatest conductor (he was active on the podium before Liszt and Wagner), perhaps the greatest organist. Had he wanted to, he could have been one of the great violinists. His ear was perfect, his memory all-encompassing. In addition, he was a humanist —cultured, widely read, interested in poetry and philosophy. As has been pointed out many times, he would have made a resounding success in anything to which he turned his attention.

But he never lived up to his initial creative promise. A certain conservatism, an emotional inhibition, kept him from reaching the heights. His music, always skillful, became more and more a series of correct, polite gestures as he grew older. For this we can blame his background. Coming as he did from a distinguished, wealthy, conservative Jewish banking family, he was taught from childhood to be correct, to observe good form, to avoid offense. A young man, no matter how ardent and full of genius, does not grow up in great wealth, dominated by a sensitive but patriarchal father, without having conservatism ingrained within him. Mendelssohn grew up a cautious man, one who sniffed suspiciously at anything that threatened the established order of things. "Do not," he told his sister, "commend what is new until it has made some progress in the world and acquired a name, for until then it is a mere matter of taste." Caution, caution. It could also be that the combination of wealth and Jewishness in a strongly anti-Semitic Berlin kept Mendelssohn unconsciously overcareful, hesitant to obtrude, anxious to be accepted. Perhaps, too, his blood pushed him into a kind of avowed German nationalism that later came to fruition in Wagner. Mendelssohn was a German and proud of it, a patriot who was convinced of German supremacy in music and the other arts. German Jews have always, when allowed, tried to be more German than the Germans; and certainly Mendelssohn regarded himself more a German than a Jew. Only once is he known to have referred to his ancestry. In any event, his parents, Abraham and Leah, were not orthodox, and had their children baptized under the name of Mendelssohn-Bartholdy. (Leah's brother had taken the name of Bartholdy on becoming a Christian.)

The Mendelssohns were integrated within Berlin society; they were "accepted," and their home was a center of musical and intellectual thought —but musical and intellectual thought of an accepted order. Felix Mendelssohn's background was not conducive to revolutionary ideas. And so he grew up to be the epitome of the wealthy German *bourgeoisie*, and he grew up with nature on his side, for he was a handsome, high-spirited young man, lithe and active, with an aristocratic bearing, a high forehead, curly black hair, and a refined, expressive face. He was well-bred, somewhat snobbish, rather priggish later in life, distrusted exuberance, enjoyed a quiet family life, had a dutiful wife, worried about his children, worked constantly, and he differed from the other wealthy *bourgeoisie* only in that he happened to be a genius.

What an extraordinary child this grandson of the great philosopher Moses Mendelssohn was! He was born in Hamburg on February 3, 1809, but the family moved to Berlin three years later, and it was there that Felix grew up in an atmosphere of almost grim culture. Grim, because both parents were determined to see that their children had every advantage money and position could provide. Leah herself was an amateur musician and artist, a student of English, French, and Italian literature, and she could also read Homer in the original. Abraham loved music and was in general a cultured, literate man. He and Leah not only directly supervised their children's education, but were also determined that the children be serious about it. This meant a great deal of work, and it was no picnic. Felix would be up at 5 A.M., ready to work at his music, his history, his Greek and Latin, his natural science, his contemporary literature, his drawing. (He was to retain that early rising hour all his life.) He thrived on the regimen, as did his talented sister Fanny. She was four years older than Felix. When Fanny was born, her mother looked at the baby's hands. "Bach fugue fingers!" she delightedly exclaimed. That was the kind of family the Mendelssohns were. Fanny and Felix: another parallel with Mozart, for Fanny was a good pianist and composer, just as Mozart's sister Nannerl was. But where Mozart later drifted away from his sister, Felix was close to Fanny all his life.

By the age of nine, Mendelssohn was playing the piano in public. Ignaz Moscheles, one of the best pianists of the day, put the finishing touches on his style. There was no question of exploiting Felix' talent, as there had been in Mozart's case, and Felix did not make many public appearances as a child. Quite the contrary. Mendelssohn's parents had doubts about Felix becoming a professional musician, and there were great family conferences about it. But it soon became evident that so enormous a gift had to be encouraged and developed. Not only did Felix have a natural instrumental talent, but by 1825, when he was sixteen, he had written four operas, concertos, symphonies, cantatas, and piano music, much of it still in manuscript. Felix tried this music out with an orchestra engaged by his parents. No wonder he developed into a flawless technician. He could grow up writing music for his own orchestra and then conducting it. On Sunday mornings there were musicales at the Mendelssohn home, attended by celebrities of European intellectual and social life. All of the children participated— Felix conducting or at the piano, Fanny also at the piano, Rebecca (born in 1811) singing, Paul (born in 1813) at the cello. Occasionally one or another of these early Mendelssohn pieces are resurrected, and they are impressive for their surety of form, their vivacity, and sheer professionalism. Already the boy was one of the better composers in Europe. When he composed the E flat Octet in 1825, he showed that he was one of the great ones.

The Octet in many ways is typical of Mendelssohn as a composer. It adheres to the established principles of sonata form and never attempts to break new ground in that respect. Never is there a suggestion that in the writing of this sixteen-year-old boy is there a revolutionary trying to break free. But with what confidence and logic is the broad opening theme presented and developed! It is a theme that contains no metrical irregularity of the kind that Berlioz, Chopin, and Schumann were to employ. Mendelssohn's mind did not run in those directions, and the opening theme of his Octet prefigures the calmly flowing, classically configured themes of his maturity, just as the working-out of the Octet theme already has the refinement, elegance, and smoothness of the later works. In the third movement, the scherzo, of the Octet, Mendelssohn did bring something new to music. That graceful, tripping, light-as-air writing was a miracle then and is a miracle now. Older writers on music invariably referred to this as "Mendelssohn's fairy music;" and there is indeed something elfin about it. This kind of writing came to its apex the following year, when Mendelssohn composed the *Midsummer Night's Dream* Overture. He was seventeen years old, and he never wrote a more perfect work. Oberon, Titania, the lovers, Bottom—all stroll through this fairy landscape. The music has remained eternally fresh, and is a perfect example of content wedded to technique. That includes the orchestration. Mendelssohn as an orchestrator, as well as a composer, represented the golden mean. He used exactly what he had to use, and no more; but what he did use, he used with taste, skill, and imagination.

Mendelssohn's early years in Berlin came to a climax with his preparation and public performance of Bach's *St. Matthew Passion* (two performances, on March 11 and March 21, 1829). The work had not been heard since Bach's day, though Bach might have had trouble recognizing his score as presented by Mendelssohn. He used a chorus of 400 and a greatly augmented orchestra. He cut some sections and modified others to make the music palatable to Berlin audiences, and he did not hesitate to supply new orchestrations when he felt they were necessary. The twenty-year-old Mendelssohn did no more or less than other composers and conductors did to early music at that time. The revival did much to spark the Bach renaissance. Throughout his life Mendelssohn was never far from Bach, and probably had all of his then-known music committed to memory. All good musicians have superior memories, but Mendelssohn's was exceptional. As a child he knew the nine Beethoven symphonies by heart and could play them on the piano. He most likely could hear a piece of music once and never forget it. Charles Hallé in a burst of extravagance said that he was convinced that Mendelssohn knew every bar of music ever written, and could reproduce it immediately.

Like all wealthy young men of breeding, Mendelssohn had to make the Grand Tour, and he started out in 1829. The trip was to last three years. He went to Italy, France, and England, meeting everybody and being liked by everybody. He wrote long, articulate letters, often illustrating them with pencil drawings. Mendelssohn has been overpraised as an artist. His drawings are all tight in line and very careful, devoid of personality, merely copies of what he had seen. When he tried to draw the human figure, his deficiencies as a draftsman showed up, though at least those figure drawings have a kind of charm that the carefully copied landscapes lack.

In 1831 he was in Paris, meeting Liszt, Chopin, Berlioz, and Kalkbrenner, listening to the first flush of romantic music and not liking it very much. Chopin, he thought, was the best of the new crop, though it took a little time for Mendelssohn to overcome his initial mistrust of Chopin's radical harmonies and his new way of playing the piano. Mendelssohn also had a high regard for Schumann as a man, but here again was distrustful of his music. It made him uncomfortable, and the conservative Mendelssohn did not like to be made uncomfortable. "He loves the dead too much," gibed

Berlioz. Mendelssohn represented the Biedermeier period: comfortable, homelike, heavy in sentiment, bourgeois, functional. But even though Mendelssohn was temperamentally opposed to romanticism, that did not keep him from conducting romantic music when he became musical director at Leipzig in 1835. It is also interesting to note that where later generations looked down upon Mendelssohn's music as being too precious, too thin, too much on the surface, the early romantics had a completely different idea about him. To Schumann, for instance, Mendelssohn was perfection itself. "I consider Mendelssohn *to be the first musician* of our time, and take off my hat to him as a master." The avant-garde Berlioz had a high regard for Mendelssohn as a composer, and so did Liszt. Part of the admiration may have been a response to Mendelssohn's phenomenal accomplishments as a practicing musician. Musicians always respond to craftsmanship, and Mendelssohn had more craftsmanship than anybody around. But there is also plenty of evidence to show that Mendelssohn's music made a decided impact on his romantic contemporaries. And the public could not get enough of it. Indeed, it is doubtful if any other composer was so universally accepted by the public as a master in his own lifetime.

Mendelssohn's standards were very high, and he had an opportunity to put them into effect in 1833, when he became director at Düsseldorf. He promptly started to program such sixteenth- and seventeenth-century composers as Lassus, Palestrina, and Leo, and directed a revival of *Don Giovanni* at the opera. Mendelssohn, however, was too sophisticated a musician for the sleepy and provincial town of Düsseldorf. When he was invited, in 1835, to take over the Gewandhaus concerts in Leipzig—Bach's town!—he was only too eager to accept. In a short time he made Leipzig the musical capital of Germany, and he also revolutionized orchestral playing in his own country. He increased the orchestra from forty to fifty players, engaged Ferdinand David as concertmaster, and saw to it that his players had ease of mind by securing a pension for each member of the orchestra. One of the first conductors to use a baton, Mendelssohn made his orchestra a precision unit. As a conductor he was sparing in gesture, inclined toward fast tempos, and insistent on accurate rhythm and smooth ensemble. Mendelssohn was probably the first modern conductor as the term is understood today. Spirited, high-strung, dictatorial, he demanded obedience from his players and was known to lose his temper if he did not get what he wanted.

He also revised the repertoire. Before he took over the Gewandhaus concerts, the most-played composers were such now-forgotten figures as Anton Eberl, Ignaz von Seyfried, Karl Reissiger, Alexander Fesca, Sigismund Neukomm, Ferdinand Ries, and other such worthies. Mendelssohn changed all that. He made Mozart and Beethoven the backbone of the repertoire, with Haydn, Bach, and Handel not far behind. Among the newer composers he introduced to Leipzig audiences were Spohr, Cherubini, Moscheles, Gade, Rossini, Liszt, Chopin, Schumann, and Schubert. He got rid of the variety programs that were customary, and began to organize programs much as they are organized today, starting with an overture, proceeding to a large-scale work, then to a concerto or another large-scale work, and ending with a shorter piece. Nor would he separate the movements of a symphony with a divertissement. Often, in programs of the day, a Beethoven symphony would be stopped after two movements, and a harpist, or cellist, or singer would entertain the audience, after which the symphony would be resumed. Sponsors of concerts clearly felt that no audience could survive the intellectual strain of listening to a Beethoven symphony straight through.

Mendelssohn worked very hard at Leipzig, but managed to find the time to get married. His wife was Cécile Jeanrenaud, daughter of a clergyman of the French Reformed Church. The marriage was happy, and was blessed with four children, but surprisingly little is known of Cécile. The Mendelssohns kept their home life to themselves, and Cécile remained in the background. She must have been an intelligent, helpful woman, and she made a good impression on Mendelssohn's sister when the two women finally met, in Leipzig. Fanny wrote home to Berlin:

At last I know my sister-in-law, and I feel as if a load were off my mind, for I cannot deny that I was very uncomfortable and out of sorts at never having seen her. She is amiable, childlike, fresh, bright and even tempered, and I consider Felix most fortunate for, though inexpressibly fond of him, she does not spoil him, but when he is capricious treats him with an equanimity which will in the course of time most probably cure his fits of irritability altogether. Her presence produces the effect of a fresh breeze, so bright and natural is she.

In addition to the Leipzig concerts, Mendelssohn took over the concerts of the Berlin Academy of Arts in 1841. As a guest conductor he appeared all over Europe and was particularly favored in London, where he was friendly with Queen Victoria and Prince Albert. The Queen liked comfortable music, and her Mr. Mendelssohn was the one to give it to her. Mendelssohn's letters are full of references to musicales and music-making at Windsor Castle. The royal family specially liked to hear Mr. Mendelssohn play the piano. Mendelssohn as a pianist represented the pure, classic style as opposed to the romantic thunderings of the Liszt school or the delicate nuances and color effects of the Chopin style. His playing was like his music— clear, elegant, precise, logical, with little use of the pedal. Probably it sounded like the playing of a Kalkbrenner with brains.

On top of all his conducting and concertizing, not to mention composing, Mendelssohn established the Leipzig Conservatory late in 1842, and it opened on April 3 the following year. He and Robert Schumann taught composition and piano. Among the faculty members was Ferdinand David, in charge of violin teaching. David, one of the best violinists in Europe, had been brought by Mendelssohn to Leipzig as concertmaster of the Gewandhaus orchestra. The two men were close friends, and Mendelssohn consulted David on a number of technical points while he was composing the E minor Violin Concerto.

And thus the middle 1840's saw Mendelssohn active as composer, conductor, pianist, teacher, administrator, family man, and traveler. He also carried on an enormous correspondence, and was instrumental in founding music festivals—at Cologne, Düsseldorf, Schwerin, Birmingham. In 1845 he asked to be released from his duties in Berlin, and that gave him more time for activity in London. He kept at his various activities day and night, constantly traveling, constantly working, constantly more irritable. His family worried about his health. Mendelssohn was physically and emotionally exhausted, but he had a compulsion to work. Early in 1847, for instance, he conducted his *St. Paul* in Leipzig and went to London, where he conducted four performances of *Elijah*. Then he conducted *Elijah* in Birmingham and Manchester. He had other obligations in England, including appearances as a pianist. He looked ill and tired when it was all over, and is reported to have said that another week in London would have killed him. He left London and arrived in Frankfort for conducting appearances.

It was there that in May, 1847, he received the news of his beloved sister's sudden death. She had had a stroke in Berlin, and died on May 14. When Mendelssohn learned about it he himself had a stroke from which he never recovered. He had to stop work—finally!—and went off with his family to Switzerland, where he tried to relax by painting water colors and working on a string quartet and other pieces. In September he returned to Leipzig, saying he was feeling better, but he had another stroke that left him partially paralyzed. He died on November 4, 1847, at the age of thirty-eight.

Mendelssohn's romanticism was by far the most restrained of any of the great composers active in the 1830's and 1840's. He had none of the romantic aspirations, none of the high-flying concepts that so delighted the romantics. "People often complain," he once wrote, "that music is too ambiguous, that what they should think when they hear it is so unclear, whereas everybody understands words. With me it is exactly the opposite. . . . The thoughts that are expressed to me by music I love are not too indefinite to be put into words, but on the contrary too definite." This is the remark of one who responds to logic in music, and most of Mendelssohn's music is nothing if not logical. Instinctively he shrank from excesses of any kind—in music. in art, in life. Naturally the extravagant-sounding music of Berlioz repelled him: "a frightful muddle, an incongruous mess . . . one ought to wash one's hands after handling one of his scores." In some of his earlier works Mendelssohn did experiment with a few advanced harmonies, but soon withdrew as though frightened. His music has almost none of the textural richness of Schumann, Chopin, and Liszt. It is devoid of those altered chords, unorthodox key relationships, irregular metrical groupings. Mendelssohn's music is largely diatonic. He and the romantics did not speak the same language.

It was this lack of harmonic bite in his music that helped make him so popular. Conventional-minded listeners, disturbed by the wild dissonances of the other romantics, were able to sit back and relax with Mendelssohn's music. It had a strong relationship with the then-popular music of Hummel, Cherubini, and even some of the salon composers. What put it miles above their music, however, was the peculiarly Mendelssohnian grace and elegance it displayed, and its clear-cut construction. Later generations would find that kind of perfection boring; would find Mendelssohn's melodies cloying and his rhythms too regular and predictable. Mendelssohn's music has less of the element of surprise in it than the music of any of the great composers. But the first half of the nineteenth century regarded Mendelssohn as close to divine. Especially in England his influence held strong throughout the century, dominating the entire British school. Mendelssohn loved England from the moment he first arrived in London, and the admiration was reciprocated. Sir George Grove, indeed, all but claimed Mendelssohn as a British national. "He has been for long looked on as half an Englishman. He spoke English well, he wrote letters and familiar notes in our tongue freely; he showed himself in the provinces; his first important work was founded on Shakespeare . . . and his *Scotch* Symphony and *Hebrides* Overture showed how deeply the scenery of Britain had influenced him."

In the twentieth century Mendelssohn's reputation took a sharp dip. Yet there never was a time when his music was not in the repertoire, and this despite the disparaging remarks of the intellectual critics. Not only was romanticism generally out of fashion, which threw Schumann, Liszt, and even Chopin into the shadow, but avant-garde critics also decided, almost to a man, that Mendelssohn's music was too unoriginal and even lacking in taste. Paul Rosenfeld, the American critic, had nothing but contempt for such scores as *Elijah* and *St. Paul*. He wrote articles suggesting that Mendelssohn was a Jewish snob trying to pass into Christian society with religious scores as his passport. Rosenfeld's view was generally accepted by avant-garde thinkers. The public, however, paid no attention to the diatribes. The Violin Concerto, the *Italian* and *Scotch* Symphonies, the *Midsummer Night's Dream* and *Hebrides* (or *Fingal's Cave*, as it is also known) Overtures were as popular as ever. Wherever there was a chamber group, the D minor and C minor Trios and several of the string quartets were never far away. The *Variations sérieuses* never left the piano literature, nor did the G minor Piano Concerto.

On the face of it, it was strange that so many musicians and critics in the period from 1920 to 1940 had so low an opinion of Mendelssohn. One can understand listeners who grew up with the antiromanticism of Stravinsky and Bartók feeling uncomfortable with the extroverted flamboyance of a Liszt or the secret soul-states of a Schumann. But Mendelssohn's music has clear lines and beautiful organization; and for the most part it completely avoids the sweeping romantic gesture. Mendelssohn should have been enthusiastically adopted by the twentieth-century antiromantics. Perhaps it was the lack of adventure in his music that made it unpalatable for a time.

In any event the latter part of the twentieth century is busy rediscovering Mendelssohn. Even the once-derided *Songs Without Words* are beginning to be regarded with respect as flawlessly written period pieces with a great deal of personality. Pianists once more are looking at the three Études, the six Preludes and Fugues and such effective virtuoso works as the F sharp minor Fantasy (Op. 28). Recent years have seen an exploration of music that Mendelssohn composed in Berlin when he was twelve years old, and listeners are amazed at the dash, sweetness, and technical expertise of the music—those symphonies for strings, concertos for two pianos, and chamber works. His songs are beginning to come back. Even—*mirabile dictu!*—the oratorios are no longer automatically regarded as stuffy examples of moralistic Victorian piety. Mendelssohn is beginning to be seen in true perspective. He was much more than a polite composer with an enormous technique. His music has sensitivity, style, and a great degree of personality; and he did compose at least one flawless specimen in each of a multiplicity of musical forms— symphony, concerto, piano, chamber music, the lied, the concert overture, oratorio. Everything, indeed, except opera. His influence can be found in music of the French school (especially Gounod and Fauré), in the young Richard Strauss, in the youthful works of Tchaikovsky. Today, there is still a little suspicion of the sentiment implicit in much of Mendelssohn's music. But as serial and postserial music runs its course and neoromanticism returns, as it seems to be returning in the 1970's, Mendelssohn's music, like Liszt's, will be accepted once again, and Mendelssohn will be recognized as the sweet, pure, perfectly proportioned master he was.

✎ 14 ✎

Voice, Voice, and More Voice

ROSSINI, DONIZETTI, AND BELLINI

From 1810, the date of Gioacchino Rossini's first opera, to 1848, the year Gaetano Donizetti died, three composers dominated Italian opera—that is, opera composed in Italy, bel canto opera, as opposed to the stately operas in Italian turned out by such composers as Cherubini in Paris. The three composers were Rossini, Donizetti, and Vincenzo Bellini.

In their kind of opera, singers and singing were the thing. Their operas for the most part aimed frankly at entertainment. Weber may have been concerned with the German people in his operas, and Beethoven in *Fidelio* was aiming at spiritual values. None of this concerned the bel canto composers. Their emotional and exhibitionistic art did not call upon listeners to think deeply. As a result, their operas were immensely popular. "Music for the Italians," complained Berlioz, "is a sensual pleasure and nothing more. For this noble expression of the mind they have hardly more respect than for the art of cooking. They want a score that, like a plate of macaroni, can be assimilated immediately without their having to think about it, or even to pay attention to it." Later, the spectacle operas of Meyerbeer, the psychological operas of Verdi, and the music dramas of Wagner pushed bel canto opera off the stage, though a handful of works survived the international circuit—Rossini's *Il Barbiere di Siviglia*, Donizetti's *Lucia di Lammermoor, Don Pasquale,* and *L'Elisir d'Amore,* and Bellini's *Norma*. In Italy, another half-dozen might have occasionally been heard. But considering that Rossini composed thirty-nine operas, Donizetti about seventy, and Bellini eleven, it was not a large representation.

After World War II there was a sudden revival of interest in bel canto opera all over Europe and America, thanks largely to two singers—Maria Callas and Joan Sutherland. Operas that had been forgotten for a hundred years or more were dragged from the shelves, and music lovers eagerly investigated the curiosities. But very few of those operas turned out to have much more than antiquarian value. Nor was it possible to give an adequate idea of what the operas sounded like. Bel canto opera demands coloratura tenors, contraltos, and baritones as well as coloratura sopranos. (There is a mistaken idea that coloratura pertains to high soprano alone.) But the tradition was gone, much as Callas and Sutherland tried to revive it, and there were no tenors or baritones anywhere in the world who could begin to sing the parts as the tenor Rubini or the bass Lablache did in the first half of the nineteenth century.

A great deal of bel canto opera was formula opera, hastily turned out, based heavily on the device of the cavatina and cabaletta. The cavatina, slow and lyric, was intended to show off a singer's line, to demonstrate the singer's ability to hold a long phrase with beauty of tone, nuance, and color. The cavatina was followed by a fast section called the cabaletta, in which the virtuosity of the singer was called into play. Bel canto, which means "beautiful singing," reflected to a large extent the eighteenth-century ideal of taste in improvisation. A singer was expected to have a flawless technique. A singer was also expected to have taste in embellishment, decoration, and cadenza. The combination of pure tone and brilliant technique constituted bel canto singing. Much of this kind of singing descended from the castrati. Baldassare Ferri, a castrato virtuoso of the seventeenth century, could insert consecutive trills for two octaves, up and down, in one breath. Such passages could take fifty unbroken seconds. Farinelli also was timed at fifty seconds in one phrase. Rossini had heard some of the great castrati and knew what they could do. He knew, too, that the great ones were not mere show-offs. Those with taste could melt their listeners with the purity, beauty, and even passion of their delivery.

The ideal—technique plus taste—did not show up very often. Opera singers above all musicians tend to abuse their prerogatives. In Rossini's early days they did whatever came into their heads. They were spoiled and pampered, and were considered much more important than the composer. The composer had to have the diplomacy of a Talleyrand to satisfy them. If two popular prima donnas were in the same opera, there would be intense rivalry and suspicion, tears and hatred. Each would count the bars of her arias to make sure she was not being cheated. Then she would go ahead and change the music to suit herself. So cavalier an attitude did the singers of Rossini's day have toward the printed note that often the baffled composer was hard put to recognize his own music. Rossini was always fighting the tastelessness of singers. He even wrote out many of the embellishments, and demanded they be closely followed. But not even Rossini expected a star soprano to follow everything exactly as written. Years after his retirement, Rossini accompanied the young Adelina Patti in *Una voce poco fa* from *Il Barbiere di Siviglia*. She embellished the aria out of recognition, and after congratulating her on her brilliant singing Rossini icily wanted to know who the composer was. A few days later Rossini told Saint-Saëns that he had no objection to his arias being altered or embroidered. "They were made for that. But to leave not a note of what I composed, even in the recitatives—well, that is too much."

In Italy during the first third of the century, the composer would arrive at an opera house, compose an opera in three weeks or so, conduct the first three performances, and move on to the next town. Italian opera had always worked this way; it was a business, and the faster the turnover, the better. Seldom were the operas published, and Rossini, for one, knowing that the next town would not have heard his last opera, would calmly appropriate sections from it and pass them off as new. Rossini's most famous opera, *Il Barbiere di Siviglia* of 1816, uses arias and ensembles from *La Cambiale di Matrimonio* of 1810, and in addition material from four other of his operas. Even the now-famous overture was lifted from a previous work. It was typical that *Il Barbiere* took the composer no more than thirteen days to finish. "I always knew Rossini was a lazy man," joked Donizetti, when told of this feat. Donizetti knew whereof he spoke, for it had taken him no more than eight days to compose *L'Elisir d'Amore*. Felix Mendelssohn, traveling in Italy, looked, marveled, and was amused at the Italian way of composing opera. "Donizetti," he wrote home, "finishes an opera in ten days. It may be hissed, to be sure, but that doesn't matter, as it is paid for all the same, and then he can go about having a good time. If in the end his reputation should be endangered, in that case he would have to work real hard, which he would not like. Therefore he sometimes spends as much as three weeks on an opera, taking considerable pains with a couple of arias in it, so that they may please the public, and then he can afford to amuse himself once more, and once more write trash." Mendelssohn, the industrious German ant, and Donizetti, the Italian grasshopper.

The bel canto composers were able to turn out scores at such speed because they were in effect composing formula operas, all constructed much the same way. An opening chorus was followed by carefully meted-out arias and ensembles, each placed with the rigidity of men in an army platoon at attention, everybody and everything in its appointed place. Each of the two acts would end with a thundering chorus, in which the principal singers advanced to the footlights and sang along, staring the audience down. In a letter to a composer, Rossini was devastatingly frank about his method of work:

Wait until the evening before the opening night. Nothing primes inspiration more than necessity, whether it be the presence of a copyist waiting for your work, or the prodding of an impresario tearing his hair.

In my time, all the impresarios of Italy were bald at thirty. . . . I wrote the overture to *La Gazza Ladra* the day of its opening in the theater itself, where I was imprisoned by the director and under the surveillance of the stagehands who were instructed to throw my original text through the window, page by page, to the copyists waiting below to transcribe it. In default of pages they were ordered to throw me out the window bodily. I did better with *Il Barbiere*. I did not compose an overture but selected for it one which was meant for a semi-serious opera called *Elisabetta*. The public was completely satisfied. [What Rossini did not add was that he had also used the *Barbiere* overture for his *Aureliano* and *L'Equivoco Stravagante* in addition to *Elisabetta*.]

Bellini, who did not have the happy-go-lucky temperament of Rossini and Donizetti, and who took his art more seriously, did break away from formula, but only slightly. His two facile contemporaries never bothered to alter their successful formula. In virtually every Rossini and Donizetti opera, and in several of Bellini's, there is slipshod work, self-plagiarism, and cynicism. That is the reason why most of their operas are dead. Donizetti: who has heard, or ever will hear, his *Chiara e Serafina*, his *L'Ajo nell'imbarazzo*, *Parisina*, *Torquato Tasso*, *Rosamonda d'Inghilterra*, or *Belisario*? Rossini: his *Elisabetta, Regina d'Inghilterra*, *Torvaldo e Dorliska*, *Adelaide de Borgogna*? Bellini: his *Bianca e Gernando*, or *Zaira*?

Rossini, who outlived Bellini and Donizetti, was the big man of the three. He had genius, he had wit and sparkle, and he had a never-failing melodic gift. "Give me a laundry list and I will set it to music," he bragged. He was born on February 29, 1792, in Pesaro, an Adriatic port. Later in life Rossini was to be called "The Swan of Pesaro." As a child he had immense facility, as so many of the great composers have had, and could play the piano, violin, and viola. He also sang in opera before his voice broke, and he was composing prolifically while a teen-ager. In 1807 he began his studies at the conservatory in Bologna. It was there that he met the Spanish soprano Isabella Colbran, who later became his wife and the great interpreter of his music. The first of his operas to be staged was a one-act farce, for Venice in 1810, named *La Cambiale di Matrimonio*. The dash, spirit, irrepressible humor of the music and its real personality immediately set it apart as something special. Rossini's first big hit, *L'Inganno felice*, was staged the following year also in Venice. Then followed such operas as *La Scala di Seta*, *Il Signor Bruschino*, *Tancredi*, *L'Italiana in Algeri*, *Semiramide*, *Il Turco in Italia*, *La Cenerentola*, and *Le Comte Ory*. At the age of twenty-one Rossini was already world-famous, and as they came out, his operas immediately entered the international repertory.

It was, above all, melody that made Rossini famous, and Wagner ruefully admitted as much. "Rossini," he wrote, "turned his back on the pedantic lumber of heavy scores and listened where the people sang without a written note. What he heard there was what, out of all the operatic box of tricks, had stayed the most unbidden in the ear: *the naked, ear-delighting, absolutely-melodic melody,* that is, melody that was just melody and nothing else." Wagner, with mingled exasperation and irony, concluded that with Rossini "the real life history of opera comes to an end," for all pretense at drama was swept away and the performer was allotted showy virtuosity as his only task. Wagner was determined to correct the situation.

Il Barbiere di Siviglia, that greatest of all buffa operas, made Rossini's music the rage of every opera house in Europe. Rossini had a certain amount of nerve writing an opera on this subject. Giovanni Paisiello, an important and very popular composer, had written a *Barbiere di Siviglia* in 1782 that was loved, admired, and immensely popular. Today, the Paisiello opera is a curiosity, one with a faded charm but essentially unadventurous harmonically and melodically. Rossini's opera, which uses almost the same libretto, sent it into rapid oblivion. Yet Rossini's *Barbiere* was a failure at its first performance, in Rome, on February 20, 1816. Apparently it was poorly sung, and there were some weird accidents that took the public's mind away from the music. A singer tripped and had to sing with a bloody nose; a cat wandered in and upstaged everybody. But the second act went well, and the work soon established itself as *the* comic opera of all time. Only nine years after its premiere it was heard in New York (though an abridged version had been presented in that city as early as 1819) in Manuel Garcia's first season at the Park Theater. Garcia had been the original Almaviva.

Rossini is remembered today primarily as a writer of opera buffa, but his serious and tragic operas were highly esteemed in their day. *Otello, Le Siège de Corinth, Moïse, William Tell*—all made the rounds to great admiration. In 1822 there was a Rossini festival at the Kärntnertor Theater in Vienna, and the city experienced a Rossini delirium. Beethoven himself admired the *Barbiere* and told Rossini to give the world many more. Schubert incorporated the famous Rossini crescendo, and other devices, into some of his scores. In Paris the Rossini operas were constantly being given at the Théâtre des Italiens and the Opéra. London in 1824 had a "Rossini season." Rossini went to London (as he had gone to Vienna) to superintend performances, and his presence added materially to the receipts. Europe was Rossini-mad. Things went very well for the volatile Italian. He married his Colbran, after having lived with her for many years, then took up with Olympe Péllisier and married her when Colbran died. Everywhere he went he was envied, feted, admired. He became corpulent, worked up some interesting ailments, was one of Europe's most famous gourmets (tournedos Rossini are one of his bequests to humanity), and when *William Tell* was performed at the Paris Opéra in 1829 the adulation was all but hysterical.

At that point Rossini stopped composing and although he lived for another thirty-nine years never wrote another note for publication.

His retirement is a mystery that has been the object of endless speculation. He did compose two large-scale religious works, the *Stabat Mater* and the *Petite Messe Solennelle* (which, as has been observed many times, is neither petite nor solennelle), and he amused himself by composing a large number of short piano and vocal pieces. But to all intents and purposes his career was over in 1829, at the height of his fame.

Several guesses can be made. For one thing, Rossini had a great deal of money. At his death he left an estate valued at approximately $1,420,000. There was no financial necessity for him to write; and Rossini was not the kind of idealist who composed from aesthetic conviction or spiritual necessity. For another, his health was not good. He had uremic troubles and on top of that was a hypochondriac and insomniac. "I have all of women's ills," Rossini told a friend. "All that I lack is the uterus." A certain amount of natural laziness, too, entered into his decision to retire.

But more than that, Rossini was distressed at the direction opera was heading. He honestly believed that with the disappearance of the castrati the art of singing was dying. As early as 1817—he was only twenty-five at the time—he was bewailing the corruption of singing: "Many of our singers, born outside of Italy, have renounced purity of musical taste. . . . Warblings, leaps, trills, jumps, abuses of semitones, clusters of notes, these characterize the singing that now prevails." At that time Rossini was also concerned about what he considered the deleterious influence of the German school. In a letter dated February 12, 1817, he sounds as conservative as the strictest academician in any conservatory:

Haydn had already begun to corrupt purity of taste by introducing strange chords, artificial passages and daring novelties. . . . But after him Cramer and, finally, Beethoven, with their compositions lacking in unity and natural flow, and full of artificial oddities, corrupted taste in instrumental music completely. And now, for the simple and majestic styles of Sarti, Paisiello and Cimarosa, Mayr has substituted in the theater his own ingenious but vicious harmonies in which the main melody is strangled in deference to the new German school.

There is no evidence that Rossini changed his mind as he grew older. His own operas, even *William Tell* with its Meyerbeerian elements, are basically classic, with elegance of melody, clarity, modesty of orchestration, and predominantly diatonic harmonies. By 1830 romanticism was on its way, and Rossini was an antiromantic. He detested the loudness, the "eccentricities," the "affectations" of the new movement. Above all he hated the new style of singing. A new breed, tenors with high notes, was the rage, and Rossini despised everything they represented. Enrico Tamberlik was astounding operatic audiences with his famous high C sharp, and there was the occasion when Tamberlik visited Rossini. "Have him come in," Rossini said. "But tell him to leave his C sharp on the coat rack. He can pick it up on the way out."

Even before *William Tell*, Rossini was thinking of quitting, and it was general knowledge. Stendhal saw Rossini in Milan. "Next April," Stendhal wrote, "Rossini will be 28 and he is eager to stop composing at 30." Then there is a letter from Rossini's father: "Gioacchino has given me his word that he wants to retire home from everything in 1830, wanting to enjoy acting the gentleman and being allowed to write what he wishes, as he has been exhausted enough." The magazines picked up the rumors and, in 1828, the *Revue musicale* in an article about the forthcoming *William Tell* noted that "he himself has asserted . . . that this opera will be the last to come from his pen."

By the 1840's Rossini, even if he had been thinking of resuming his career, must have asked himself whether or not his public would desert him in favor of the new gods, especially Giacomo Meyerbeer. Rossini, who had been the king of European opera for so many years, would not have relished the possibility of being called a has-been. Herbert Weinstock, Rossini's biographer, sums it up: "Nothing about him suggests that he would have competed—or would have wanted to compete—with the composer of *Les Huguenots* and *Le Prophète* and the composer of *Nabucco* and *Ernani* in order to supply audiences whose tastes he did not share with operas that he could not wholly like." The Rossinian opera world, in short, no longer existed.

So Rossini retired. He had homes in Bologna and Paris and a summer home in Passy. He found a new mistress. He busied himself with the Liceo Communale in Bologna, trying to raise the standards of that provincial conservatory of music. He was courted and flattered, and was recognized as The Grand Old Man of music. Witty, civilized, urbane, sharp-tongued, he was feared for his opinions, and his offhand remarks were gleefully quoted everywhere. "I have just received a Stilton and a cantata from Cipriani Potter. The cheese was very good." Or, "Wagner has some fine moments but some bad quarters of an hour." He said, after hearing the *Symphonie fantastique* by Berlioz, "What a good thing it isn't music." Another comment by Rossini about Berlioz concerned the *Song of the Rat* from *La Damnation de Faust*. It did not please, Rossini explained, because there was no cat in the house. Or—he loved making puns—when he overheard somebody praising the Credo of Liszt's *Gran* Mass as the fairest flower in the garland, Rossini said: "Yes, in fact a *fleur de Liszt.*" The tiny piano pieces and songs that he composed—many are still unpublished—he called the sins of his old age. These pieces have a Chabrier and Satie kind of surrealism, especially in the titles: *Les Hors d'oeuvres,* with individual pieces in the set named radishes, anchovies, butter, and so on; or *Mon Prélude hygienique du matin,* or *Gymnastique d'écartement,* or *L'Innocence italienne suite de la candeur française.*

In Paris he established one of the most glittering salons in Europe. On Saturday nights he formally entertained. There would be music, and often Rossini himself would go to the piano to accompany a famous singer. He was a pianist of the old school, using little or no pedal, letting his fingers drift elegantly over the keys. Printed invitations were sent to guests, and there were printed programs for the musical part of the evening. Rossini had a few talented pianists on call, to play or to accompany when he was not in the mood. Charles Camille Saint-Saëns was one of them, and the brilliant Louis Diémer was another. Eduard Hanslick, writing for the *Neue Freie Presse* in Vienna, described one of Rossini's soirées. Hanslick said that the house was too small to accommodate the number of guests:

> The heat was indescribable and the pressure so great that the most desperate efforts were always necessary whenever a fair vocalist (especially one of the weight of Madame Sax) had to make her way from the seat to the piano. A host of ladies, sparkling with jewels, occupy the entire music room; the men stand, so jammed together as to be unable to move, at the open doors. Now and then a servant with refreshment worms his way through the gasping crowd, but it is an odd fact that only very few persons (and those mostly strangers) take anything worth mentioning. The lady of the house, it is said, does not like their doing so.

When Rossini died, on November 13, 1868, it was the death of an emperor.

In his operas, Rossini was never part of the romantic world. But he listened to everything, and in such works as the *Stabat Mater* or the *Petite Messe Solennelle,* he used harmonies much more adventurous than anything that can be found in his operas. The *Messe,* with its chromaticisms alongside its classic melodic outline, is a fascinating amalgam of the old and the new. In its original scoring, for chorus, four soloists, two pianos, and organ, the work exerts a peculiar charm. It is a masterpiece just as the *Péchés de vieilesse—Sins of My Old Age—*are masterpieces in miniature. As for those bubbling pre-1829 operas, there remains the *Barber.* But who today can sing it, or sing those other enchanting frivolities? What would Rossini, the ultimate connoisseur of singing, have had to say had he encountered the strained, throaty, hooty, spread, loud, vulgar, heavy, maladroit singing that today passes, *faute de mieux*, as "the Rossini style?"

Gaetano Donizetti (November 29, 1797–April 7, 1848) was even more prolific than Rossini. He studied in Bergamo, the city of his birth, went to Bologna, returned to Bergamo, and then started to turn out operas with the fluency of a matchstick machine. In addition to some seventy operas there came from his pen twelve string quartets, seven masses, songs, piano music, cantatas, motets, and psalms. He had flair, he had style, and he constantly was abusing his talent, writing too much too fast. Yet *Lucia* (1835), *Don Pasquale* (1843), and *L'Elisir d'Amore* (1832) remain very much with us, and *Anna Bolena* (1830), *La Fille du Régiment* (1840), and *La Favorite* (1840) are occasionally revived. Donizetti's mad scenes were especially admired. Audiences liked to hear his heroines expiring in showers of trills, arpeggios, scales, leaps, and high notes, all augmented with interpolated cadenzas. French opera adopted the Donizetti mad scenes. And Donizetti was a strong influence on the young Verdi, much more so than were Rossini and Bellini. Throughout the century, great singers from Pasta, Rubini, Lablache, and Duprez to Lind, Sontag, Grisi, Patti, Mario, and Albor.i, loved the Donizetti operas. In those mid-nineteenth-century days of great singing, *Anna Bolena* (1830) was regarded as Donizetti's masterpiece.

Like all Italian opera composers, Donizetti was constantly on the move. He went up and down Italy, staging his operas. Many were enthusiastically received, and after *Anna Bolena* he was famous. *L'Elisir d'Amore* illustrates the conditions under which Donizetti had to work, and the speed with which he filled his commissions. The manager of the Teatre della Canobbiana in Milan needed a new opera at short notice because of the failure of a composer to deliver a promised work. Donizetti was approached two weeks before the scheduled premiere. The desperate manager suggested that Donizetti patch up an old work and pass it off as new. Donizetti probably took this as a challenge. What? Do you think I cannot compose an opera in two weeks? He sent for the librettist, Felice Romani, and is supposed to have said: "I am obliged to set a poem to music in fourteen days. I give you one week to prepare it for me. We'll see which of us two has more guts!" Romani supplied the libretto in time, and Donizetti dashed off the music. It was a success at the premiere and has remained one of his most popular operas. Berlioz heard it in Milan shortly after the premiere. His account gives an idea of the behavior of Italian audiences. He found the theater full of people, but they were "talking in normal voices with their backs to the stage. The singers, undeterred, gesticulated and yelled their lungs out in the strictest spirit of rivalry. At least I presumed they did, from their wide-open mouths; but the noise of the audience was such that no sound penetrated except the bass drum. People were gambling, eating supper in their boxes, etc., etc. Consequently, perceiving it was useless to expect to hear anything of the score, which was then new to me, I left."

The years after *L'Elisir d'Amore* saw Donizetti in Paris, in Vienna, still constantly on the move. *Lucia di Lammermoor* was produced in Naples in 1835. It turned out to be one of the most popular operas of the century. In 1837 Donizetti lost his wife, whom he adored, and he never recovered from the shock. In addition, he had periodic bouts of ill health. He had a stroke in 1845, slowly lost control of his mind, and died three years later. There was general sorrow. Not only had the world lost a talented composer, but also a gentle, good-natured man of whom it was said he never had the least trace of jealousy or viciousness. At his best, he was a composer of grace, and his comic operas have the kind of melodic invention, gusto, and brio that only Rossini has brought to music.

Vincenzo Bellini (November 3, 1801–September 23, 1835) composed an opera semiseria, *La Sonnambula* (1831), a tremendous favorite in its day and still in the repertoire. It has its moments of charm, but the works more representative of Bellini are *Norma* (1831) and *I Puritani* (1835). These are full of the arias that are the essence of Bellini—the long, arched, slow melody over an arpeggiated bass. Bellini was obsessed by melody. Once, playing through Pergolesi's *Stabat Mater,* he told a friend: "If I could write one melody as beautiful as this, I would not mind dying young, like Pergolesi." Even Wagner, who detested most Italian music, responded to *Norma.* He said of Bellini's operas that they were "all heart, connected with words." Rossini and Donizetti had also written long, slow melodies, but without Bellini's peculiar intensity. Rossini's melodies, for instance, are classically oriented, while Bellini's are romantic, and it was with good reason that Bellini and Chopin were close friends. They had something musically in common, and a Chopin nocturne has a type of melody and bass that comes very close to the Bellinian kind of melody. (They had other things in common. Both were slim, slight, aristocratic-looking men. Both had the fashionable romantic disease, tuberculosis, and both died young.) Even in the early Bellini operas, such as *Il Pirata* of 1827 and *La Straniera* of 1829, a new, long-breathed, somewhat sentimental voice was heard. Verdi was to exclaim over Bellini's "long, long melodies, such as no one before has written."

His music attracted the great singers more than the music even of Rossini. They responded to the romanticism implicit in the Bellini arias. And he had some remarkable voices with which to work, notably the heroic tribe of mezzo-sopranos active in the first half of the nineteenth century. It was for them that Rossini, Donizetti, and Bellini wrote many of the roles now sung by sopranos (the role of Rosina in *Il Barbiere,* for instance, was created for low voice). But those bel canto mezzos were protean. They could sing the lightest coloratura role one night and at their next performance sing Norma or the heaviest Meyerbeer role. Maria Malibran, who died in 1836 at the age of twenty-eight after a fall from a horse, was confidently thought by her contemporaries to have been the greatest singer who ever lived. She was a mezzo-soprano who could go down to a low F and up to an easy high C. The same was true of Marietta Alboni and Giulia Grisi. The high sopranos, such as Giuditta Pasta and Henriette Sontag, could reach an F or G. Then there were tenors like Mario (he was known by this name alone), baritones like Antonio Tamburini, and basses like Luigi Lablache, who has come down in history as the greatest of his tribe. Luigi Lablache: he with the voice of thunder and yet the flexibility of "a coiled snake." Bellini wrote for those singers. Probably what was the greatest vocal quartet of all time—Grisi, Rubini, Tamburini, and Lablache—would appear all together in his operas. The great Jenny Lind also achieved her first fame as a Bellini exponent, as did Adelina Patti.

Not necessarily the best, but surely the most electrifying of all Bellini singers, was Giovanni Battista Rubini, the tenor who also had been identified with some of the Rossini and Donizetti operas. "Rubini and Bellini were born for each other," said the *Musical World*. Rubini was especially famous for his interpolated F above high C in *I Puritani*. He sang it falsetto. Léon Escudier, the French critic, once heard Rubini, in Donizetti's *Roberto Devereux*, "leap even to G. He himself has never ascended so high, and he himself, after that *tour de force,* appeared astonished at the feat." He was not a good actor, but nobody went to any of his performances expecting to be thrilled by his acting. They went to be thrilled by his singing. *La Revue des Deux Mondes,* in the obituary notice of Rubini (who died in 1854), gives an idea of his powers:

> The astonished ear followed the singer, in his triumphal ascent, to the highest limits of the tenor register without noticing any interruption of continuity in this long spiral of notes. . . . To this almost incredible power of passing without a break from chest to head register, Rubini added another no less important—namely, a breath control, the force of which he had learned to economize. Gifted with a broad chest, where his lungs could dilate with ease, he took a high note, filled it successively with light and warmth, and when it was completely expanded, threw it forward into the house, where it burst like a Bengal rocket in a thousand colors.

The writer goes on to rhapsodize over Rubini's "prodigiously flexible" coloratura technique—scales, arpeggios, trills taken on the highest notes, grupetti, appogiaturas. Small wonder that the Bellini operas are unable to make their full effect in the twentieth century. The breed of singers for whom they were composed is extinct.

Bellini spent some years in Paris, where he was one of the most romantic figures in a city of romantic figures. Slight, delicate, handsome, languishing, talented, he attracted worshipers, mostly of the opposite sex. Heinrich Heine, sharp and cynical as always, saw Bellini as

> . . . a tall, up-shooting, slender figure who always moved gracefully; he was coquettish, ever looking as though just removed from a bandbox; a regular but large, delicately rose-tinted face; light, almost golden hair worn in many curls; a high, very high, marble forehead, straight nose, light blue eyes, good-sized mouth and rounded chin. His features had something vague in them, a want of character, something milk-like; and in this milk-like face flitted sometimes a painful-pleasing expression of sorrow. This expression in his face took the place of the fire that was lacking; but it was that of a sorrow without depth. It glanced, but un-poetically, from his eyes. It played, but without passion, upon his lips. It was this poutless, shallow sorrow that the young maestro seemed most anx-ious to represent in his whole appearance. His hair was dressed so fanci-fully, his clothes fitted so languishingly around his delicate body, he car-ried his cane so idyll-like, that he reminded me of the young shepherds we find in our pastorals with their crooks decorated with ribbons. . . . The whole man looked like a sigh, in pumps and silk stockings. He has met with much sympathy from women but I doubt if he ever produced strong passion in any one. . . .

Norma is conceded to be his greatest work, though *I Puritani* has more brilliance (including the high D's for Rubini). A poised, infinitely long mel-ody like the *Casta Diva* from *Norma*, building from measure to measure, perfectly proportioned, chaste yet full of passion, makes an unforgettable impact when well sung. Norma is not an easy role. It calls for a dramatic so-prano of unusual flexibility. Later in the century the German soprano, Lilli Lehmann, was to say that she would rather sing three Brünnhildes in a row than one Norma. *Norma* is the only Bellini opera steadily in the interna-tional repertory. To many it is the very essence of the bel canto tradition.

❧ 15 ❧

Spectacle, Spectacle, and More Spectacle

MEYERBEER, CHERUBINI, AUBER

While the Germans were concentrating on sonata form and absolute music, the French were providing a form of music that the public and the aristocracy from Lisbon to St. Petersburg found titillating and agreeable enough to keep in the active repertory throughout the nineteenth century and even a little beyond. The French grand opera of Meyerbeer and his contemporaries, which succeeded the bel canto operas of Rossini and Bellini, swept the world. Wagner may have had his theories, his great orchestra and his leitmotifs, his daring harmonies and far-reaching vision, but the French knew how to satisfy the palate. This was music to enjoy! Meyerbeer, Auber, Halévy, Hérold—these were composers who could give you melody and singing! And the Opéra in Paris could supply the spectacle.

The Académie Royale de Musique had been founded in 1671 as an institution for serious lyric drama. By the turn of the eighteenth century it had developed into an outlet for opera. Some important composers were active there (and elsewhere in Paris theaters), and many of the operas they produced were markedly preromantic, and much more anticipatory of romanticism than the instrumental music of the time. As early as Jean Jacques Rousseau's *Le Devin du village* (1752) a feeling towards nature was expressed. André Grétry's *Zémire et Azor* (1771), *La Caravane du Caire* (1783), and *Richard Coeur de Lion* (1784), went in for the kind of medievalism and interest in exotic subjects so beloved by the romantics. The operas of Nicolas Dalayrac, especially *Les deux petits Savoyards* (1788) and *Adolphe et Clara* (1799), were popular. Luigi Cherubini, in his *Lodoiska* (1791), *Médée* (1797), and *Les deux journées* (1800), anticipated spectacle opera, with great fires and other natural phenomena simulated on stage. These three Cherubini operas were first presented at the Théâtre Feydeau and later were done at the Opéra. At the Théâtre Favart, François Boieldieu was setting to music such exotic librettos as *Zoraïne et Zulnar* (1798) and *Le Calife de Bagdad* (1800). No comparable operatic school existed anywhere else in the world at the time. German opera was isolated, and only a few works —Mozart's *Die Zauberflöte* and *Don Giovanni*, Weber's *Der Freischütz*, and, later, Nicolai's *Die Lustigen Weiber von Windsor* (1849) attracted much international attention. The operas of Heinrich Marschner, Ludwig Spohr, and Albert Lortzing, popular in Germany, were local phenomena, whereas French opera and light opera captivated all of Europe.

During the 1830's, with Meyerbeer riding high, the Opéra was big business. It was a bourgeois affair. In 1831 the businessmen who had come in with the Citizen King turned the Opéra over to a director-entrepreneur "who should manage it for six years at his own risk and fortune." In effect, it was his house. He could pocket the gains, bear the losses, select repertory and casts. With all that, he enjoyed a subsidy from the State—710,000 francs in the 1830's. The director ran the Opéra as a business enterprise. He supplied a commodity in hope of a profit. Naturally he too was bourgeois, with bourgeois tastes. Louis Véron, the first of the great directors of the Opéra, actually entitled his autobiography *Mémoires d'un bourgeois de Paris*. In that, he reflected the complacency of the real ruling class—the bankers, industrialists, and *bourgeoisie* who ran Paris and the country. The King himself prided himself on being bourgeois, and to many the reign of Louis-Philippe was intolerably dull. *"La France s'ennuie,"* complained Lamartine.

Véron, born in 1798, was trained as a physician and actually practiced medicine. Then he went into journalism and founded the *Revue de Paris*. Shrewd, publicity-conscious, knowing what the people wanted, he also knew what was expected of him. This fat man lived in extreme elegance, dressed like a fop, wore expensive clothing and jewels, went in heavily for advertising, and paid off the critics with a lavish hand. Appointed director of the Opéra in 1831, he straightened out the administration and brought in his own people. He also had some new ideas about repertory, and for the four years he was there, Véron made the Paris Opéra the most prestigious house in Europe. In those days the Opéra was in the Rue Le Peletier. The building had been erected in 1821, and the auditorium seated 1,954.

Composers such as Meyerbeer, Auber, and Halévy supplied the music for many of the operas in Véron's administration. Eugène Scribe was the official librettist. As chief conductor there was François Habeneck, the Beethoven specialist who also was conductor of the Conservatoire concerts. The dancers were headed by the great Marie Taglioni, later to be joined by the equally great Fanny Elssler. Edmond Duponchel and Pierre Cicéri were the stage directors. Among the singers were such stars as Adolphe Nourrit, Louis Duprez, and Cornélie Falcon. There was strong vocal competition from the Théâtre des Italiens, which specialized in Italian opera and had such giants as Malibran and Sontag. But not even they attracted as much attention as Duprez, one of the first great dramatic tenors. He sang high notes from the chest instead of in falsetto; and, says a contemporary report, when "he brought out the high C in the chest voice with all the might of his colossal organ, it was all over with the fame of all his predecessors. Nourrit, till then the favorite of the Parisians, a distinguished tenor, recognized his rival's power. His day was over, and in despair over his lost and irrecoverable glory, he flung himself from an upper window down upon the pavement, and so made an end to his life."

Heading the *corps de claque* was an imposing man known to the world simply as Auguste. His full name was Auguste Levasseur. Of Auguste it was written: "He lived—indeed, he could only live—at the Opéra. . . . Large, robust, a veritable Hercules in size, gifted with an extraordinary pair of hands, he was created and put into the world to be a claqueur." No singer, no composer, not Véron himself, felt safe unless Auguste was directing the applause, creating a success on the spot. The claque remained an institution in Paris throughout the century, and the position of *chef de claque* was eagerly sought after. It was a profitable job. The *chef de claque* could make money by being engaged by singers and composers, and he could also sell the forty free seats he received gratis for each performance. By 1860 the *chef de claque* was no longer paid by the Opéra; instead, he was paying the manager for the job. Not only the opera but every theater had its *chef de claque*. Each made a café his headquarters. As the *Musical World* in London explained the operation, the *chef de claque* would put in an appearance towards 5 or 6 o'clock, "and is mobbed by the forty or fifty people anxious to be enrolled for the evening. As a rule, the first thing the *chef de claque* looks at is the dress of his candidates. He accepts no blouses and no slovens. If he sees a man well arrayed, hearty looking and florid of countenance, endowed with broad shoulders and big hands, he enlists him at once." The *Musical World* went on to say that it would be folly for a new singer to appear without engaging the *chef de claque*. "So long as the French mind evinces a sly relish for furtive hisses and takes overt pleasure in dramatic rows, so long will the *chef de claque* be at his post, crying in a stage whisper to his honorable troops, '*Allons, mes enfants, tous ensemble; chaudement, et à bas la cabale.*'"

Just as the singers felt they needed Auguste, so many composers of French opera would have felt naked without a Scribe libretto. Eugène Scribe (1791–1861) took a law degree in 1815, but never practiced. He was too busy writing successful plays and becoming rich and famous. As early as 1811 he was on the boards, and between 1820 and 1830 about a hundred of his plays were given. During his life he turned out an incredible amount of material, and his complete works fill seventy-six volumes. He had been engaged as librettist for the Opéra in 1828, before Véron's appointment, and he supplied the librettos for some of the most sensational successes of the period.

Scribe's material was largely original and did not follow classical models. He had little to do with the mythology and the classic subjects of lyric tragedy so dear to the heart of the Académie. He echoed the new, popular romantic taste. He wrote about the supernatural, he could supply Gothic romances, and he dealt also with medieval legends. He delighted above all in historical melodrama. Among the famous librettos he wrote were *Robert le Diable, Le Prophète, Les Huguenots,* and *L'Africaine* (Meyerbeer); *La Juive* (Halévy); *La Dame Blanche* (Boieldieu); *Le Comte Ory* (Rossini); *I Vespri Siciliani* (Verdi); *Ali Baba* (Cherubini); *La Favorite* (Donizetti); and *Fra Diavolo* (Auber). Scribe wrote thirty-eight librettos for Auber alone. In addition, many librettos, such as Verdi's *Un Ballo in Maschera,* were fashioned from Scribe plays.

Today his writing is faded, but contemporary audiences saw social significance in his plays and librettos about oppressed peoples and minority groups. Working closely with his composers, Scribe developed a formula. Generally, as in Italian opera, his librettos opened with a chorus. Arias and ensembles were carefully allotted. Everything was calculated to lead to some kind of superspectacle, such as the great ballroom scene in Auber's *Gustav III* or the festival scene in Halévy's *La Juive.* In 1835 the *Courier Français* wrote of *La Juive* as the eighth wonder of the world. "The costumes of the warriors, civilians, and ecclesiastics are not imitated but reproduced in their smallest details. The armor is no longer pasteboard; it is made of real metal. One sees men of iron, men of silver, men of gold! The Emperor Sigismond, for instance, is a glittering ingot from head to foot. The horses, not less historically outfitted than their riders, turn and prance."

That was grand opera. That was Scribe. That was Véron.

Scribe's first libretto was written for Auber in 1828. The opera, *La Muette de Portici* (also called *Masaniello*), was a turning point in the history of the lyric stage. It was grand opera, more elaborate by far than anything hitherto produced. Among its technical features were a cyclorama and mobile panoramas. *La Muette* also had a fine, tuneful, richly instrumented score, one that held the stage throughout the century. The next great hit after the Auber was Rossini's *William Tell,* in 1829. This too was a tremendous stage spectacle, and many listeners thought it contained Rossini's best music. Véron, when he took over the Opéra, wanted to duplicate those two smash hits, and he came up with Meyerbeer's *Robert le Diable* in 1831. It was a romantic opera in that it had to do with medieval knights and the Devil. The costumes outdid even those in *La Muette de Portici;* and for the first time, gas

202

illumination was used on a French stage. *Robert le Diable* was a success that eclipsed anything ever seen in Paris up to that time. So popular was it, and the following Meyerbeer operas, that they all but wiped out the Rossini craze in Europe. Up to then Rossini had been *the* opera composer; but, *William Tell* excepted, how could Rossini's slender, thinly scored music stand up against the cannonades of the heroic Meyerbeer orchestra? It couldn't. Having seen *Robert le Diable,* the public demanded that all other new operas come up to its level as a spectacle.

Meyerbeer, who achieved such fame in Paris, was born in Berlin on September 5, 1791. His real name was Jakob Liebmann Beer. Like Mendelssohn, he came from a rich Jewish banking family. Like Mendelssohn, too, he was a prodigy and one of the most talented pianists in Europe. But unlike Mendelssohn he had a flair for the theater and was only happy composing operas. He went to Italy, where he came under the influence of Rossini, and in 1824 composed a successful opera named *Il Crociato in Egitto.* Then he went to Paris, where the important men were Auber, Méhul, Cherubini, and Spontini. Gasparo Spontini (1774–1851) was a sort of pre-Meyerbeer composer whose two most famous operas, *La Vestale* and *Fernand Cortez,* had been produced at the Opéra in 1807 and 1809 respectively. Berlioz always thought *La Vestale* to be the greatest opera since Gluck. Every once in a while it enjoys a revival, even today. It is an early specimen of grand opera. Musically it is noble and static, very Gluck-like in its diatonic harmonies and lack of modulation.

On Meyerbeer's first visit to Paris, in 1826, opera was in the doldrums. The opera house was the plaything of the aristocracy. Productions were shabby, performances listless, and the previously popular operas by François Philidor, Pierre Monsigny, and André Grétry seldom played. So miserable was the Opéra that François Castil-Blaze in 1824 used the Odéon Theater to stage operas by Mozart, Weber, and Rossini. His intentions were good, but he tampered so heavily with the scores, even inserting his own or some other new music, that the results were monstrous distortions. Rossini in 1826 was called in by the Opéra as a consultant, and he supervised productions of his own *Le Siège de Corinthe, Moïse,* and *Le Comte Ory.* But even he could not overcome the inertia and bureaucracy. It was Véron who had the flair and administrative ability to revitalize the Opéra and bring new works into its repertoire. When Meyerbeer returned to Paris in 1830, he had almost a clear field. All he had to do was compose something on the order of *Muette* or *Tell.* It is to the credit of Véron's imagination that he was willing to take a chance on this little-known composer.

Meyerbeer was not a fast worker. *Robert le Diable* of 1831 was followed by *Les Huguenots* in 1836, *Le Prophète* in 1849, *L'Etoile du Nord* in 1854 (this one at the Opéra-Comique), *Dinorah* in 1859, and the posthumously produced *L'Africaine* in 1865. There was no reason for Meyerbeer to be in a rush. Every one of his operas took Europe by storm, and never had a composer achieved such incredible popularity, not even Rossini. *Robert le Diable* in its first eight years was performed in 1,843 European theaters. "We could fill a library," a British magazine writer said, "with the pieces arranged by a thousand composers from the airs of this opera. . . . Everywhere, at the theater, in the tavern, at military parades, in the churches, at concerts, in the cottage and in the palace, was and is to be heard the delicious music of *Robert*. . . . In London it has been played in four theaters at the same time." Not until the great Verdi successes in the early 1850's was there a composer of operas who could compete with Meyerbeer.

Meyerbeer knew what the public wanted, and he put his operas together determined to satisfy them. There had to be spectacle. There had to be brilliant vocal parts, but the arias were not to last very long. Nobody should be bored. To bore the public was the worst sin. Leave characterization and developments to the Germans. Leave bel canto to the Italians. The orchestration had to be glittering and powerful, with massed superfortissimos. There had to be imposing choruses. There had to be a ballet. Scribe was most accommodating, and gave Meyerbeer exactly what he wanted. The *Journal pour Rire* presented an imaginary dialogue between Meyerbeer and his librettist:

M. MEYERBEER: I should like a libretto for a comic opera having for its subject the amours of Czar Peter the Great and the vivandière [canteen manager] Catherine.

M. SCRIBE: . . . First let us find our three acts. Nothing easier. In the first, Peter the Great, simple ship carpenter, loves Catherine, simple vivandière; in the second, Peter the Great, in the tumult of camps, continues to love Catherine; in the third, Peter the Great, in the bosom of grandeur, always loving Catherine, decides to marry her. Let us occupy ourselves, if you please, with the first act. It is the only important one. Good or bad, the public is obliged to see the other two. We say then that Peter the Great, simple carpenter, loves Catherine, simple vivandière. Here we have the motive for: (1) a chorus of carpenters at the rising of the curtain; (2) a grand aria for Peter's declaration to Catherine; (3) a finale of carpenters. . . .

M. MEYERBEER: I should like to introduce in the first chorus a chanson or ballade like that in *La Dame Blanche*.

M. SCRIBE: Nothing easier. We will bring in some chocolate or cake merchant, who shall offer his refreshments and gay refrains. And then?

M. MEYERBEER: I should also like a wedding like that in the first act of *Macon*.

M. SCRIBE: Nothing easier. We'll celebrate the wedding of one of Peter's companions.

M. MEYERBEER: With an arietta for soprano.

M. SCRIBE: Expressive of the bride's beating heart: tic, tac, tic, tac.

M. MEYERBEER: And a drinking song for the basses.

M. SCRIBE: Chorus of drinking guests: glu, glu, glu, glu. It's done. And then?

M. MEYERBEER: We must find some variation, some military song, like that of Max in *Le Chalet*.

M. SCRIBE: Nothing easier. A troop of recruiters, beating the drum, shall break into the wedding. . . .

M. MEYERBEER: And do you think that will suffice for the intelligence of the public?

M. SCRIBE: Oh, mon Dieu! For the public, the important thing is not to comprehend but to be amused. Besides, if a comic opera contained common sense, it would not be a comic opera.

M. MEYERBEER: And how much time will you require to put all that into verse?

M. SCRIBE: Only a few hours. . . .

The better musicians of the day realized that the Meyerbeer operas were nothing more than skillful collages. Mendelssohn sneered. Yes, he said, the Meyerbeer operas are full of great effects. But of what did they consist? "Melodies for whistling, harmony for the educated, instrumentation for the Germans, contra dances for the French, something for everybody—but there's no heart in it." Something for everybody: Mendelssohn put his finger directly on it. Some doubted if the Meyerbeer operas were even music. The composer-pianist Ferdinand Hiller was asked what he thought of the Meyerbeer operas. "Oh," Hiller said, "let us not talk politics." Others took a stronger view. George Sand said of *Les Huguenots* that she did not care to go to the opera to see Catholics and Protestants cut each other's throats to music set by a Jew. She also said that there was more music in Chopin's tiny C minor Prélude than in the four hours of the trumpetings in *Les Huguenots*. (Claude Debussy, many years later, got off a gibe close to Sand's. He wrote of *Les Huguenots:* "The music is so strained that even the anxiety to massacre unfortunate Protestants does not altogether excuse it.") Berlioz, who never completely made up his mind about the Meyerbeer operas, described them testily (but with a certain amount of respect and even envy) as consisting of

high C's from every type of chest, bass drums, snare drums, organs, military bands, antique trumpets, tubas as big as locomotive smokestacks, bells, cannon, horses, cardinals under a canopy, emperors, queens in tiaras, funerals, fêtes, weddings . . . jugglers, skaters, choirboys, censers, monstrances, crosses, taverns, processions, orgies of priests and naked women, the bull Apis and masses of oxen, screech-owls, bats, the five hundred fiends of hell and what have you—the rocking of the heavens and the end of the world interspersed with a few dull cavatinas and a large claque thrown in.

To the pure Robert Schumann, Meyerbeer was the archfiend of composers, the perverter of taste. When Schumann first became acquainted with *Les Huguenots* he brought up his heaviest artillery: "I am no moralist, but it enrages a good Protestant to hear his dearest chorale shrilled out on the boards, to see the bloodiest drama in the whole history of his religion degraded to the level of an annual fair farce . . ." Schumann concluded that *Les Huguenots* exemplified "commonness, distortion, unnaturalness, immorality and unmusicality." The Germans were not the only opponents of the Meyerbeer operas. Almost to a man the lovers of bel canto accused Meyerbeer of ruining the art of singing. "Meyerbeer," said one critic, "has on his conscience all this screaming and unlovely exaggeration of the effects of song, all ths feverish excitement of the nerves in over-refined declamation. . . . To the consequences of his operas must it be ascribed that our singers no longer sing but scream."

But criticism was to the Meyerbeer operas what the sting of a hornet is to an armored car. For most of the century, even through Wagner's day, Meyerbeer was one of the two most popular operatic composers. Verdi was the other.

Naturally Meyerbeer became rich and famous, moving with great dignity between Berlin (where he was head of the opera) and Paris, with frequent trips to London to supervise productions there. He had more decorations, more orders from nobility, than any man not of royal blood. For one of his influence and wealth, he had surprisingly few personal enemies, though of course many musicians attacked the art he represented. Heine called Meyerbeer "the man of his age," and Heine as usual was correct. Meyerbeer's music, as Heine pointed out, was more social than individual. "Rossini would never have acquired his great popularity during the revolution and empire. Robespierre would have accused him perhaps of being antipatriotic. . . . Men in the old time had convictions; we moderns have only opinions." Meyerbeer had a notoriously thin skin, and with some glee Heine relates how Meyerbeer would try to mold critical opinion: "As the Apostle thinks neither of toils nor sufferings to save a single lost soul, so Meyerbeer, when he learns anybody rejects his music, will expound it to him indefatigably until he has converted him; and then the single saved lamb, were it only the most insignificant soul of a feuilletonist, is to him more dear than the whole flock of believers who have always worshipped him with orthodox fidelity." The careful Meyerbeer, anxious to keep the press on his side, always would invite the critics, before every one of his premieres, to a splendid dinner at the Hotel des Princes or the Trois Frères Provençaux. No critic is on record as ever having turned down the invitation. They staggered away from those meals with grand feelings of fellowship. "How can a chap of decent feeling," Spiridion in the *Evening Gazette* wanted to know, "write harshly of a man who has been pouring the choicest vintages of France and the most delicate tidbits of sea, air, forest, orchard and garden down one's throat? Try it. You will find the thing impossible. . . . There were few music critics in Paris who were not in receipt of annual pensions of several hundred dollars, and in one or two instances they exceeded $1,000 annually. There were critics here who had been in receipt of large pensions from Meyerbeer since 1831. Meyerbeer did not content himself with giving them pensions and good dinners. He also made it a point of duty to give them costly presents on their birthdays and on New Year's Day. Meyerbeer used to defend this by saying that he did not put these gentlemen under obligations. He was the person obliged, and he could not see anything wrong in giving evidence of his gratitude to them." (The critic who above all carried extortion to a fine art was P. A. Fiorentino, who wrote for *Le Moniteur, La France,* and *L'Entr'acte,* among others. Again quoting Spiridion: "He left an estate of over $300,000, although he lived expensively. . . . He levied blackmail with a ferocity unknown even in this capital of blackmail. . . . The managers of the Italian, Lyric and Opéra-Comique paid him considerable sums annually, and as for the costly presents he received there was no end of them. Meyerbeer always paid him a large pension with government punctuality." Fiorentino died in 1864.)

Today, on the rare occasions we hear a Meyerbeer opera, it is difficult to see what all of the excitement was about. Meyerbeer's admirers to the contrary notwithstanding, the music is extremely conventional, all the more so in that there are no heroic singers around who can trumpet forth the music as Caruso, the de Reszkes, Schumann-Heink, and Nordica used to do at the turn of the century. The music sounds synthetic, flabby, and overcalculated, and the melodic ideas are second-rate. Even the once-brilliant orchestration and the once-daring harmonies sound pallid because they are used for so cynical a purpose. The Meyerbeer operas are period pieces. But in their day, great musicians and critics took them very seriously. Bizet all but equated Meyerbeer with Beethoven and Mozart, and called him "a thundering dramatic genius." Heine wrote that the mother of Meyerbeer was the second woman in history to see her son accepted as divine. All over Europe, composers rushed to imitate the Meyerbeer formula. Wagner did, in *Rienzi,* and Verdi as late as *Aïda* in 1871. Gounod and Massenet also were influenced by the Meyerbeer operas.

But Meyerbeer was a dead end. Nobody could seem to imitate him with much success, try as they did. Nobody could follow him, and he had a monopoly on spectacle opera. As Berlioz ruefully said—Berlioz, whose *Troyens* never had any success—"Meyerbeer's influence and the pressure exerted on managers, artists, critics and the public as well by his immense fortune, at the very least as great as that exercised by his genuine eclectic talent, makes any serious success at the Opéra almost impossible." Berlioz also said that Meyerbeer not only had the luck to be talented, but also the talent to be lucky. And Berlioz burst out in genuine admiration over *Les Huguenots*. He was so moved by "this masterpiece" that he longed to be a great man "in order to place one's glory and one's genius at the feet of Meyerbeer."

Wagner, too, soon decided that Meyerbeerian opera was not his line. "It is impossible to surpass him." Wagner hated Meyerbeer—a competitor, a wealthy and successful competitor, and worst of all a wealthy, successful, and *Jewish* competitor. Meyerbeer seems to have been a rather retiring man, interested in the work of young composers, and generous with his money (he helped Wagner among others), but Wagner made him an object of derision. Meyerbeer, he wrote, was "like the starling who follows the plowshare down the field and merrily picks up the earthworm just uncovered in the furrow." Or, "Meyerbeer . . . wanted a monstrous, piebald, historico-romantic, diabolico-religious, fanatico-libidinous, sacro-frivolous, mysterio-criminal, autyloco-sentimental dramatic hodgepodge, therein to find material for a curious chimeric music—a want which, owing to the indominatable buckram of his musical temperament, could not be quite suitably applied." And on, and on, page after turgid page. Wagner's prose was much worse than Meyerbeer's music. It so happens that Wagner was largely correct in his opinions, but his writings about Meyerbeer drip such venom that they are uncomfortable to read. Yet Wagner used many of Meyerbeer's devices as building blocks for his own music. In a curious way Meyerbeer, who died on May 2, 1854, was one of the seminal forces of nineteenth-century operatic music.

Luigi Cherubini (1760–1842) is as little played today as Meyerbeer, though in his day he was considered by many, including Beethoven, to be not merely one of the masters but one of the immortals. The only one of his thirty operas holding the edge of the twentiety-century repertory, however, is *Médée*. And every once in a great while his *Anacreon* Overture turns up on a symphony program.

In the Louvre hangs a portrait of Cherubini painted by Ingres in 1842. Ingres, his good friend, shows him seated deep in thought, accompanied by his constant companion, the Muse of Music. She is giving him her benediction. He accepts it as a matter of course, like accepting dinner from his cook. Ingres has painted the face of a strong man—Roman nose (Cherubini was Italian-born and settled permanently in Paris in 1788), firm thin lips, cold eyes: a face of character, determination, and power.

But others saw him differently. He had a reputation for intolerance, for a temper and a cutting tongue, and he could be cruel. Adolphe Adam, later an important composer, was presented to the great Cherubini as a young boy. Cherubini's only remark was: "My! What an ugly child!" Berlioz, who considered Cherubini his complete enemy, tells about his run-in with the *directeur du Conservatoire*. Cherubini had been appointed the head of that institution in 1822. He was a martinet, and his rules extended even to such piddling details as having separate entrances for men and women. When Berlioz once entered the Conservatory through the wrong door, the porter told Cherubini, who burst into the library and confronted Berlioz "looking more wicked, cadaverous and dishevelled even than usual." The two got into an argument, and Cherubini chased Berlioz around the tables. At least, that is the way Berlioz tells the story. The two men could never hit it off, and Berlioz writes, with satisfaction, that if Cherubini chastized him with whips, "I certainly returned the compliment with scorpions."

If ever there was a textbook teacher and composer, it was Cherubini. That was his trouble. Everything in his music is unutterably, definitively, pulverizingly correct. Chordal progressions move exactly as the books say they should move. A glance at any one of his scores—the operas, the D minor Requiem, the chamber music—shows severe and correct melodies over a very conservative harmonic framework. When he modulates it is to a safe, closely related key. His most daring harmony is the diminished seventh chord, and that already was threadbare in his own day. As a result, his "white-key" music seldom moves. It is this harmonic timidity that afflicts even his most famous work, *Médée*. To attempt to explain his lack of vitality by saying that Cherubini was a classicist will not do. Mozart, just as much a classicist, achieved in *Don Giovanni* what Cherubini could not begin to envision in *Médée*. Basically Cherubini (and also his contemporary, Spontini) merely followed Gluck. After four or five hearings, *Médée* becomes more and more a Gluckian façade, a set of frozen attitudes in which the figures are permanently congealed.

Cherubini's mind was too rigid, and at basis too commonplace, ever to allow him to depart from the rules. What Beethoven, of all people, saw in him is hard to conceive. Probably it was technique. Beethoven, a consummate technician himself, respected technique in others. And in the one area where Beethoven was relatively weak—the human voice and opera (imagine Cherubini writing such an impossible-to-sing chorus as the *Et vitam venturi* from the *Missa Solemnis!*)—Cherubini moved with technical surety and, even, brilliance. Beethoven was far too good a musician not to respond with admiration. He and his contemporaries had no doubt about Cherubini's sublimity. The Director of the Conservatory was considered on a par with the other great composers of the day—Ignaz Moscheles, Ludwig Spohr, Johann Nepomuk Hummel, and Friedrich Kalkbrenner. All were destined for immortality.

The composers of the 1830's and 1840's who were able to write operas that held the stage even against the competition of Meyerbeer include, in addition to Auber, Ferdinand Hérold, with *Zampa* (1831; the overture is still played), and Fromental Halévy, with *La Juive* (1835). Halévy was a one-opera man who turned out work after work without ever coming near his great success. But that one success made him world-famous. For that one opera he was so venerated that his face was in every print-shop window and every photographer's showcase. At Halévy's death the Baron de Rothschild settled upon the widow of the composer of *La Juive* an annuity; and, reported Spiridion in the *Gazette,* "M. Rodriques, a wealthy stockbroker, sent her 8000 francs for the dowry of her two daughters, which sum, he said, was raised by several friends as a tribute of admiration and respect for her husband's memory. . . . A few days ago the Emperor sent a bill to the Council of State conferring upon her an annuity." *La Juive* remained extremely popular through the century and up to the death of Enrico Caruso in 1921. Bizet married Halévy's daughter; and Ludovic Halévy, a nephew, was one of the *Carmen* librettists.

At the Opéra-Comique, a house with a history that goes back to 1715, there was equal activity. During the 1830's and 40's, the repertoire of the Opéra-Comique was light in nature and the operas had spoken dialogue. (Spoken dialogue was the one requisite of a work for the Opéra-Comique.) Later in the century the line became obscured, and at the Comique there were operas, such as *Carmen* in 1875, that actually were tragedies. Even spoken dialogue was sometimes dropped. The better composers of the Opéra-Comique turned out a witty, skillful, civilized product. Works like Adam's *Le Postillon de Longjumeau* (1836), Boieldieu's *La Dame Blanche* (1825), Auber's *Fra Diavolo* (1830) and *Domino Noir* (1837) were played everywhere, and some of them still are.

Daniel François Auber (1782–1871) was the dominating force of his time at the Opéra-Comique. His first work there came out in 1805 and his last, forty-four operas later, in 1869. What with turning out this large number of works and in addition active as the head of the Conservatory, he was a busy man. After his death a critic had some recollections:

Auber was always composing. You met him sauntering down the boulevards: he was working. At the theater you had a stall next to his, and in which he was soon asleep: he was working. You pass along the Rue St. Georges after midnight. The street looked black on all sides except for a window through which the light of a modest lamp percolated: he was working. You knocked at his door at 6 A.M. A concierge as decrepit as the fairy Urgéle directed you to the first floor. A housekeeper old as Baucis referred you to a valet as old as Philemon. The valet showed you into a hospitable drawing room where the sounds of the piano already reached you: he was working.

At the age of eighty-seven he was still turning out stage works. He died rich and showered with honors, and not from overwork. He contributed to the lyric stage a handful of charming light operas. In the long run, the grace and sophistication of music like Auber's and Adam's have proved more durable than Meyerbeer's spectacles and big orchestral sounds; more durable, indeed, than anything produced at the Opéra or other grand opera stages in Paris until *Faust* came along in 1859, though nobody at the time would have thought so; or, having thought so, would have had the nerve to say it aloud.

❧ 16 ❧

Colossus of Italy

GIUSEPPE VERDI

As opera composers go, Giuseppe Verdi made his success early in life. He was born on October 10, 1813, in Le Roncole (almost five months after the birth of Richard Wagner in Leipzig). His first opera, *Oberto*, was well received in Milan in 1839, and his third, *Nabucco*, made him famous in 1842. Thirteen years after that, with *Rigoletto*, *Il Trovatore*, and *La Traviata* on the boards, he was the most popular composer of operas in the world, edging out even the fabulously successful spectacle operas of Meyerbeer. Verdi was a specialist who gave the public a commodity, and he never pretended to be a learned musician. Even when he was at the height of his fame he claimed that he was a pragmatist. In a letter of 1869 he said that "There is hardly any music in my house. I have never gone to a music library, never to a publisher to examine a piece. I keep abreast of some of the better contemporary works not by studying them but through hearing them occasionally at the theater. . . . I repeat, therefore, that I am the least erudite among past and present composers." This was true; it was not a *façon de parler*. Nor did Verdi speak much about his own work, except to those directly concerned—his publisher, conductors, singers. He wanted his music to do the talking, and he almost indignantly turned down a request for an autobiography. "Never, never will I consent to write my memoirs!"

Certain it is that as a child he gave no indication that he would develop into the musical colossus in the Italy of his time. He did display talent, but not a spectacular talent on the order of a Mozart or a Mendelssohn. In his town of Le Roncole, near Busseto in the duchy of Parma, he had studied with the village organist. His father, an innkeeper and grocer, was pleased with his son's talent and managed to purchase a used spinet for him. When Giuseppe was ten, his father sent him to live with a cobbler friend in Busseto. There he was noticed by Antonio Barezzi, a rich local merchant and a generous man. Barezzi took him into his own house as an apprentice, and also saw to it that the boy received the best musical training Busseto had to offer. It was not much. Verdi worked with the local organist, who also was the conductor of the local orchestra, and soon was deputizing for him. Then Barezzi saw to it that Verdi was sent to Milan, to study at the conservatory. At the age of eighteen the young musician arrived in that city—a short, intense, taciturn person, with brown hair, black eyebrows and beard, a very pale complexion, and a pock-marked face.

Whatever hopes he may have had were immediately dashed. The kind of training he had received in Busseto was not enough to get him into the conservatory. His piano playing was weak, his knowledge of theory insufficient. For two years he remained in Milan, studying privately. He even started work on an opera, *Oberto*. In 1834 he returned to Busseto, and two years later married Barezzi's daughter, Margherita. He finished *Oberto* and it was brought to the attention of Bartolomeo Merelli, the impresario of La Scala. Merelli took a chance on the opera by an unknown composer, and was rewarded when *Oberto* was well received. In a farsighted move, Merelli offered Verdi a contract to compose three operas at eight-month intervals. *Un Giorno di Regno* was the first commission. It was a comic opera, and Verdi had to turn it out during a period in which he lost both of his children and then his wife. Small wonder that *Un Giorno di Regno* failed. The failure not only left a mark on Verdi; it almost stopped his career for good. He seriously thought of giving up composition. It is clear that he had completely lost faith in himself. A dour man, he hid his disappointment about the *Giorno di Regno* disaster, but for years it rankled, and it also helped establish his own inner relations with the public. "It may be," he wrote, "that it is a bad opera, though many no better are tolerated and even applauded. Had the public not applauded, but merely endured my opera in silence, I should have had no words enough to thank them! . . . I do not mean to blame the public, but I accept their criticisms and jeers only on condition that I do not have to be grateful for their applause." Verdi lived up to this statement all his life.

Un Giorno di Regno fiasco or not, Merelli saw something in the young composer. He pressed on Verdi a libretto that Otto Nicolai, the promising German composer, had refused. Verdi reluctantly set to work. Then came idea after idea, and the opera was finished in three months. It had its premiere on March 9, 1842, and a new operatic hero was hailed by Italy.

The opera was *Nabucco,* short for *Nabucodonosor.* Today it may sound like unformed Verdi, and in many ways it is. It straddles the bel canto school and the coming dramatic school. Donizetti's influence can be heard in *Nabucco,* and also the Rossini of the serious operas. But the formulae take on new breadth, new life, in Verdi's opera. It is hard to put ourselves back in time and realize the impact that *Nabucco* made in 1842. What today sounds derivative came then as an explosion. During the rehearsals of *Nabucco* the theater was, according to contemporary accounts, "turned upside down." Nobody had ever dreamed of this kind of music. It was "so new, so unknown, the style so rapid, so unusual, that everybody was amazed. . . . It was impossible to work offstage while the rehearsals were going on, for employees, workmen, painters, machinists, excited by the music they were hearing, left their tasks to stand open-mouthed and watch what was taking place on stage."

Naturally word-of-mouth reports flooded Milan, and the public was beside itself to hear the opera. The connoisseurs—and everybody in the city considered himself a connoisseur of opera—immediately realized that a new and original talent had arrived. "With this opera," Verdi said, "my artistic career can truly be said to have begun." Verdi's competition also realized it. Some of his colleagues were jealous, and some took it gracefully. Donizetti was one of the latter. "The world wants new things," he said. "Others, after all, have yielded the place to us, so we must yield it to others. . . . Delighted to yield it to people of talent like Verdi." Donizetti predicted that his new rival would soon occupy "one of the most honored places in the cohort of composers."

What Verdi did in *Nabucco,* and what struck musical Italy, was to open up and expand the formula bel canto opera. He used a larger orchestra, with a consequently larger tonal thrust. The music itself is much broader and more forceful than in any bel canto opera, and it moves more directly. There is no lingering over empty vocal display. There are, to be sure, plenty of vocal fireworks, but always for an emotional rather than exhibitionistic reason. The role of Abigaille is one of the most difficult in the repertory; it needs a dramatic coloratura soprano with a mezzo-soprano ability to take chest tones and an ability to project raw power—the power of the character itself, and the power of Verdi's writing. There is terrific personality all through *Nabucco*. Even when Verdi touched on the bel canto conventions and mannerisms, he made them sound bigger and stronger. In this opera he found himself, and the music contains many anticipations of later Verdi. Zaccaria's "D'Egitto là sui lidi" anticipates the elder Germont's arias in *La Traviata,* just as the third-act duet between Nabucco and Abigaille brings to mind the Aïda-Amonasro duets.

In addition, there were political implications in *Nabucco,* and the opera made Verdi a symbol of the resistance to the Austrian domination. The "Va, pensiero" chorus, which concerns the longing of the Jewish exiles for home, was identified by all Italian listeners with their own longing for freedom. Whether or not Verdi deliberately set this chorus as a politically oriented message is not known. He himself was strongly nationalistic, as pro-Italian as Wagner was pro-German. Verdi lived in hope of a united Italy, and he lived to see it. But whatever his motivation for the "Va, pensiero" chorus, the tune immediately made its way through Italy and was sung as a symbol of the resistance. To many Italians, Verdi himself symbolized that spirit, and years later an acrostic was made on his name: *Vittorio Emmanuele, Re d'Italia.*

Verdi followed *Nabucco* with two more hits—*I Lombardi* in 1843 and *Ernani* in 1844. The latter made him known outside of Italy. In Paris it was staged at the Théâtre des Italiens and Verdi went there to supervise the production. Now in a position to demand large fees, Verdi did not hesitate to do so. He was a solid businessman, determined to make the best bargain he could. Several lesser hits or even failures followed *Ernani,* and then came *Macbeth* in 1847. Verdi, who was to conclude his career with two settings of Shakespeare plays, took special pains with *Macbeth,* which had its premiere in Florence. It was the drama of the play he wanted to emphasize; and even if his librettists distorted Shakespeare, Verdi strove with all his power to approximate Shakespeare's kind of terror and pity. It is a strange opera, dark and moody, unconventional and often unsatisfactory. But it does have the "Sleepwalking Scene," an episode that ranks with the great ones of his later operas. At the time he wrote *Macbeth,* Verdi had all but broken free from the Italian operatic conventions. He did not even *want* pretty singing in *Macbeth.* He wanted song to be subsidiary to situation; he wanted the sounds produced by the singers to reflect their inner turmoil and psychological stresses. This was unheard-of in opera at the time. When *Macbeth* in 1848 went into rehearsals in Paris, Verdi write a long letter to the director, and it is a revealing document, telling a great deal of what Verdi was looking for:

> I know you are rehearsing *Macbeth,* and since it is an opera that interests me more than all the others, you will permit me to say a few words about it. They gave the role of Lady Macbeth to [Eugenia] Tadolini, and I am very surprised that she consented to do the part. You know how much I admire Tadolini, and she knows it herself; but in our common interest we should stop and consider. Tadolini has too great qualities for this role. Perhaps you think that is a contradiction! Tadolini's appearance is good and beautiful, and I would like Lady Macbeth twisted and ugly. Tadolini sings to perfection, and I don't wish Lady Macbeth to sing at all. Tadolini has a marvellous, brilliant, clear, powerful voice, and for Lady Macbeth I should like a raw, choked, hollow voice. Tadolini's voice has something angelic. Lady Macbeth's voice should have something devilish. . . .

The point is that Verdi was, in his way, moving toward the direction of music drama. The difference between his approach and Wagner's, musical considerations aside, is that of melodrama opposed to drama. Many Verdi operas are outright melodramas, of wretched literary quality: studies in black and white, with characterization down to a minimum. Sophisticates have always sneered at the Verdi librettos. The subject of Verdi and his librettos is an interesting one. He was not a sophisticate, not an intellectual (though he had as much common sense as any composer in history), and until the end of his career did not seem very concerned about the literary qualities of his librettos. To put it bluntly, he set some ridiculous stuff to music. Or was it that his choice of librettos was conditioned by the taste of the public? Verdi always was responsive to public opinion. "In the theater the public will stand for anything but boredom," he said. He never pretended to be more than a craftsman, giving the public what it wanted. Perhaps Verdi himself believed that he could set only blood and thunder librettos. Whatever the reason, Verdi only too often used librettos that are no credit to his taste. An argument has been advanced that Verdi's librettos are not that bad; that they "work," that they depict raw emotion in great primary colors: love, hate, revenge, lust for power. But this is the stuff of melodrama, and is anything but a subtle literary form. Fortunately, Verdi's power as a composer was such that he could take a melodramatic situation and set it to unforgettable music. This music makes one ignore how conventional and wretched the words can be. Looked at dispassionately, a large number of Verdi librettos are literary trash. It makes no difference. The operas continue to live because they *do* have drama, no matter how primitive, and most of all because they do have great music.

Macbeth was followed by a series of operas that, except for *Luisa Miller* (1849), no longer hold the stage. Then, in 1851–1853, came the first three operas of his maturity—*Rigoletto* (1851), *Il Trovatore*, and *La Traviata* (both 1853). They were epoch-making in their day, and they made Verdi the only opera composer who could approach Meyerbeer in popularity. The public could not seem to get enough of those three operas. As an example: the Théâtre des Italiens in Paris gave eighty-seven performances in the 1856–57 season. Of those, fifty-four went to the three Verdi operas. In London, the clamor for Verdi was so great, and those three operas were done so often, that *Punch* objected:

> Three Traviatas in different quarters,
> Three Rigolettos murdering their daughters,
> Three Trovatori beheading their brothers,
> By the artful contrivance of three gypsy mothers.

The London *Musical World* pondered the phenomenon in 1855 and presented a more considered view than many critical journals were prepared to give. Verdi, the article pointed out, "has revolutionized the musical stage in his native country; for his operas, all others are forgotten. In time he made himself a name on the other part of the Alps. Other mobs caught up the enthusiasm, which spread from kingdom to kingdom, until new countries were invaded and conquered, and the mob-idol of one land became the mob-idol of all. Is this, or is it not, the secret of Signor Verdi's career? Could this have been effected without talent, and is Verdi the nonentity that musicians make him out?"

Singers fell in line as enthusiastically as the public. Marie Wieck, Clara Schumann's sister and herself also a prominent pianist, had a few words to say on the subject in 1855. She describes the glories of bel canto singing as practiced by the old exponents, Sontag, Lind, and the others, and then writes: "This style of singing is seldom heard. . . . The youthful, vigorous singers of today have only *one* name on their lips, and that is Verdi. Upon his operas rests the whole art of music—for the present time as well as for the future—and for this reason many singers under certain circumstances sacrifice the remains of their voices, sometimes even their health and constitution. All are ambitious only to be called Verdi singers, and they claim their title with glorious pride." Wieck, in this discussion of the Verdi operas in relation to singing, was more even-tempered than many critics. In their early years Verdi and Wagner were lumped together as irresponsible creators at whose feet lay the bleeding body of the Muse of Singing. Traditionalists sighed for the good old days of Bellini where—gad, Sir!—a singer was a singer and not a bellows. Meyerbeer had been attacked for his role in the death of singing, but those attacks were as nothing compared to the artillery brought up against Verdi and Wagner. Henry Fothergill Chorley in England wrote venomously of "the years during which singers' music was being stamped into such trash by the Wagners of New Germany and bawled into premature destruction by the Verdis of infuriate Italy."

It is interesting to note that while the public went crazy over the Verdi operas, and while singers jostled one another in their eagerness to be heard in the juicy Verdi roles, the conservatives and the critics were unhappy. They were used to the old conventions, and the furious dramatic onrush of Verdian movement made them uncomfortable. They were also used to mythological and historical characters in their operas, not hunchbacked jesters, consumptive courtesans, and dirty gypsies. Chorley scoffed. "Consumption for one who is to sing! A ballet with a lame Sylphide would be as rational." Sensibilities were offended. In New York, in 1855, two gentlemen started legal action against the impresario Max Maretzek. They sought to prevent the showing of *Rigoletto* on the ground that it was a lewd and licentious work, and that "by its singing, its business, and its plot, was then and there such an exhibition of opera as no respectable member of the fair sex could patronize without then and there sacrificing both taste and modesty." In Boston, where *La Traviata* was given in 1857, John S. Dwight attacked the opera on moral grounds before concluding that in any case it was no good musically: ". . . his old effects tried over and over again, as if with a nightmare inability to move beyond them. Nowhere, in one single point, of song or instrumentation, does this opera add a little to what we all know of Verdi. Invention seems exhausted, and only an intense craving for production left." But the young composers of Europe knew better, and Bizet put his finger on the essential Verdi: "He has marvellous bursts of passion. His passion is brutal, true, but it is better to be passionate that way than not at all. His music is sometimes exasperating but never boring."

Had the ex-Unitarian minister John S. Dwight known more about Verdi's private life, his darkest suspicions would have been proved. During the years that brought forth his three great operas of 1851–1853, Verdi was living with a woman named Giuseppina Strepponi. She was a soprano, and he had met her as early as 1839, when she sang in his very first opera, *Oberto*. Two years younger than Verdi, Strepponi in the 1830's and 1840's was recognized as one of the best singers in Italy—a soprano with a pure, clear voice, a good actress, and a musician of sensitivity. She shared his great triumph in *Nabucco,* singing the role of Abigaille at the premiere, she later sang other Verdi roles, she advised him on contractual and monetary matters, and in 1848 they began to live together. Three years later they moved into a new home, near Busseto. Verdi had purchased property there, had a house built, and named it the Villa Sant' Agata. There was head-wagging, finger-pointing, and soon an open scandal. In Busseto, in 1851, man and woman did not live openly together unless they were married. Verdi was outraged at the gossip. He got off a letter to his old friend and ex-father-in-law, Antonio Barezzi, and it reveals an independent, strong, scrappy, and unconventional man. In effect, Verdi told Barezzi and the town of Busseto to mind its own damn business. "In my house lives a lady, free and independent, and possessed of a fortune that places her beyond reach of need, who shares my love of seclusion. Neither she nor I need render account of our actions to any man." And, "In my house she has the right to be treated with even greater respect than is due to myself, and nobody is allowed to forget it." And, "This long and rambling letter is only designed to establish my claim to that liberty of action to which every man has a right. My nature shrieks against submitting to the prejudices of other people." Some writers suggest that there were two reasons for Verdi's defiant flaunting of the conventions. One was his strong anticlericalism. Who was the Church to tell *him* what to do? Verdi never was a believer, and Frank Walker, whose researches into Verdi's life and thought have opened more areas than those of any previous biographer, flatly says that Verdi was an atheist. The other reason might have been Giuseppina's diffidence. Her past life had not been beyond reproach, and it has been hazarded that she had guilt feelings about marriage.

In any case, having established his point, Verdi finally married Giuseppina in 1859. It was a happy though childless marriage. To compensate for the lack of children, there were animals: cats, dogs, parrots, peacocks, and the undisputed ruler of Sant' Agata—the Maltese spaniel, Loulou.

After the 1851–1853 trinity, the Verdi operas began to change in style. They grew broader, richer in sound, longer, more ambitious. Instead of turning out an opera every year, Verdi took much more time. No longer was there the "guitar" accompaniment of the orchestra that so amused the Germans. Verdi was feeling his way toward something bigger, and he experimented along that line. There was the Meyerbeerian *I Vespri Siciliani*, composed in 1855 for Paris. *Simon Boccanegra*, composed for Venice in 1857, was a failure. The impossibly disjointed libretto did not help. Yet *Simon Boccanegra* had a brooding quality, and some ravishingly sensuous ensembles, which Verdi had not achieved up to then. The year 1859 saw *Un Ballo in Maschera*, which had its premiere in Rome. This was a singing opera, full of bubbling ideas: one of the most sustained flights of lyricism in the entire Verdi canon. *La Forza del Destino*, composed for St. Petersburg, came in 1862 and turned out to be one of Verdi's most popular operas, wretched libretto and all.

The libretto of *Don Carlo* (Paris, 1867) is equally confused. Verdi tinkered with this opera for years. It never has been one of his most popular ones, and not until after World War II did it enter the repertoire with any degree of regularity. But it is a masterpiece. A feeling of black fate lies over the work—a work dominated not by the hero but by the tormented Philip of Spain. The auto-da-fè scene has unparalleled intensity and even a type of chromaticism rare for Verdi. When those trombones come in, heavy, marchlike, and menacing, it is as if the weight of the Inquisition were pressed on the listener's shoulders. The justly admired Inquisitor's scene that follows, with its great "Dormirò sol" for Philip, his confrontation with the blind Inquisitor, and Eboli's "O don fatale," ranks with anything Verdi ever composed. *Don Carlo* is a panorama that swirls around Spain and The Netherlands and, different though it is from Mussorgsky's *Boris Godunov* (which came out only a few years after the Verdi opera), the two works have points in common. Both deal with the responsibilities of rule, aspiration for freedom, countries being ripped apart. They are epic works.

Don Carlo is, indeed, a more striking and original work than *Aïda* of 1871. *Aïda*, composed for Cairo as part of the festivities attendant on the opening of the Suez Canal, is in a way a throwback. It may be the most popular of the Verdi operas, and it is the opera most people think of when the expression "grand opera" is used, but the Meyerbeerian panoply of the first two acts contains some of Verdi's weakest music, and the marches and ballet music of the second act can be listened to, these days, at best with indulgence. Not until the "Nile Scene" does Verdi show what he can do, and from that point to the end the opera is a masterpiece. Mussorgsky, for one, fell in love with *Aïda* and raved about Verdi: "This one pushes ahead on a grand scale; this innovator doesn't feel shy. All his *Aïda* . . . outdistances everyone, even himself. He has knocked over *Trovatore*, Mendelssohn, Wagner."

Even that arch-Teuton, Hans von Bülow, finally came around. Bülow at first had a low opinion of Verdi. After hearing the Requiem in 1874—the Requiem was the next important work by Verdi to follow *Aïda*—he called it rubbish. But shortly after, Bülow sent a hysterical *mea culpa* letter to Verdi (Bülow was never the one to do things by halves), casting dust on his head, beating his breast, and asking for forgiveness. The Requiem, he had now decided, was one of the greatest works of the century.

Bülow never wrote a truer word. Verdi composed the Requiem in honor of Alessandro Manzoni, the poet and novelist. To Verdi, Manzoni could be equated with that other "gloria d'Italia," Rossini. At Rossini's death in 1868, Verdi proposed that the most important Italian composers, including himself, collaborate on a requiem mass in his honor. Nothing came of the project, though Verdi did write a "Libera me" as his contribution. After Manzoni's death in May, 1873, Verdi decided to compose a Requiem Mass, to be performed in Milan, where Manzoni was buried, on the first anniversary of the death. For this work Verdi used—or said that he used (some authorities doubt it)—the "Libera me" that had been composed for Rossini. The long Requiem turned out to be all blazing passion: a colossal work, glorious in sound. Some attacked it for being too theatrical, and even today there are those who feel uncomfortable about its frank drama, which to them suggests opera rather than a religious experience. Giuseppina sprang to Verdi's defense:

> They talk a lot about the more or less religious spirit of Mozart, Cherubini, and others. I say that a man like Verdi must write like Verdi, that is, according to his own way of feeling and interpreting the text. The religious spirit and the way in which it is given expression must bear the stamp of its period and its author's personality. I would deny the authorship of a Mass by Verdi that was modeled upon the manner of A, B, or C.

Critical remarks after the premiere of the *Manzoni Requiem*—remarks to the effect that the music was tawdry, sensational, cheap, unreligious, irreligious, melodramatic—were representative of the critical attitude that faced

Verdi most of his life. His operas received unprecedented critical attack, especially in England and America. Many critics simply could not take Verdi seriously as a composer. The more the public loved his music, the more the critics screamed and lectured about the "obvious" nature of the writing, its "unvocal" quality, its "primitive" orchestration. They assured one another and the public that this music had only a temporary appeal and could not live. The critic of the London *Telegraph* had to take notice of the tremendous reception that the Requiem received at its Milan premiere. But, he gravely explained, that had nothing to do with the music. The ovation occurred because Verdi was so loved as a man, because of Manzoni, because Italians were so proud of Verdi's fame. "Now that the Peninsula is one State, every inhabitant of the most remote district assumes with pride his share in the honor paid to every Italian celebrity." It could not occur to the *Telegraph* critic that the music of the Requiem could have had a bearing on the case. He had been brainwashed for too many years.

Verdi was not disturbed by the negative reaction from some of the critics. He seems to have been one composer who honestly cared little about what critics said. He faced failure and success with equanimity. "You are wrong," he wrote to a friend, "to defend *Ballo in Maschera* from the attacks of the press. You should do as I always do: refrain from reading them and let them sing what tune they please. . . . For the rest, the question is this: Is the opera good or bad? If it is good and they have not thought so owing to their prejudices, etc., one must let them have their say and not take it to heart." And, elsewhere: "As for the newspapers, does anybody force you to read them? . . . The day of justice will come, and it is a great pleasure for the artist, a supreme pleasure, to be able to say: 'Imbeciles, you were wrong!' "

After the *Manzoni Requiem,* about fourteen years passed before Verdi's next major work. He spent some time visiting Vienna, Paris, and London, supervising productions of his operas, then returned to Sant' Agata to lead a life of retirement. He could look at the world and be pleased about certain things. Italy was now united. The Kingdom of Italy had been created in 1860, Venice was restored after Austria was defeated by the Prussians in 1866, and then Garibaldi freed Sicily and Naples. Rome became Italian in 1870. As one who had always hoped for the independence of Italy, Verdi was happy. For a few years he even sat in the Parliament as a member from Busetto. At first, in 1860, he took the job seriously and attended every session in Turin. He did not participate in the debates, but did try to push through a scheme for government subsidy of lyric theaters and conservatories. But soon the political mind started to bother him, and he did not like the politicians with whom he was in constant association. Once, at a session in Turin, he amused himself by setting to music a couple of parliamentary outbursts. One wonders what happened to that manuscript. It might be fun.

Verdi, in retirement at Sant' Agata, could also look at the musical scene in Italy and well realize his place in it. Never in the history of music has an era and a country been so dominated by one man. Wagner in Germany, the opposite number to Verdi in Italy, at least had a Brahms as a counterpoise. Verdi had nobody. Between the death of Donizetti and the emergence, in the 1870's, of Amilcare Ponchielli, there was only *one* important composer in Italy, and that was Verdi (Boito composed the impressive *Mefistofele* in 1868, but he was really a one-work man). No other Italian music survives. The Italian opera houses dutifully staged new operas every year, and the operas were invariably forgotten after a few performances. Take 1869. There were new operas by Sampieri, Mancini, Ricci, Monti, Petrella, Morales, Vera, Montuoro, Marchetti, Perelli, Vezzossi, Battista, Germano, Alberti, Seneke, Zecchini, Tancioni, Libani, and Grondona, among others. Not one of those composers rates even a footnote in any history of music. No; for about thirty years in Italy there was one giant, and then there was nobody— nobody at all.

Verdi in retirement also might have considered his place vis-à-vis Wagner. Certainly he must have heard about Wagner's glorious success with his first Bayreuth season in 1876. It is surprising that the two men never met, for they traveled much and they lived long lives. And they were the most important and famous composers of operas of their time. But Wagner's attitude toward Verdi was one of complete indifference—a lion shrugging off a gnat. Wagner must have heard some of the Verdi operas, but in all his vast correspondence there is virtually no mention of them except for a few slighting references expressed in terms of detached Olympian amusement. Verdi was more generous. Apparently he never heard a note of Wagner's music until 1865, when he encountered the *Tannhäuser* Overture (and did not like it very much). Later he had some words of praise for Wagner, though he detested Wagnerism and was bothered by the theories of symphonic development surrounding the Wagner operas. "Opera is opera," he said, "symphony is symphony."

One charge that strongly irritated Verdi was to hear his operas accused of 'Wagnerism," and that kept happening more and more as the Verdi operas grew longer, more powerfully scored, and cunningly put together. Verdi insisted that there was such a thing as an Italian temperament, as opposed to a German temperament, and he looked with dismay as such young composers as Arrigo Boito attempted a style of composition that had Wagnerisms in it. In Verdi's opinion, those composers were imitating Wagner's structure, harmony, and leitmotif development without fully understanding what they were doing. "If the Germans, setting out from Bach and arriving at Wagner, write good German operas, well and good. But we descendants of

Palestrina commit a musical crime when we imitate Wagner. We write useless, even deleterious music. . . . We cannot compose like the Germans, or at least we ought not to; nor they like us. . . . If we let fashion, love of innovations, and an alleged scientific spirit tempt us to surrender the native quality of our own art, the free natural certainty of our work and perception, our bright golden light, then we are simply being stupid and senseless." Yet when he heard of Wagner's death in 1883, Verdi wrote to his publisher: "Sad, sad, sad! Frankly, when I received the news yesterday, I was crushed. Let us say no more about it. A great personality has gone, a name that will leave a most powerful impression on the history of art."

During the period following the *Manzoni Requiem* it was assumed that Verdi was finished with composition. He let the world know that he would never again write another work for the stage. And he might have kept his promise had he not been thrown into close association with Arrigo Boito.

Boito (February 24, 1842–June 10, 1918) was a literary man and composer. To most non-Italian music-lovers he is known as the man who furnished Verdi with librettos for *Otello* and *Falstaff.* Others know him as the composer of *Mefistofele,* his only musical work of any importance. But in his youth, around 1865, he was one of the Young Turks of Italian music, and this even though he composed next to nothing. He was always torn between literature and music, wavering uncertainly between the two for many years. *Mefistofele,* composed in 1868 and revised seven years later, was his only completed opera. He worked on another called *Orestiade* but never offered it to the public. A third, *Ero e Leandro* got only as far as a libretto. There remains *Nerone,* which Boito started thinking about in 1862. All his life he worked on that opera, and it remained unfinished at his death in 1918.

Yet Boito had immense talent and perhaps genius. Was it the overpowering force of Verdi that held him down? The two men crossed in the early 1860's. When Boito was twenty years old, fresh from his studies at the Milan Conservatory (where great things were expected of him), he wrote the text for Verdi's *Hymn of the Nations.* But relations between the two men were touchy for a long time. Verdi was notoriously sensitive, and he got the idea that Boito was an enemy.

No doubt this stemmed from Boito's critical writings, in which he kept agitating for a reform in Italian opera. Boito was an intellectual, and one of the very few Italians of his day to propagandize for Beethoven, Wagner, and German music. He wrote a great deal about the necessity for "true form" in opera. As practiced in Italy, opera, he insisted, was merely formula. "The hour has come for a change in style. Form, largely developed in the other arts, must develop too in our own." Boito was thinking in terms of Wagnerian operatic form, and to Verdi this was treason. The Italian spirit, Verdi felt, could never accommodate itself to German form and metaphysics. And as Verdi was in effect the only major composer of Italian opera from the death of Donizetti to the 1890's, even a less sensitive figure than Verdi would have felt that Boito's attacks were directed against him. Verdi grumbled to his publisher, Tito Ricordi, "If I too among the others have soiled the altar, as Boito says, let him clean it and I shall be the first to light a candle."

Thus, when *Mefistofele* had its premiere at La Scala in 1868, many in the audience had a chip on their shoulder. Between Boito's admirers and enemies, the performance ended in the kind of riot so dear to the hearts of the emotional Latins. There was screaming in the theater, fights broke out, and there were demonstrations in the streets. After a second performance the chief of police banned all further presentations in the interests of public safety. Verdi did not hear the opera until more than ten years later. In 1879 he attended a performance in Genoa and had some tart remarks to make: "I had always heard it said, and always read, that the Prologue in Heaven was cast in a single piece, a thing of genius . . . and I, listening to the harmonies of that piece, based almost entirely on dissonances, seemed to be . . . not in *heaven*, certainly."

But Verdi was being cruel. Even for its time the harmonies of *Mefistofele* were not very adventurous, though it is true that the Prologue is an altogether original conception. Boito was trying for higher things than Gounod in his saccharine *Faust* of 1859. Gounod composed a French formula opera, whereas Boito, true to his tenets, was aiming for a kind of intellectual synthesis that would draw together both parts of the Goethe play. Boito's Devil is not a stock figure of evil. He is an elemental force who confronts his Adversary with dignity. In his preoccupation with new operatic forms, Boito anticipated some writing of a future era. The Prologue, for instance, is in classic form, with a scherzo and trio predominating. (Much later, in *Wozzeck*, Alban Berg was to write an opera in which classic forms—variation, sonata, suite, passacaglia, invention—are the actual basis on which the entire opera is constructed.) Boito's entire approach was different from Verdi's, and considering that Boito was only twenty-six years old when *Mefistofele* was staged, one would have thought that the world was his, that the great Verdi would be faced with some real competition. That was not to be. Boito, who on the evidence of so tremendous an achievement at so young an age could conceivably have gone on to magnificence, in effect put down his musical pen. He contributed to intellectual journals, he taught, he became director of the Parma Conservatory, he wrote librettos (*La Gioconda,* for Ponchielli, is his under a pseudonym), he occupied himself with *Nerone.* Something in him held back his musical creativity, and his was one of the strange psychological blocks in musical history. He could not write music, and toward the end he was unable to write so much as a letter.

This was the man who became Verdi's incomparable librettist. The idea for *Otello* came in 1879. At a dinner in which Verdi and Boito were guests, Giulio Ricordi (who had succeeded his father, Tito, as head of the publishing firm), turned the conversation to the Shakespeare play, and Verdi reacted as Ricordi had hoped. Boito and Verdi were brought together to discuss the possibility of an opera on *Othello*. Verdi seemed encouraging, and Boito dropped everything to provide a libretto. He gave it to Verdi later that year, and Verdi put it aside. Then he read it again, made some suggestions, received a new libretto, and again put it away. Finally he set to work, in 1884, at the age of seventy. Everybody concerned with the project walked on tiptoe. Boito wrote to Ricordi: "I have good news for you, but for charity's sake, don't tell anybody, don't tell even your family, don't tell even yourself. I fear I have already committed an indiscretion. The Maestro is writing, indeed he has already written a good part of the opening of the first act and seems to be working with fervor." There were some hitches along the way. Boito had to write and rewrite. There was a silly misunderstanding that had to be cleared up. Finally the opera had its premiere, at La Scala on February 5, 1887, and the seventy-three-year-old composer shared the applause with his librettist.

In *Otello*, the greatest of his tragic operas, Verdi brought to fusion everything that he had learned in a lifetime. He had the best libretto ever submitted to him, and he poured into it a combination of drama, rapture, and compassion unprecedented even for him. There is not a single weak passage in *Otello*, not one false gesture, nothing but a fusion of word, action, and music. Even such normally melodramatic episodes as Iago's "Credo" or the Otello-Iago "Sì, pel ciel" duet fall naturally within the movement of the drama. Verdi's musical impulse had deepened and richened. The first-act love duet is all ardor and sensuousness, expressed in music that is the essence of desire. It is not the exultant music of young lovers. Rather it is the radiant music of man and wife. Iago's is two-faced music: hearty and bluff, or subtle, insinuating, and of shattering venom. The last act, with Desdemona's hushed "Salce, salce" and "Ave Maria," is all impending doom suggested by the simplest of means. *Otello* is much more than a collection of arias and ensembles. It is a through-composed opera, every element carefully joined to make a unity. Nor had Verdi ever before handled his orchestra with such mastery. It does not merely accompany singers. It underlines the action, hints at the tragedy to come, describes what the characters are thinking and feeling. Often there are mottos and figures instead of themes. *Otello* is to Italian opera what *Tristan* is to German.

Nevertheless *Otello* is a logical continuation of what Verdi had done from *Nabucco* through *La Traviata, Don Carlo,* and *Aïda*. With his last opera, something new enters the picture. *Falstaff* is almost a freak, what the biologists call a sport. Nobody had expected Verdi to compose another opera. And, even granting that there might be another work, who would have expected it to be a comedy, and the most atypical opera Verdi ever wrote?

Falstaff is an opera that always has been part of the standard repertory, but never an integral part. Musicians keep crying its praises. The word customarily used with this opera is "miracle." Yet it has never fully captured the public imagination as *Otello* and the others have. Audiences, for the most part, listen politely, waiting for something to happen, for the big arias that never come. The opera has always been more a *succès d'estime* than anything else, even in Italy, where Verdi is a god.

Admittedly *Falstaff* does not have the immediate emotional appeal of *Otello* or *Aïda*. Verdi's wife, Giuseppina, described it as "a new combination of poetry and music." Indeed it was new. Nowhere in opera had there been an equivalent type of condensation in which words and music are so intertwined. What *Otello* had merely hinted at, *Falstaff* accomplishes. Gone are the arias in which the tenor advances to the footlights, glares down the audience, and stuns it with a high C. Gone is the broad canvas. Gone is the melodrama. Gone are the primary colors. Instead, all is subtle, fast-moving, full of glints, mocking laughter, high humor. *Falstaff* is a commentary on life, a summation of a career, a jest—and such a civilized one!—with its undertone of sadness. Verdi knew it was to be his last opera. *"Tutto è finito. Va, va, vecchio John . . ."*

Verdi had been persuaded by Boito to undertake the task after the success of *Otello*. In 1889 the two men were deep in the Shakespeare comedy. The failure of Verdi's one comic opera, *Un Giorno di Regno* in 1840, had continued to be a sore spot with him all his life. Perhaps he undertook *Falstaff* with the idea of erasing that failure. And, deep down, could he have undertaken *Falstaff* to show the world that Wagner had no monopoly on music drama, that another composer could write an opera with continuous melody and inner development—but in the Italian and not the German manner? Anyway, Verdi worked on *Falstaff* with great enjoyment. He played it down, pretending that he was working on it only to pass the time. Almost eighty, he could spend no more than two hours a day on the opera. But that does not mean he approached *Falstaff* with anything less than his usual thoroughness. From the very beginning he did his homework. Before reading Boito's first script he read the three *Henry* plays and the *Merry Wives of Windsor*. Then he carefully went through the Boito draft, worrying about the last act, which "in spite of its touch of fantasy will be trivial." There was an exchange of letters with Boito in which Verdi actually became coquettish, putting up some token resistance against the idea of writing another opera. Was he too old for such a task? Would he live to complete it? Boito brushed this aside as "not valid and no obstacle to a new work."

A letter from Verdi to Boito in 1889 is interesting. "You are working, I hope? The strangest thing is that I am working too. I am amusing myself by writing fugues. Yes, sir, a fugue—and a comic fugue." This must refer to the conclusion of the opera. So Verdi, the old rascal, already had the end of *Falstaff* in mind. By March, 1891, Verdi was all involved with the fat man. "Big belly is going crazy. There are days when he doesn't move, but sleeps and is in a bad humor. At other times he shouts, runs, jumps, causes a devil of a rumpus. I let him indulge his whims a bit. If he continues, I'll put on a muzzle and a strait-jacket."

The world premiere took place on February 9, 1893, at La Scala. It was a success, of course. Verdi was such a revered figure that any opera of his would have been enthusiastically received. He was an Old Master, and long gone were the days when the critics snapped at him. Notables from all over Europe attended the premiere, and also the performance in Rome that followed soon after. The critics wrote learned reviews. Many of them did wonder if an opera with so little in the way of clear-cut melody would ever attract the public. But the critics also were entranced with the translucence of the writing, the wit of the music, the technical mastery evident in every measure. The shades of Mozart (*Figaro*) and Wagner (*Meistersinger*) were invoked, as they are to this day. For *Falstaff* is the third in that trinity of great comic operas, and it is in no way inferior to either.

In 1893, George Bernard Shaw, the music critic for the *World* in London, looked through the score of *Falstaff* and had some observations to make:

I have noticed one or two exclamations of surprise at the supposed revelation in *Falstaff* of a "hitherto unsuspected" humorous force in the veteran tragic composer. This must be the result of the enormous popularity which *Il Trovatore* and *Aïda* afterwards attained in this country. I grant that these operas are quite guiltless of comic relief; but what about *Un Ballo* with its exquisitely light-hearted *È scherzo od è follia,* and the finale to the third act, where Renato is sarcastically complimented on his domestic virtue. . . . Stupidly as that tragi-comic quartet and chorus has always been mishandled on our wretched operatic stage, I cannot understand anyone who knows it denying Verdi's gift of dramatic humor.

Shaw may not have been surprised at the humor in *Falstaff,* but the public remained perplexed. *Falstaff* does have arias and ensembles, but they move so fast that no sooner does the listener start to enjoy them than they are gone. Falstaff's "Quand'ero paggio" lasts thirty seconds—the entire aria. The duet between Nannetta and Fenton takes a minute and a half (though it is later repeated). Wonderful melodic inspirations seem to be dropped as soon as they are introduced. It is almost as though Verdi is writing a kind of musical shorthand. As a result *Falstaff* gives many listeners the feeling of an opera without development, without anything to seize.

What the listener comes to realize, if *Falstaff* is given a chance, is that the opera is not only continuously melodic from beginning to end, but that it is also full of related melody. *Falstaff* is full of thematic linkages, and that is what gives the work its extraordinary unity. When, at her first appearance, Alice sings "Escivo appunto," it is accompanied by a little six-note motto that is immediately dropped—only to turn up prominently an act later when the words "Dalla due alla tre" are used. As one becomes familiar with the music, linkages like this spring into high relief.

The orchestra plays a more important role in *Falstaff* than in any Verdi opera, *Otello* included. The vocal line of *Otello* is primarily song; in *Falstaff* it is a mixture of song and song-speech (parlando). But when the characters in *Falstaff* are using a parlando line, the orchestra picks up the melody or somehow manages to supplement the action. Nowhere is this better illustrated than in Falstaff's "Honor" monologue. Singer and orchestra are one. When Falstaff builds up to "Che ciancia! Che baja!" the orchestra laughs with a trill: all the strings and lower winds. Then, as if suddenly waking up, the oboes, clarinets, and bassoons suddenly start trilling too, all alone. The effect, if one realizes what is going on, is indescribably witty. When Falstaff sweeps his precious retainers out of the way at the end of the act, the orchestra again his its say. Once more comes a trill, but what a trill! An impolite horse laugh, a Bronx cheer in music, as the orchestra razzes Falstaff and the world.

Everywhere in *Falstaff* come surprises, and the biggest of all is kept for the end. The opera concludes with a fugue. Verdi had been building up to this. *Aïda*, for example, has an unusual amount of polyphony. But nowhere else in the Verdi operas is there a full-fledged fugue, and there is something symbolic in the fact that the old Verdi rounded off his greatest and most revolutionary opera with one of the oldest and severest of musical forms. Only this fugue has nothing severe in it. "Everything is a farce," sing the characters, their voices rising and rising until abruptly cut off. Verdi was having his little joke.

Although *Falstaff* completed his cycle of operas, Verdi was not through writing. He composed a *Te Deum* and finished four religious pieces (two of them written before *Falstaff*), later published under the title of *Quattro Pezzi Sacri*. Boito kept urging him to write another Shakespeare opera. *Antony and Cleopatra? King Lear?* All his life Verdi had toyed with the idea of setting *Lear* to music. Giuseppina fended off Verdi's beseechers. "Verdi is too old, too tired." So was Giuseppina, and she died in 1897. When Verdi received the news he stood erect, mute, refusing to sit down. Most of his remaining years he spent at Sant' Agata, but occasionally visited Milan to be near Boito and other old friends. When death came, it was in Milan. He had a stroke, lingered unconscious for a week, and died on January 27, 1901. Several months later Boito wrote to a friend describing Verdi's last hours. "Poor Maestro, how brave and handsome he was up to the last moment! No matter; the old reaper went off with his scythe well battered. . . . Now it is all over. He sleeps like a King of Spain in his Escurial, under a bronze slab that completely covers him."

❧ 17 ❧

Colossus of Germany

RICHARD WAGNER

If it was Beethoven who dominated music in the first half of the nineteenth century, it was Richard Wagner who loomed over the second half. It was not only that Wagnerian opera changed the course of music. There was also something messianic about the man himself, a degree of megalomania that approached actual lunacy—and that raised the concept of the Artist-as-Hero to an unprecedented degree. He was a short man, about 5 feet, 5 inches tall, but he radiated power, belief in himself, ruthlessness, genius. As a human being he was frightening. Amoral, hedonistic, selfish, virulently racist, arrogant, filled with gospels of the superman (the superman naturally being Wagner) and the superiority of the German race, he stands for all that is unpleasant in human character.

No composer ever demanded so much from society, and Wagner was altogether unblushing about his needs. "I am not made like other people. I must have brilliance and beauty and light. The world owes me what I need. I can't live on a miserable organist's pittance like your master, Bach." His egoism approached madness. He thought nothing of writing to a young man he hardly knew, asking for money. "It would be rather hard for you to provide me with this sum, but it will be possible if you *wish* it, and do not shrink from such a sacrifice. This, however, I desire. . . . Now let me see whether you are the right sort of man!" Then follows an inducement: "The assistance you give me will bring you into very close touch with me, and next summer you must be pleased to let me come to you for three months at one of your estates, preferably in the Rhine district." The young man, Robert von Hornstein, refused to give the money to Wagner, who actually was surprised. How could such a pipsqueak refuse to subsidize a man like him? He sent a note to Hornstein, writing him off for good: "It probably will not happen again that a man like me will apply to you."

No composer, and few human beings, have had Wagner's sense of mission. "I let myself be guided without fear by my instinct. I am being used as the instrument for something higher than my own being warrants. . . . I am in the hands of the immortal genius that I serve for the span of my life and that intends me to complete only what I can achieve." Such was Wagner's ego that it is not stretching a point to suggest that he secretly regarded himself as a god. He was sent to earth by mysterious forces. He gathered disciples unto Himself. He wrote holy scriptures in word and music (the Sacred Writings eventually to be gathered in ten large volumes of prose and twenty more of letters). He caused a temple at Bayreuth to be created, in which His works could be celebrated and He Himself worshiped. He cast out all who did not agree with His divinity.

But his egomania was supported by genius; and, after him, music was not the same.

Richard Wagner was born in Leipzig on May 22, 1813. Some mystery attaches to his paternity. There is strong evidence that his true father was an actor named Ludwig Geyer. There is indirect evidence that Geyer was a Jew. The true facts may never be known. In any case, Wagner's legal father died when he was six months old, and his mother married Geyer the following year. The family moved to Dresden, where Richard went to school. From childhood he was surrounded by actors, musicians, and artists, but he showed no unusual aptitude in any direction. Not until he was fifteen, when he heard the Beethoven Ninth Symphony and *Fidelio,* did he decide to become a composer. The Ninth Symphony seems to have shaken him psychically, releasing all the latent musical ferment that was bottled up in him, and the Ninth Symphony remained his ideal throughout his life. Wagner was to maintain that his operas were a continuation of the Ninth Symphony. "The last symphony of Beethoven," he wrote, "is the redemption of music from out of her peculiar element into the realm of universal art. It is the human evangel of the art of the future. Beyond it no further step is possible, for upon it the perfect art work of the future alone can follow: the universal drama for which Beethoven forged the key."

When Wagner at fifteen decided to become a composer, he was completely untrained. In many respects he developed into a self-taught composer, and like many self-taught composers, or composers who came to music late in life, he always lacked certain requirements that normally are considered basic. Like Berlioz, he had no professional skill on any instrument. Even when he was a conductor and a great composer, he could do little more than pick at the piano, and he admitted that he was an indifferent score reader. He made up for his deficiencies by instinct and a profound musicality. His learning seemed to be automatically absorbed. While a teen-ager, he did take a few harmony lessons with a local musician in Leipzig, but he learned much more by himself during the hours he spent poring over scores of the Beethoven symphonies. Then he started composing. His early works show no talent, and of all the great composers he was the one who developed latest in life.

In 1831 he was for a brief time at the University of Leipzig, where he made himself well known by his compulsive, nonstop talking, his dogmatism, and his drinking and gambling. Yet underneath was that enormous pool of musicality, ever rising, finally to overflow. Soon everything was neglected in favor of music. Wagner finally decided he needed discipline, and in 1831 he worked with Theodor Weinlig, the cantor of St. Thomas. Weinlig stopped the lessons because, he said, he could teach Wagner nothing more about harmony or counterpoint. Once Wagner decided to concentrate, he learned with amazing rapidity. As far as is known, the short time he spent with Weinlig constituted his only professional instruction. No great composer has had as little formal training. When Weinlig dismissed him, Wagner immediately started a series of compositions, most of them academic juvenilia, including a piano sonata and a symphony. An opera named *Die Hochzeit* was started but never finished, but in 1833 came *Die Feen*, and Wagner was launched as a composer of operas. (*Die Feen* was never produced in his lifetime, and not until 1888 did it receive a performance.) It was around this time, 1834 to be exact, that Wagner started his series of polemical writings. He wrote an article praising the French style of opera composition ("facile . . . melodious") over the German ("too learned and intellectual"). With that in mind he worked out a libretto based on Shakespeare's *Measure for Measure*, named it *Das Liebesverbot*, and started composing the music. Later that year he accepted a position as musical director of a company in Magdeburg. Now he was a professional. His career had started.

In Magdeburg he established a pattern that was to be his normal way of life. He ran up enormous debts, made many enemies, and tried to impose his will on the musical life of the company and the city. In Magdeburg, too, he fell in love with an actress in the company. Her name was Minna Planer, and he frightened her with his intensity. He had great plans. He would marry her; his opera, *Das Liebesverbot* would achieve a great success and wipe out his debts; he had been promised a position with the opera company at Riga, where he would make a great reputation. *Das Liebesverbot* was produced, in 1836. It failed. Nevertheless Wagner and Minna got married, in November of that year. They lived in Königsberg, where she had an engagement. Wagner ran up more debts. His creditors from Magdeburg pursued him to Königsberg. This frightened the Königsberg creditors, who also presented bills. Minna could not stand it. She left him, to go to her parents in Dresden. Fortunately the position in Riga came through, and Wagner went there in September, 1837, to be joined by Minna.

The pattern repeated itself in Riga. Wagner started work on another opera that would make him famous. This was *Rienzi,* modeled on the grand-opera formula that Meyerbeer had established. More debts were run up, more enemies made. Wagner tried to vitalize the musical life of the city, demanding more rehearsal time, an expansion of the repertoire, and the inclusion of symphony concerts into the musical program. In 1839 Wagner was discharged. He fled to France by boat (legend has it that the trip was the inspiration for *Der fliegende Holländer*), leaving his creditors behind. He and Minna settled in Paris, where he tried to make himself known. Meyerbeer received him, looked at the first act of *Rienzi,* and introduced him to important members of the musical establishment. Nothing happened, and soon the Wagners ran out of money. They pawned everything, and Wagner had to resort to hack work to keep alive. He put the final touches to *Rienzi* toward the end of 1840, and started work on *Der fliegende Holländer.* Then came good news. *Rienzi* was accepted by the Dresden Opera. Meyerbeer had recommended it, as had several other musicians, and the opinion of Meyerbeer carried enormous weight. Wagner and Minna had to borrow still more money to leave Paris. He was, literally, on his uppers; his shoes had no soles, and he had to stay indoors, working on *Holländer.* Finally they were able to say good-bye to Paris. He and Minna went to Dresden for the premiere, which took place on October 20, 1842. Wagner well knew how much was at stake, and he must have been a frightened man on opening night. Heinrich Heine was there and sent off a report to Paris. Wagner, Heine said, "looked like a ghost; he laughed and wept at the same time and embraced everybody who came near him, while all the time cold perspiration ran down his forehead." *Rienzi* turned out to be an enormous success, and Wagner was suddenly a famous man. The Dresden Court Theater immediately secured rights to *Der fliegende Holländer,* which was staged early in 1843. It did not make as big an impression as *Rienzi,* and ran for only four performances. But Wagner made enough of an impression to be appointed second kapellmeister at the Dresden Opera. He was given a salary that would have been comfortable for anybody but a Wagner. As usual he was able to hold on to none of it, spending far more than he earned. In addition, as word of his appointment got out, he was bedeviled by creditors from his previous travels—creditors from Leipzig, Magdeburg, Königsberg, Riga, Paris. It was a story that was to be repeated throughout much of his life.

Wagner settled into his duties and began to conduct some of the operas in the Dresden repertoire. Inevitably he ran into trouble. Trying to do away with the seniority system, he antagonized the entire orchestra. Trying to conduct such great works as *Don Giovanni* according to his inner vision, he alienated the public. The Dresden public was used to comfortable tem-

233

pos in *Don Giovanni,* and Wagner's dashing attack unsettled the listeners. He was reproved, and he had to promise, in his own words, "to alter nothing in the hitherto accepted interpretation of tempo, etc., when conducting older operas, even when it goes against my artistic judgment." But there were compensations. In Dresden he was admired and respected, and he started work on a new opera, *Tannhäuser,* finishing the libretto in 1843 and the score two years later. The premiere took place on October 19, 1845, and audiences at first were bewildered. Soon, however, *Tannhäuser* achieved popularity, and Wagner started to think about a new opera, *Lohengrin.* The next two years saw *Lohengrin* come into shape and Wagner's financial position disintegrate. He was desperate for money. He also supervised a production of *Rienzi* in Berlin. It failed, and that added to his gloom.

A few years later he got into political in addition to his financial trouble. Stimulated by the collapse of the French monarchy, and influenced by the theories of the anarchist Mikhail Bakunin, Wagner came out on the side of the revolutionaries during the uprising in Dresden. Perhaps he was sincerely interested in the plight of the working man. Or perhaps he looked for a social upheaval that would wipe out the capitalists, thus automatically eliminating his enormous debts. He made speeches demanding the end of money and the abolition of royalty, and he wrote violent tracts: "I will destroy the existing order of things. . . . So up, ye peoples of the earth! Up, ye mourners, ye oppressed, ye poor!" When the Dresden uprising was put down in 1849, Wagner fled to Weimar and his friend Liszt, one of the few musicians who had encouraged him. (Schumann and Berlioz never were attracted to Wagner's music.) After a short stay in Weimar, Wagner made his home in Zurich. *Lohengrin* had been completed in 1848, and Liszt conducted the world premiere in Weimar, 1850. Wagner was not present. He was thinking about new projects in Zurich, His revolutionary period was over. Soon he was writing about "the vulgar egotism of the masses."

Rienzi had been a huge spectacle opera. *Der fliegende Holländer, Tannhäuser,* and *Lohengrin* went to German myth for their subject. But none of these operas fully expressed what Wagner was trying to do. For six years Wagner lay fallow, thinking about the problem, working out his artistic theories, writing a big libretto based on the Teutonic *Nibelungenlied,* and turning out one treatise after another: *Art and Revolution* (1849), *The Art Work of the Future* (1850), *Judaism and Music* (1850), *Opera and Drama* (1851), *A Communciation to My Friends* (1851), and assorted essays.

He arrived at the concept of a unified art work, the *Gesamtkunstwerk,* and decided that all great art must be based on mythology. As early as 1844 he was writing: "It is the province of the present-day dramatist to give expressive and spiritual meaning to the material interests of our own time; but to the operatic poet and composer falls the task of conjuring up the

holy spirit of poetry as it comes to us in the sagas and legends of past ages."
He wrote that "God and gods are the first creations of man's poetic force."
Myth, then, was the ideal stuff of which poetry was made. It was necessary
to go to a pre-Christian period, for Christianity had diluted the *mythos*.
"Through the adoption of Christianity the folk had lost all true understand-
ing of the original, vital relations of the *mythos*."

But how to get back to the *mythos*? What kind of language should be
used? A new speech had to be created, Wagner decided. The poet must use
Stabreim, which resembles the poetry found in the sagas. This is a highly al-
literative kind of poetry, with "a kinship of vowel sounds." Soon Wagner, in
his *Nibelung* libretto, was writing like this:

> Mächt'ger Müh'
> müde nie,
> stau'ten starke
> Stein' wir auf;
> steiler Thurm,
> Thur' und Thor,
> deckt und schliesst,
> im schlanken Schloss den Saal.

The language once secured, the music must meet it on equal terms. The
music must grow out of the libretto. There must be no pandering to the
public, no vocal display for its own sake, no set arias and ensembles in
which the action comes to a halt. Leitmotifs can be used as an organiza-
tional force. Leitmotifs are short descriptive tunes, capable of being meta-
morphosed, that describe characters or states of mind. These leitmotifs are
put through a process of constant manipulation and quasi-symphonic development. (Debussy later was to jibe that "the leit-motif system suggests a
world of harmless lunatics who present their visiting cards and shout their
names in song.") Because in this style of composition there is no stop for
arias, and because there is none of the feeling of transition that there had
been in previous opera, mention began to be made of Wagner's "endless
melody." Unbroken drama expressed in unbroken music was his goal, and
as early as *Lohengrin* he was pleased to be able to point out that nowhere
in the opera "have I written the word *recitative* over a passage. The singers
are not to know there are any recitatives in it."

Above all, there was the new use of the orchestra. More than any composer in history up to that point, Wagner made the orchestra an equal part
of the drama. It is in Wagner's big, resonantly scored orchestra where much
of the action of the opera is explained—where psychological changes of the
characters, their motivations, drives, desires, loves, hates, are all underlined.

Singers had to learn how to carry over an operatic orchestra of this unprecedented size. During the last half of the century there were great arguments about Wagner and the human voice. Many professionals cried that Wagner, even more than Verdi and Meyerbeer, was killing the singer by imposing such "unnatural" demands. George Bernard Shaw took Wagner's part, pointing out that Verdi's habit "of taking the upper fifth of the compass of an exceptionally high voice and treating that fifth as the normal range, has a great deal to do with the fact that the Italian singer is now the worst singer in the world." Wagner, Shaw said, used the voice all over its compass, with the result that Wagnerian singers "are now the best in the world."

Not only did Wagner work out the main lines of the *Gesamtkunstwerk* during his years in Zurich, but in the process he also changed his musical style. Up to then his music had tended to be rhythmically four-square, but with *Tristan und Isolde* and the *Ring* cycle came a kind of rhythm that depended more on the phrase than on the bar line. In addition, Wagner's harmonic ideas became intensely chromatic, and key relationships began to become very vague. Wagner was an eclectic who synthesized the techniques of early romanticism. He took ideas about the orchestra from Berlioz. Weber's operas, especially *Der Freischütz,* played a great part in Wagner's final synthesis. He took harmonic ideas from Chopin, Mendelssohn, and, above all, Liszt, and he was even influenced to a certain extent by Meyerbeer. And there was the overriding ethical idea implicit in Beethoven's last works. Wagner welded all of this material into something uniquely his own, creating his own world, a world of myth surrounded by the most advanced music known at the time. It is interesting to note that he himself did not fully carry through on his own theories of the *Gesamtkunstwerk. Das Rheingold* comes closest, whereas *Die Meistersinger* breaks most of his own rules. When a musical idea collided with Wagner's theory of the music drama, it was music that always won over theory. Indeed, the three most "Wagnerian" operas, the three that most closely approach the *Gesamtkunstwerk* that Wagner was talking about, are Verdi's *Falstaff,* Debussy's *Pelléas et Mélisande,* and Berg's *Wozzeck.*

In the meantime, the years that Wagner spent in Zurich were also years that saw the early Wagner operas making their way through Europe. Wagner's genius was recognized almost from the beginning, and it would be a mistake to assume that he was working in a vacuum. From *Rienzi* on, the Wagner operas were the talk of Europe. Verdi's operas were more popular, but there was one significant difference. The Verdi operas did not excite the avant-garde, nor did they drive a wedge into the public. When a Wagner opera was given, it generally was to great excitement and polemics. People may have gone around *whistling* the famous Verdi tunes, but they were constantly *talking* about the Wagner operas—in derogation, in admiration, in derision,. in praise, but always talking, and loudly talking. It was realized that Wagner was an elemental force—a destructive force, to some, and the ultimate hope of music to others. The impresario Max Maretzek joked about the furor: "I never discuss politics, religion, or Wagner. It always makes for bad blood and originates quarrels." Not only was Wagner's music a subject for heated conversation. His prose writings achieved very wide circulation, and were even being read in the United States as early as the 1850's. They were promptly translated and published in *Dwight's Journal of Music*. Liszt and his friends loudly beat the drum for Wagner, and the conservatives thought there was an international conspiracy under way. The French write⁻, François Joseph Fétis, summed up the anti-Wagner feeling in 1855:

> . . . A party has been formed only a few years ago that has the audacity to proclaim itself as the creator of the only true and complete art, and anything previous to it has been mere preparation. . . . The disdain which they affect towards form proceeds from the difficulty they have adhering to it without betraying poverty of matter. Disorder, phrases merely sketched and without construction, are more to their liking because nothing is more irksome to the logic of ideas for sterile and lazy imaginations. . . . In Germany they have taken control of magazines to ensure the triumph of their revolutionary attempt. A silence as of death reigns in these same writings about the work of artists who follow other ways. Some serious men have tried to enlighten public opinion by a rational criticism of this shameful socialism, but have not been able to make their voices heard. All approaches to the press have been closed to them. It would take too long to relate the means used by the brethren and friends for the glorification of their chief: their maneuvers to get possession of theaters; their falsehoods to smother truth when it tries to make itself heard; their concerted plans to blacken and eliminate those not with them . . .

The British critics, headed by the ineffable Henry Fothergill Chorley, were especially vicious. Chorley fought every Wagner opera as it appeared. *Rienzi* he called "simply noise." *Der fliegende Holländer* left "an impression of grim violence and dreary vagueness." Chorley wrote of *Tannhäuser* that he had "never been so blanked, wearied, *insulted* even (the word is not too strong) by a work of pretension as by this same *Tannhäuser*." Chorley also predicted the "utter ruin which must overtake vocal art if composers followed in the wake of their idol [Wagner] and, for the sake of the orchestra, like him utterly debased and barbarized the cantilena under pretext of truth in declamation." But, ending his description of *Tannhäuser*, Chorley found a ray of hope: "There is comfort, however, in thinking that beyond

Herr Wagner in his peculiar manner it is hardly possible to go. The saturnal of licentious discord must have here reached its climax." Chorley never reviewed the later operas, unfortunately. They would have inspired him to inimitable outbursts of prose. The British critics, more than any in Europe, continually attacked Wagner, even in the 1870's, after his battle obviously was won.

During his years in exile, Wagner lived mostly off other people's money. Often the money came from impressionable women. Julie Ritter and Jessie Laussot helped him in 1850. (He planned to leave Minna and elope with Laussot, but she became frightened and returned to her husband.) To augment his income Wagner did a great deal of conducting, and he turned out to be the strongest influence on conducting in his time. At the beginning of his career, he had been an opera-house conductor. Later he conducted only symphony orchestras. His interpretations were original and highly personal, with insistence on nuanced playing and a complete range of dynamics. Never a purist, he was always more concerned with the spirit than the letter of the score. He also introduced the concept of tempo fluctuation. Most conductors of his period were time-beaters of the Mendelssohn school. Wagner substituted a rise and fall, slowing and speeding, a constant variation of tempo with the use of ritards to link contrasting passages. It was an approach that drove academicians out of their minds. From all evidence, it was also an approach that would sound extremely eccentric to twentieth-century ears. The more classic, restrained conducting of a Mendelssohn or a Berlioz would be preferred. Nevertheless it was the Wagner style of conducting that dominated the last half of the nineteenth century. Not only did Wagner himself set the example on the podium, but the world was full of Wagner-trained conductors. The most famous were Hans Richter, Anton Seidl, Hans von Bülow, Felix Mottl, and Hermann Levi. Probably the most popular conductor of the day was Artur Nikisch, and while he had not worked directly under Wagner's supervision, he had been weaned on the Wagner operas, and his first big assignment was as a conductor of the Wagnerian repertoire. Not until a classic reaction set in, with the advent of such conductors as Felix Weingartner and Arturo Toscanini, was there a counterrevolution. At that, the Wagner type of highly personal conducting continued until 1954 when Wilhelm Furtwängler died.

It was during his Swiss exile that Wagner started work on the four operas of the *Ring des Nibelungen*. An opera on the death of Siegfried was his original conception. Unable to contain the story in one opera, he started a series. In 1852 he finished the complete libretto, and *Das Rheingold* was composed in 1854. A conducting tour to London in 1855 broke into the composition of the *Ring,* but Wagner managed to finish *Die Walküre* in 1856. During these years Wagner was having an affair with Mathilde Wesendonk. She was the young wife of a silk merchant. Otto Wesendonk not only had money, but he also was a patron of the arts. It was a combination very pleasing to Wagner. Mathilde and he had met in 1852, and by 1854 they were in love. She inspired him, while her husband supplied Wagner with money. Matters came to a head when Minna intercepted a love letter. She sent some bitter words to Mathilde: "Before my departure I must tell you that you have succeeded in separating my husband from me after nearly twenty-two years of marriage. May this noble deed contribute to your peace of mind, to your happiness." The Wagners and Wesendonks remained neighbors in Zurich, but relations began to grate. Finally, in 1858, Minna, who was suffering from a heart condition, went to Dresden, ostensibly to be treated. Wagner went to Venice and worked on *Tristan und Isolde.* He had temporarily dropped the *Ring* cycle. The Wesendonk affair had given him a different kind of inspiration, and the shadow of Mathilde hovers over *Tristan,* which was started in 1857. (There are autobiographical elements in many Wagner operas. In the *Ring,* Wagner identified himself with Siegfried. In *Der fliegende Holländer,* the first draft has the heroine named Minna. Wagner changed it to Senta, and the inference is that he felt that Minna could not redeem the Holländer [Wagner]. In *Die Meistersinger,* he is Walther von Stolzing, just as Beckmesser is the Viennese critic, Eduard Hanslick. It was with difficulty that Wagner was talked out of naming the character Hans Lich.)

Nothing Wagner had done had hinted at the operatic miracle named *Tristan und Isolde.* Never in the history of music had there been an operatic score of comparable breadth, intensity, harmonic richness, massive orchestration, sensuousness, power, imagination, and color. The opening chords of *Tristan* were to the last half of the nineteenth century what the *Eroica* and Ninth Symphonies had been to the first half—a breakaway, a new concept. Nor is the impact of the opera yet over. *Tristan und Isolde* has been analyzed and psychoanalyzed almost as much as *Hamlet* (Wagner has been written about more than any composer in history, and *Tristan* occupies a major share of the bibliography). The very opening chords, with their harmonic vagueness, create a certain amount of controversy to this day, and analysts dispute their "spelling." Are they fourths or sevenths? In *Tristan,* harmonic relationships are pushed to their breaking point, and twentieth-century scholars see in the opera the beginnings of atonality. Wagner claimed to have been in something like a trance when he wrote it: "Here, in perfect trustfullness, I plunged into the inner depths of soul-events and from the innermost center of the world I fearlessly built up to its outer form. . . . Life and death, the whole meaning and existence of the outer world, here hang on nothing but the inner movements of the soul." What *Tristan,* that most static of operas and yet the most relentless in building up to its doom, does is to describe inner states, with a kind of power and imagination that peels off layer after layer of the subconscious. It abounds in symbols—symbols of Night, Day, Love, eroticism, the dream world, Nirvana. Whatever its meaning or meanings, *Tristan und Isolde* brings together man and woman, and probes their deepest impulses.

The influence of Schopenhauer was a strong factor in *Tristan und Isolde*. Wagner started to read the German philosopher in the early 1850's, and Schopenhauer's ideas about music entered into a good deal of Wagner's thinking. Schopenhauer wrote that music "is entirely independent of the phenomenal world, ignores it altogether, could to a certain extent exist if there was no world at all, which cannot be said of the other arts." Music, continued Schopenhauer, "is the copy of the will itself. . . . That is why the effect of music is so much more powerful and penetrating than that of the other arts, for they speak only of shadows, but music speaks for the thing itself." In melody Schopenhauer found "the unbroken significant connection of *one* thought from beginning to end representing a whole." This Schopenhauer equated with "the objectification of will, the intellectual life and effort of man." The creator of music "reveals the inner nature of the world." Schopenhauer claimed that if music is too closely connected to word, "it is trying to speak a language not its own." By 1855 Wagner was echoing Schopenhauer and writing that music was "the proto-image of the world itself." Wagner eventually was to assign to music the highest hierarchy in his operas; he decided, as had Schopenhauer, that music was, after all, more important than the Word. Another aspect of Schopenhauer that interested Wagner was his doctrine of the redemption of the soul through the medium of art, and also through renunciation and the ascetic life. Wagner was no more ready to live the ascetic life than Schopenhauer himself had been, but in theory it was a grand and ennobling revelation. The concept of renunciation and redemption, which was present in the Wagner operas as early as *Tannhäuser*, is greatly intensified in the *Ring* and *Parsifal*.

Tristan und Isolde was finished in 1859, but no productions were in sight. The last measures of the opera were written in Lucerne, where Wagner settled—alone, for Minna was still in Dresden—after leaving Venice. They were corresponding, however, and Wagner decided to go to Paris with her. Wesendonk supplied the money for the move by purchasing the completed portion of the *Ring* for 24,000 francs, and the Wagners arrived in Paris toward the end of 1859. It was characteristic that in Paris he rented an expensive house, paid the rent for three years in advance, paid for repairs on the house, had all his furniture sent from Lucerne, and hired a servant for Minna and a valet for himself. Wesendonk's money did not last long. A performance of *Tannhäuser* was arranged for the Opéra in 1861, and it ended in one of the most famous of all operatic scandals, with the Jockey Club booing the opera off the stage. Much has been made of this disaster, but while it might have hurt Wagner's pride, it meant little in the long run. Wagner had gone far beyond *Tannhäuser*.

The next few years were difficult. Vienna promised to stage *Tristan und Isolde* and then backed down: a bitter blow. Wagner ran out of money, had to give up his big house, and moved into menial quarters on the Quai Voltaire, where he started working on a new opera, *Die Meistersinger*. The publishing firm of Schott advanced him money for it, and he soon ran through that. An amnesty allowed him to go back to Germany, and he and Minna moved to Biebrich, on the Rhine. Again his money ran out. He raged: "Mine is a highly susceptible, intense, voracious sensuality, which must somehow or another be indulged if my mind is to accomplish the agonizing labor of calling a non-existent world into being." His next move, in 1862, was to Vienna. Again he was alone. Minna had left him for good. Conducting engagements in Russia, 1863, brought in a good deal of money, but his spending was on a cosmic scale, and what would have sufficed to keep most men happy could not begin to keep Wagner in furs, silks, and perfume. Creditors pressed him, and he had to flee to Switzerland in 1864. The alternative was going to a debtors' prison.

In the darkest hours of 1864, salvation appeared to the desperate Wagner in the person of the homosexual King Ludwig II of Bavaria, who was in love with Wagner's music and very possibly with Wagner himself. Ludwig gave Wagner carte blanche to produce his operas in Munich under ideal conditions. The entire resources of the opera house there—more, the entire resources of Bavaria, as it turned out—were turned over to Wagner. There is no record of any surprise from him. He thought it was his due. "I am the most German of beings. I am the German spirit. Consider the incomparable magic of my works."

Wagner immediately summoned Hans von Bülow to Munich and made him the conductor of the Munich Court Opera. Bülow, trained as a pianist by Liszt, had come under Wagner's spell as early as 1850. In 1857 he married Liszt's daughter, Cosima. One of the best pianists in Europe, Bülow also was a brilliant conductor and one of the sharpest musical minds of his period. His tongue was as sharp as his mind. A tiny, tart, driving, dyspeptic man, he was famous for the intellectual vigor of his interpretations. Some called him all mind and no soul. Wagner, as a friend of Liszt, had seen much of Bülow through the years. He knew that Bülow, who idolized him, would work night and day in his behalf. And Wagner was very, very interested in Cosima. She became his mistress soon after the arrival of the Bülows in Munich, in the spring of 1864. If Bülow knew that he was being made a cuckold, he gave no sign. When a girl, named Isolde, was born to

Cosima in April, 1865, Bülow accepted the infant as his own child.

Rehearsals for *Tristan und Isolde* started. There is an amusing caricature of Wagner and Cosima, who towers over him, walking down the street, with a tiny Bülow, clutching the score of *Tristan*, creeping humbly behind them. Bülow antagonized the musicians with his demands and his tantrums, but from all accounts he conducted brilliantly at the premiere, on June 10, 1865. Three performances rapidly followed.

It took time for *Tristan und Isolde* to establish itself in the European repertoire. The opera was too long, too "uneventful," too "dissonant," too "modern." All many critics could see were two large people screaming at each other. Another reason for the slow progress of *Tristan* was the inability of most singers to cope with the two major roles. At the Munich performances the role of Tristan was sung by Ludwig Schnorr, a tenor who was Wagner's ideal as a singer—young, handsome, heroic in build, intelligent, with a bronzelike, steady voice. Three weeks after the fourth performance of *Tristan und Isolde*, Schnorr was dead at the age of twenty-nine. Rheumatic fever carried him away. Wagner, Ludwig, and all musical Europe grieved.

Wagner was busily engaged in digging his own grave in Munich, and he did not have many months to remain there after the *Tristan* premiere. Faced with an unlimited supply of funds for the first time in his life he ran wild, indulging himself with an incredibly lavish hand. Had he shown any finesse, he could have lorded it over King and court, but his combination of arrogance, recklessness, selfishness, and dishonesty was too much. He even started to dabble in politics, and that really scared some of the most important members of the Bavarian establishment, who gathered together to stop him. They whipped up a public outcry over Wagner's spending, his insane extravagance, his morals (everybody at court knew about his relationship with Cosima, and now the public was told), and his domination over the King. On December 10, 1865, Wagner was forced to leave. It was banishment. Ludwig suggested that it might be better if he disappear for a while—on full allowance, of course. Wagner went to Geneva, where he worked on *Die Meistersinger*. In January, 1866, he learned of Minna's death. Cosima joined him, and they found a palatial estate at Triebschen, on Lake Lucerne. It was there that she bore him their second child, Eva, in 1867.

At Triebschen, Wagner lived surrounded by the luxury he needed. The living room, which contained portraits of Beethoven, Goethe, and Schiller, had walls covered with yellow leather traced with gold. The gallery was a long, narrow room hung in violet velvet, lined with statues of Wagnerian heroes, and draped with tapestries portraying scenes from the *Ring*. In one corner of the gallery was a butterfly collection; in another, a gilded Buddha, Chinese incense burners, and other Orientalia. In the carefully kept gardens lived a great dog, a Newfoundland named Russ. (Wagner always had a dog or dogs. In more or less chronological order, there were two black poodles, Dreck and Speck; the Newfoundland, Robber, who accompanied Wagner and Minna from Riga to London and Paris; a spaniel named Peps; another spaniel, Fips; a brown hound, Pohl; two more Newfoundlands, Mark and Brangäne; several terriers; and a Spitz named Putzi. Wagner idolized them.)

Now and then Cosima, for the sake of appearances, joined her husband in Munich, where *Die Meistersinger* was in rehearsal. Bülow and Hans Richter were preparing the opera. Richter, a Hungarian, had come to Triebschen in 1866 as Wagner's secretary and copyist. Later he became, with Mottl and Seidl, the first of the Wagner-trained conductors to emerge from Bayreuth. Many considered him the greatest. It was to Richter that the honor of conducting the *Meistersinger* premiere fell, on June 21, 1868. A few months later, Richter resigned from the Munich Opera, claiming that rehearsals of *Das Rheingold* were scandalously inadequate. Everybody knew that Richter would not have resigned without Wagner's blessing, and Ludwig for once was furious. Franz Wüllner conducted the *Rheingold* premiere (and also the premier of *Die Walküre* in 1870).

Bülow meanwhile was in an intolerable position. All Germany by now knew of his marital problems. Cosima refused to return to him, and in 1869 she bore Wagner a third child, Siegfried. Bülow had enough. Divorce proceedings were set in motion, and the decree became final in 1870. On August 25 of that year, Wagner and Cosima were married. *Siegfried* was finished in 1871 and *Götterdämmerung* substantially completed in 1872 (though the scoring was not finished until 1874).

The early 1870's saw two other major events in Wagner's life—his relationship with Nietzsche, and the inception of Bayreuth.

Friedrich Nietzsche had met Wagner in 1868 and had all but drowned himself in worship of the man and his music (especially *Tristan und Isolde*). In 1872 he published *The Birth of Tragedy from the Spirit of Music*, in which Greek tragedy was interpreted along Wagnerian lines. Nietzsche's concept of Apollonian (pure, classic) and Dionysian (wild, romantic) opposites, as set forth in his book, made a deep impression on contemporary aesthetic thinking. Later, Nietzsche was to reconsider his adoration of Wagner and eventually swung out of the orbit, calling Bizet's *Carmen* the perfect opera. But for a long time Wagner had the support of the most widely read German philosopher.

As early as 1870 Wagner was thinking seriously about a festival theater that would be dedicated to his works alone. He found his ideal site at the quiet little Bavarian town of Bayreuth. Ludwig at first was cold to the idea. But Wagner Societies were formed all over Germany, and Wagner's friends exerted themselves to raise money for the cause. Wagner sent out a circular, dated November 12, 1871, advising that the *Ring des Nibelungen* would open Bayreuth in 1873. Those who donated money "will receive the name and rights of patrons of the festival stage play at Bayreuth, while the carrying-out of the enterprise itself will be left exclusively to my knowledge and my exertions. The real estate accruing from this common enterprise shall be placed at my disposal and subject to such future arrangements as I shall consider most appropriately serviceable to the sense and ideal character of the undertaking." Wagner left Triebschen, had a villa built near the festival theater in Bayreuth, and supervised the work. In Vienna, Hanslick was amazed. "Wagner," he wrote, "is lucky in all things. At first he raves against all monarchs; and a magnanimous King meets him with flattering love and prepares for him an existence free from care and even lavish. Then he writes a pamphlet against the Jews; and all Jewry, both in and outside of music, pays him all the more zealous homage, through newspaper criticisms and purchase of Bayreuth promissory notes."

The Bayreuth project received world-wide publicity, but money was slow coming in. Wagner had to cancel his plans for an 1873 season. Less than half the necessary funds were on hand. Wagner put all his hopes in Ludwig, and was not disappointed. In 1874 the King advanced enough money to start things moving again. There was a great deal of opposition in Bavaria to the project. It was attacked as folly, as a testament to Ludwig's madness. When Ludwig's money ran out, Wagner embarked on conducting tours to raise funds. For a while the future of Bayreuth was in doubt. Nevertheless the building was completed, and the first Bayreuth Festival was given in 1876. *Der Ring des Nibelungen,* Richter conducting, was given three times. The first season showed an enormous deficit, and the future of Bayreuth was once again in doubt. Not until 1882 could a second Bayreuth Festival be undertaken.

The first Bayreuth season was the musical event of the decade. Some 4,000 visitors, including sixty newspaper correspondents from all over the globe, inundated the tiny village. In attendance were the Emperor of Germany, the Emperor and Empress of Brazil, the King of Bavaria, Prince George of Prussia, a Hohenzollern prince, Prince Wilhelm of Hesse, Grand Duke Vladimir of Russia, the Grand Duke of Mecklenburg, the Duke of Anhalt-Dessau, and other nobility. Such was the interest in the festival that the two critics from New York—both the *Times* and the *Tribune* sent reporters— were allowed to use the new transatlantic cable to get their stories through instantly. Among the things they reported was the unhappiness about creature comforts. "The great distance from the town over a dirty road with no shade and no restaurant accommodations caused much discontent. The discontent in these regards is daily increasing," said the *Times*. Audiences listened to the music with some puzzlement but also with honest enthusiasm. At the end of each opera there was an ovation, but no singer was allowed to take a curtain call. "The reason for so declining was explained by Herr Wagner and the leading artists, who said that appearances before the curtain would tend to violate the unity of the representation." At the end of the festival there was a great party for over 500 people. Wagner made a long speech, was cheered, and bent his head to receive a silver crown of laurel leaves. Wagner then paid tribute to Liszt, saying he owed everything to him; whereupon Liszt got up to make *his* speech. "Other countries," he said, "greet Dante and Shakespeare. So," turning to Wagner, "I am your most obedient servant."

Musically the Bayreuth season was the turning point in Wagner's European fortunes. Not only did the audience consist largely of Wagner admirers, but the critics (including the ones from New York) were also for the most part supporters. (Brahms and his group ostentatiously stayed away.) They spread the word about the glories of the new music; and the many composers who came to Bayreuth, especially the French contingent, were overwhelmed. For the first time words like "melodious," "tuneful," "lyric" and "beautiful" began consistently to appear in reviews of the Wagner operas. The chorus of praise drowned out the cries of the doubters. Even Hanslick hedged, though he was bothered by the underlying aesthetic of Wagnerism. "The plastic energy of Wagner's fancy, his astonishing mastery over the orchestral technique, and numerous musical beauties reign in the *Nibelungen* with a magical power to which we willingly and thankfully yield ourselves captive. These single beauties that creep, as it were, behind the back of the system do not prevent this *system*, the tyranny of the word, of unmelodious dialogue, from planting in the whole the seeds of death." Joseph Bennett, in the London *Musical Times*, echoed Hanslick, saying that the music might very well be beautiful, full of genius, full of melody—but "Something of Milton's Fallen Spirit surrounds Wagner, with a strange mixture of attraction and repulsion. Among the gods of his native heaven he might have been great, and in that which is now his own place he lifts himself in Titanic grandeur. But let us not forget he is powerful chiefly for evil." Bennett, like the other old critics, could feel the ground slipping from him, but he went down bravely, firing as he went.

Stimulated by the furor, *Punch* added its contribution. It ran a long imaginary interview on "Music—of the Present and of the Future." Mrs. Hazy Highfaluter was being questioned. "Will you define the tone-art of the future?" Her answer: "It defies definition. I should describe it as a mighty system of spiritual aëronautics, meant to lift up the soul to the sublime regions of supersensuous harmony, above the gross and earthly restraints of received form in composition, and the vulgar attractions of sustained melody."

Everybody in Europe was writing or talking about Wagner. But, more important, the opera houses were staging his works, and not only the early ones. After Bayreuth there was a run on Wagner. At the Berlin Opera, for example, there were 223 performances during the 1877–78 season. Wagner headed the list with thirty-eight performances of five operas. Next was Mozart, with twenty-nine of six works, followed by Verdi with nineteen of four works. These ratios were to prevail for many years in German opera houses. Within a decade after Bayreuth, opera houses in Germany, Austria, England, and the United States were bidding eagerly for the Wagnerian operas, and Wagner was beginning to show up even in such unsympathetic centers as France and Italy.

Die Meistersinger quickly made its way as the most "human" of the Wagner operas. German audiences especially identified with medieval Nuremberg, and with Hans Sachs's plea for German art. This is the sunniest of Wagner's operas, and if the humor is heavy-handed and all the cards stacked against poor Beckmesser, the glorious sweep of the music is irresistible. The message of *Die Meistersinger* is clear and direct, altogether different from the murky symbolism of the *Ring*. The four operas of the *Ring* may outwardly be concerned with gods, goddesses, earth-mothers, and Aryan heroes, all manipulated so that the theme of redemption through love wins out, but the characters end up being archetypes, capable of being interpreted any number of ways. George Bernard Shaw, for one, took the *Ring* in terms of capitalism versus Fabian Socialism. The post-World War II stagings at Bayreuth present the *Ring* in terms of sun-god myths, mother-images, father-images, closed and broken circles, and the whole Jungian apparatus. But a miracle happens when the *Ring* is heard. Exegesis disappears, and the listener is swept into something primal, timeless, and is pushed by elemental forces. The *Ring* is a conception that deals not with women but Woman; not with men, but Man; not with people, but with the Folk; not with mind, but with the subconscious; not with religion, but with basic ritual; not with nature, but with Nature.

Wagner had triumphed. He had had his way. Now he was the most famous composer in the world. He could, with relative peace of mind, spend much of his time at the Villa Wahnfried in Bayreuth and devote himself entirely to the things that interested him. That included working on *Parsifal* and writing pamphlets and articles for the official Wagner publications. His personal life became even more eccentric. Among other things, he became a vegetarian and came to the conclusion that the world would be saved if everybody ate vegetables instead of meat. He lived like an Oriental pasha, bathed in incense, dressed in violently clashing colors, with only the softest silk touching his skin. Secure in his all-embracing wisdom, he wrote reams of prose on every conceivable subject. Sometimes his articles approached idiocy, as in the section of an essay on Beethoven dealing with the composer's cranial characteristics:

If it is held to be an axiom of physiology for high intellectual endowments that a great brain must be enclosed in a thin, delicate skull, as if to facilitate the immediate cognition of external things, we saw, nevertheless, on the inspection of the remains a few years ago, in conformity with the entire skeleton, a skull of unusual thickness and firmness. So did nature guard in him a brain of extreme tenderness, in order that it might look towards the interior only, and carry on in undisturbed repose the world contemplation of a great heart. What that exceedingly robust strength enclosed and preserved was an inner world of such conspicuous delicacy that, left defenceless to the rough touch of the external world, it would have gently dissolved—as did Mozart's genius of light and love.

His anti-Semitism and screams for racial purity approached madness. He even compared Brahms's music to that of "a Jewish czardas player." In one of his last tracts, *Heldentum und Christentum*, he claimed that the Aryans had sprung from the gods. But inferior peoples had deprived the Aryans of their godhead, especially the Jews, "former cannibals, educated to be the business leaders of society." Christ was not a Jew. He was basically an Aryan. Small wonder that Hitler was to say: "Whoever wants to understand National Socialistic Germany must know Wagner."

. Work on *Parsifal* continued, alternating with racist treatises, studies of what had happened to Christianity, and a love affair with Judith Mendès, she about forty years younger than he was. Judith, noted for her beauty, was the daughter of Théophile Gautier, the French poet and critic who had been one of Wagner's earliest admirers. She was married to the poet Catulle Mendès, and they first met Wagner at Triebschen. He was fascinated with her, and when they met again during the first season in Bayreuth, the attraction became physical. She moved into Villa Wahnfried, and Cosima pretended not to notice. Judith returned to Paris and her husband, but she and Wagner corresponded until 1878. It was Wagner's last love affair, and it is hard to resist reading into the sensuous music of the second act of *Parsifal* the erotic stimulation that Judith had given him.

Parsifal, finished in 1882, is commonly taken to be a religious opera, and there is something ironic in the sight of audiences attending it as a Christian rite. It is, however, an opera capable of many interpretations. The accepted theme is that of Christian mysticism, purity, and redemption. Others have found in it the essence of anti-Christianity; and Robert W. Gutman, one of Wagner's recent biographers, has proved, to his satisfaction at least, that *Parsifal* is "an allegory of the Aryan's fall and redemption." In this interpretation, Klingsor represents not only the Jews but also the Jesuits. That, specifically, is what Wagner once said to Cosima. Debussy had his own ideas about *Parsifal*. He wrote, only half jokingly, that Klingsor was "the finest character" in the opera:

He knows what men are worth, and weighs the solidity of their vows of chastity in scales of contempt. From this one may safely argue that this cunning magician, this hardened old criminal, is not merely the only human character, but the only normal character in this drama which contains the falsest of moral and religious theories—theories of which the youthful Parsifal is the heroic and foolish champion. In fact, in this Christian drama, no one wants to sacrifice himself. . . .

One thing can be said of *Parsifal* with complete accuracy. Its composer was not a religious man. Wagner detested religious orthodoxy of any kind, and he dismissed Christianity as stemming from the Jews. If he had any religious feeling at all, it was a vague pantheism, a longing for the heroic deeds of Teutonic myth. The pan-Germanism of Richard Wagner was one of the governing forces of his life.

Parsifal, Wagner decided, should be restricted to Bayreuth for thirty years, after which the work would be released to the world. (The Metropolitan Opera did not care to wait that long, and staged *Parsifal* in New York in 1903. "Heresy!" shrieked the Wagnerians in Bayreuth and elsewhere.) Wagner made an exception for King Ludwig, and there were several private performances in Munich. The world premiere took place at Bayreuth on July 26, 1882. Hermann Levi was the conductor. He was chief conductor at the Munich Opera—and he was a Jew. Wagner spent a great deal of time pleading with this son of a rabbi to undergo baptism. Levi was so disgusted that he wrote a letter asking to be relieved of the assignment, and Wagner, who admired Levi's artistry, had to spend that much more time patching things up. After *Parsifal*, Wagner was exhausted, and he had premonitions of death. He went to Venice to recuperate, and it was there that he died, on February 13, 1883. His body was brought back to Bayreuth, and as the coffin was being lowered into the grave an orchestra played the funeral march from *Götterdämmerung*.

The years after Wagner's death—indeed, the years after the first Bayreuth season of 1876—saw Wagner's music penetrate the intellectual life of Europe. He was a potent influence on all composers who worked in the 1870's, and upon those who followed—on Richard Strauss, on Bruckner and Mahler, on the French school, on Dvořák, even on Debussy. Wagnerism lived on in Schoenberg's *Verklärte Nacht*, with its post-*Tristan* harmonies, and in such later Schoenberg works as *Erwartung*, which is a post-*Tristan* song of love that even has the equivalent of a *Liebestod*. Alban Berg's music is saturated with Wagner. Wagner lived on in the profusion of books that were, and still are, written about him: books to explain the leitmotifs, the message of the operas, the implications in them (from Schopenhauerian thought to Jungian psychology to the impact on National Socialism). In France, during the last two-thirds of the nineteenth century, Wagner was probably the supreme figure in all the arts. The symbolist poets took up his cause, and such important painters as Whistler, Degas, and Cézanne were Wagnerians. Redon and Fantin-Latour painted canvases based on the operas. Daudet described the phenomenon: "We studied his characters as if Wotan held the secret of the world and Hans Sachs was the spokesman for free, natural, and spontaneous art." Mallarmé and Baudelaire were enthusiasts, and the latter went around saying that Wagner in music was the equivalent of Delacroix in painting. The French literature of the day was full of allusions to Wagner.

Early in the twentieth century, strong anti-Wagnerian schools began to make themselves felt. Debussy, who originally has been a Wagnerian, broke away and defiantly signed himself "musicien français." Even Debussy, however, was not able to shake entirely free. He poked fun at the wordy librettos and their length—"All this is inadmissible for those who love clarity and conciseness"—but had to admit that the Wagner operas were full of passages of "unforgettable beauty" that "silence all criticism." Debussy fought the music of the siren from Bayreuth, and in his own scores did make a considerable breakaway. Stravinsky was probably the first completely successful anti-Wagnerian, in that he discarded the entire Wagnerian apparatus in favor first of Russian nationalism and then of neoclassicism.

With the prevalent antiromanticism in all the arts that set in after 1920, Wagner slipped a little from his position. Suddenly the Wagner operas were found by musicians and intellectuals to sound thick, old-fashioned, verbose, faintly (or not so faintly) ridiculous. Coincidentally, the delights of bel-canto opera and early Verdi were rediscovered. As Wagner began to slip, the international repertoire began to include Verdi operas that in some instances had not been staged for generations. There was something in Verdi's emotional health, clarity, and directness that appealed to the age. It was also realized that Verdi and Wagner, once considered so apart from each other, did have some points in common, and *Falstaff* was held up as an example—*Falstaff*, in which set arias are all but abolished, in which the orchestra is completely integrated with the text, in which something very close to leitmotifs glint, disappear, and reappear. Thus was the circle closed. The two great men, so far apart, came near touching in *Falstaff*. In the future Wagner and Verdi will live together, as they have lived together in the past. But one thing seems certain. Verdi will never again be underrated, as he once was; and Wagner will never again be taken as seriously as he was taken at the turn of the century, when he all but dominated the intellectual life of the Western world.

❦ 18 ❧

Keeper of the Flame

JOHANNES BRAHMS

The only German composer of Wagner's lifetime who was big enough to stand with him on more or less an equal footing was Johannes Brahms. But they are antipodal. Wagner was the revolutionary, the man of the future. Brahms was the classicist who dealt with abstract forms and never wrote a note of program music in his life, much less an opera. Wagner was to exert enormous influence on the future. With Brahms the symphony as handed down by Beethoven, Mendelssohn, and Schumann came to an end. Brahms, like Bach, summed up an epoch. Unlike Bach, he contributed little to the development of music, though some of his textures and harmonies find a faint echo in Arnold Schoenberg. Even in Brahms's own day the progressives thought little of him. Mahler called Brahms "a mannikin with a somewhat narrow heart." Such Wagner-dominated hotheads as Hugo Wolf gleefully jumped on each new Brahms composition, poking fun at it. Wolf, reviewing the Third Symphony for the *Wiener Salonblatt,* proclaimed that "Brahms is the epigone of Schumann and Mendelssohn and, as such, exercises about as much influence on the history of art as the late Robert Volkmann [a once-popular, now forgotten academic composer], that is, he has for the history of art just as *little* importance as Volkmann, which is to say *no* influence at all. . . . The man who has written three symphonies and apparently intends to follow with another six . . . is only a relic from primeval ages and no vital part of the great stream of time."

But for a relic Brahms has turned out to have remarkable endurance. The major part of his *oeuvre* has remained an active part of the repertory, and shows no diminution in public favor. Quite the contrary. Brahms, in the 1960's, was elbowing Beethoven as the most popular of symphonic composers. His four symphonies, the two piano concertos, the Violin Concerto and even his Double Concerto are basic repertory, as are the *Haydn Variations* and the *Academic Festival Overture.* Pianists are regularly playing the

F minor Sonata, the *Handel* and *Paganini Variations* and the various rhapsodies, intermezzi, and caprices of his late period. Chamber groups find indispensable the Clarinet Quintet, the Piano Quintet, the three string quartets and other chamber music. His songs are regularly on recital programs. The *German Requiem* is steadily performed. Violinists would be lost without the three sonatas. Considering that the major percentage of Mendelssohn's, Schumann's, and Liszt's music lies untouched in the Collected Editions, considering that great reputations have come and gone, Brahms's record is amazing. Clearly he had something very pertinent to say to future generations.

Brahms was a conscious classicist, occupying in the last half of the nineteenth century a position analogous to Mendelssohn's in the first half. Like Mendelssohn, he was content with the old forms, and he knew more about them than anybody in his period. As conductor of the Gesellschaft der Musikfreunde he placed a great deal of early music on its programs, and he was one of the very few musicians of his day who refrained from romanticizing and rewriting. Only a man well versed in baroque counterpoint could have written the propulsive, heroic fugue that concludes the *Handel Variations*, and only so strong an individualist as Brahms could at the same time have kept it from being a mere copy of an old formula. Bach he loved above all. He wrote to Clara Schumann of the Chaconne: "On a system for a small instrument, a man writes a whole world of the deepest thoughts and the most tremendous emotions. If I could imagine that I could have accomplished such a thing, could have conceived it within myself, I know surely that the excitement and the shock would have driven me insane." And he told Eusebius Mandyczewski: "When the new Handel edition comes out and is sent to me, I put it in my library and say, 'As soon as I have time I will look it over.' But when a new Bach edition appears, I let everything else go." He knew the classic period almost as well, and was a profound student of Beethoven's music. The violent romantic currents around him, the "music of the future," he largely ignored. He was content to work the way the old masters had worked, employing counterpoint, variation, and sonata form. He had a strong feeling for German folksong and often used it, but his is not a nationalist music. It is a music of immense weight and solidity, especially at the beginning of his career; a music marked with Schumannesque cross-rhythms, with a Beethovenian feeling for development, with a Bachian feeling for polyphony.

Above all it is essentially a serious music, even if Brahms could be as lyric as any romantic composer when he wanted to be. From the beginning he set himself to write a "pure" music, an absolute music, a music that would be a corrective to the extravagant ideas of Liszt and Wagner. His music could be complicated and difficult, but it was never showy except in one bravura set, the *Paganini Variations*, and even there the virtuosity is governed by strict musical logic. His music deliberately avoided anything suggestive of superficial prettiness. For many years Brahms had the reputation of being a "difficult" composer, a philosopher in sound.

Definitely he was an uncompromising composer; but, then again, he was an uncompromising man. Prickly, tough, ultrasensitive, cynical, bad-tempered, he created almost as much fear as the dyspeptic Hans von Bülow. He had his generous side; if he was interested in a composer, as he was in Dvořák or Grieg, he would move heaven and earth to help him. But he was interested in very few living composers. Liszt and Wagner were alien to him, and he had little respect for Bruckner, Mahler, Tchaikovsky, Verdi, or Richard Strauss. The contemporary composer he probably loved best was the Waltz King, Johann Strauss, the younger. He never had any hesitation speaking his mind, and sometimes his comments could be brutally contemptuous. Max Bruch, a well-thought-of composer of the day (his G minor Violin Concerto still is played), sent Brahms the manuscript of an oratorio, *Arminius*. Brahms looked it over. One day shortly thereafter, Bruch and Brahms were dining, and they heard a hurdy-gurdy across the street. "Listen, Bruch!" Brahms shouted. "That fellow has gotten hold of your *Arminius!*" Even Brahms's closest friends could be impaled on the spike of Brahms's testiness. At a party in the composer Ignaz Brüll's house, the poet and biographer of Brahms, Max Kalbeck, started making an anti-Wagner speech. Brahms suddenly shot forth: "For God's sake, stop talking about things you don't understand." Brahms's remark was that of the professional irritated by the amateur, but it was tactless, and Kalbeck left the room. The critic Richard Specht, who relates this story, says that he met Kalbeck a few days later, and Kalbeck bitterly complained of Brahms's ingratitude. "This is what I get for such devotion!" But, said Kalbeck, "This time I did not tolerate such an attack by the lord and master. I wrote him a long letter and told him off in no uncertain terms." Specht wanted to know what Brahms's reaction was. "Of course," Kalbeck grinned, "I never sent the letter." There was a story current in Vienna that Brahms left a party saying, "If there is anybody here I have not insulted, I apologize." The Viennese critic Max Graf says that while the story *should* be true, it was invented by a man named Béla Haas, a friend of Brahms and Hanslick.

All of Brahms's biographers are unanimous in saying that beneath the gruff exterior was a heart of gold. That appears to be true, but it did not make it easier for his friends, who had to put up with a kind of bluntness that often was all but antisocial. Even with such devoted and lifelong friends as Clara Schumann and Joseph Joachim there were occasional ruptures. Brahms knew the kind of man he was. "I let the world go the way it pleases. I am only too often reminded that I am a difficult person to get along with. I am growing accustomed to bearing the consequences of this." His frank and even crude way of talking, and his inability to see any point of view but his own, cost him many friends. He would blurt out things without thinking. On tour in Denmark in 1868 he was asked by his hosts if he had seen the Thorwaldsen Museum. "Yes, it's quite extraordinary. It's only a pity that it's not in Berlin." This tactless remark got out, and the public outcry was such that Brahms had to leave the country.

In his youth he was a handsome man, slim, with fair hair, very blue eyes, and a high voice that annoyed him. In his mature years he became a heavy-set man with an enormous beard. He constantly smoked cigars and had an appearance of hopeless sloppiness. And he *was* sloppy. He hated to buy clothes, and his old, baggy, patched trousers were invariably too short. In Vienna, there were many who pointed out the resemblances with Beethoven (could Brahms have played these up?): both were short men, both loved the country, both had fierce tempers, both were bachelors. They even had a similar way of walking, head forward and hands clasped behind the back. Over his shoulders Brahms would wear a plaid shawl secured by a safety pin. In his hand, a hat that he seldom put on his head. All his life he observed humble habits. Even when he was financially well off he ate at cheap restaurants, lived very simply, and spent next to nothing on himself. Generally he could be found at his favorite tavern, The Red Hedgehog. He liked the coffee there. His biggest indulgence was his collection of original music manuscripts, among which could be found Mozart's G minor Symphony. He even owned the autograph score of Wagner's *Tannhäuser*, which he got as a gift from the pianist Karl Tausig. (It turned out that the score was not Tausig's to give away. Wagner asked for its return and, with great and guarded politeness, Brahms did return it. Wagner sent him in its stead an autograph of *Das Rheingold*.)

Between Wagner and Brahms was a certain grudging admiration. They were the leaders of opposed schools, and while they had little to do with each other, there was no overt hostility between them. Wagner had a few ill-tempered remarks to make about Brahms, but for the most part ignored him as studiously as Brahms avoided *him*. In a way that was surprising, for both were fighters, and as early as 1860 Brahms, with Joachim, Julius Otto Grimm, and Bernhard Scholz had signed a proclamation against the "so-called music of the future." Nobody paid any attention to the proclamation. The signers for the most part were young and unproved musicians. Brahms never again signed a manifesto or made a public utterance about music. If he was set up as the leader of the classic school, it was none of his own doing and Brahms even was exasperated with the whole thing. It was Eduard Hanslick, his friend and the influential critic of the *Neue freie Presse*, who was instrumental in casting Brahms as the "foe" of Wagner, as the flag-

253

bearer behind whom marched the "pure" musicians—Clara Schumann, Joseph Joachim, and the other upholders of the classic tradition.

On the whole Brahms lived an uneventful life. Most of it was spent in Germany and Vienna. He did little traveling and little to promote his music. He was born in Hamburg on May 7, 1833. His father was a double-bass player. When Brahms was six years old it was discovered that he had perfect pitch and an extraordinary musical talent. By good luck he fell into the hands of Eduard Marxsen, a fine musician and teacher who gave him a heavy diet of Bach. It was clear to Marxsen that Brahms was something special, and his faith never wavered. When he heard of Mendelssohn's death in 1847, he said: "A master of the art has gone; a greater one arises in Brahms." Brahms was fourteen at the time, and it took a prescient man to make such an accurate prediction. Marxsen and Brahms remained close friends throughout life, and the Piano Concerto in B flat is dedicated to him. He died ten years before Brahms, in 1887.

At the age of ten Brahms was playing the piano in public. He also, to bring money into the family, played in waterfront dives and bordellos. This left psychic scars. All his life he was uncomfortable with virtuous women, and his sex life seems to have been confined to prostitutes. (Max Graf tells the story of the great Brahms coming into a dubious café in the 1880's and being asked by a well-known prostitute to go to the piano. "Professor, play us some dance music." The composer of the C minor Symphony obediently went to the battered upright and entertained the company.) The experiences he went through as a child undoubtedly kept him from marriage. He was tempted many times but always pulled back. Altogether characteristic was his relationship with Agathe von Siebold. After becoming engaged to her, he sent her a hysterical letter: "I love you. I must see you again. But I cannot wear fetters . . ." Naturally Agathe acted like any prudent girl, and broke off the engagement. A man who could write a letter like this would not have made a good husband. Later in life, in a confidential moment, Brahms told a friend about some of the things he had gone through as a child. "That was my first impression of women. And you expect me to honor them as you do!"

Brahms at the age of twenty had composed several major piano works, including the Scherzo in E flat minor, and the C major and F minor Piano Sonatas. Like all of the Brahms piano music up to the *Handel Variations,* they were serious and thick, with rumbling basses, awkward figurations, and an almost complete lack of charm. But they radiated bigness; there was something monumental about them. Not many pianists were interested in this kind of music. Like the late Beethoven works, they were written as much against the piano as for the piano. They spurned the virtuosity of Liszt and the sweet decoration of Chopin, and were concerned primarily with idea instead of texture. Brahms was not going to achieve overnight fame as a composer with such music.

He was, however, recognized as an accomplished pianist, and in 1853 he toured with Eduard Reményi as an accompanist. Reményi was a Hungarian violinist who played à la tzigane. A showman rather than a musician, he unabashedly catered to his audiences, and his repertory consisted mostly of short encore pieces and his own transcriptions of Chopin nocturnes and mazurkas. (As late as 1879, Reményi was touring the United States—not with Brahms—and he amused a critic no end: "This class of music was about what I expected to hear, but I was not prepared for *Swanee River* and, horror of horrors! must it be told? *Grandfather's Clock.*") What Brahms felt playing for this gentleman, history does not relate. It was on this 1853 tour with Reményi that Brahms met Joseph Joachim (1831–1907). The young but already famous violinist was very much impressed with Brahms's piano playing, and even more with his music. They became friends. At that time, Joachim was a member of the Liszt circle, and he took Brahms to Weimar with him. Brahms brought his music along, but was too shy to play it. Liszt, who gloried in acting as a patron of young composers, and who most likely was the greatest sight reader who ever lived, took Brahms's manuscripts to the piano and played at sight the E flat minor Scherzo and some of the C major Sonata. Whatever Brahms thought of Liszt as a composer, he had nothing but admiration for him as a pianist. "We others can play the piano," he later said, "but we all of us have only a few fingers of his hands." Liszt then played for Brahms his B minor Sonata. There is a story that Liszt looked at Brahms to see how the young man was taking it, and found him fast asleep. It sounds apocryphal. Nobody slept while the great Franz Liszt was storming up and down the keyboard.

If there was one living composer the young Brahms loved, it was Schumann. In 1853 the two men came together in Düsseldorf. Joachim had told Schumann about his new friend, and had been instrumental in arranging the meeting. There is a note in Schumann's diary dated September 30, 1853: "Brahms to see me (a genius)." Schumann was so impressed he wrote a long article about Brahms in the *Neue Zeitschrift für Musik*, calling him a young eagle and predicting that great things would come from him. It was Schumann's last article for the publication he had founded. Another concrete gesture by Schumann came when he introduced Brahms to Breitkopf and Härtel, who published his early works. So great was the attraction between Schumann and Brahms that he insisted the younger man move into his house. Brahms was at Clara's side after Schumann tried to commit suicide, and he was at her side after he died, in 1856. Brahms ended by falling in love with her. There are stories that the relationship between them was more than platonic, but it is hard to believe that Clara would have given herself to Brahms. Her mind, from everything we know about her, did not work that way. She was the widow of the great Robert Schumann, and she became a professional widow who wore mourning clothes all her life. That is not to say she and Brahms were anything but close. If nothing else, the memory of the man they both loved would have kept them together. They needed each other and they inspired each other. They also thought alike about music, had much the same ideals and aspirations, and were, intellectually and emotionally, much closer to each other than most husbands and wives.

The other great friendship of his life was with Joseph Joachim, who was to the violin what Clara Schumann was to the piano—an upholder of the faith, a bastion of classicism in the romantic kingdom. Joachim perceived the steel in Brahms as early as 1854, as witness a letter to a friend:

> With Brahms, who stayed with me for a few days, sleeping on the black couch, I could not feel perfectly at ease, even though I again recognized his good, even extraordinary, qualities. . . . Brahms is the most intransigent egotist imaginable, although he himself does not realize it. Everything oozes out of his sanguine nature quite spontaneously, but at times with a lack of consideration (not a lack of reticence, which would suit me fine!) that causes injury because it betrays uncouthness. . . . He recognizes the weakness of people with whom he deals, and he exploits them. . . . All he cares is to write music without interference; and his faith in a more sublime world of fantasy, and his manner of keeping all the unhealthy sensations and imaginary sufferings of others at arm's length borders on genius. . . . His compositions, so rich and ruthlessly rejecting all earthly woes, are such an effortless game in the most complex disguise. Never have I encountered such talent. He has surpassed me by far.

Brahms's first great orchestral work was the D minor Piano Concerto, which had its premiere in 1859 with the composer at the piano. Its opening, bold and daring, with a magnificent, defiant theme that still raises shivers, announced a major talent. It was not a work calculated to get many performances, for it was too difficult, too uncompromising, too big, too demanding intellectually. The initial consensus could be found in the remark of a critic that "the public was wearied and the musicians puzzled." At the Leipzig premiere another critic called the concerto "a symphony with piano obbligato" (not an original thought, for many years previously E. T. A. Hoffmann had called the concertos of Mozart and Beethoven "not so much concertos as symphonies with piano obbligato"). The critic went on to say that "the solo part is as ungrateful as possible and the orchestral part a series of lacerating chords." Leipzig was the headquarters of the neo-Mendelssohn party of archconservatives. But Leipzig's criticism was echoed elsewhere. Anton Rubinstein expressed what many musicians were thinking when Brahms's music first appeared: "For the drawing room, he is not graceful enough, for the concert hall not fiery enough, for the countryside not primitive enough, for the city not cultured enough. I have but little faith in such natures." Even such progressive composers as Édouard Lalo in Paris were bothered twenty and more years after the D minor Concerto was written. In a letter to the Spanish violinist Pablo de Sarasate, Lalo said that he had heard the D minor Concerto five times: "I maintain that when a soloist is set on the stage he must be given the main role and not be treated as a soloist within the orchestra. If the solo genre displeases the composer, then let him write symphonies or something else for the orchestra alone, but don't let him bore me with fragments of solo constantly interrupted by the orchestra." Many pianists felt that way. The D minor Concerto never received many performances, and not until the 1950's did it become one of the most popular of all concertos.

No matter what the critics and some of the musicians thought, it was evident that a new and powerful voice was being heard, and some important people in musical Germany took note. Little by little Brahms's reputation grew. Clara Schumann and Joachim played his music, and Julius Stockhausen began to sing his lieder. In 1862 Brahms visited Vienna, returned the following year, and made the city his home for the rest of his life. A decision by the Hamburg Philharmonic was instrumental in the move. Brahms wanted to become conductor of the orchestra, but was turned down—a rejection that rankled within him as long as he lived.

On his arrival in Vienna, Brahms became conductor of the Academy of Singing, and remained in that position for two years. After that, he concentrated on composing, breaking up his creative work by short concert tours as pianist or conductor. He made many friends in Vienna, including the pianist Julius Epstein, the violinist Joseph Hellmesberger, and the singer Amalie Weiss (whom Joachim married). Hellmesberger, who was the leader of a prominent string quartet, loudly acclaimed Brahms as Beethoven's heir. In the Brahms circle were also the great surgeon and amateur musician Theodor Billroth; the conductor Hermann Levi (who later moved to Munich, became a Wagnerian, and thus lost Brahms's friendship); the poet Max Kalbeck (who wrote the first important biography of Brahms); and the musicologist and Beethoven specialist, Gustav Nottebohm. Brahms lived in various apartments until 1871, when he took permanent lodgings at Karlgasse 4, over which his housekeeper, Frau Celestina Truxa, presided. It was in that house that he died, twenty-six years later.

The work that made Brahms famous was the *German Requiem*. It was first performed in Dresden in 1868 with one section missing, and the complete work had its premiere the following year in Leipzig. The text is in German, from the Lutheran Bible, and has no relation to orthodox rites. Even the name of Christ is avoided. Brahms was a freethinker, and this disturbed his religious friends. "Such a great man! Such a great soul! And he believes in nothing!" lamented the appalled Dvořák. After the success of the *German Requiem,* Brahms all but stopped touring as a pianist. For several years, 1872–1875, he conducted the concerts of the Gesellschaft der Musikfreunde, and after that he no longer professionally conducted except to pick up the baton for his own music. He kept his publisher, Fritz Simrock, plentifully supplied with new material. Until 1876, he wrote in all forms except symphony and opera. Opera did not interest him, although every now and then he said he would like to write one. Nobody took him seriously. But symphony was another matter. His friends kept urging him to write one, but he held off. As with all the romantics, he had before him the fearsome specter of the Beethoven Ninth, against which all symphonies had to be measured.

Finally, in 1876, came his Symphony No. 1. Brahms had been working on it for years, and was not to be rushed. Beethoven at the equivalent age of forty-three had composed eight of his nine symphonies, but Brahms, who was being hailed as Beethoven's successor, was not going to put himself in competition with the greatest of all symphonists until he was sure of his command over the medium. "Composing a symphony is no laughing matter," he would tell those friends who kept insisting he must give birth. And, "You have no idea of how it feels to hear behind you the tramp of a giant like Beethoven." Sure enough, musical Europe instantly set up the Brahms C minor Symphony against Beethoven, all the more in that a theme in the last movement of the Brahms bore some resemblance to the "Ode to Joy" theme in the Ninth. Hans von Bülow excitedly called Brahms's symphony "The Tenth." Brahms was half pleased, half irritated, by Bülow's outburst.

Having taken the plunge, Brahms followed with another symphony the next year. Then came masterpiece after masterpiece—the Violin Concerto in 1879, the B flat Piano Concerto in 1881, the Third Symphony in 1883, the Fourth Symphony in 1885, the Concerto for Violin and Cello in 1887. A large quantity of piano music and lieder, and three violin sonatas, came after the First Symphony. There was a remarkable series of works for the clarinet—the Clarinet Trio and Clarinet Quintet (both in 1891), and two clarinet sonatas (1894). These clarinet works were the result of Brahms's friendship with Richard Mühlfeld, the first clarinetist of the Meiningen Orchestra. In the 1880's, the greatest interpreter of Brahms's orchestral music was Hans von Bülow, who had taken over the Meiningen Orchestra in 1880 and proceeded to make it the precision instrument of European orchestras. Bülow was constantly on tour with the orchestra, and was constantly programing Brahms's music. All the devotion he previously had lavished on Wagner now was placed at the feet of Brahms. If a story related by Kalbeck is true, he, Brahms, and Bülow were walking in Vienna, Brahms a little ahead. Bülow clutched Kalbeck's arm, telling him to look at Brahms. "How broad and secure and healthily he stalks in front of us. I have him to thank for being restored to sanity—late, but I hope not too late—in fact, for still being alive. Three quarters of my existence has been misspent on my former father-in-law, that mountebank, and his tribe, but the remainder belongs to the true saints of art, and above all to him, to him." Bülow wrote to his fiancée, Marie Schanzer, that after Beethoven, Brahms was "the greatest, the most exalted of all composers. I consider his friendship my most priceless possession, second only to your love. It represents a climax in my life, a moral conquest." Unfortunately the friendship foundered on Brahms's tactlessness. Bülow had intended to conduct the Brahms Fourth Symphony on tour with the Meiningen Orchestra in Hamburg. It would have been the Hamburg premiere. Instead Brahms got there a few days earlier and conducted the premiere with the local orchestra. There undoubtedly was a psychological reason for this, for Brahms had a love-hate relationship with Hamburg, and on this occasion he must have been anxious to show the city how the local boy had made good. Nevertheless he did step on Bülow's toes, and the conductor was so insulted he not only refused to lead the Meiningen Orchestra in Hamburg; he also, in a typically quixotic gesture, resigned from the orchestra.

Bülow was not the only friend Brahms lost. Relations between him and the faithful Joachim were strained after the violinist's divorce from Amalie Weiss, in 1881. Brahms took Amalie's side, and Joachim was understandably hurt. In 1887 Brahms and Joachim were reconciled, though the friendship was never as close as it had been. Brahms tried to joke about it. "Now I know what I've missed all these years. It was the tone of Joachim's violin." (As a point of historical interest, it is worth noting that Joachim made a few recordings around 1905, and at least one of them, the first movement of Bach's unaccompanied G minor Sonata, shows the noble style and pure tone that made him the greatest classical violinist of the century.) Brahms grew more difficult, more sarcastic, as he grew older, and Billroth complained that Brahms made it impossible for anybody to come close to him, much less love him. In a letter to his daughter written in 1892 Billroth says that after all those years he still cannot figure out Brahms's behavior. "He occasionally enjoys baiting or teasing people. It seems to be a necessity for him. It may be a remnant of the resentment that remained in him from early youth, when he, knowing how serious his work was, was not recognized."

Clara Schumann died in 1896. It was a great blow to Brahms, who expressed his sorrow in the noble and brooding *Vier ernste Gesänge*. A greater blow came almost immediately afterward. Brahms developed cancer of the liver, the same ailment from which his father had died. He wasted away, and his friends sorrowed. "It is tragic," wrote Heinrich von Herzogenberg, "that a forceful personality like Brahms is condemned to observe with a clear mind every phase of the destruction of his body. . . . Brahms flat on his back!" The husky Brahms had never been seriously ill in his life. He dragged himself out of bed on March 7, 1897, to hear Hans Richter conduct the Fourth Symphony, and he received a great ovation. On April 3 he died.

As with so many composers, there are three well-defined periods in Brahms's creative life. At the beginning he was preoccupied with a struggle for form. His music was big, had the utmost seriousness of purpose and a self-conscious nobility that was curiously engaging. It also was a music that did not flow with much ease. It could be clumsy, and even his admirers admitted as much. In 1863 a writer for the *Rezensionen* in Vienna had some words to say about the turgidity of Brahms's early music, and noted with satisfaction that Brahms had been able "to extricate himself from the mystical fogs of that somewhat dense and darkly seething cloudiness of feeling." The article, however, did settle on what was the central point of the Brahms style: "It is the awful dignity, the profound and, at the same time, honest seriousness with which Brahms devotes himself to all he undertakes that raises him above the ordinary level."

Later in life Brahms was just as happy if his early music was not played. Not only does his Beethoven fixation show too strongly, but such works as the three Piano Sonatas, the B major Trio, or the B flat Sextet tend to be controlled by formal ideas. Form dominates the composer rather than the composer dominating form. If the music is full of originality and striking ideas, it also sounds thick and labored. Even later, as in the great F minor Piano Quintet of 1864, there is a thickness that weights down the music; and granted that Brahms was not the least interested in making "pretty" sounds, there nevertheless are miscalculations in balances.

With the *Handel Variations* (1861), and the two books of *Paganini Variations* (1862–63), Brahms entered on a new phase of piano writing, culminating in the Eight Pieces of 1878 and the two rhapsodies of 1879. There is more security, confidence, and ebullience; more brilliance without any concession to frivolity. The eight short pieces of Op. 76 are the first he composed along that line, and all of his subsequent piano works were to be short. The pieces are varied, extremely sophisticated harmonically and rhythmically, and they carry Schumann's lovely sketches, such as in the *Davidsbündlertänze,* one step further. Another characteristic of the middle-period music of Brahms, as in the three string quartets, is grace. The early works of Brahms are too serious to be graceful, but in the middle-period music he is infinitely more relaxed, and a quality of unexpected charm can

260

be felt. In the *Liebeslieder* waltzes, those lovely evocations of the Strauss family, Brahms carries this charm almost to excess. The music verges on the sentimental. In his songs, of which he composed some 250, Brahms strikes a perfect balance. His songs are very much in the Schumann tradition, even with the frequently thick piano parts, and they exhibit a lyricism comparable to Schumann's.

It is interesting to note that Brahms often composed in sets of two. Thus there were, only a few years apart, two sextets, two quartets, the two most famous sets of piano variations, two orchestral serenades, two sets of vocal waltzes, two overtures (the *Tragic* and the *Academic Festival*), two clarinet sonatas, two piano quartets, two symphonies. As he wrote the first, he seemed to get interested in the problems and they overflowed into a companion work. He kept this habit up to the very end. His late works take a different course than one might have expected. Where Beethoven went on to music of ever-increasing intensity and daring, Brahms seemed to relax more and more, and the word that invariably is used to describe his last works is "autumnal." His style became ever more gentle and reflective, especially after the Fourth Symphony of 1885.

The four symphonies are so familiar that no extended description is necessary. No. 1 in C minor came after years of anguished experiment: Bülow's nickname, "The Tenth," did more harm than good. Beethoven-lovers resented it, and took it out on Brahms rather than Bülow. The Second, in D major, the most lyric, came in 1877, a year after the First. It was criticized for being too light and superficial, and Brahms's admirers were disappointed. The second movement, however, sounded very mysterious and knotty to its contemporaries. At the London premiere in 1878, all of the critics dodged the issue of the slow movement. In the *Times* review could be read: "It is almost impossible to judge of this movement from a first hearing." The *Standard:* "Of the adagio we shall make no effort to speak in detail." The *Daily Telegraph:* "The boldest critic might well speak with diffidence after but one hearing." Only the *Daily Chronicle* made a flat statement: "In every respect a masterly composition." The D major Symphony is to the C minor what the Brahms A minor String Quartet is to the C minor, that is, lyricism after drama. But after the C minor Symphony something equally heroic had been expected, and everybody seemed much happier with the Symphony No. 3 in F of 1883. This was promptly named by some critics "The Heroic," a name that never took hold. Two points about this symphony are not generally known. At the very end of the last movement, Brahms brings back the opening theme of the first movement in a gentle, quiet reminiscence. Many think this was original with Brahms. But Joachim Raff, a composer of the Liszt school who wrote popular program-symphonies, had previously ended his *Im Walde* Symphony (1869) exactly the same way. (Until the end of the century Raff's *Im Walde* together with Rubinstein's *Ocean* Symphony were the two most-played of all symphonic works in the repertoire.) It also has not been noticed that the theme with which Brahms starts his symphony, after the two opening chords, comes from Schumann, where it turns up twice. In the second movement of Schumann's First Symphony, measures 74–78, it is stated, never to reappear again during the course of the work. Exactly the same thing happens in the first movement of the Schumann Third (pages 49 and 50 of the Eulenburg score). In both cases the key of the movement is in E flat, and in both cases the mysterious theme is in G major. Presumably the theme had a special meaning to Schumann, although its symbolism is not known. Perhaps Brahms knew what Schumann was driving at. In any case, he used the theme for the F major Symphony. His last symphony, No. 4 in E minor, was relatively unsuccessful for a while. It was considered too "secretive;" and its key of E minor—rather unconventional—bothered some musicians. Also its finale, a chaconne (variations over a recurrent bass), was considered dry.

Another complaint registered against the music of Brahms was that it was too hard to play. Both of the piano concertos and the violin concerto are full of unusual and uncomfortable stretches, and there are spots in each work that are all but impossible to negotiate. There also are extended sections of mixed rhythms, where the right hand may play threes against the left hand's fours. Listeners in Brahms's day said these rhythms made them seasick. ("But this was probably the start of the polyrhythmic structure of many contemporary scores," Arnold Schoenberg later was to write.) Brahms's instrumental technique is anything but flashy, and demands an ability to handle wide stretches and awkward figurations. But what can be played *can* be played, as later virtuosos proved. Eugen d'Albert, one of Liszt's greatest pupils, was the first to adopt the B flat Concerto. People were astonished that he could play so long and demanding a work by heart. Today all of the Brahms concertos and instrumental music are tossed off by the young. If the music no longer poses insuperable technical problems—though nobody would claim that the Brahms concertos are easy—it still poses musical problems that continue to challenge artists.

In his last years, Brahms wrote a very tender, personal kind of music. That does not mean the music lacks tension. But such works as the D minor Violin Sonata, the Clarinet Quintet, the Intermezzi for piano, and his very last work, a set of eleven chorale preludes for organ, have a kind of serenity unique in the work of any composer. The late Haydn symphonies, for instance, could still be the product of a young man, but there is nothing suggesting youth or ardor in the late music of Brahms. It is the twilight of romanticism, and the peculiar glow of this setting sun is hard to describe. It beams a steady, warm light, not flaring up as it does in the music of Mahler, not looming big halfway over the horizon as in the symphonies of Bruckner, not erupting with solar explosions as in the music of Richard Strauss. It is the music of a creative mind completely sure of its materials, and it combines technique with a mellow, golden glow. In a day when the gigantic operas of Wagner dominated the opera house, when the shocking symphonic poems of Richard Strauss were the talk of Europe, the music of Brahms continued to represent in an intensified way what it had always represented— integrity, the spirit of Beethoven and Schumann, the attitude of the pure and serious musician interested only in creating a series of abstract sounds in forms best realized to enhance those sounds.

❧ 19 ❧

Master of the Lied

HUGO WOLF

The year of Brahms's death also saw the disappearance of the strange Hugo Wolf from the local scene. The greatest song composer of his day and, many think, of all time, was placed in a sanitorium—a euphemism for lunatic asylum. Wolf had burned himself out, and even had his nervous system not been affected by the syphilis he had picked up at the age of seventeen, he was the kind of manic-depressive who in any event could not have lasted long. There are many photographs of Wolf, and they all look much the same. He stares at the photographer with those burning and hypnotic black eyes mentioned by so many of his contemporaries, dressed usually in a velvet jacket and flowing artist's tie: slim, handsome, aristocratic-looking, unsmiling, consumed. He looked, and was, a man out of the ordinary. Within the space of a few years this tortured creature left the world a legacy that carried the German art song to its highest point.

He did write other things than songs. There is an interesting opera, *Der Corregidor,* almost never staged. There are also some choral works, a long string quartet, and the *Italian Serenade* for string quartet (later expanded for string orchestra), a handful of piano works, and a long symphonic poem named *Penthesilea,* which hardly anybody knows but which Wolf authorities assure us is a masterpiece (it isn't). But it was as a song composer that Wolf achieved whatever little fame he had in his own day, and it is as a song composer that he lives.

No greater songs exist. Wolf, the rebel who led such a stormy life, the bohemian and malcontent, the genius who died mad at the age of forty-three, was able to direct a musical stream of laser-bright strength on poetry. In the 242 songs he wrote, there often is a serenity at complete odds with his day-to-day life. And no composer had such an acute feeling for poetry. It has been pointed out many times that where such great song writers as Schubert, Schumann, and Brahms were musicians with a feeling for poetry, Wolf was a poet who thought in terms of music. Nobody has to be reminded of the extreme beauty of the great lieder from Schubert through Brahms. But the Wolf songs are not only more original and more advanced harmonically, they also have more point, a stabbingly intense correlation of text and music. Wolf achieved what the Elizabethan song writer, Thomas Campion, expressed as the ideal: to couple words and notes lovingly together. Wolf did this so unerringly that the term "psychological song" has been used to describe his music. Some of this extraordinary meeting of word and music —this ability to pick up the high point of a poem through an unexpected modulation, or through an accompaniment that heightens the verbal meaning, or through a melody that can be searing in its purity and rightness— some of this came from Wagner, who was Wolf's idol. Some came from Liszt, whose prophetic songs have been so unaccountably neglected by recitalists. In many respects the Liszt songs prefigure those of Wolf.

It might be that Wolf's admiration for Liszt and Wagner, and his detestation of Brahms, came about for personal reasons. Wolf was born in Windischgraz, Styria (now Slovenjgrade, Yugoslavia), on March 13, 1860. Over his father's objections he left home in 1875 to study at the Vienna Conservatory. While Wolf was a student there, Wagner visited Vienna. The fifteen-year-old Wolf hung around him and finally worked up the nerve to show the great man some of his music. Wagner was amused by the young man's hero-worship. But he did not dismiss Wolf out of hand, which Brahms apparently did. When Wolf approached Brahms, the older man suggested that Wolf study counterpoint with Nottebohm. Wolf was furious. "It's only Brahms's North German pedantry that makes him thrust Nottebohm on me." From that moment, Brahms was his enemy. Wolf amply paid him off during the three years he was music critic for the Wiener *Salonblatt*.

A friend got him the job. Wolf, highly strung and nervous, had never been able to hold down any position up to then. Nor could he stay long in any one place. At school in Windischgraz he easily became bored and did well only in the one subject that interested him, music. He left the Vienna Conservatory after only two years, telling Joseph Hellmesberger, the director, that he was forgetting more than he was learning. Hellmesberger immediately expelled him. Wolf always claimed he left before being expelled, though for a time he seriously considered bringing legal action against the Conservatory. He did not have the patience to teach, and when he did teach he was not very good at it. For the most part he moved from one cheap lodging to another, and lived on food parcels sent by his family. As amanuensis to the conductor Karl Muck at Salzburg, and then as assistant chorus master there, he made enemies, got into trouble, and left, calling the place a "pigsty." He probably was not good enough for the job. But he did seem to enjoy his work as a music critic, and he made a name for himself with his violent attacks on Brahms and the entire Viennese establishment. He wrote with fury and venom: "Through this composition"—the D minor Concerto of Brahms—"blows an air so icy, so dank and misty, that one's heart freezes, one's breath is taken away. One could catch a cold from it. Unhealthy stuff!" Or, on the Brahms Fourth Symphony, "He has, to be sure, never been able to raise himself above the level of mediocrity, but such nullity, emptiness and hypocrisy as prevail in the E minor Symphony have come to light in none of his other works. The art of composing without ideas has decidedly found its most worthy representative in Brahms." It could very well be that Wolf's reviews were a corrective in a musical Vienna that was dominated by the conservative opinions of Brahms's friend Hanslick. It also was a fact that Wolf's intemperately expressed opinions and his unabashed propaganda for Liszt and Wagner were a decided setback to his career.

Being a composer-critic put him in an awkward position. On the one hand he was attacking the (to him) staid and uninteresting programs of the Vienna Philharmonic. On the other hand he was going, hat in hand, to such important members of the orchestra as its famous concertmaster, Arnold Rosé, and the violinist-violist Sigismund Bachrich, both of whom he had roughly handled in print. He wanted their help in getting his music played; he wanted the Rosé Quartet to play his quartet, and he wanted the Philharmonic to play his *Penthesilea*. Rosé gleefully let him dangle and then polished him off with an insulting letter: "We have attentively gone through your D minor String Quartet and unanimously resolved to leave the work for you with the doorman of the Opera House. Will you have the kindness to send for it as soon as possible? He may easily mislay it. With kindest greetings." Finally *Penthesilea* was rehearsed by the Philharmonic under Hans Richter. According to Wolf, the conductor led it through to the end because, as he told the orchestra, he wanted to see for himself the work of the man "who dares to write in such a way about *Meister* Brahms." Richter later denied that he had said any such thing, but the story does sound true. In any case, Wolf was very naïve in thinking that an attacking critic would be welcomed by the people he attacked. He was only sticking his neck out. He also could be unethical about his critical work, ready to use his column to castigate enemies on a personal basis. After the *Penthesilea* fiasco he ran about swearing vengeance. "I will publish an article about Richter that shall make the devil himself grow pale." And he did.

Wolf started writing songs around 1875, but he came into maturity thirteen years later. From 1888 to 1891 he composed over 200 songs to poems by Mörike, Eichendorff, Goethe, Geibel, Heyse, and Keller. From 1895 to 1897 there were another thirty or so songs. His mind snapped in 1897 and he spent the last four years of his life in an asylum. Thus his song-writing career is confined to seven years. The major collections are the fifty-three songs to Mörike poetry (published 1889), the *Gedichte von Eichendorff* (1889), the *Spanisches Liederbuch, nach Heyse und Geibel* (1891), *Alte Weisen: Sechs Gedichte von Keller* (1891), the *Italienisches Liederbuch, nach Paul Heyse* (2 volumes, 1892 and 1896), and *Drei Gedichte von Michelangelo* (1898). There are over a hundred additional miscellaneous songs set to Heine, Lenau, Chamisso, and others. The period of his mastery starts with the Mörike songs of 1888. He wrote them at white heat—two, sometimes three, songs a day. In three months he turned out forty-three songs. Later in the year he turned his attention to Goethe and in three and a half months composed fifty songs. It was as if an outside force had grabbed his pen and guided it. Wolf knew the songs were good. "What I now write, I write for posterity, too. They are masterpieces." He would get drunk on his songs and describe them as though intoxicated: "*Erstes Liebeslied eines Mädchen* is by far the best thing I have done up to now. . . . The music is of so striking a character and of such intensity that it would lacerate the nervous system of a block of marble." But the very next day: "I retract the opinion that *Erstes Liebeslied eines Mädchen* is my best thing, for what I wrote this morning, *Fussreise*, is a million times better. When you hear this song you will have only one wish—to die."

These songs were immediately recognized as great works by a discriminating group. Rosa Papier and Ferdinand Jäger began to sing them in public. Generally Wolf, a good pianist, accompanied them. Even Wolf's enemies admitted that he might have something to say. The music represented something new in lieder composition. Some Wolf songs, of course, are as easily assimilated as the songs of Schubert, Schumann, and Brahms. But there are some difficult ones in which the secrets do not reveal themselves on first hearing. They can sound austere, unmelodic, too declamatory. It is necessary to hear some Wolf songs many times before the exquisite joinings and subtle expressive content are clear.

Wolf worked on the theory that the form of the poem must dictate the form of the music. He summed up his ideas in a letter to Rosa Mayreder, the librettist of *Der Corregidor*:

> There's something gruesome about the intimate fusion of poetry and music in which, actually, the gruesome role belongs only to the latter. Music has decidedly something of the vampire about it. It claws its victim relentlessly and sucks the last drop of blood from it. Or one could also compare it with a greedy suckling, who relentlessly demands fresh nourishment and becomes plump and fat while its mother's beauty wilts away. But this comparison is valid only with regard to the effect that music, in league with poetry, has upon the public. . . . Nothing has shocked me more than this groundless injustice in the preference of one art over the other . . .

In the process of sucking out the poetry the music itself filled out and took shape. Most song composers have always been interested in melody primarily as melody. Wolf was interested in melody as merely one of the elements needed to underline the meaning of a poem. It might be said that each of his songs is a tiny word painting. Each one is different; each one is subtle; each is full of unexpected ideas. In *Dass doch gemalt* there is the quiet and touching conclusion, where a less imaginative composer would have rattled the piano with chords after the declaration of love that ends the poem. There is *Wer rief dich denn*, where the singer says one thing and the accompaniment indicates that what she is saying is false. There is the hushed, almost monotonal vocal line of *Nun wandre, Maria*, where the accompaniment suggests—so delicately, yet so persistently—a kind of blind, purposeless walking. There is *Gesegnet sei*, where on the words *Erschuf die Schönheit* there is a blaze of glory. There are the last three songs he composed, the *Michelangelo Lieder*, where the circle comes full turn: in *Wohl denk' ich oft*, a *Meistersinger* theme is heard at the end, and in *Sag mir, wie ich's erwerbe*, a motive from *Tristan*. In his last songs, Wolf recalled the great musical influence of his life and paid homage.

He never had any luck with his opera. In 1895 he began work on *Der Corregidor*, friends donating money to subsidize him. He had to be subsidized, for never in his life did he have a cent. He did not even have a home. In an effort to correct the situation he would come up with all kinds of impractical ideas. Among them was emigration to the United States, a country in which, as every European knew, every citizen was a millionaire. Wolf said that he was going to settle in "the land of gold, to lay the foundations of a decent existence on a safe basis of dollars." Of course nothing came of it. For years he drifted from one friend to another, and not until 1896 did he find an apartment of his own. He enjoyed it for only a year. Wolf, who had lived off his friends, did not hesitate to accept money from his friends to keep him going while he worked on his opera. "High time! High time that occurred to somebody. Really it should be the cursed liability and obligation of the State to support musicians and poets." Schubert, whose life Wolf's so resembled in many aspects, had said the same thing. Wolf worked rapidly on *Der Corregidor* and had it substantially completed in fourteen weeks. He looked at it with characteristic joy and optimism. "People will no longer talk about anything but this opera. All of them, Mascagni, Humperdinck *e tutti quanti* will be unable to compete and will fade away."

When *Corregidor* had its premiere at Mannheim in 1896, it achieved a modest success. But soon it was dropped, and it never has entered the repertory. The following year Wolf went mad. He had delusions that he had been appointed director of the Vienna Opera, and he went around the city saying that Mahler had been discharged and that he, Wolf, would immediately reorganize the organization. He burst into the house of the opera singer, Hermann Winkelmann, introduced himself as the new director and said that he wanted to make use of his services that very afternoon. Winkelmann pretended to be called to the telephone, did not return, and Wolf was very angry. "He shall suffer for that, refusing the first request of his director." Wolf's friends gathered around him, not knowing what to do, and Wolf looked at their glum faces. "A fine lot of friends you are. When one for once accomplishes something in life, you are not a bit pleased." When the carriage for the asylum drew up, Wolf thought it was going to take him to Prince Liechenstein, the intendant of the Court Opera, so he carefully got into his dress clothes. From the madhouse he wrote detailed reports of his plans, and discussed the operas he wanted to compose. He had been working on one, *Manuel Venegas*, when he was stricken. Only a fragment remains. Released in 1898, Wolf wandered from one place to another, tried to drown himself, and had himself recommitted. He died in the asylum on February 22, 1903. A death mask was made. The face, fanatic and beautiful, thin, with a pointed beard, high cheek bones, and sunken eyes, looks like the face of Don Quixote as conceived by Doré.

A Selected Bibliography
of Books in English

1

Blume, Friedrich *Renaissance and Baroque Music* (New York, 1967)
Bodky, Erwin *The Interpretation of Bach's Keyboard Works* (Cambridge, Massachusetts, 1960)
Bukofzer, Manfred *Music in the Baroque Era* (New York, 1947)
Dart, Thurston *The Interpretation of Music* (New York, 1963)
David, Hans T., and Mendel, Arthur *The Bach Reader* (New York, 1966)
Donington, Robert *The Interpretation of Early Music* (New York, 1963)
Geiringer, Karl *The Bach Family* (New York, 1954)
            Johann Sebastian Bach (New York, 1966)
Hutchings, A. J. B. *The Baroque Concerto* (New York, 1961)
Rothschild, Fritz *The Lost Tradition in Music: Rhythm and Tempo in J. S. Bach's Time* (New York, 1953)
Schweitzer, Albert *J. S. Bach*. 2 vols. (New York, 1966)
Spitta, Philip *Johann Sebastian Bach* (London, 1884–85)
Terry, Charles Stanford *Johann Christian Bach* (London, 1933)

2

Abraham, Gerald (ed.) *Handel: A Symposium* (London, 1954)
Burney, Charles *A General History of Music,* ed. Frank Mercer. 2 vols. (New York, 1967)
Dean, Winton *Handel's Dramatic Oratorios and Masques* (London, 1959)
Dent, Edward J. *Handel* (London, 1934)
Deutsch, Otto Erich *Handel: A Documentary Biography* (New York, 1954)
Lang, Paul Henry *George Frideric Handel* (New York, 1966)
Myers, Robert Manson *Handel's Messiah* (New York, 1948)
Pleasants, Henry *The Great Singers* (New York, 1966). See chapter on the castratos.

3

Asow, Hedwig, and E. H. Mueller von *The Collected Correspondence and Papers of Christoph Willibald Gluck* (New York, 1962)

Berlioz, Hector *Memoirs*, ed. David Cairns (New York, 1969)

Burney, Charles *An Eighteenth-Century Musical Tour in France and Italy*, ed. Percy A. Scholes. 2 vols. (London, 1959)

Cooper, Martin *Gluck* (London, 1935)

Einstein, Alfred *Gluck* (London, 1936)

Grout, Donald Jay *A Short History of Opera*. 2 vols. (New York, 1965)

Howard, Patricia *Gluck and the Birth of Modern Opera* (New York, 1963)

Nettl, Paul *The Book of Musical Documents* (New York, 1948). See excerpts from the Mannlich memoirs.

Tovey, Donald *The Main Stream of Music and Other Essays* (New York, 1949)

Weisstein, Ulrich *The Essence of Opera* (New York, 1964)

4

Geiringer, Karl *Haydn: A Creative Life in Music* (New York, 1963)

Nettl, Paul *Forgotten Musicians* (New York, 1951). See pp. 161–203 for autobiography of Karl Ditters von Dittersdorf, which has source material on Mozart and Haydn.

Newman, William S. *The Sonata in the Classic Era* (Chapel Hill, North Carolina, 1963)

Robbins-Landon, H. C. *The Symphonies of Joseph Haydn* (New York, 1956)
The Collected Correspondence and London Notebooks of Joseph Haydn (New York, 1959)

Somfai, Laszlo *Joseph Haydn: His Life in Contemporary Pictures* (New York, 1969)

Tovey, Donald *The Main Stream of Music and Other Essays* (New York, 1949). See pp. 1–64 for essay on the string quartets of Haydn.

5

Anderson, Emily (trans. and ed.) *The Letters of Mozart and His Family*. 3 vols. (London, 1938)

Badura-Skoda, Paul and Eva *Interpreting Mozart on the Keyboard* (London, 1962)

Brion, Marcel *Daily Life in the City of Mozart and Schubert* (New York, 1962)

Dent, Edward J. *Mozart's Operas* (London, 1947)

Deutsch, Otto Erich *Mozart: A Documentary Biography* (Stanford, California, 1965)

Einstein, Alfred *Mozart: His Character, His Work* (New York, 1945)

Girdlestone, Cuthbert *Mozart and His Piano Concertos* (New York, 1964)

Kelly, Michael *Reminiscences*. 2 vols. (London, 1826)

King, A. Hyatt *Mozart in Retrospect* (London, 1955)

Medici, Nerina, and Hughes, Rosemary (eds.) *A Mozart Pilgrimage: Being the Travel Diaries of Vincent and Mary Novello in the Year 1829* (London, 1955)

Nettl, Paul   *Mozart and Masonry* (New York, 1957)

Ponte, Lorenzo da   *Memoirs* (New York, 1929)

Robbins-Landon, H. C., and Mitchell, Donald (eds.)   *The Mozart Companion* (New York, 1956)

Rothschild, Fritz   *Musical Performance in the Times of Mozart and Beethoven* (New York, 1961)

Schenk, Erich   *Mozart and His Times* (New York, 1959)

Turner, W. J.   *Mozart: The Man and His Works* (New York, 1954)

6

Anderson, Emily (trans. and ed.)   *The Letters of Beethoven.* 3 vols. (New York, 1961)

Chorley, Henry F.   *Modern German Music* (London, 1954). Also valuable for impressions of Schumann, Wagner, Verdi, and Mendelssohn.

Cooper, Martin   *Beethoven: The Last Decade* (New York, 1970)

Marek, George   *Beethoven: Biography of a Genius* (New York, 1969)

Misch, Ludwig   *Beethoven Studies* (Norman, Oklahoma, 1953)

Moscheles, Ignaz   *Recent Music and Musicians* (New York, 1873). Also valuable for impressions of Chopin, Mendelssohn, Liszt, and the early romantics.

Pleasants, Henry (trans. and ed.)   *The Musical Journeys of Louis Spohr* (Norman, Oklahoma, 1961)

Schindler, Anton Felix   *Beethoven as I Knew Him* (London, 1966)

Sonneck, O. G.   *Beethoven: Impressions by His Contemporaries* (New York, 1926)

Spohr, Louis   *Autobiography* (London, 1878)

Sterba, Richard and Edith   *Beethoven and His Nephew* (New York, 1954)

Thayer, Alexander Wheelock   *The Life of Beethoven, revised and ed. by Elliot Forbes.* 2 vols. (Princeton, New Jersey, 1964)

Tovey, Donald Francis   *Beethoven* (London, 1945)

7

Abraham, Gerald (ed.)   *The Music of Schubert* (New York, 1947)

Brown, Maurice J. E.   *Schubert: A Critical Biography* (New York, 1958)

Essays on Schubert (New York, 1966)

Capell, Richard   *Schubert's Songs* (London, 1928)

Deutsch, Otto Erich   *The Schubert Reader* (New York, 1947)

Schubert: Memoirs by His Friends (New York, 1958)

Einstein, Alfred   *Schubert: A Musical Portrait* (New York, 1951)

Grove, George   Article on Schubert in his *Dictionary of Music and Musicians.*

Schumann, Robert   *Music and Musicians.* 2 vols. (London, 1891). Also valuable for reviews and commentaries on Mendelssohn, Berlioz, Chopin, Liszt, and many of the minor early romantics.

8

Carse, Adam   *The Orchestra from Beethoven to Berlioz* (New York, 1949)

Courcy, G. I. C. de   *Paganini.* 2 vols. (Norman, Oklahoma, 1957)

Einstein, Alfred   *Music in the Romantic Era* (New York, 1947)

Hallé, Charles *Life and Letters* (London, 1896). Valuable for source material on many of the early romantics.

Lenz, Wilhelm von *The Great Pianists of Our Time* (New York, 1899)

Newman, William S. *The Sonata Since Beethoven* (Chapel Hill, North Carolina 1969)

Schonberg, Harold C. *The Great Pianists* (New York, 1963)

Stevens, Denis (ed.) *A History of Song* (New York, 1961)

Warrack, John *Carl Maria von Weber* (New York, 1968)

9

Barzun, Jacques *Berlioz and the Romantic Century*. 2 vols. (Boston, 1950)

Berlioz, Hector *Evenings With the Orchestra*, trans. Jacques Barzun (New York, 1956)

Berlioz, Hector *The Memoirs of Hector Berlioz*, trans. David Cairns (New York, 1969)

10

Abraham, Gerald (ed.) *Schumann: A Symposium* (London, 1952)

Brion, Marcel *Schumann and the Romantic Age* (New York, 1956)

Chissel, Joan *Schumann* (London, 1948)

Cooper, Martin *Ideas and Music* (London, 1965). See pp. 163–208 for essay on Schumann songs.

May, Florence *The Girlhood of Clara Schumann* (London, 1912)

Pleasants, Henry *The Musical World of Robert Schumann* (New York, 1965)

Sams, Eric *The Songs of Robert Schumann* (New York, 1969)

Schumann, Robert *Music and Musicians*. 2 vols. (London, 1891)
        Early Letters (London, 1888)

11

Abraham, Gerald *Chopin's Musical Style* (London, 1939)

Boucourechliev, A. *Chopin: A Pictorial Biography* (New York, 1963)

Chopin, Frédéric *Selected Correspondence,* trans. and ed. Arthur Hedley (London, 1962)

Cortot, Alfred *In Search of Chopin*, trans. Cyril and Rena Clarke (New York, 1952)

Delacroix, Eugene *The Journal of Eugene Delacroix*, trans. Walter Pach (New York, 1937)

Hedley, Arthur *Chopin* (New York, 1962)

Holcman, Jan *The Legacy of Chopin* (New York, 1954)

Huneker, James *Chopin: The Man and His Music* (London, 1901)

Liszt, Franz *Frédéric Chopin,* trans. Edward N. Waters (New York, 1963)

Walker, Alan (ed.) *Frédéric Chopin* (New York, 1967)

Wierzynski, Casimir *The Life and Death of Chopin* (New York, 1949)

12

Beckett, Walter *Liszt* (London, 1956)

Fay, Amy *Music Study in Germany* (New York, 1903)

Friedheim, Arthur *Life and Liszt* (New York, 1961)

Grove's Dictionary of Music and Musicians, 1955 edition. The catalogue of Liszt works compiled by Humphrey Searle is indispensable.

Huneker, James *Franz Liszt* (New York, 1911)

Liszt, Franz *Letters to Marie zu Sayn-Wittgenstein*, trans. Howard E. Hugo (Cambridge, Massachusetts, 1953)

Mason, William *Memories of a Musical Life* (New York, 1901)

Newman, Ernest *The Man Liszt* (New York, 1934)

Searle, Humphrey *The Music of Liszt* (New York, 1966)

Sitwell, Sacheverell *Liszt* (New York, 1956)

Walker, Bettina *My Musical Experiences* (New York, 1893)

13

Glehn, M. E. von *Goethe and Mendelssohn* (London, 1874)

Haweis, H. R. *My Musical Life* (London, 1888)

Jacob, Heinrich Eduard *Felix Mendelssohn and His Times* (Englewood Cliffs, New Jersey, 1963)

Mason, Lowell *Musical Letters from Abroad* (New York, 1854)

Mendelssohn, Felix *Letters from Italy* (New York, 1865)
                              Letters (New York, 1945)

Moscheles, Ignaz *Recent Music and Musicians* (New York, 1873)

Petitpierre, Jacques *The Romance of the Mendelssohns* (New York, n.d.)

Radcliffe, Philip *Mendelssohn* (London, 1954)

Werner, Eric *Mendelssohn* (New York, 1963)

14

Dwight's Journal of Music, 1852–1881. 41 vols. Reprinted by Arno Press (New York, 1968)

Fitzlyon, April *The Price of Genius: A Life of Pauline Viardot* (New York, 1964)

Moscheles, Felix *Fragments of an Autobiography* (New York, 1899). See pp. 271–299 for essay on Rossini.

Pleasants, Henry *The Great Singers* (New York, 1966)

Russell, Frank *Queen of Song: The Life of Henrietta Sontag* (New York, 1964)

Schultz, Gladys Denny *Jenny Lind, the Swedish Nightingale* (New York, 1962)

Stendhal *Life of Rossini* (New York, 1957)

Toye, Francis *Rossini* (New York, 1947)

Weinstock, Herbert *Donizetti* (New York, 1963)
                           Rossini (New York, 1968)

15

Crosten, William L. *French Grand Opera: An Art and a Business* (New York, 1948)

Dieren, Bernard van *Down Among the Dead Men* (London, 1935). See pp. 142–174 for essay on Meyerbeer.

Dwight's Journal of Music, 1852–1881. 41 vols. Reprinted by Arno Press (New York, 1968)

Goldman, Albert and Sprinchorn, Evert (eds.) *Wagner on Music and Drama* (New York, 1964). See pp. 111–121 *et passim* for essay on Meyerbeer.

16

Abraham, Gerald   *A Hundred Years of Music* (Chicago, 1964)

Dwight's Journal of Music, 1852–1881. 41 volumes. Reprinted by Arno Press (New York, 1968)

Gatti, Carlo   *Verdi: The Man and His Music* (New York, 1955)

Hussey, Dyneley   *Verdi* (New York, 1962)

Martin, George   *Verdi: His Music, Life, and Times* (New York, 1963)

Osborne, Charles   *The Complete Operas of Verdi* (New York, 1970)

Shaw, George Bernard   *London Music in 1888–89* (London, 1937)
                       Music in London, 1890–94. 3 vols. (London, 1949)

Toye, Francis   *Giuseppe Verdi: His Life and Works* (New York, 1946)

Walker, Frank   *The Man Verdi* (New York, 1962)

Werfel, Franz, and Stefan, Paul (eds.)   *Verdi: The Man in His Letters* (New York, 1942)

17

Bekker, Paul   *Richard Wagner* (London, 1931)

Bülow, Hans von   *Early Correspondence* (London, 1896)

Burk, John (ed.)   *Letters of Richard Wagner* (New York, 1950)

Donington, Robert   *Wagner's Ring and Its Symbols* (New York, 1963)

Dwight's Journal of Music, 1852–1881. 41 vols. Reprinted by Arno Press (New York, 1968)

Goldman, Albert, and Sprinchorn, Evert (eds.)   *Wagner on Music and Drama* (New York, 1964)

Gutman, Robert W.   *Richard Wagner: The Man, His Mind, and His Music* (New York, 1968)

Hanslick, Eduard   *Vienna's Golden Years of Music*, trans. and ed. Henry Pleasants (New York, 1950)

Jacobs, Robert   *Wagner* (New York, 1962)

Newman, Ernest   *The Life of Richard Wagner.* 4 vols. (London, 1933–46)

Shaw, George Bernard   *London Music in 1888–89* (London, 1937)
                       Music in London, 1890–94. 3 vols. (London, 1949)
                       The Perfect Wagnerite (London, 1898)

Wagner, Richard   *My Life.* 2 vols. (New York, 1911)

Zuckerman, Elliott   *The First Hundred Years of Wagner's Tristan* (New York, 1964)

18

Barkan, Hans (trans. and ed.)   *Johannes Brahms and Theodor Billroth: Letters from a Musical Friendship* (Norman, Oklahoma, 1957)

Gal, Hans   *Johannes Brahms: His Work and Personality* (New York, 1963)

Geiringer, Karl   *Brahms* (New York, 1947)

Hill, Ralph   *Brahms* (New York, 1948)

Latham, Peter   *Brahms* (New York, 1949)

Mason, Daniel Gregory   *The Chamber Music of Brahms* (New York, 1933)

May, Florence   *The Life of Johannes Brahms* (London, 1905)

Schauffler, Robert Haven   *The Unknown Brahms* (New York, 1933)

Schoenberg, Arnold   *Style and Idea* (New York, 1950). See pp. 52–104 for essay on
   Brahms.

19

Newman, Ernest   *Hugo Wolf* (London, 1907)
Rolland, Romain   *Essays on Music* (New York, 1948). See pp. 341–361 for essay
   on Wolf.
Sams, Eric   *The Songs of Hugo Wolf* (New York, 1962)
Walker, Frank   *Hugo Wolf* (New York, 1968)

Index